THE CAMBRIDGE COMPANION TO LITERATURE AND CLIMATE

Investigating the relationship between literature and climate, this *Companion* offers a genealogy of climate representations in literature while showing how literature can help us make sense of climate change. It argues that any discussion of literature and climate cannot help but be shaped by our current – and inescapable – vantage point from an era of climate change, and uncovers a longer literary history of climate that might inform our contemporary climate crisis. Essays explore the conceptualisation of climate in a range of literary and creative modes; they represent a diversity of cultural and historical perspectives, and a wide spectrum of voices and views across the categories of race, gender, and class. Key issues in climate criticism and literary studies are introduced and explained, while new and emerging concepts are discussed and debated in a final section that puts expert analyses in conversation with each other.

Adeline Johns-Putra is Professor of Literature at Xi'an Jiaotong-Liverpool University. She is a past president of the Association for the Study of Literature and Environment, UK and Ireland (ASLE-UKI). Her books include *Climate Change and the Contemporary Novel* (2019) and *The History of the Epic* (2006), and the edited volumes *Climate and Literature* (2019) and *Cli-Fi: A Companion* (2018).

Kelly Sultzbach is a Professor at the University of Wisconsin, La Crosse, and was a Fulbright Scholar with the University of Liverpool in 2019. She is the author of *Ecocriticism in the Modernist Imagination: Forster, Woolf, and Auden* (2016). Recent work also includes articles in *Modernist Cultures*, the ASLE-UKI journal *Green Letters* (2019) and a chapter in *Understanding Merleau-Ponty, Understanding Modernism* (2018).

T0381637

THE CAMBRIDGE
COMPANION TO
LITERATURE AND CLIMATE

EDITED BY
ADELINE JOHNS-PUTRA
Xi'an Jiaotong-Liverpool University

KELLY SULTZBACH
University of Wisconsin, La Crosse

CAMBRIDGE
UNIVERSITY PRESS

CAMBRIDGE
UNIVERSITY PRESS

University Printing House, Cambridge CB2 8BS, United Kingdom

One Liberty Plaza, 20th Floor, New York, NY 10006, USA

477 Williamstown Road, Port Melbourne, VIC 3207, Australia

314–321, 3rd Floor, Plot 3, Splendor Forum, Jasola District Centre,
New Delhi – 110025, India

103 Penang Road, #05–06/07, Visioncrest Commercial, Singapore 238467

Cambridge University Press is part of the University of Cambridge.

It furthers the University's mission by disseminating knowledge in the pursuit of
education, learning, and research at the highest international levels of excellence.

www.cambridge.org
Information on this title: www.cambridge.org/9781316512166
DOI: 10.1017/9781009057868

© Cambridge University Press 2022

First published 2022

A catalogue record for this publication is available from the British Library.

Library of Congress Cataloging-in-Publication Data
NAMES: Johns-Putra, Adeline, 1973– editor. | Sultzbach, Kelly, 1972– editor.
TITLE: The Cambridge companion to literature and climate / edited by Adeline Johns-
Putra, Kelly Sultzbach.
DESCRIPTION: Cambridge ; New York, NY : Cambridge University Press, 2022. | Includes
bibliographical references and index.
IDENTIFIERS: LCCN 2021041368 (print) | LCCN 2021041369 (ebook) | ISBN
9781316512166 (hardback) | ISBN 9781009057868 (ebook)
SUBJECTS: LCSH: Climatic changes in literature. | Climatology in literature. |
Environmental literature – History and criticism. | Ecocriticism.
CLASSIFICATION: LCC PN56.C612 C36 2022 (print) | LCC PN56.C612 (ebook) | DDC 809/
.9336–dc23/eng/20211222
LC record available at https://lccn.loc.gov/2021041368
LC ebook record available at https://lccn.loc.gov/2021041369

ISBN 978-1-316-51216-6 Hardback
ISBN 978-1-009-06081-3 Paperback

CONTENTS

Contents

Contents

FIGURES

NOTES ON CONTRIBUTORS

THOMAS BRISTOW is an editor, researcher, and writer. Editor-in-chief of the journal *PAN: Philosophy Activism Nature*, and environmental humanities series editor for Routledge's 'Literature, Media and Communication', Bristow authored *The Anthropocene Lyric* (2014) and co-edited *The Cultural History of Climate Change* (with Thomas H. Ford, 2016). He is currently an honorary fellow at the University of Western Australia and Roderick Research Fellow at James Cook University. Forthcoming work from Bristow will include a chapter on the perceptual space of Australian fiction in *The Cambridge Companion to the Australian Novel* (2021) and a chapter on ecopoetics for *The Cambridge History of Australian Poetry* (2022).

GERRY CANAVAN is Associate Professor of Twentieth- and Twenty-First-Century Literature in the Department of English at Marquette University, Wisconsin, USA, and the author of *Octavia E. Butler* (2016). He is the co-editor of *Green Planets: Ecology and Science Fiction* (2014), *The Cambridge Companion to American Science Fiction* (2015), and *The Cambridge History of Science Fiction* (2018), and also serves as an editor at two academic journals focused on science fiction studies: *Extrapolation* and *Science Fiction Film and Television*.

SARAH DIMICK is Assistant Professor of English at Harvard University, USA. She received her PhD in English Literature from the University of Wisconsin-Madison and spent two years as the Andrew Mellon Postdoctoral Fellow in Environmental Humanities at Northwestern University. Her research focuses on environmental writing of the twentieth and twenty-first centuries, concentrating on literary representations of climate change and environmental justice.

THOMAS H. FORD is Lecturer of English at La Trobe University in Melbourne, Australia. His *How to Read a Poem: Seven Steps* (2021) and *Wordsworth and the Poetics of Air* (2018) won the British Association for Romantic Studies First Book Prize for 2017–19. His other publications include *A Cultural History of Climate Change* (2016), co-edited with Tom Bristow, and a translation from the German of *The Communist Postscript* by Boris Groys (2010).

Notes on Contributors

ISABEL GALLEYMORE is Lecturer in Creative Writing at the University of Birmingham, UK. Her monograph, *Teaching Environmental Writing: Ecocritical Pedagogy and Poetics*, was published by Bloomsbury Academic in 2020 and her poetry collection, *Significant Other* (2019), won the John Pollard Foundation International Poetry Prize in 2020.

JENNIFER MAE HAMILTON is Lecturer in English on unceded Anaiwan lands at the University of New England, Australia, co-founder of the 'Composting Feminisms and Environmental Humanities' group, and author of *This Contentious Storm: An Ecocritical and Performance History of King Lear* (2017).

HSINYA HUANG is Distinguished Professor of American and Comparative Literature, National Sun Yat-Sen University (NSYSU), Taiwan. She is former Dean of Arts and Humanities and Provost of Academic Affairs and Faculty Advancement, NSYSU. She served as Director General of International Cooperation and Science Education, Ministry of Science and Technology, Taiwan, 2018–19. She is the author or editor of books and articles on Native American and Indigenous literatures, ecocriticism, and transnational studies, including *(De)Colonizing the Body: Disease, Empire, and (Alter)Native Medicine in Contemporary Native American Women's Writings* (2004) and *Native North American Literatures: Reflections on Multiculturalism* (2009), *Aspects of Transnational and Indigenous Cultures* (2014), *Ocean and Ecology in the Trans-Pacific Context* (2016), and *Chinese Railroad Workers: Recovery and Representation* (2017). She serves on the advisory board of *The Journal of Transnational American Studies* and Routledge series on Transnational Indigenous Perspectives and on the editorial board of *Transmotion: A Journal of Vizenorian Indigenous Studies*. Her current research project investigates the Anthropocene in trans-Pacific Indigenous and Arctic Writing.

ADELINE JOHNS-PUTRA is Professor of Literature at Xi'an Jiaotong-Liverpool University, China. She was President of the Association for the Study of Literature and Environment UK and Ireland (ASLE-UKI) from 2011 to 2015. She is the author of *Heroes and Housewives: Women's Epic Poetry and Domestic Ideology in the Romantic Age* (2001), *The History of the Epic* (2006), and *Climate Change and the Contemporary Novel* (2019). She is the editor of *Climate and Literature* (2019) and co-editor of *Process: Landscape and Text* (2010), *Literature and Sustainability: Concept, Text, and Culture* (2017), and *Cli-Fi: A Companion* (2018).

JENNY KERBER is Associate Professor in the Department of English and Film Studies at Wilfrid Laurier University in Waterloo, Ontario, the lands of the Haudenosaunee, Anishinaabe, and Neutral Peoples and part of the Haldimand Tract of 1784. She teaches Canadian literature, Indigenous literatures, border studies, and the literature of sport, and is the author of *Writing in Dust: Reading the Prairie Environmentally* (2010), as well as articles in *Canadian Literature, Studies in Canadian Literature, ISLE,* and *Western American Literature,* among other venues.

CHERYL LOUSLEY is Research Chair in Environmental Humanities and Associate Professor, English and Interdisciplinary Studies, Lakehead University Orillia, Canada, with a focus on contemporary Canadian, Indigenous, and postcolonial environmental justice writing and cultural studies. She lives, learns, and teaches among Anishinaabe and Métis neighbours, students, and elders on lands and waters unjustly appropriated for settler cultures to benefit. She is past president of the Association for Literature, Environment, and Culture in Canada, and the founding series editor for the Environmental Humanities book series published by Wilfrid Laurier University Press since 2007.

GREGORY LYNALL is Professor and King Alfred Chair in English Literature, and co-director of the Literature and Science Hub Research Centre at the University of Liverpool, UK. His publications include *Swift and Science: The Satire, Politics, and Theology of Natural Knowledge, 1690–1730* (2012) and *Imagining Solar Energy: The Power of the Sun in English Literature, Science and Culture* (2020).

THERESA J. MAY is a director, playwright, and Professor of Theatre at the University of Oregon, USA. She is a leading voice in ecological and community-based theatre, and the praxis of ecodramaturgy. She is author of *Earth Matters on Stage: Ecology, Environment and American Theater* (2021) and *Salmon Is Everything: Community-Based Theatre in the Klamath Watershed* (2019); co-editor of *Readings in Performance and Ecology* (2012); and co-author of *Greening Up Our Houses* (1994), the first book on sustainable theatre management. She is the co-founder and executive director of the EMOS Ecodrama Festival.

ELIZABETH MAZZOLINI is Associate Professor of English at the University at Buffalo, SUNY, USA. She is the author of *The Everest Effect: Nature, Culture, Ideology* (2015), and articles appearing in *The Minnesota Review, The Goose,* and *Cultural Critique.* She is co-editor of the collection *Histories of the Dustheap: Waste, Material Cultures, Social Justice* (2012). She directs the Academic and Professional Writing Program at the University at Buffalo.

JOHN PARHAM is Professor of Environmental Humanities at the University of Worcester, UK. He has authored or edited six books, including *Green Media and Popular Culture* (2016) and the *Cambridge Companion to Literature and the Anthropocene* (2021). He was until recently co-editor of the journal *Green Letters: Studies in Ecocriticism.* John has published widely on 'Victorian ecology', contemporary literature, and 'green' media and popular culture. He is currently examining the cultural imagination of photosynthesis in the context of climate change and the Anthropocene.

FIONA PROBYN-RAPSEY is Professor in the School of Humanities and Social Inquiry at the University of Wollongong, Australia. Probyn-Rapsey's research connects feminist critical race studies and animal studies, examining where, when and how gender, race and species intersect. She is the author of *Made to Matter: White Fathers, Stolen Generations* (2013), and co-editor of three books, *Animal Death* (2013), *Animals in the Anthropocene: Critical Perspectives on Non-Human Futures* (2015), and *Animaladies: Gender, Species, Madness* (2018) with Lori Gruen. She is also Series Editor (with Melissa Boyde and Yvette Watt) of the Animal Publics book series through Sydney University Press.

CHITRA SANKARAN is Chair of Literature in the Department of English at the National University of Singapore. Her research interests are South and Southeast Asian fiction, feminist and postcolonial theories, and ecocriticism. Her publications include three monographs, ten edited volumes on Asian literatures, chapters in books and articles in journals including *ISLE, Journal of Commonwealth Literature, ARIEL,* and *Theatre Research International.* Her recent monograph, *Women, Subalterns and Ecologies in South and Southeast Asian Women's Fiction* was published in 2021. She is the founding and current president of the Association for the Study of Literature and Environment in ASEAN (ASLE-ASEAN) and the Chief-Editor for the *Journal of Southeast Asian Ecocriticism.*

SAM SOLNICK is Senior Lecturer in English Literature at the University of Liverpool, UK, where he co-leads the Literature and Science Hub and the Environmental Humanities research theme. He has published widely on aspects of environment and ecology in poetry, fiction, visual culture and performance. His first monograph, *Poetry and the Anthropocene,* was published in 2016.

SHELLEY STREEBY is Professor of Ethnic Studies and Literature at the University of California, San Diego, USA. Her book *Imagining the Future of Climate Change: World-Making through Science Fiction and Activism* was published by the University of California Press in the American Studies Now! Series in 2018. She is also author of *Radical Sensations: World Movements, Violence, and Visual Culture* (2013) and *American Sensations: Class, Empire, and the Production of Popular Culture* (2002), which received the ASA's Lora Romero Prize. She is co-editor (with Jesse Alemán) of *Empire and the Literature of Sensation: An Anthology of Nineteenth-Century Popular Fiction* (2007) and, with Ramzi Fawaz and Deborah Whaley, of the forthcoming *Keywords for Comics Studies.* Since 2010 she has directed the Clarion Science Fiction and Fantasy Writers' Workshop. She is currently working on a new book, *Speculative Archives: Hidden Histories and Ecologies of Science Fiction World-Making.*

KELLY SULTZBACH is a Professor at the University of Wisconsin, La Crosse, USA, and was a Fulbright Scholar with the University of Liverpool, UK, in 2019. She is author of *Ecocriticism in the Modernist Imagination: Forster, Woolf, and Auden* (2016). Recent work also includes articles in *Modernist Cultures* (forthcoming), the ASLE-UKI journal *Green Letters* (2019), and a chapter in *Understanding Merleau-Ponty, Understanding Modernism* (2018). Her current monograph project is *Green Thinking: Imagining a Collective Environmental Consciousness in 20th Century Literature and Beyond.*

ALEXA WEIK VON MOSSNER is Associate Professor of American Studies at the University of Klagenfurt in Austria. Her research explores contemporary environmental culture from a cognitive ecocritical perspective. She is the author of *Cosmopolitan Minds: Literature, Emotion, and the Transnational Imagination* (2014) and *Affective Ecologies: Empathy, Emotion, and Environmental Narrative* (2017), the editor of *Moving Environments: Affect, Emotion, Ecology, and Film* (2014), and the co-editor of *The Anticipation of Catastrophe: Environmental Risk in North American Literature and Culture* (with Sylvia Mayer, Winter, 2014).

DEREK WOODS is Assistant Professor of English at the University of British Columbia, Canada. He is writing a book about 'ecotechnology' in the context of ecological sciences and science fiction. His articles look at topics such as the philosophy and aesthetics of scale, biopolitics, and modern Anglophone literature. He recently completed a postdoctoral fellowship in the Society of Fellows at Dartmouth College. His future work will continue to address questions of scale and be devoted to (the mediation of) fungi and lichens.

ADELINE JOHNS-PUTRA AND
KELLY SULTZBACH

Introduction

The relationship between 'climate' and 'literature' seems a simple one, but only deceptively so. Literature, one might argue, depicts climate in its settings – the atmospheres or climes in which storyworlds are embedded, or the conditions that inspire lyrical effusions. Or weather events might play a part in plot (a storm waylaying a journey, perhaps) and imagery (a storm representing emotional or psychological breakdown). But to go this far is already to consider that literature helps to shape, and not simply reflect, our ideas about climate (how much is one's response to a tempest 'real' and how much 'imaginary'?). Moreover, climate is itself an elusive term determined by various sets of written records: discrete meteorological occurrences or phenomena, prevailing atmospheres, and statistical averages. So, language and text – literary texts included – are where we parse and apply these different concepts. Increasingly, 'climate' refers to a set of physical forces jolted out of kilter, shockingly so, and on a massive, global scale: climate as climate change, as climate crisis. Here, too, literature plays a role, airing anxiety or expressing hope, giving voice to alarm or channelling grief, alerting us to damage, suffering, and injustice.

'Climate' is not just a slippery term or innocent scientific word; it has become an emotionally and ethically violent one. It is, then, our contention in this volume that any analysis of climate and literature must not only deal with the many ways in which climate has been conceptualised but also frame those conceptualisations as a pre-history to climate emergency. We chronicle here the vexed genealogy of climate and literature, before turning to consider the literary and literary-critical field in a time of climate crisis. We then introduce the chapters in this volume, which look both back on this terrain and forward into a fraught world.

A Genealogy of Climate and Literature

Climate, as is often observed, is not just weather; it is weather measured, averaged, quantified. At the same time, it refers to meteorological conditions or events in a given location; it can be correlated to cultural attitudes and habits; it interacts with human experiences, emotional responses, and memories. To borrow the distinction made by James Fleming and Vladimir Jankovic, although one might think of climate as numerical *index*, it has also long been treated in terms of its *agency*. As Fleming and Jankovic put it, climate in its 'exclusive association with the atmospheric sciences' is 'abstract[ed] from the "lived" experience and construct[ed] as a derived entity, a statistical index of averaged parameters across time and space'; yet, 'Outside this context one is more likely to encounter climate as an agency rather than an index. Climate has more often been defined as what it *does* rather than what it *is*.'[1] To this study of the chronology of conceptualisations of climate, however, we will add a crucial third term. As we shall show below, in the light of twentieth-century developments in climatological science, climate is no longer just an index, no simple aggregate or data-driven patterning of weather. The conceptualisation of climate as index has led to it being now chiefly regarded as a *system* – in the words of Paul Edwards, 'a dynamic system, intricately interconnected, articulated, but ultimately fragile and vulnerable'.[2] As we show, the history of climate and literature is a history of these three distinct but interlocking definitions of index, agency, and system. Looking back on this history, it pays to understand how these ideas have developed, how they are linked, and – now – how they have each played a role in our arrival at the current moment of global climate crisis.

To consider the genealogy of literary engagements with climate is to see how climate has always been textual – as agency and index at least. The written record of human understandings of climate begins with descriptions of massive and extreme weather events, from the deluges of rain that cause the great floods in both the story of Gilgamesh and the Bible's Old Testament, to the storms that waylay Odysseus. Such dramatic accounts present climate as utterly agential – a non-human force and natural power to be reckoned with.

However, what is also discernible in the earliest ancient written texts is the recording of climate as index. These offer, on the one hand, phenological descriptions that quantify weather events into predictable processes and, on the other, chronicles of distinctive local patterns and thus the first recorded discussions of the world's differing climates. Examples of the first kind include classical Greek tablet almanacs or *parapegmata* (third century BC) used in fishing and farming, that echo the advice given in Hesiod's *Works and Days* (ca. 700 BC) on how agricultural practices should pay heed to the different weather patterns that pertain in different regions.[3] Similarly, ancient Chinese records provide purviews of the seasonal shifts in diverse parts of the nascent Chinese empire. These include the magisterial, multi-authored *Chunqiu* or 'Spring and Autumn Annals', consisting of brief records of significant events that cover a period from 722 to 481 BC, and *Lu Shi Chun Qiu* or 'Master Lu's Spring and Autumn Annals' (*ca.* 239 BC), which offer more detailed phenological observations, such as variations in the timing of crop harvests year on year.[4] In the second category, one could place the medical treatise *On Airs, Waters, and Places*, attributed to Hippocrates (460–377 BC), which connects seasonal and regional weather variations to people's physical and psychological conditions. One could include, too, Aristotle's *Meteorology* (384–322 BC), which not only attempts to investigate all manner of meteorological and geological phenomena, but helps to introduce the concept of climatic zones, or *klimata*, dividing the world latitudinally into five bands, much as Ptolemy would go on to do with seven climatic zones in his *Geography* (*ca.* 150 CE). Meanwhile, in both Hindu and Tamil poetries from the first few centuries CE (such as Kalidasa's 'Garland of the Seasons' and the *thinai* poetry of early Tamil *Sangram* literature), climatic states are explicitly linked to emotional ones, so much so in *thinai* that climatic settings are assigned their own predetermined poetic tropes, topics, and themes.[5]

Here, then, we see the earliest attempts to quantify weather over space and time as climate, and thus the beginnings of an understanding of climate as index. Even so, these indexical records consistently relate climatic conditions to human activity, in both correlational and causal terms, and thus retain a belief in climate as agency. Such human–climate causation works both ways in these records: not only do meteorological events determine how humans could and should behave but humans were also capable of provoking natural catastrophes, events often believed to be divine punishment for transgressive human behaviour meted out by wrathful gods.

As this history continues into the early modern and modern eras, there is still no clear demarcation between climate as agency and as index, the usurpation of the latter over the former being a gradual shift. Broadly speaking, climate data-keeping begins with the practice of chorography – the regular recording of physical, including meteorological, conditions. There is evidence of distinct traditions of this in both Europe and Asia from the sixteenth century onwards. Keeping weather diaries is a continent-wide habit encompassing Britain, Italy, Iberia, Poland, Germany, and Switzerland,[6] while the emperors of China's Qing dynasty (1644–1911) increasingly demanded weather reports from the many corners of their kingdom, contained in what Quansheng Ge *et al.* call the 'Memos-to-Emperor'.[7] But, as Jankovic points out, however, although weather diaries attempt a record of weather, they still tend to emphasise the subjective encounter between human and climatic agency, since first-hand knowledge and eye-witness accounts were yet considered the most reliable sources of information: 'personal inspection, scrutiny, and observation played a critical role'.[8]

Nonetheless, chorographical records were the preface to the reification of climate away from ideas of agency and into the objective state of index – or, perhaps more accurately, the transformation of climate's agential characteristics into an entity knowable primarily through its indexical qualities. This occurs in what one might call the 'quantifying spirit' of the Enlightenment – that is, the privileging of ostensibly impartial, calibrated measurement.[9] With climate, this expresses itself as the systematic comparative study of not just long-term weather patterns but regional similarities and differences, now emblematised by Alexander von Humboldt's first use of the isotherm in cartography in 1817. As Deborah Coen has shown, in the late nineteenth century, large land-based empires, from the Hapsburg territories to Russia and British India, began to record and compare regional climatic variations.[10] Certainly, climate could still be defined, in Humboldt's words, in terms of its agential relationship with human and non-human life – 'with respect to the increased radiation from the Earth, the organic development of plants, and the ripening of fruits, but also with reference to its influence on the feelings and mental condition of men'. But, above all, it described general meteorological conditions – 'all the changes in the atmosphere which sensibly affect our organs, as temperature, humidity, variations in the barometrical pressure, the calm state of the air or the action of opposite winds, the amount of electric tension, the purity of the atmosphere or its admixture with more or less noxious gaseous exhalations, and, finally, the degree of ordinary transparency and clearness of the sky' – that could only be known through exhaustive quantification and the subsequent extrapolation of data.[11]

Such an understanding expresses itself in the nineteenth-century novel as an awareness of how the diverse operations of climate could come together to produce a local condition, much in the same way as character actions and interactions contribute to the plot, mood, and drive of narrative. For this reason, as Jesse Oak Taylor puts it, the Victorian realist novel serves as the kind of 'climate model' that contemporary science was in the process of developing and deploying.[12] From Emily Brontë's *Wuthering Heights* (1847) to Thomas Hardy's *The Return of the Native* (1878), the novel's accumulation of descriptions of weather alongside longitudinal climate observations represents the same epistemological operation found in contemporary scientific practice: they both serve to collapse discrete events and features into a coherent, stable state known as a climate.

It might seem easy to draw a straight line from the Enlightenment and nineteenth-century practice of climate quantification and extrapolation to modern climatology and its understanding of global climate dynamics. Certainly, the kind of massive, multi-scalar climate analysis that Coen describes meant that, by the beginning of the twentieth century, scientists understood that large, regional climates were composed of complex and interdependent ecological, geological, and meteorological processes, an understanding that became 'crucial to the development of the understanding of the earth as a whole'.[13] And, certainly, in literature too, particularly in the science fiction of the late nineteenth and early twentieth centuries, ideas of relatively stable regional climates are expanded to depictions of planetary ones, such as the Martian atmosphere of Edgar Rice Burroughs's 'Under the Moons of Mars' (1912), and are discussed as part of a complex and interconnected Earth system in more ambitious works, such as Jules Verne's *The Purchase of the North Pole* (1889) and Camille Flammarion's *Omega: The Last Days of the World* (1893).

However, climate's elevation from index to system required some important further steps. As Spencer Weart shows in his valuable history of the development of what was first known as 'global warming', the mid-twentieth century saw an important change of emphasis in climate science. One reason for this lay in the even wider changes in public understandings of the considerable scale of environmental damage inflicted by humans in terms of radioactive fallout or chemical pollution – the outcomes of the dawn of the nuclear age and the birth of modern environmental awareness so eloquently heralded by Rachel Carson's *Silent Spring* (1962). Other reasons lay in the enormous investment into meteorology made by a (cold-)war-ready United States, eager to gain any advantage in military intelligence, an attitude that benefited scientists, such as those at the University of Chicago, who, from the 1940s onwards, 'were determined to make the study of climate truly scientific', who sought to replace 'traditional climatology [which] merely listed descriptions of the "normal" climate in each geographical region' with 'a more complex understanding of climate from basic principles of physics'.[14] Thus, by 1965, the not-quite-coherent field of climate study (a broad church comprising – among others – meteorologists, atmospheric physicists, biochemists, and geologists) came together at Boulder, Colorado, to discuss, for the first time, the 'Causes of Climate Change'. As they did so, these scientists were becoming aware that global climate 'could not be treated in the old fashion, like some simple mechanism that kept itself stable'; they were ready to conclude, in other words, that the world's climate was really 'a complex system, precariously balanced'.[15] By the 1980s, what Edwards calls the *'global knowledge infrastructure'* of climate science – that 'collects data, models physical processes, tests theories, and ultimately generates a widely shared understanding of climate and climate change' – had evolved, effectively maintaining and constantly reproducing climate as system.[16]

The significance of the twentieth-century conceptualisation of climate as system (and how it relates back to agency) is best grasped if framed in terms of climate's designation as divinely ordained. In the dislodging of climate as agency that took place – gradually, but eventually – through the Enlightenment, the ancient idea that climate expressed the ways and will of God or nature writ large remained surprisingly durable. It persisted in the history of understandings of climate as index, as statistical average, for this meant it was really a norm held in place by nature, or what Weart terms 'a universal principle: the Balance of Nature'.[17] In this case, the shock appeal of extreme weather is merely the flipside to understanding climate as innately a state of balance and normality. Literature responds to this idea by depicting climate catastrophe as an opportunity for dramatic effect, signalling a step outside the ordinary. In early modern and modern literature, this has been the case from Shakespeare's storms to Daniel Defoe's sensational reporting in *The Storm* (1703), to the atmospherically induced moodiness and meditations of William Cowper's *The Task* (1785). Even in twentieth-century tellings, from what Weart calls 'old folk's tales' of the Dust Bowl to John Steinbeck's literary evocations of the same, catastrophe was 'something transient; things revert to normal after a few years'.[18] In contrast, the shift from climate as index – 'stable by *definition*' – to climate as system punctures the idea that climate offers humans a perpetual, God-given stability: 'The system showed a dangerous potential for dramatic change, on its own or under human technological intervention, and quicker than anyone had supposed.'[19]

Thus, to understand climate as system is to allow the return of climate as agency – this time, with a relentless focus on human agency. The twentieth century's deepened comprehension of climate, brought on by the discovery of climate change, recognised anew humans as a player – and a major one at that – amidst the diffuse and numerous agential forces of the climate system. Human agency, of course, is what distinguishes climate change (or, to give it its full name, 'anthropogenic climate change') from other global climatic phenomena, such as glaciation and the transition into and out of geological epochs. This is also what makes climate change a component of the Anthropocene, along with other devastating, human-caused processes, such as ocean and atmospheric pollution, careless bioengineering, ozone depletion, and nuclear fallout. If the Anthropocene names a possible new geological epoch in which human damage to the environment has become so great as to leave its mark in the stratigraphic record, then climate change at least is its 'most prominent feature'.[20] At the same time, and in terms of its effect on human psychology and action, climate change awareness is not simply a subset of Anthropocene anxieties, for we can now recognise it as one of the earliest forms of worldwide attention to a specific fabric of human-generated issues and impacts, from the loss of permafrost to species extinction.

For this reason, the literature of climate change is tightly entangled with literary and critical responses to the Anthropocene. It is perhaps most deeply entangled with that knotty ethical dilemma of the Anthropocene: how to dislodge a vision of human exceptionalism that paints us as benefactors of God-given environmental harmony and yet still retain a sense of human responsibility for reversing the profound disharmony we have visited upon the planet. Or, to put this another way, if the Anthropocene names the recognition that human agency is part of the delicate system of climate, we must now work within that system, not against it. This, in part, underlies Fleming's and Jankovic's call to return to the ancient idea of agency – which they invoke under its Greek name, *Klima* – and to disown that of index.[21] And, yet, Fleming and Jankovic do not quite heed the distinction between *Klima* and what we term here the idea of climate as system: that the one merely returns us to questions of the interconnectedness of human and climatic agencies while the other demands a new form of human agency to preserve the fragile balance that locks them together. It is, then, in the literary sphere that such a balance might be struck. Perhaps it is in the new climate imaginings that we might come to terms with the dilemma of how to decentre ourselves from old ideas of observing, utilising, or exploiting climate, while calling to each other to collectively act in ways that respect it.

Literature in the Age of Climate Change

As climate change has become increasingly researched and reported, and the vulnerability of the climate system has become alarmingly apparent, voices from the humanities, sciences, and the popular press have urged writers and scholars to help create a collective, cultural imagination for grappling with the potential futures of a warming planet. As a recent study points out, 'the arts and humanities inhabit the (usually fractured) join between "fact-making" and "meaning-making"'.[22] Indeed, what the seemingly benign figure of 2°C warming might mean in terms of bodies and places can be profoundly difficult to absorb without imaginative scenarios and careful, hermeneutic study. As earlier climate literature engaged with indexical measures of agricultural statistics and temperature recordings, current literary engagements with the hyperobjects of climate-changed systems respond to new indexical measures of alarm, such as the United Nations' IPCC reports. Contemporary stories also contend with the paradox of human agency in the Anthropocene – both as a source of anthropocentric hubris open to critique and as a political body to motivate societies towards a more ethical partnership with nature's agency. Although awareness of anthropogenic climate change accentuates scientific manifestations of human agency, older forms of human agency, including the fear of incurring divine punishment and roles inherited from creation stories, are still at stake as well. As Ursula Heise reminds us, no matter how devoted an individual environmentalist or conservation scientist may be, their work will only 'gain sociocultural traction to the extent they become part of the stories that human communities tell about themselves: stories about their origins, their development, their identity, and their future horizons'.[23] How literature depicts the diverse agencies of cultural climates is now bound up with geophysical and ecological outcomes. From this contemporary vantage point, the historical and conceptual interdependency of agency, index, and system becomes more real and poignant than was popularly understood in earlier eras of climate literature. Given that any literary engagement with climate is, now and unavoidably, also an engagement with climate change, we apply the term 'climate change literature' to literature written within the context of cultural awareness of anthropogenic agency and global warming, rather than the more encompassing 'climate literature', which refers to a myriad of different forms of climate awareness in any period, from ancient texts through the present day.

The study of climate change literature usually centres on fiction, since fictional, narrative treatments of climate change, or climate fiction, have historically been more prevalent than dramatic or poetic ones.[24] It has also tended to focus on some genres of fiction over others, for example, on science fiction – indeed, climate fiction is sometimes designated as a subgenre of science fiction.[25] Yet, that emphasis risks occluding the sheer explosion of climate change literature now occurring across a wide range of creative outputs and modes. For sure, one can distinguish broadly between climate novels 'set in a recognisable, realist present (or very near future)' and those set 'in a futuristic climate-changed world' (for example, in Sylvia Mayer's distinction of 'anticipatory' and 'catastrophic' forms of climate fiction).[26] But to hold too fast to this divide, turning it into a line between the categories of realist novels and science, or speculative, fiction, is to ignore the extent to which climate fiction straddles boundaries. Climate fiction, which can be defined primarily by its 'thematic focus' on anthropogenic climate change, emerges in 'thrillers, science fiction, disaster novels, crime and conspiracy novels, young adult novels of personal development, social satire, and even work in the genres of cyberpunk, horror and fantasy', ranging from 'serious' or 'highbrow' novels to so-called genre fiction.[27] And, although early fictional engagements with global warming from the 1970s and 80s, such as Ursula K. Le Guin's *The Lathe of Heaven* (1971), Arthur Herzog's *Heat* (1977), and George Turner's *The Sea and Summer* (1987), tended to be futuristic in their settings, the second decade of this century onwards has seen a spate of climate fiction in which present-day narratives also abound, for example, Ian McEwan's *Solar* (2010) and Barbara Kingsolver's *Flight Behaviour* (2013). This proliferation has seen climate fiction occur increasingly in non-Anglophone literatures as well, such as Finnish and German, in the novels of Antti Tuomainen (*Parantaja*, 2010) and Ilija Trojanow (*EisTau*, 2011), for example.[28] Significantly, a rich spectrum of views and voices has emerged: in the work of writers such as Alexis Wright, Nnedi Okorafor, Alexis Pauline Gumbs, and Wu Ming-yi, climate fiction has moved well beyond Anglophone (and predominantly white) perspectives, to incorporate the experiences of people of colour, Indigenous communities, and the Global South; readers are being alerted to the intertwining of environmental (in)justice with issues of climate devastation, for example, the real impact of sea-level rise on pelagic and archipelagic communities, or the new and frightening shapes taken by settler–colonialist attitudes in the Anthropocene.

Yet the field itself is molten and mutable. As many scholars have pointed out, the global scope of climate change challenges the traditional structure of storytelling, whether decentring its conventional focus on a single human protagonist with a personal conflict, distending its scales of space or time, or reinventing wholesale its ideas about nature or wilderness.[29] Climate change literature can still be highly localised, drawing attention to particular phenological shifts, migration patterns, or watersheds, recalling earlier indexes, but it may also use cognitive animal science to construct sentient, non-human characters. Alternatively, its plots or characters could sprawl across generations or continents, and in some futuristic fiction, planets and galaxies. Representing how readers experience climate change today involves multiple layers of encounter: from the immediacy of embodied sensation (such as a welcome breeze on sweaty skin) to the abstract symbols of climate science in popular culture (hockey-stick graphs and blue-to-orange temperature stripes). Further, the lived experience of climate change – with its forcings and feedback loops – also increasingly mandates an awareness of something akin to Lorenz's metaphor for chaos theory, how the wings of a butterfly in Texas can cause a tornado in China, seemingly minor events cascading into larger states of disorder.[30] As a result, climate change literature is also a place for working through problems of privilege, suffering, and inequity. 'Who is the we?', Dipesh Chakrabarty asks, when 'we humans never experience ourselves as a species'.[31] Indeed, climate change is imbricated in a lack of understanding and empathy for fellow humans. Kathryn Yusoff traces the 'geomateriality of race', suggesting, for example, how slavery in sugar and coal production 'weaponized the redistribution of energy around the globe through the flesh of black bodies', attesting to the way climate change literature and criticism is grappling with geological, anthropological, historical, and storied antecedents.[32] Thus, climate change literature's primary characteristics are less foundational properties than they are reactive elements.

Similarly, in contrast to the *relative stability* of natural fluctuations in pre-change literature, texts written from the late twentieth century to the present reflect the *current instability* of both literal and literary climates – and, further, express awareness of the causes of that instability. This awareness emerges as an anxiety, registered particularly in a heightened call for consciousness-raising, a new set of conflicting emotional paradigms, and even political rancour and passionate cries for environmental and social justice. As a result, there can be an expectation from readers that contemporary climate change literature is or should be a platform for advocacy and protest. Some authors certainly do align themselves with a sense of moral urgency and hope to encourage a public will for the sacrifices required to curb greenhouse emissions. Although writers have long penned pleas for direct action – from William Wordsworth, who bemoaned the cultural devaluation of a once deified nature in a world of 'getting and spending', to Kathy Jetñil-Kijiner, whose lyrics enshrine the beauty of the Marshall Islands as ocean levels rise – the contemporary tone has become more urgent, sometimes more elegiac.[33] Richard Powers, speaking in a recent interview about how *The Overstory* (2018) makes trees sacred beings, defends his overtly political themes while acknowledging that they are often shunned in the literary circles of high art: 'Moral passion hasn't been cool for some time; much better to gird yourself in irony and fatalistic detachment.'[34] Of course, that was before *The Overstory* won the 2019 Pulitzer Prize. Others, like Ian McEwan, express concern that 'fiction hates preachiness . . . Nor do readers like to be hectored'.[35] In addition to these debates about politically charged content, Robin Wall Kimmerer, a citizen of the Potawatomi nation, reminds readers that cultural assumptions about environmental ethics are already embedded in the power dynamics of the English language: 'Saying *it* makes a living land into "natural resources." If a maple is an *it*, we can take up the chain saw. If a maple is a *her*, we think twice.'[36] This anthology makes space for a broad range of political positioning in climate-oriented literatures.

The feelings evoked by climate change literature are also in flux, embroiled in conflicted emotional reactions. For some, the experience of droughts, floods, unparalleled fires, and choking ocean plastics are not just the stuff of apocalyptic fiction, but happening in their lives here and now; others may see little change to their local place, creating a situation where climate change is 'cognitively and discursively ever-present, and yet experientially and even materially invisible, at least in any direct form'.[37] As a result, while coiling the springs of catharsis is inherent to all literary art, and such pulleys have historically leveraged moral themes and elevated some cultural values over others, the effect of using those emotional levers in climate change literature can be more tricky to predict. When Raymond Williams wrote *The Country and the City* in 1973, his survey of roughly three hundred years of pastoral literary tradition, the return of the urban speaker from their rural retreat would often provoke some kind of healing respite, either as an idealised reverie or (in a more critical pastoral mode) as an opportunity for raising an ethical awareness of class inequity or over-commodification of nature. In climate change literature, the retreat is unlikely to be so green or so pleasant. What once produced glib nostalgia can now trigger stress or panic. And the ethical issues a character learns during the retreat and return (that is, if they get to return at all) are now more likely to unmask environmental justice failures on a global scale, an experience capable of catapulting a reader into overwhelming inertia rather than goading reformation. In the same spirit as Jonathan Skinner's 2001 manifesto for ecopoetry in the inaugural issue of *Ecopoetics*, which both connects and distinguishes the genre from earlier nature poetry, Terry Gifford has devised a new set of six critical post-pastoral questions for contemporary readers, including 'What are the implications of realizing we are part of nature's creative–destructive processes?' and 'Is the exploitation of our planet aligned with the exploitation of minorities?'[38] Perhaps even more starkly illustrating the acuteness of emotional discordance, Timothy Clark, looking back at Wendell Berry's 1968 poem 'The Peace of Wild Places', now categorises it as 'an example of the kind of work many people no longer find credible'.[39] Instead, Clark draws attention to the power of Juliana Spahr's 'Unnamed Dragonfly Species', a poem about an anonymous 'they' virtually witnessing the breaking of glaciers, interspersed with bolded names of different species, some threatened, others extinct, noting how it creates 'anxiety and denial in relation to the reality of climate change, a complex of contradictory emotions'.[40] Rather than offering restoration and peace, encounters with nature prove unsettling. Glenn Albrecht is the philosopher who invented the word for the paradoxical emotion that poems like 'Unnamed Dragonfly Species' provoke: solastalgia.

Solastalgia appears in several chapters of this volume, confirming its prevalence in the lexicon of climate writing. It is defined as 'the pain or distress caused by the loss or lack of solace and the sense of desolation connected to the present state of one's home and territory. It is the lived experience of negative environmental change. It is the homesickness you have when you are still at home'.[41] More often than not, hopeful representations of a society that mitigate the doom and despair of a climate-changed world have been found to be more psychologically motivating than narratives that rely on fear and apocalypse to incite cultural change, yet an overly optimistic representation can encourage complacency or minimise the collective conflicts inherent in setting emission limits and enforcing economic penalties.[42] Author Paolo Bacigalupi warns readers, 'Human beings are wired to react quickly and exquisitely when it comes to the visceral, but we remain primitive as apes when it comes to the abstract, the complex, and the long-term', thus highlighting climate change stories that seem less focused on 'easy' 'fantasy techno-fixes' and more oriented towards 'hard and complicated' 'social fixes'.[43] What kind of species can humans be in a multispecies world, at our worst, and at our best? What lies between the choices of ecotopian fantasies or apocryphal doom? Can we 'stay with the trouble' and enter the mess of 'generative, joy, terror, and collective thinking'?[44] How writers deploy and readers react to triggers of fear, remorse, or some form of hope-as-work, is yet another unstable barometer of climate change literature.[45]

Criticism in an Age of Climate Change

Literary-critical approaches in an age of climate change were initially associated with the wider field of ecocriticism.[46] The field has since evolved rapidly, registering the huge shifts in scientific knowledge, political responses, and public consciousness. Moreover, as we map it here, the growth has been uneven, with overlaps between bodies of critical thought – our description here can capture only some of this complex and ongoing development.

It is a commonplace that the history of ecocriticism took place in waves – for example, a first wave invested in evocations of untouched or even wild 'nature' and a second wave concerned with the imbrications of urban and non-urban environments, as well as with filtering readings of the non-human through the lenses of race, gender, and class.[47] But, as others have pointed out, the wave model of ecocritical historiography does not quite do justice to the distinctly untidy nature of the field's development.[48] Whatever one makes of first, second, or even third waves, though, one can identify a move, since the 1990s at least, to re-evaluate received notions of human and non-human agency, ontology, and identity.

One could characterise this as a shift from physical concerns to metaphysical ones, from investigations into human relationships with and understandings of the non-human to interrogations of what it is to be human amidst the tangle of these relationships. As Glen Love linked ecocriticism to the life sciences, so new materialism and material ecocriticism benefit from Karen Barad's references to quantum physics as well as political and philosophical inheritances traced by Jane Bennett.[49] New materialism's examination of the agency of matter as it works within assemblages of the non-human and human, in turn relates to the insights of Donna Haraway on the imbricated nature of non-human and human ecology (or 'naturecultures') and on the human condition as, if anything, cyborgian.[50] One might include here, too, Stacy Alaimo's influential work on 'trans-corporeality', which reminds us of the permeability of the human body.[51] Although these ecocritical movements are not directly related to critical interrogations of climate and climate change, they have worked in fruitful dialogue with them, opening as they do on to questions of the interdependency of climatic with human agency, and therefore directly on to concerns of the Anthropocene. Also discernible in this broad shift – and more closely connected with climate concerns – is a deconstructionist approach to climate change, which, generally speaking, considers climate change (and the wider Anthropocene) as themselves constituting a deconstructive force, undoing conventional ideas of human agency. These include Clark's work on scale effects and Anthropocene disorder and Claire Colebrook's investigations into extinction.[52] Probably the most influential of this strand is Timothy Morton's object-oriented ontology, which argues, among other things, that climate change is a prime example of the category of hyperobjects, 'objects massively distributed in time and space relative to humans'.[53] At the same time, however, critical attention is also now being paid to particularised, embodied, human victims in 'the mesh' of climate violence and what Rob Nixon terms 'slow violence'.[54] The conversations that have followed Chakrabarty's arguments for a species-historical awareness, for example, are concerned with instituting questions of intra- and inter-species justice together.[55] Theories of social and material relations pertaining to postcolonialism, feminism, eco-Marxism, and race theory percolate through approaches to environmental justice as they unravel the coeval concerns of cultural and ecological othering within histories of capitalist imperialism. One might place the strands of critique mentioned here under the rubric of 'climate change criticism' or 'critical climate change', although not all these thinkers have directly associated themselves with the term.[56] Finally, of course, the rise of the climate change novel as the most prominent example of literary engagements with climate change has led to a body of textual scholarship that we would call 'climate fiction studies', focused on interrogating, interpreting, and exploring this literary category.[57]

Most recently, within climate change criticism and climate fiction studies there is emerging the conviction that a climate-inflected – or Anthropocene – reading is not just one more way to read but might perhaps be *the* primary mode of twenty-first-century reading. That is to say, authors, readers, and critics cannot now fail to acknowledge humans' place in the climate as system and their own vantage point from within the Anthropocene, as they write, read, and critique that system. Thus, Tobias Menely and Jesse Oak Taylor identify 'two interconnected imperatives: to read the Anthropocene as a literary object and at the same time to recognize the Anthropocene as a geohistorical event that may unsettle our inherited practices of reading'.[58]

Such an awareness also gives way, in a corresponding move, to an acknowledgement of political and ethical, as well as emotional and psycho-logical, investments, on the part of all of us now doing that writing and reading. Thus, this volume unapologetically returns ecocritical scholarship to some of the thorny questions of value and objectivity with which it has grappled in the past. After all, if the ecocritical study of environmental literature more broadly originally emerged from 'subaltern' disciplines such as feminism and postcolonialism, then ecocriticism and climate change criti-cism within it have always intended to create more value and care for the non-human environment.[59] More than one treatise on climate literature goads critics to 'explore well beyond our disciplinary comfort zones', sug-gesting that not only may critics need to engage with forms of literature that are pointedly activist, but also the role of the literary scholar in terms of climate literature is less certain, amidst a growing scholarly unease with speaking in a voice of expert assurance or singular interpretation.[60] Yet, other environmental humanities scholars have plumped for 'profoundly political' critique that avoids overt 'consciousness-raising' in favour of 'greater reflexivity', even if this puts such critique at odds with 'conserva-tionist and other environmental activist communities, which do not always welcome debate that challenges some of the key terms in which they have long understood their missions'.[61] In other words, while some may have voiced concerns that overt advocacy may detract from literary analysis, literary engagements with representations of climate change are, now more than ever, steeped in expectations of consciousness-raising.

Swings of climate feeling are also influencing the voices of literary critics, some of whom are now more likely to discard the traditional stance of authoritative objectivity to insert the context of their localised environmental perspectives, create themes that are explored as queries rather than concre-tised thesis statements, or use fictocritical methods of folding a witnessing 'I' into the prose of scholarly critique. In this volume, contributors were writing about climate literature as 'the black summer' scorched land and animals in

Australia, wildfires raged in California, and Antarctica measured its single hottest day ever recorded; all this is not even to mention that revisions took place through the unfolding tragedy of the Covid-19 pandemic, whose zoonotic origins offer a stark and deadly testimony to the follies of human exceptionalism. Increasingly, scholars of climate literature are acknowledging their own embeddedness in a lived reality of climate change. Although still avoided as a guise of bias to some scholars, for others, acknowledging subjective positioning is a necessary exercise in place-based specificity and emotional transparency. Thus, while this collection encompasses a broad variety of situated positions and formal strategies, it does not deny the moral positions that often frame literary responses to climate change. Instead, the chapters that follow demonstrate the complicated nexus of art and ethics, emphasising that such literature and criticism speak in many voices: pain, anger, fear, defiance, grief, and hope.

The Chapters in This Volume

Part I: Historical Shifts in Climate Consciousness

The first part sets out how climate has been conceived both in and through literary texts, shaping and being shaped by them. Each chapter engages with a key meteorological concept or theme – seasons, atmosphere, weather – and charts its messy history. Rather than simply rehearsing existing historiographical narratives of climate and literature (such as an abrupt Enlightenment-era shift from weather to climate), these essays speak directly to the volume's core argument that the history of our conceptualisation of climate proceeds unevenly through expectations around, variously, climate's agency as a felt presence, its status as data or index, and its betokening of an impossibly complex global system.

In the opening chapter on 'Seasonal Processions', Sarah Dimick begins from the premise that cultural expectations around seasons, forged not just by very real climatic phenological shifts but also by literature, are no longer a sign of climatic stability but a psychologically and politically charged measure of anthropogenic damage; yet, throughout, Dimick understands seasonal imaginaries not as irrevocably lost but as a powerful source of Anthropocenic awareness and advocacy. Subsequently, in his chapter on 'Literal and Literary Atmospheres', Thomas Ford troubles distinctions between the (literal) idea of atmosphere as air, or a physical accumulation of gases, and (literary) notions of atmosphere in its metaphorical sense of mood or aura. Ford shows how nineteenth-century scientific discoveries of atmosphere gave new impetus to atmospheric metaphors, rather than dislodging them, resulting in a specifically modern literary understanding of atmosphere as simultaneously figurative and physical. Then, Jennifer Mae Hamilton's analysis in 'Weathers of Body and World' picks up this theme, enacting readings of literary representations of weather both as literal descriptions and as figurative evocations. In ultimately demonstrating that literature enables both at once, Hamilton draws out the complexities – and political forces – at play when we connect weather with climate, arguing that to mistake one as visible and the other as invisible is akin to ignoring how individual events occur within larger power structures.

Part II: Current Issues in Climate Change Criticism

This part develops the history of thinking about key issues in the study of climate and literature and, more recently, climate change criticism. Major themes within the field coalesce around several complex systems dynamics that predominate discussions of global warming's causes and effects: methods for comprehending multiple scalar dimensions of climate; the politics of petrocultures; the remorse and terror of species extinction; and the grave social injustice of climate burdens faced by those least to blame for their environmental causes, particularly in the Global South. These chapters both assess the prevailing analytical frameworks and innovatively update them.

In 'Scales: Climate versus Embodiment', Derek Woods plots the development of scalar orientations through the era of the Anthropocene across four major topics: the 'superorganism', the climate theory of race, the concepts of 'hyperobject' and 'trans-corporeality', and the idea that literature can 'model' anthropogenic climates. Similarly, Elizabeth Mazzolini's 'Capitalist Cultures: The Taste of Oil' complicates contemporary environmental vilification of the petroleum industry by using the history of the 'boom narrative' to expose how the sticky nexus between resource extraction and class stratification has evolved from television shows like *Dallas* to novels such as *Heat and Light* (2016) by Jennifer Haigh. Drawing from the broader animal turn in posthumanism, 'Animals and Extinction' by Fiona Probyn-Rapsey coins the term 'zoo cli-fi' for literature that represents the perspectives of non-human animals, especially points of view readers are reluctant to imagine, such as animals' potential desire for humanity's own extinction. Long-term social justice problems and environmental challenges dominate Chitra Sankaran's 'Climate Justice and Literatures of the Global South', which features literature from the Philippines, Pakistan, India, and Sri Lanka to reveal the complexity of slow violence and climate refugeeism through a multiplicity of voices, both multi-national and intergenerational.

Part III: Ways of Telling Climate Stories

This part shifts the focus from climate prose and poetry, directing the reader instead to theatre, digital media, and film, to reflect the increasing range of imaginative responses to climate crisis. Theresa May's discussion of 'Climate Theatre' presents us with a comprehensive look at the field, demonstrating not only how theatre as an art form is uniquely placed to enact the lived experience of climate and climate crisis, but also how playwrights are innovating with existing theatrical conventions to push further the ethical and democratic potential of climate theatre. John Parham discusses 'Digital Cli-Fi', from blogs to citizen-science websites. Arguing that the medium of cyberspace helps to recreate climate's diffuseness, ubiquity, and polysemy, Parham considers how these sometimes maligned or 'lowbrow' cultural forms instead offer an effective means of advocacy in the current climate crisis. Finally, in 'Climate on Screen', Alexa Weik von Mossner surveys the field of climate film, drawing out its two different affective modes – the apocalyptic and the ecotopian – to examine these for their psychological and ethical efficacy.

Part IV: Dialogic Perspectives on Emerging Questions

The protean nature of climate change literature's still evolving form creates a rich environment for emerging issues. This section highlights some of the most dynamic new sub-fields and features a pair of contributors writing two separate chapters on each issue to show the dialectical potential and plurality of approaches to these nascent areas of critique. While the writers' arguments do not necessarily present opposing 'sides', each essay articulates a distinctly different approach to the issue, illustrating the inspiring fecundity of climate change literature's growing, branching, mycelium-network of writing and research.

Science Fiction and Future Fantasies: With the spectre of climate change in mind, Fredric Jameson has recently identified science fiction as the new 'realist' novel for our times.[62] Gerry Canavan investigates how science fiction has registered the changes to our ideas of the future, once presumed limitless but now increasingly curtailed by the realities of ecological catastrophe; science fiction's consensus future of technological marvels is increasingly now a 'consensus apocalypse'. Although renewable energies might seem to portend a brighter future vision, Gregory Lynall shows how the countercultural 'solarpunk' genre bends as much towards potential futures of solastalgia and enforced homogeneity as it does towards sustainable optimism.

Collective Climate Action: These essays raise the possibility that climate fiction and other forms of climate change literature might be a new form of protest literature, or that activism might itself be a narrative for our times. Shelley Streeby shows that many Indigenous and Black authors and authors of colour connect climate change to cultural practices that are inextricable from activism, and in their writing model inclusive knowledge and collaborative meaning-making in ways that inherently dismantle colonial power and ecological racism. Kelly Sultzbach looks at the way Richard Powers and Vandana Singh provide two alternative models for imagining a collective that combines humans, non-human animals, and AI, as well as the different forms of 'action' such a hybrid, multispecies collective might create.

Love Letters to the Planet: While love and pastoral yearning are long-standing tropes within environmental literature, they have often been disparaged as subjects of serious scholarly enquiry. More recently, however, their durability is affirmed by innovative forms of expression and new modalities of climate emotion. In the midst of witnessing the ravages of Australia's most devastating wildfire season to date, Thomas Bristow uses fictocriticism to create an affective and personal study of bodies, places, and texts as he analyses climate fiction by writers in the Global South. Offering a corollary to the immediacy of those encounters, Isabel Galleymore draws from environmental psychology and the poetry of Jorie Graham to explore whether virtual reality promotes perspective-taking and empathy, or forces us to reckon with our inability to fully connect.

Diverse Indigenous Responses to Climate: The literature of Indigenous cultures, long marginalised or erroneously mythologised by Western empires, counter mainstream discourses about climate and climate change. However, from an international perspective, not all Indigenous communities share the same assumptions, values, or economic stakes in the climate debate. Hsinya Huang amplifies trans-Pacific Indigenous literature, united in the threats they face as island cultures with rising ocean levels, diminished aquatic ecologies, and increasingly militarised seas. Their poems and stories re-centre Indigenous agency and propose multispecies solutions. Jenny Kerber and Cheryl Lousley focus on Indigenous writers in Canada, responding to settler states and extraction economies with texts and practices that advocate for the reoccupation of Indigenous land, and expand mainstream genres to construct a more enduring legacy of land-based justice.

Redefining 'the Real': These essays speculate on what a renovated sense of history might mean for literary realism: what possibilities might a climatological understanding of time open up for realist narrative in the Anthropocene? Might the Anthropocene's demand that we recognise ourselves as inhabiting geological, planetary, and multispecies scales also be a demand for a new kind of realism, for a new range of storyworlds that would re-enact this experience? Adeline Johns-Putra argues that, if we include what Gerard Genette theorised as the transtexts of literature – from author interviews to fan fiction – within the ambit of realist storyworlds, we might gain a clearer understanding of what it means to write, read, and build multi-scalar collectives in the Anthropocene. Starting from the premise of what he terms 'critical climate irrealism', Sam Solnick combines Michael Löwy's notion of 'critical irrealism' with the climate crisis, analysing how the weird, the Gothic, and the uncanny become literary methods of representing climate change's non-local effects and distorted temporalities.

*

What new questions of systems, index, and agency are at play as more readers internalise anthropogenic climate change? How might that engender further evolutions within climate literature? Most readers know that individual choices alone are not going to make a significant, timely impact on greenhouse emissions, yet cultural and literary messaging often valorises personal responsibility (with its corollary after-effects of guilt and stuplimity) rather than systemic solutions. There is a dearth of climate change literature depicting how the larger algorithmic cogs of corporations and economies might be re-tooled, or conceptualising the machinations of enforceable climate penalties and legal retributions. So how does literature depict systems *conversion* – not merely the future potential for disastrous failure, which is painfully abundant in climate change literature, but rather the means to re-invent it? How might stories motivate rather than simply critique or estrange conglomerate actors? Nathaniel Rich's *Odds Against Tomorrow* (2013) and the work of Kim Stanley Robinson are notable examples of views from inside these monolithic structures, but more imagining of this sort could be an area of expansion within climate change literature. New indexes are emerging too, from Indigenous peoples measuring the carbon-offset capacities of tropical forests to the publicly amassed data of citizen-science projects tracking species migration; these collective indexes pose challenges and opportunities to the meaning of 'authoritative sources' both in terms of authority and authorship. As this volume attests, story-making is already becoming a more interactive process that might value cross-textual pollination between works over the identification of a single authoritative text, or favour hybrid spaces of collective storytelling modelled on indigenous forms. Similarly, how will Covid-19 and other indexes of viral pandemics erupting from the way we treat other animals or the ancient microbes unleashed from melting glaciers influence ways we understand 'community'? Additionally, a recent study notes that readers aged eighteen to thirty-four are being drawn to climate texts in higher percentages.[63] How might that augur new forecasts of mood and agency in climate literature?

Whether it be those who join Greta Thunberg's voice in decrying a house on fire or the Sunrise Movement's Gen Z campaigners for a Green New Deal, future readers might demand more direct confrontation of scientific realities or be more responsive to registers of tone and feeling which reflect hot emotions and righteous anger, as opposed to their parents' solastalgic remorse. Volatility disrupts all coordinates. Power dynamics, indexes, systems, and agencies continue to react as stability cedes to instability and 'Change!' becomes the cry of fear and hope, alike.

Notes

1 J. R. Fleming and V. Jankovic, 'Revisiting *Klima*', *Osiris* 26.1 (2011), 3–4.

2 P. N. Edwards, *A Vast Machine: Computer Models, Climate Data, and the Politics of Global Warming* (Cambridge, MA: MIT Press, 2010), 2.

3 D. Lehoux, *Astronomy, Weather, and Calendars in the Ancient World: Parapegmata and Related Texts in Classical and Near Eastern Societies* (Cambridge University Press, 2007).

4 K. Zhu, 'A Preliminary Study on the Climatic Fluctuations during the Last 5000 Years in China', *Scientia Sinica* 2 (1973), 115–20.

5 For a description of *thinai*, see C. Sankaran, 'Retrieving the Margins: Use of *Thinai* by Three Contemporary Tamil Women Writers', *ISLE: Interdisciplinary Studies in Literature and Environment* 28.1 (2021).

6 C. Pfister *et al.*, 'Daily Weather Observations in Sixteenth-Century Europe', *Climatic Change* 43 (1999), 111–50; F. Domínguez-Castro *et al.*, 'An Early Weather Diary from Iberia (Lisbon, 1631–1632)', *Weather* 70.1 (2015), 20–24; V. Jankovic, *Reading the Skies: A Cultural History of English Weather, 1650–1820* (University of Chicago Press, 2000); D. Camuffo, 'History of the Long Series of Daily Air Temperature in Padova, 1725–1998', *Climatic Change* 53 (2002), 7–75; J. Golinski, *British Weather and the Climate of Enlightenment* (University of Chicago Press, 2007).

7 Q.-S. Ge *et al.*, 'Reconstruction of Historical Climate in China: High Resolution Precipitation Data in Qing Dynasty Archives', *Bulletin of the American Meteorological Society* 86.5 (2005), 671–9; see also P. K. Wang and D. Zhang, 'An Introduction to Some Historical Governmental Weather Records of China', *Bulletin of the American Meteorological Society* 69.7 (1988), 753–8.

8 Jankovic, *Reading the Skies*, 91.

9 T. Feldman, 'Late Enlightenment Meteorology', in T. Frängsmyr *et al.* (eds.), *The Quantifying Spirit in the Eighteenth Century* (Berkeley, CA: University of California Press, 1990), 145–6.

10 D. R. Coen, *Climate in Motion: Science, Empire, and the Problem of Scale* (University of Chicago Press, 2018).

11 A. von Humboldt, *Cosmos: A Sketch of the Physical Description of the Universe* (New York, 1877), quoted in Fleming and Jankovic, 'Revisiting *Klima*', 5–6.

12 J. O. Taylor, *The Sky of Our Manufacture: The London Fog in British Fiction from Dickens to Woolf* (Charlottesville: University of Virginia Press, 2016), 14.

13 Coen, *Climate in Motion*, 83.

14 S. R. Weart, *The Discovery of Global Warming* (2003; Cambridge, MA: Harvard University Press, 2008), rev. ed., 20.

15 Weart, *Discovery of Global Warming*, 39.

16 Edwards, *Vast Machine*, 8.

17 Weart, *Discovery of Global Warming*, 8.

18 Weart, *Discovery of Global Warming*, 8.

19 Weart, *Discovery of Global Warming*, 10, 39.

20 T. Clark, *Ecocriticism on the Edge: The Anthropocene as a Threshold Concept* (London: Bloomsbury Academic, 2015), 10.

21 Fleming and Jankovic, 'Revisiting *Klima*', 1–15.

22 R. Tyszczuk and J. Smith, 'Culture and Climate Change Scenarios: The Role and Potential of the Arts and Humanities in Responding to the 1.5 Degrees Target', *Current Opinion in Environmental Sustainability* 31 (2018), 56–64, 60.

23 U. K. Heise, *Imagining Extinction: The Cultural Meanings of Endangered Species* (University of Chicago Press, 2016), 5.

24 While we use the term 'climate fiction', essays in this volume also employ the term 'cli-fi', which has risen in popularity and recognisability; we note, however, that it is increasingly surrounded by controversy, not just around its origins but because of the way in which it has sometimes been policed on social media.

25 A. Milner and J. R. Burgman, *Science Fiction and Climate Change: A Sociological Approach* (Liverpool University Press, 2020).

26 A. Goodbody and A. Johns-Putra, 'The Rise of the Climate Change Novel', in A. Johns-Putra (ed.), *Climate and Literature* (Cambridge University Press, 2019), 229–45, 234; S. Mayer, 'Explorations of the Controversially Real: Risk, the Climate Change Novel, and the Narrative of Anticipation', in S. Mayer and A. Weik von Mossner (eds.), *The Anticipation of Catastrophe: Environmental Risk in North American Literature and Culture* (Heidelberg: Universitätsverlag Winter, 2014), 21–37.

27 Goodbody and Johns-Putra, 'Rise of the Climate Change Novel', 231, 237.

28 A. Johns-Putra, 'Climate Change in Literature and Literary Criticism: From Cli-Fi, Climate Change Theater and Ecopoetry to Ecocriticism and Climate Change Criticism', *WIREs Climate Change* 7 (2016), 268.

29 See, for example, the arguments that underpin Clark, *Ecocriticism on the Edge*; A. Trexler, *Anthropocene Fictions: The Novel in a Time of Climate Change* (Charlottesville; University of Virginia Press, 2015); and A. Bracke, *Climate Crisis and the Twenty-First-Century British Novel* (London: Bloomsbury Academic, 2016).

30 E. N. Lorenz. 'Deterministic Nonperiodic Flow', *Journal of the Atmospheric Sciences* 20 (1963), 130–41.

31 D. Chakrabarty. *The Crises of Civilization: Exploring Global and Planetary Histories* (Oxford University Press, 2018), 188.

32 K. Yusoff, *A Billion Black Anthropocenes or None* (Minneapolis: University of Minnesota Press, 2018), 14–15.

33 W. Wordsworth, 'The World Is Too Much with Us', in S. Gill (ed.), *Selected Poems* (London: Penguin, 2004), 144–5; K. Jetñil-Kijiner, *Kathy Jetñil-Kijiner*, www.kathyjetnilkijiner.com.

34 M. A. Rose, 'Richard Powers: The Biggest Questions in Literature', *BookPage* (April 2018).

35 B. Tonkin, 'Ian McEwan: I Hang onto Hope in a Tide of Fear', *The Independent* (20 April 2007).

36 R. W. Kimmerer, *Braiding Sweetgrass: Indigenous Wisdom, Scientific Knowledge, and the Teachings of Plants* (Minneapolis, MN: Milkweed, 2013), 57.

37 T. Bristow and T. H. Ford, 'Climates of History, Cultures of Climate', in Bristow and Ford (eds.), *A Cultural History of Climate Change* (Abingdon: Routledge, 2016), 6.

38 J. Skinner, 'Editor's Statement', *Ecopoetics* 1 (2001): 5–8; T. Gifford. 'Pastoral, Antipastoral and Postpastoral as Reading Strategies', in S. Slovic (ed.), *Critical Insights: Nature and the Environment* (Armenia, NY: Salem Press, 2013), 57, 59.

39 T. Clark, *The Value of Ecocriticism* (Cambridge University Press, 2019), 58.

40 Clark, *The Value of Ecocriticism*, 58.

41 G. Albrecht, *Earth Emotions: New Words for a New World* (Ithaca, NY: Cornell University Press, 2019), 38.

42 M. Schneider-Mayerson, 'The Influence of Climate Fiction: An Empirical Survey of Readers', *Environmental Humanities* 10.2 (2018), 473–500.

43 P. Bacigalupi, foreword, in J. J. Adams (ed.), *Loosed upon the World: The Saga Anthology of Climate Fiction* (New York: Saga, 2015) xiii, xiv.

44 D. J. Haraway, *Staying with the Trouble: Making Kin in the Chthulucene* (Durham, NC: Duke University Press, 2016), 31.

45 K. Sultzbach, 'How Can Scholarly Work Be Meaningful in an Era of Lost Causes?', *Green Letters* 23.1–2 (2019), 19–38.

46 A. Trexler and A. Johns-Putra, 'Climate Change in Literature and Literary Criticism', *WIREs* 2 (2011), 192.

47 L. Buell, *The Future of Environmental Crisis and Literary Imagination* (Malden, MA: Blackwell, 2005), 1–28; S. Slovic, 'The Third Wave of Ecocriticism: North American Reflections of the Current State of the Discipline', *Ecozon@* 1.1 (2010), 4–10.

48 H. Bergthaller *et al.*, 'Mapping Common Ground: Ecocriticism, Environmental History, and the Environmental Humanities', *Environmental Humanities* 5 (2014), 269.

49 G. Love, *Practical Ecocriticism* (Charlottesville: University of Virginia Press, 2003); K. Barad, *Meeting the Universe Halfway: Quantum Physics and the Entanglement of Matter and Meaning* (Durham, NC: Duke University Press, 2007); J. Bennett, *Vibrant Matter: A Political Ecology of Things* (Durham, NC: Duke University Press, 2010).

50 D. J. Haraway, *The Companion Species Manifesto: Dogs, People and Significant Otherness* (Chicago, IL: Prickly Paradigm Press, 2003), and 'A Cyborg Manifesto : Science, Technology, and Socialist-Feminism in the Late Twentieth Century', in *Simians, Cyborgs and Women: The Reinvention of Nature* (London: Free Association Books, 1991), 149–81.

51 S. Alaimo, *Bodily Natures: Science, Environment, and the Material Self* (Bloomington: Indiana University Press, 2010).

52 T. Clark, 'Scale', in T. Cohen (ed.), *Telemorphosis: Essays in Critical Climate Change*, vol. 1 (Ann Arbor, MI: Open Humanities Press, 2012) 148–66, and see also his *Ecocriticism on the Edge*; C. Colebrook, *Death of the Posthuman: Essays on Extinction* (Ann Arbor, MI: Open Humanities Press, 2014).

53 T. Morton, *Hyperobjects: Philosophy and Ecology after the End of the World* (Minneapolis: University of Minnesota Press, 2013), 1.

54 R. Nixon, *Slow Violence and the Environmentalism of the Poor* (Cambridge, MA: Harvard University Press, 2011).

55 See not just D. Chakrabarty, 'The Climate of History: Four Theses', *Critical Inquiry*, 35 (2009), 197–222, and 'Postcolonial Studies and the Challenge of Climate Change, *New Literary History* 43 (2012), 1–18, but also Chakrabarty, *The Crises of Civilization* and R. Emmett and T. Lekan (eds.), 'Whose Anthropocene? Revisiting Dipesh Chakrabarty's "Four Theses"', *RCC Perspectives: Transformations in Environment and Society* 2 (2016).

56 The term was first employed by Tom Cohen in founding the Institute of Critical Climate Change, or IC³, at Albany and was subsequently used in Cohen, *Telemorphosis*.

57 See, for example, Trexler, *Anthropocene Fictions*; Bracke, *Climate Crisis and the Twenty-First-Century British Novel*; A. Mehnert, *Climate Change Fictions: Representations of Global Warming in American Literature* (London: Palgrave Macmillan, 2016); A. Johns-Putra, *Climate Change and the Contemporary Novel* (Cambridge University Press, 2019); and G. Andersen, *Climate Fiction and Cultural Analysis: A New Perspective on Life in the Anthropocene* (London: Routledge, 2020).

58 T. Menely and J. O. Taylor, Introduction, in Menely and Taylor (eds.), *Anthropocene Reading: Literary History in Geologic Times* (University Park, PA: Penn State University Press, 2017), 5.

59 G. Garrard, *Ecocriticism*, 2nd ed. (London: Routledge, 2012), 3–4; Trexler and Johns-Putra, 'Climate Change in Literature and Literary Criticism', 192.

60 G. D. Wood, foreword, in Johns-Putra *et al.* (eds.), *Literature and Sustainability: Concept, Text and Culture* (Manchester University Press, 2017), xv.

61 Bergthaller *et al.*, 'Mapping Common Ground', 268.

62 F. Jameson, *The Antinomies of Realism* (London: Verso, 2015), 298.

63 Schneider-Mayerson, 'Influence of Climate Fiction', 473–500.

PART I

Historical Shifts in Climate Consciousness

I

SARAH DIMICK

Seasonal Processions

In *The End of Nature* (1989), widely hailed as one of the first monographs confronting anthropogenic climate change, Bill McKibben asks: 'What does it mean that we have destroyed the old spring and replaced it with a new one of our own devising?'[1] What does it mean that climate change is altering a sense of reliable seasonal procession? Within literary and artistic scholarship, a seasonal procession is typically understood as a representation of each season's timely appearance and fulfilment over the course of a year, but McKibben is calling attention to an entirely different type of seasonal shift. Rather than tracking the procession of spring into summer, and summer into autumn, he signals the transition from 'old spring' into what might be thought of as anthropogenic spring. Similarly, he argues, 'summer is going extinct, replaced by something else that will be called "summer"'.[2] I suspect that McKibben's emphasis on threatened seasonality in *The End of Nature* derives partially from ecological fact and partially from literary tradition. 'The air around us, even where it is clear and smells like spring, and is filled with birds, is *different*, significantly changed', he notes.[3] In an ecological sense, of course, this statement references the imperceptible atmospheric shifts well underway by the 1980s, the steadily rising CO_2 levels altering the experience of spring in the northeastern region of the United States where McKibben resides. But literary context is just as important: McKibben's statement invokes Rachel Carson's *Silent Spring* (1962), gesturing towards the commingling of birdsong and environmental threat and disturbed seasonality that generates the power of Carson's title. Returning again and again to questions of seasonality as the world warms, McKibben claims his place in a tradition of seasonal literature, images of threatened seasonality accentuating his warning. Seasonality, long a feature of environmental non-fiction, enters the age of anthropogenic climate change.

To think through the resonances and complexities of seasonal literature and media in the time of anthropogenic climate change, I turn to two case studies in this chapter. First, to examine the experience of reading seasonal prose drafted before widespread awareness of anthropogenic climate change, I revisit Carson's oeuvre, paying particular attention to her ocean trilogy. I contextualise this trilogy within American seasonal writing of the mid twentieth century, take a brief foray into seasonality within the blue humanities, and then speculate on the marked tendency of environmental critics to return to Carson's work when confronting the climate crisis. What, I ask, drives these currents of nostalgia towards seasonal writing crafted prior to widespread awareness of anthropogenic climate change? I then pivot from this seasonal retrospective to consider the contemporary production of seasonal media, using the British Broadcasting Corporation (BBC) series *Springwatch* as a second case study. I locate *Springwatch* within a British tradition of seasonal media, reflect on how environmental and cultural seasonality intersect in this series, and then examine how *Springwatch* actively works to generate seasonal data for climate research in the United Kingdom. Analysing this show, I am curious about the possibilities of seasonal media unfolding within – and responding to – perceptible season creep. Placed beside each other, Carson's writing and *Springwatch* allow for a comparison of seasonal literature and media produced before and after what Lynn Keller calls the 'self-conscious Anthropocene', the 'pervasive cultural awareness of anthropogenic planetary transformation' that emerges at the turn of the twenty-first century.[4] These two cases offer a glimpse of how seasonal representations are also undergoing a form of season creep, the meanings and capacities of seasonal literature and media adjusting in response to rising awareness of anthropogenic seasonality.

Rachel Carson: Seasonal Retrospectives in the Age of Anthropogenic Climate Change

Prior to the publication of *Silent Spring*, Carson was known as an oceanic writer, but she was also an established seasonal writer.[5] Carson was unusually well versed in seasonal literature – copies of Henry David Thoreau's *Journal* and Richard Jeffries's nature essays had a permanent place on her bedside table.[6] And yet, Carson's proclivity for seasonal prose is unsurprising – perhaps even a bit conventional – within the genre of mid-twentieth-century American nature writing. As the cultural historian Michael Kammen notes, Carson was part of a cohort of seasonal writers working between the 1940s and 1970s, including Aldo Leopold, Joseph Wood Krutch, Donald Culross Peattie, Edwin Way Teale, Gladys Taber, and Hal Borland.[7] Carson employs seasonality more subtly in her oeuvre than many members of this cohort – Teale, for instance, would publish a seasonal quartet, one book dedicated to each of the four seasons of the American temperate zone. Nonetheless, Carson's first book,

Under the Sea-Wind: A Naturalist's Picture of Ocean Life (1941), exhibits a clear if understated seasonal cycle, its chapters subtly processing through the year: 'Spring Flight' is followed by 'Summer's End', 'Indian Summer of the Sea', and 'Winter Haven'. As Kammen suggests, Henry Beston's *The Outermost House: A Year of Life on the Great Beach of Cape Cod* (1928) may be the model for Carson's seasonal procession: Carson was an avid reader of Beston's work, and even visited the Massachusetts site depicted in *The Outermost House* while she drafted *Under the Sea-Wind*.[8] Identifying Beston as one of Carson's key influences usefully positions her within a distinct genealogy of oceanic seasonal prose.

Before turning to the particularities of oceanic seasonal writing, it is worth observing that Carson's clearest affinity with other seasonal writers of the mid-twentieth century is her sentimental treatment of the seasons, her tendency to describe annual recurrences as emotionally reassuring or sustaining. For instance, in her 1956 essay, 'Help Your Child to Wonder', published in the magazine *Woman's Home Companion*, Carson reflected on the certainties of seasonal repetition: 'There is symbolic as well as actual beauty in the migration of birds; in the ebb and flow of the tides; in the folded bud ready for the spring. There is something infinitely healing in these repeated refrains of nature – the assurance that dawn comes after night, and spring after winter.'[9] The publication context – an essay on observational practices to cultivate in children – suggests a link between Carson's seasonal philosophy and her childhood upbringing within the nature study movement of the early twentieth century. Nature study enthusiasts like Carson's mother, Maria, sought to instil 'a sympathetic attitude towards nature' in their young pupils through regular observations of the natural world.[10] The heavy sentimentality of Carson's seasonal work – her conviction that seasonal processions are representative of assurance and order – may be an offshoot of nature study's core tenets. Indeed, Carson insisted: 'I am not afraid of being thought a sentimentalist … I believe natural beauty has a necessary place in the spiritual development of any individual or any society.'[11] Carson, like other nature writers of this period, did not shy away from heavy-handed seasonal sentimentalism: annual processions were not simply ecological occurrences but rather symbols of steadiness and assurance.

While the emotional tenor of Carson's seasonal prose aligns with other seasonal writing of this period, her work differs from the dominant tradition insofar as it focuses on the sea. Studies of American seasonal literature are so often populated with terrestrial works – highlighting Edwin Way Teale's automobile trip across the United States in pursuit of seasonal change or Annie Dillard's hyperlocal observations in a valley of Virginia's Blue Ridge

Mountains – and part of the reward of returning to Carson's sea trilogy is the crucial reminder that some of the most powerful works of seasonal prose fall within the purview of the blue humanities.[12] In *The Sea around Us* (1951), the second work in Carson's sea trilogy, she cautions against assuming that 'the passage of the seasons, the procession of the years, are lost in [the ocean's] vastness, obliterated in its own changeless eternity', and indeed, tracking oceanic seasonality requires an alternate set of gauges.[13] Carson's eye, for instance, is drawn to the processions of light that play across the ocean's surfaces. She notes that the summer sea is marked by 'a hard, brilliant, coruscating phosphorescence' caused by protozoa or by bioluminescent shrimp glittering like 'a thousand thousand moving pinpricks of light, like an immense swarm of fireflies moving through a dark wood'.[14] These summer light shows are reprised in autumn, 'when every wave crest is aflame' with the flowering of the dinoflagellates.[15] In addition to tracking processions of luminescence, Carson also notes regular surfacings and submergences, charting seasonality along a vertical axis: 'glassy globules' of cod eggs slowly rise in the spring, while minuscule crustacea descend for winter hibernation.[16] In Carson's estimation, the careful observer of these seasonal movements is rewarded with a sense of oceanic seasonality: 'seen with an understanding eye', she insists, 'the signs are there'.[17]

As Carson works to attune her readers to oceanic seasonal processions, she inevitably emphasises topics now bound to anthropogenic climate change. For instance, even in the short booklets she produced during her employment with the US Fish and Wildlife Service, Carson's depictions of oceanic seasonality emphasise movements and migrations. In 'Chincoteague: A National Wildlife Refuge', the booklet that Carson researched and drafted in 1946, simultaneously with her ongoing research for *The Sea around Us*, she depicts the seasonal patterns of bird migrations along the Atlantic flyway, particularly as they manifest on a wildlife refuge located on a barrier island just off the coast of Virginia.[18] 'The changing seasons at Chincoteague are reflected in the changing populations of the birds', Carson explains.[19] Beginning in May and proceeding until June, she offers prospective visitors a migratory almanac:

> September brings the first of the returning waterfowl, and toward the end of the month flocks of small land bird migrants appear. One morning tree swallows by the thousand are lined up, wing to wing, on the Coast Guard telephone wires for miles along the beach ... Then in October, when the marshes are silvered with frost in the mornings, the waterfowl begin to pour in from the north. ... the refuge suddenly takes on new life as flocks of canvasbacks, redheads, teal, and baldpates rise into the air in noisy thousands.[20]

Beyond her characteristically fluid prose, two elements of Carson's migratory almanac are worth noting. First, the seasonality depicted in this booklet is a seasonality of the shoreline, a depiction of arrivals and departures in both the marshes and the waters just offshore. Second, for Carson, avian migratory patterns have something of the oceanic about them, the birds' movements recalling the advance and return of the salt water: 'the activities of the refuge have reached their lowest point by mid-summer', she notes, 'the ebb between the flood tides of migration'.[21] To conceptualise seasonality as tidal is to indelibly link seasonal writing as a genre with the ocean itself.[22]

But most crucially, Carson's oceanic seasonal writing resists the tendency towards small-scale, stationary observation that defines much of terrestrial seasonal writing, opting instead for a planetary conceptualisation of seasonality.[23] Carson tracks hemispheric migrations and global currents, working to articulate – for a general audience – the way that these vast earth systems function and interact. In *The Sea around Us,* she observes that 'a very slight winter warming of the eastern Atlantic temperatures means, for example, that the snow cover of northwestern Europe will melt earlier, that there will be an earlier thawing of the ground, that spring plowing may begin earlier, that the harvest will be better'.[24] As Carson's prose forges connections between warming ocean currents, precipitation patterns, and agricultural yields, it seems to anticipate the concerns of current climate models. And yet, as Hester Blum notes, even as Carson's description of the ocean as a 'global thermostat' foreshadows current climate discourse, her emphasis on the equilibrium of these planetary systems is a reminder that her research and writing predate widespread awareness of anthropogenic climate change.[25] In Carson's sea trilogy, the ocean is 'the great regulator, the great stabilizer of temperatures', and its currents exhibit 'a beautifully balanced system – as long as it remains in balance'.[26] The global scale of seasonal patterns generated by the ocean – the expansiveness of these annual circuits and patterns – is, for Carson, an assurance against their alteration.

I would argue, however, that with the publication of *Silent Spring* in 1962, Carson inverts the literary seasonality of mid-twentieth-century American nature writing, anticipating seasonal writing informed by anthropogenic climate change insofar as she utilises disrupted seasonality to signal environmental threat. The pastoral ideal of Carson's famous opening fable is generated through a subtle seasonal procession:

> in spring, white clouds of bloom drifted above the green fields. In autumn, oak and maple and birch set up a blaze of color that flamed and flickered across a backdrop of pines .... Even in winter the roadsides were places of beauty,

where countless birds came to feed on the berries and on the seed heads of the dried weeds rising above the snow.[27]

After lulling her readers with the reassurance of this procession, Carson represents chemical threat by undercutting spring's arrival: 'It was a spring without voices. On the mornings that had once throbbed with the dawn chorus of robins, catbirds, doves, jays, wrens, and scores of other bird voices there was now no sound.'[28] Bees are absent from blooming orchards and the window for pollination closes. Newborn piglets die in a matter of days. Carson effectively reverses the sentimentality of seasonal nature writing, offering readers a poisoned, hollow rendition of a season. Drawing on seasonal tropes of spring as a time of vitality and rebirth, she crafts a season of unease. To be clear, Carson is not depicting altered phenologies: her fable is less concerned with seasonal timing than with seasonal absences. And yet, as she narrates a spring that fails to fully manifest, Carson's image of threatened seasonality is a clear precedent for the kind of anthropogenic seasonality found in McKibben's work and other climate writing produced at the turn of the twenty-first century.

It is tempting, as Rob Nixon suggests, to read Carson's writing 'anachronistically', searching for signs of a shifting climate in texts written decades before widespread concern about global warming.[29] And indeed, as Blum notes, reading works like *The Sea around Us* in the twenty-first century, 'when both ecocritical scholarship and environmental policy are increasingly turning to more oceanic and planetary modes of thinking, compels responses both startling and familiar'.[30] But even as Carson's research balances on the precipice of contemporary concerns, I suspect this desire to return to Carson's work as the climate crisis intensifies, this yearning for an ahistorical reading that allows her to speak to current anxieties, is only partially due to her subject matter. As Jenny Price notes, Carson 'was a visionary', someone who not only shaped the modern environmental movement but 'has remained its conscience'.[31] Facing the uncertainties of the climate crisis, I often find myself wishing for Carson's insight, but the closest possibility is a rough historical analogy. In 1951, shortly after the publication of *The Sea around Us*, Carson explained that she received 'a great deal of mail ... people everywhere are desperately eager for whatever will lift them out of themselves and allow them to believe in the future'.[32] She attributed this outpouring of correspondence to the anxieties of living under nuclear threat, to readers 'finding in [*The Sea around Us*] something that is helping them face the problems of these difficult times'.[33] Falling back on the sentimentalism that characterised so much of her seasonal prose, Carson hypothesised that, in periods of duress, 'release from tension can come through the contemplation of the beauties and mysterious rhythms of the natural world'.[34] For Carson, the observation of seasonal processions was a method of retaining equanimity in the face of drastic environmental uncertainty. But for readers returning to Carson's oeuvre in the face of anthropogenic climate change, that reassurance becomes difficult to access: these patterns of seasonality are now subjects of uncertainty in their own right.

Springwatch: Seasonal Media Unfolding in the Age of Anthropogenic Climate Change

Pivoting from this retrospective on Carson's seasonal writing, I turn now to seasonal media produced with a full awareness of anthropogenic climate change. My focus is on *Springwatch*, a television series produced annually by the BBC that regularly garners close to 4 million viewers.[35] The first season of *Springwatch* aired in 2005, followed in subsequent years by the spin-off programmes *Autumnwatch* and *Winterwatch*. Beginning on the Spring Bank Holiday, which typically falls on the last Monday in May, *Springwatch* is broadcast four evenings a week for three weeks. The show offers viewers a cheerful collage of footage from live webcams – which capture Glasgow's urban foxes, the annual cuckoo migration, swallows nesting in a barn on an organic farm in Devon, and muntjacs at Birmingham Airport. At its inception, *Springwatch* seemed like programming designed to convey sentimental reassurance, its seasonal footage of cute animals emphasising feel-good nature: like portions of Carson's writing, *Springwatch* aimed to generate a sense of environmental wonder. However, *Springwatch* coincided with perceptible season creep in Britain. As global temperatures spiked, altering blooming times and migratory arrivals, the very events that *Springwatch* set out to document became destabilised. It became impossible for the BBC to produce a seasonal nature documentary without also producing a climate change documentary: the two genres inevitably converged.

Springwatch emerged from an array of British natural history programming. In the late 1970s, live webcams focused on a badger den in the Cotswolds provided night-time footage for a show called *Badgerwatch*, while a series called *Birdwatch* highlighted the vast range of bird species residing in Britain.[36] These progenitors were produced by the BBC's Natural History Unit, also responsible for the more widely recognised *Planet Earth*, as well as *Springwatch* itself. While these earlier series acclimated British audiences to curated live footage, *Springwatch* and its seasonal spin-offs were distinct in that their focus was not just spatial but also temporal: they featured ecological processions, they documented a season unfolding.

Additionally, in contrast to *Planet Earth* and other BBC nature programming that tracked exotic species in far-off locales, *Springwatch* stayed close to home, skirting the colonialist tendencies that often mark travelogue-expedition nature documentaries.[37] Instead, *Springwatch* relishes the particularities of British seasonality. Rather than reverting to hyperlocal observations or trying to encompass the global seasonal patterns of Carson's work, *Springwatch* is invested in cultivating a sense of seasonality on the level of the nation. The series ultimately constructs, commercialises, and nationalises a period of environmental time.

Just as it emerged from prior renditions of televised nature, *Springwatch* emerged from a long British tradition of cultural seasonality. Other scholars, notably Tess Somervell, have undertaken the task of contextualising British seasonal writing within a more extensive history of European cultural production, ranging from Ovid's description of an everlasting spring to Vivaldi's *Four Seasons* concerti.[38] Indeed, as Somervell's work attests, seasonality suffuses British writing: the pilgrimage in *The Canterbury Tales* commences 'whan that Aprill with his shoures soote / the droghte of March hath perced to the roote', the influence of James Thomson's eighteenth-century poem cycle *The Seasons* can be traced through nineteenth-century works like John Keats's 'To Autumn', and on to Scottish writer Ali Smith's *Summer*, the fourth novel in her lauded seasonal quartet, published in 2020. In relation to this vast corpus, *Springwatch* continues a particular vein of British seasonal pastoralism: it emphasises appreciation for seasonal processions, participating in what Raymond Williams calls 'a renewed intensity of attention to natural beauty' undertaken not by labourers but rather by 'the scientist or the tourist'.[39] The series generates and promotes a carefree enjoyment of the passage of the year, rendering the British seasons as visual pleasures rather than analysing their agricultural or economic implications. How, then, does this television series working within the genre of the seasonal pastoral incorporate anthropogenic climate change? How is it possible to revel in the first blooms of a particular flower, while also noting that blooming is occurring earlier and earlier? This tension lies at the core of *Springwatch* and can exacerbate what Williams calls the tendency to set 'an ordered and happier past ... against the disturbance and disorder of the present'.[40] The act of watching, even with the aim of seasonal appreciation, reveals change.

A season is an environmental occurrence, a period of time in which particular environmental and climatic events are expected to unfold, but seasons can also signify cultural periods, a schedule of performances or airtimes, and *Springwatch* entangles these two definitions. The show, as British scholars Peter Coates and Susie Painter note, has 'become as much a part of our spring as the bluebells, wild garlic, frogspawn, and nesting blue-tits'.[41]

In one sense, spring's seasonal procession within the United Kingdom brings a cultural season into being, environmental events occasioning the BBC's documentary serial. And springtime, as an ecological procession unfolding over the course of weeks, is uniquely suited to seriality: each nightly instalment of *Springwatch* provides an update on spring's development. In a reciprocal sense, though, the cultural season of *Springwatch* draws attention to – and heightens awareness of – the environmental season the show seeks to engage. As it generates interest in seasonal observation among its audience, *Springwatch* cultivates alert viewers not only of a show but also of the season outdoors. The hosts ask viewers to report on their experiences of the season – what they are noticing in their backyards or what they have observed on their commutes to work. For instance, in the ninth season, which aired in 2013, Martin Hughes-Games, one of the three hosts, directly solicits engagement from viewers: 'But we would like to know how spring has been for you. Can you tell us what's your experience of spring? What have you seen? As ever, we'd love to hear from you.'[42] *Springwatch* the show adheres to a more fixed schedule than the environmental season it seeks to portray: it airs according to the calendar rather than according to phenological events. Therefore, the entanglement of these two kinds of seasonality – environmental and cultural – in combination with the way *Springwatch* repeats annually on a precise schedule, positions the show to highlight changes in spring's arrival in the United Kingdom. During the same three weeks each year, a substantial population of viewers becomes particularly attuned to environmental events, primed to note repetitions or discrepancies in timing from year to year.

These appeals for viewer responses set the stage for citizen science – the amassing of vast sets of data through the voluntary observations of amateur naturalists. Enthusiasm for *Springwatch* as a media phenomenon motivated thousands of Britons to record their own sightings of the arrivals and occurrences that became known as the '*Springwatch* six': sighting of frogspawn, the arrival of the peacock butterfly, the flowering of hawthorn, the sighting of swifts, the appearance of red-tailed bumblebees, and the arrival of seven spot ladybirds. The Woodland Trust, an environmental organisation that partnered with the BBC in the show's early seasons and coordinated these observations, notes that *Springwatch* enabled seasonal data collection on a mass scale. As the hosts urged viewers to send in their records, the Woodland Trust 'received literally tens of thousands of observations ... to put this in perspective, in a standard year we receive around a *tenth* of this number of observations'.[43] According to *The Guardian*, in 2005, when

Springwatch and *Autumnwatch* actively promoted this citizen-science effort, more than 93,000 observations were submitted to the Woodland Trust's Nature's Calendar Survey. Moreover, there are now 40,000 people in the United Kingdom who have registered as recorders with the Woodland Trust.[44] In this way, a televised nature programme amplified seasonal observation across the United Kingdom, generating a data set far more extensive than what would have otherwise existed.

*

It's crucial to note, though, that *Springwatch* and the Woodland Trust not only amass seasonal data but also report on the degree to which the climate is changing. When contemporary data from the Nature's Calendar Survey is placed alongside records from the Royal Meteorological Society taken between 1875 and 1947, or when current observations are compared with records taken by the eighteenth-century naturalist Robert Marsham, phenologists can demonstrate that each time the global temperature rises by one degree Celsius, plants bloom five days earlier in Britain.[45] These comparative records indicate that climate change has dramatically shifted spring's arrival. *Springwatch* regularly airs these findings, completing the feedback loop between seasonal media and seasonal data: for instance, in 2010, an episode called 'Signs of Change' followed the host Chris Packham as he outlined historical phenological efforts in Britain and explained how they compare to present observations. In essence, *Springwatch* now bridges seasonal nature footage and the climate change documentary, commingling genres. The pastoral charm of spring's arrival may initially attract viewers who crave footage of blooming daffodils or downy hatchlings, but as these viewers contribute their own observations, they generate alarming climatic data that is then featured on future episodes. In *Springwatch*, as in much seasonal media produced in an age increasingly conscious of the climate crisis, spring is simultaneously pastoral and catastrophic.

Although the repercussions of anthropogenic climate change permeate literature and media, they are particularly acute in seasonal works. To consider literary and cultural seasonality in the early decades of the twenty-first century, as season creep becomes a tangible experience, is to watch a literary and cultural mode shift in response to alterations in the physical world. Reflecting on earlier renditions of seasonality – like those exemplified in Carson's work – often generates a degree of nostalgia, made all the more intense by seasonal literature's association with affects of reassurance. Meanwhile, contemporary seasonal media productions – like *Springwatch* – that actively document and track changes in seasonal timing often mix a sense of unease or apprehension into the easy aesthetics of appreciation that have traditionally characterised the seasonal mode. In this sense, it becomes possible to think of season creep – environmental timings shifting earlier or later as the climate changes, bloomings, and migratory arrivals creeping into timespans they have previously not occupied – not only in an ecological sense, but also as a literary and cultural phenomenon. The seasonal mode itself is creeping into new territory and affects. If tracking season creep in the physical world involves comparing the timing of past and present seasonal events, noting how the dates of leaf burst and frogspawn have shifted, then tracking literary or cultural season creep involves comparing past and present seasonal works. Reflecting on past seasonal writing in light of current seasonal productions allows us to trace the ways that seasonality has shifted culturally: a mode of reassurance is becoming a mode of keen observation and heightened anxiety.

Notes

1 B. McKibben, *The End of Nature* (New York: Random House, 1989), 79.
2 McKibben, *End of Nature*, 59.
3 McKibben, *End of Nature*, 18.
4 L. Keller, *Recomposing Ecopoetics: North American Poetry of the Self-Conscious Anthropocene* (Charlottesville: University of Virginia Press, 2017), 8–9.
5 Notable studies of Carson's engagement with seasonality include M. Kammen, *A Time to Every Purpose: The Four Seasons in American Culture* (Chapel Hill: University of North Carolina Press, 2004) and S. Kaza, 'Rachel Carson's Sense of Time: Experiencing Maine', *ISLE: Interdisciplinary Studies in Literature and the Environment* 17.2 (2010), 291–315.
6 W. Souder, *On a Farther Shore: The Life and Legacy of Rachel Carson* (New York: Crown, 2012), 155–6.
7 Kammen, *A Time to Every Purpose*, 176–86.
8 Kammen, *A Time to Every Purpose*, 146.
9 R. Carson, 'Help Your Child to Wonder', *Woman's Home Companion* (July 1956), 48. This passage also appears in a 1954 speech Carson gave to Theta Sigma Phi, a sorority of women journalists; see L. Lear, *The Lost Woods: The Discovered Writing of Rachel Carson* (Boston, MA: Beacon Press, 1998), 163.
10 The phrase is Cornell University horticulturalist Liberty Hyde Bailey's. It appears in K. C. Armitage, *The Nature Study Movement: The Forgotten Popularizer of America's Conservation Ethic* (Lawrence: University of Kansas Press, 2009), 1. For more on Carson's connection to the nature study movement, see Armitage, 209–11.
11 Lear, *Lost Woods*, 160.
12 See E. W. Teale's *North with the Spring* (New York: Dodd, Mead & Company, 1951), *Autumn across America* (New York: Dodd, Mead & Company, 1956), *Journey into Summer* (New York: Dodd, Mead & Company, 1960), and

Wandering through Winter (New York: Dodd, Mead & Company, 1965). Also see A. Dillard's *A Pilgrim at Tinker Creek* (New York: Harper & Row, 1974).

13 Carson, *The Sea around Us* (New York: Oxford University Press, 1951), 28.

14 Carson, *Sea around Us*, 32.

15 Carson, *Sea around Us*, 33.

16 Carson, *Sea around Us*, 36.

17 Carson, *Sea around Us*, 29.

18 For a biographical account of this period of intense research and travel, see L. Lear, *Rachel Carson: Witness for Nature* (New York: Henry Holt, 1997), 131–51.

19 Carson, 'Chincoteague: A National Wildlife Refuge', *Conservation in Action* (Washington, DC: Fish and Wildlife Service, Department of the Interior, 1947), 12.

20 Carson, 'Chincoteague', 12.

21 Carson, 'Chincoteague', 13.

22 As Kammen notes, descriptions of seasonality as akin to tides can be found in the writing of Henry David Thoreau, John Burroughs, and May Sarton; *A Time to Every Purpose*, 153. Carson, however, was one of the few writers to think of oceanic patterns not simply as metaphor but as intertwined with the experience of seasonality itself.

23 Examples of terrestrial localism include Leopold and Dillard. For more on Carson's planetary perspective in comparison with her contemporaries, see Kammen, *A Time to Every Purpose*, 181.

24 Kammen, *A Time to Every Purpose*, 171–2.

25 H. Blum, '"Bitter with the Salt of Continents": Rachel Carson and Oceanic Returns', *WSQ: Women's Studies Quarterly* 45.1–2 (2017).

26 Kammen, *A Time to Every Purpose*, 172, 175.

27 R. Carson, *Silent Spring* (Boston, MA: Houghton Mifflin, 1962), 1–2.

28 Carson, *Silent Spring*, 2.

29 R. Nixon, 'Rachel Carson's Prescience', *The Chronicle of Higher Education* (3 September 2012).

30 Blum, 'Bitter with the Salt', 287.

31 J. Price, 'Stop Saving the Planet! – and Other Tips via Rachel Carson for Twenty-First-Century Environmentalists', in L. Culver *et al.* (eds.), *Rachel Carson's* Silent Spring: *Encounters and Legacies*, special issue of *RCC Perspectives*, 7 (2012), 11.

32 Lear, *Lost Woods*, 88–9.

33 Lear, *Lost Woods*, 88.

34 Lear, *Lost Woods*, 89.

35 B. Dowell, 'TV Ratings: Springwatch Return Watched by 3.9m', *The Guardian* (26 May 2009).

36 P. Lee-Wright, *The Documentary Handbook* (London: Routledge, 2010), 359.

37 For an excellent discussion of the rise of travelogue-expedition wildlife films in American cinema, see G. Mitman, *Reel Nature: America's Romance with Wildlife on Film* (Seattle: Washington University Press, 1999).

38 T. Somervell, 'The Seasons', in A. Johns-Putra (ed.), *Climate and Literature* (Cambridge University Press, 2019), 45–59.

39 R. Williams. *The Country and the City* (New York: Oxford University Press, 1973), 20.

40 Williams, *Country and City*, 45.

41 P. Coates and S. Painter, 'How *Springwatch* Was Sprung', *Arts and Humanities Research Council Blog* (14 June 2018).

42 *Springwatch*, season 9, episode 1, 2013.

43 K. Lewthwaite, 'Ten Years of Nature's Calendar', *Springwatch, Autumnwatch and Winterwatch Blog* (4 June 2014), www.bbc.co.uk/blogs/natureuk/entries/17cc4d9a-de72-3d55-ba48-9c014b9b96ca.

44 'Britain Blooming Earlier Thanks to Rising Temperatures, Study Says', *The Guardian* (7 April 2010).

45 'Britain Blooming Earlier'.

2

THOMAS H. FORD

Literal and Literary Atmospheres

Taken at its most literal, a literal atmosphere is one made of letters. A literary atmosphere is equally a written one. Both *literal* and *literary* come from the Latin word *littera*, which meant a letter of the alphabet, and which referred to texts, documents, records, inscriptions, scholarship – in short, 'letters'. Literary and literal atmospheres are at least in this etymological sense always textual, matters of writing as much as matters of air. Yet despite this shared etymology, the two phrases are far from synonymous. If someone speaks of a literal atmosphere, we are much more likely to understand them to be referring to the real thing, the atmosphere itself, rather than to writing. The converse is true of literary atmospheres, which suggest something to be found between the pages rather than in the open air. So although they share a common derivation, the two phrases frame a loose opposition in contemporary language.

On one side is the physical atmosphere. This is the atmosphere comprehended scientifically in chemistry, meteorology, climatology and so on; it is the thin diffuse fluid of the troposphere, thinning out further up through the stratosphere; it is the stuff I am currently breathing in; it includes, today, around 412 parts per million of carbon dioxide; and where I am writing in late 2019 it smells of the smoke of catastrophic bushfires. On the other side, there are the atmospheric representations, effects and techniques to be found in poems, novels, plays and other literary texts. These might be taken to include such things as evocatively realist references to the weather, breathy lyric sighs like 'ah' and 'oh', and tonal unities of scene, episode, or work. Such literary atmospheres seem quite different in nature from the air itself, not least in that, inasmuch as they are textual, a matter of letters on a page or screen, they are literally airless. These words, for example, don't smell of smoke.

For much of the twentieth century, atmosphere considered as a literary or cultural phenomenon tended to be discussed in isolation from the environmental chemistry and physics of the atmospheric sciences. Jesse Oak Taylor has observed that 'the absence of a correlation between literary atmosphere and literal atmosphere in the meteorological sense has long been considered a given of literary language'.[1] Tim Ingold has described this division, similarly, as one between a scientific meteorology that 'gives us a notion of atmosphere evacuated of all traces of moods and affects' and a cultural atmospherics understood as 'a system of affects that appears to exist in a vacuum'.[2] Indeed, although atmosphere has a long and complex literary history, until quite recently it was a minor and relatively under-theorised category in literary criticism and cultural analysis. In 1983, Luce Irigaray went so far as to characterise twentieth-century philosophy as the 'forgetting of air'.[3] Literary atmospheres, it seemed, were not really atmospheric and not really very interesting either.

From around 2000, however, atmosphere has become one of the critical keywords of the present, prominent in fields from geography to anthropology to law to queer theory to media and cultural studies. This research has drawn heavily on accounts from phenomenology and affect theory in which atmosphere has been understood to subvert a series of foundational binary distinctions, including those between subject and object, interior experience and outer world, and mind and body.[4] And this sense of atmosphere as an in-between phenomenon – as a fluid medium of transit that blurs traditional oppositions into indiscernibility – has taken on new force as climate change has come to occupy an ever more central place in public concern. Atmosphere is hot across research fields of the humanities today in large part because anthropogenic global warming puts unprecedented pressure on any assumption of a secure epistemological or ontological distinction between cultural and physical atmospheres. The aim of most recent critical accounts of atmosphere has then been to deconstruct this opposition. By 'staging the intersection of literal and literary atmosphere', they have sought to demonstrate 'the ultimate impossibility' of distinguishing between them.[5]

This chapter reviews how literary and literal atmospheres have cut across each other in complex transactions of meaning and practice over the past four hundred years. To organise the history of these intersections, it introduces two additional terms into the discussion. For in most contexts and in common parlance, *literal* and *literary* are not strictly contradictories. This is because they normally function as different kinds of categories. *Literal* tends to operate as a way of specifying a particular type of meaning. It is usually opposed to terms like *figurative* or *metaphoric*. But while *literal* is a semantic category, *literary*, by contrast, is primarily a discursive one. It refers to literature – a particular mode of discourse and set of accompanying discursive practices – and so is implicitly opposed not to other kinds of meaning but to other discourses like those of philosophy or science. The story of literal and literary atmospheres is then equally a story of figurative and technical atmospheres: of their development, separations, junctures, and transformations.

THOMAS H. FORD

Literal Atmosphere

An atmosphere is literally a fog-ball. The word derives from a 1608 Dutch neologism, *dampcloot*, which was translated in the same year as *atmosphaera* – a Latin word made up of the Greek terms for vapour (ἀτμός) and sphere (σφαῖρα) – from whence it was taken up by the languages of modern Europe.[6] It was, to begin, a speculative term of astronomy and mathematical natural philosophy. In its first appearance in English, in John Wilkins's 1638 *The Discovery of a World in the Moone*, 'Atmo-sphaera' was glossed as 'an orbe of vaporous aire', which, as Wilkins set out to prove, is 'immediately encompassing the body of the Moone'.[7] Only through a second movement, later in the seventeenth century, was this originally extraterrestrial concept applied in English to the air surrounding the Earth. Atmosphere was, then, a hypothetical, purely conceptual category before it became an empirical one. Throughout the eighteenth century it remained a technical term, one found exclusively in works of early modern science.

The new word provided an erudite Graeco-Latinate alternative for an already existing common term, *air*. Atmosphere was air abstracted and experimented upon; air weighed, decomposed, and analysed; air as a matter of inquiry for astronomy, medicine and chemistry; the air of other planets. The old word *air* continued to be available for these kinds of technical uses. It can be found from Robert Boyles's 'the spring of the air' of 1660, for instance, to Joseph Priestley's 'dephlogisticated air' of 1775. But the emergence of the new word signalled a larger-scale disambiguation of air that was occurring through this period, in which new scientific meanings were progressively differentiated from what would come, in retrospect, to be recognised as pre-scientific semantic residues. It was a process in which, in defining its terms, science came also to define itself. Looking back, the scientific history of air from Boyle's spring to Priestley and Antoine Lavoisier's discovery of oxygen has then appeared as a series of epistemological boundary disputes: conflicts through which the nature and status of modern scientific knowledge were articulated and secured.[8]

In Enlightenment philology, comparable projects for disambiguating air were also under way. Thomas Hobbes, Baruch Spinoza, Priestley, and others argued that the key terms of theological tradition, which had interwoven spiritual and physical references, should in fact be read purely literally. For example, the word *spirit* (in Latin: *spiritus*) could be shown always to have a material referent in scripture. It meant a breath or breeze or air but never God or the soul. Both scientifically and hermeneutically, air was then literalised through early modernity: translated down to earth and empirical investigation. The sense of the literal – of literalness – was also transformed in this process. In the middle ages, *literal* had named a type of meaning and a way of reading. It meant to read for the letter rather than for the spirit; it referred to the grammatical sense of a passage as opposed to its figurative or allegorical senses. This medieval opposition of *sensus literalis* and *sensus spiritualis* was a hierarchy, on the scriptural basis that 'the letter killeth, but the spirit giveth life'.[9] From the mid 1600s, just as the word *atmosphere* entered the lexicon and as the word *spirit* was being critically redefined by materialist philology, *literal* likewise took on a new sense. No longer referring to one relatively subordinate kind of textual meaning amongst others, *literal* came instead to signal a language of pure denotation. It signalled, that is, reference to the thing specified, to the thing being talked about, to the actual thing itself. In this new sense, to speak literally was to employ a mode of communication that sought to subtract its own communicative activity from its referential functioning.[10] To speak literally of air was to give voice to a self-erasing figure of atmosphere.

Figurative Atmosphere

The literal meaning of *atmosphere* was consolidated around 1800, when meteorology was reformulated as the modern science of the global atmospheric system. Remarkably, this was also the precise moment in which the word began to circulate in non-scientific contexts, and we find, for the first time, such formulations as 'political atmosphere', 'mental atmosphere', and 'poetic atmosphere'. The entrance of the word into the language 150 years earlier had marked an initial moment of air's disambiguation, its literalisation. At the start of the nineteenth century, *atmosphere* became ambiguous all over again. It remained a technical word that was used with specific reference in scientific contexts. But it also now became very widely available for figurative uses. In effect, the word was split into a literal sense elaborated in the sciences, and a metaphoric sense, in which the properties of that scientific atmosphere were employed for the imaginative redescription of language, culture, and society.

Many words in *atmosphere*'s immediate semantic neighbourhood had figurative and extended uses that were well established and long-standing. *Spirit*, as we have seen, had a complex and multi-layered meaning that included physical substances alongside sacred dimensions. In his 1755 *Dictionary of the English Language*, Samuel Johnson listed no fewer than eighteen different meanings for *spirit*, which ranged from the material, as in 'breath', 'wind in motion', and 'an inflammable liquor', to 'an immaterial substance', 'the soul of man', and 'intellectual powers distinct from the body'.[11] In its primary meaning, *air* was essentially synonymous with *atmosphere* for Johnson, both words referring to 'the element encompassing the terraqueous globe'. But *air* also had a series of extended meanings having to do with communication, including 'publication', 'intelligence', 'information', and 'poetry'. Linked to *aria*, it was potentially musical, naming a melody or song. Through its link to *aura*, it also claimed a spiritual sphere of reference. It could refer further to the characteristic manner, expression, or appearance of a person, or to 'the artificial or practised motions of a managed horse'.[12] Air was, then, global, but also potentially very particular and local. It was both a surrounding exterior element and something radiated or communicated from within, a kind of personal emanation. *Cloud*, meanwhile, named a mass of vapour floating in the air. But in a transferred sense it also referred to any state of obscurity, darkness or gloom. Minds and faces could be clouded as well as skies; the word was used just as commonly with reference to intellectual and affective states as to atmospheric ones. And from the 1750s, *climate*'s reference to a delimited region of the Earth – which had from classical geography into early modernity been understood as a natural set of culturally determining conditions – was extended figuratively to encompass non-natural (which is to say, cultural and historical) conditions: 'the political climate', for example.

As atmosphere became metaphoric at the end of the eighteenth century, it then moved into a densely prepopulated semantic field. Early modern air was abundantly figurative; it was already the vehicle of innumerable interchanges and transits of meaning between the empirical and the numinous, the physical and the ideal, and nature and culture. Figurative atmospheres post-1800 traded on these already existing metaphors. As they came to stand in for climates of mind, personal airs, cloudy intellects, and stormy passions, they drew on ready-made networks of expressive resources. But if metaphoric atmospheres often repeated existing figures of air, they did so with a difference. For, unlike most of the other words in its semantic family, *atmosphere* was a term drawn from the increasingly specialised lexicon of the natural sciences. So even as these new atmospheric metaphors remobilised older figures, they also marked their now non-literal nature more insistently. They occurred as specifically modern re-uptakes, ones taking place after air's empirical literalisation, and after the larger disentanglement of natural scientific knowledge from humanist traditions in which that literalisation had played so prominent a part. As air became more literal, aerial metaphors then became more clearly metaphoric: more identifiable as such, more fictive – and so potentially more literary.

Take weather, for example. As Michael Gamper has outlined, weather underwent 'a gradual semantic abstraction' through the eighteenth century.[13] No longer primarily a word for extraordinary and violent events – for storms, above all else – it came increasingly to refer to the state of the atmosphere quite generally. A discontinuous tradition of textual records of tempests, whirlwinds, and floods was gradually replaced by continuous quantitative data sets that were collected using a whole array of new instruments, from thermometers to anemometers and barometers. Enlightenment weather was weather standardised, smoothed, and normed: 'the sky was emptied of portent, and weather, sliced and secularized, came to mark time's movement in its most prosaic register'.[14] But this same moment also witnessed an unparalleled upsurge of aesthetic interest in weather. As M. H. Abrams observed, 'there is no precedent to the way the symbolic wind was used by poet after poet, in poem after poem, all within the first few decades of the nineteenth century'.[15] With Romanticism, the imagination turned atmospheric, being itself imagined as a visionary state that, as Samuel Taylor Coleridge remarked, 'spreads its influence and colouring over all, that co-exists with the exciting cause, and in which

> The simplest and the most familiar things
> Gain a strange power of spreading awe around them'.[16]

In 1856, John Ruskin went so far as to define modern art and poetry as 'the service of clouds'.[17] The weather that was aesthetically revalorised in this service – re-enchanted, and laden with new symbolic meanings – was modern weather: that is to say, weather as environment, familiar, secular and literalised, rather than weather as event.

A century earlier, in his volume on the great storm of 26–7 November 1703, Daniel Defoe had sought to interweave weather reportage with heavenly providence in an effort to 'reconcile Christian apocalypticism with empirical observation'.[18] But providential and empirical structures of atmospheric meaning were being pulled apart in early modernity. Weather as transcendentally meaningful could no longer be integrated symbolically with weather as what happens. In consequence, Defoe's *The Storm* presented at best 'complex, dialectical, and even incoherent visions of "Nature"'.[19] The 'service of clouds' outlined by Ruskin offered an alternative resolution to this historical dilemma. For Ruskin, a newly literal spirit of observation and representation was central to modern art. The appearances of cloud and mist, for instance, and of objects seen through clouds and mist, became 'a subject of science with us'.[20] But this literalised and empirically observed weather was equally the prime vehicle for what Ruskin famously named 'the pathetic fallacy'.[21] This is the unwarranted projection of human feelings onto the natural world. It is the fallacy of the aesthetic anthropomorphisation of nature – of the rain falling because you're sad. It was a specifically modern fallacy for Ruskin, characterising the contemporary poetry of Wordsworth, Coleridge, Scott, Percy Shelley, Keats, Byron and Tennyson. And for Ruskin it was only a fallacy – a critical flaw in the artwork – to the extent that the poem failed to include an immanent principle of reflection on the metaphoric status of its affective anthropomorphisation of the weather. That is to say, if the metaphor – 'it's raining women's voices', for example – was appropriately acknowledged and motivated within the work itself in some way, then it wasn't a pathetic fallacy any more but instead potentially part of a very good poem. The weather of human feeling would have turned from falsehood to fiction, from impossible wish or even lie to literature.

Literary Atmosphere

Weather in such a poem would be at once literal – 'a subject of science', in Ruskin's words – and metaphoric. Its signs would function at once denotatively and evocatively, both referentially and figuratively. They would indicate events and states out there in the world and interior affects within. And, to avoid falling victim to the pathetic fallacy, the poem would also need to figure this division within itself. It would need, that is, to reflect the fictive metaphoricity of its atmospheres and also to mark, at least negatively, their simultaneous empirical and literal status.

As a critical category, literary atmosphere could refer to atmosphere considered as a literary theme or subject, as background or setting, as a kind of *genius loci* or distinctive spirit of place, as the similarly distinctive quality of a transient moment, as a collective affective state, as a unifying emotional mood or tonality, as a mode of literary sociability, as a set of environmental conditions, as aesthetic aura, and doubtless as more besides. The model presented by Ruskin identifies a structure that potentially underwrites all of these alternatives. In it, literary atmosphere specifically involves a practice of double troping. As we have seen, modern figurative atmospheres reworked older figures of air, reinscribing them in a newly secular register. They also drew on contemporary meteorological, chemical, and medical understandings of air, translating scientific concepts into new imaginative schemas of cultural understanding. In Ruskin's model, literary atmosphere involved a further semantic operation as well, that of re-figuring these already complex figurations in order to mark both the metaphoricity and the empiricism of their aerial representations. At once figurative and literal, such an atmospherics was 'a powerful epistemological tool', as Antonio Somaini has described, for the investigation of environments and mediations of all kinds.[22] As such, literary atmosphere was integral to the development of both modernist poetry and the modern novel.

Charles Baudelaire – an indispensable reference point in the history of modernist poetics – provides a good case in point. Modern poetry's problem as confronted by Baudelaire closely paralleled the problem of the pathetic fallacy discussed by Ruskin in the same years. For Baudelaire, the aim of 'pure art according to the modern idea' was 'the creation of an evocative magic, containing at once the object and the subject, the world external to the artist and the artist himself'.[23] The poetry of modernity was also for Baudelaire a big-city poetry, one responsive to the shocks, rhythms and disorientations of urban life. Paris was for him rich in undiscovered poetic motifs: 'the marvellous envelops and saturates us like an atmosphere; but we fail to see it'.[24] But as Ross Chambers has noted, 'the factitious character of urban existence as a historical phenomenon' meant that such a poetry had to reject any presumption of a sympathetic correspondence between the human subject and the non-human world. City life, in other words, was a daily demonstration that the pathetic fallacy was only ever a fallacy: 'as a man-made environment the city can offer, as substitutes for the nature that is now absent, only such categories as the material, the useful, and the ordinary'.[25] Atmosphere in Baudelaire's poetry was, then, denatured. It was a site of non-correspondence, disorientation, and alienation: the disillusioned atmosphere of the everyday, of a city street in which nothing is happening, of a desacralised, manufactured world.

In his 1857 urban pastoral 'Landscape' (*Paysage*), Baudelaire observes the blending notes of a Parisian dusk:

> How sweet to watch the birth of the star in the still-blue
> Sky, through mist; the lamp burning anew
> At the windows; rivers of coal climbing the firmament
> And the moon pouring out her pale enchantment.

But in the poem's conclusion, this environing urban atmosphere of smoke and mist and moonlight is bracketed out: 'I'll draw the blinds and curtains tight.' Only when atmosphere has been reduced to zero in this way can the work of poetic creation proceed, and the poet make 'Out of my fiery thoughts a tepid atmosphere'.[26] In the influential terms provided by Walter Benjamin, Baudelaire's poetry was one that had been stripped of aura. It set out system-atically to negate the trappings and airs of poeticisation – drawing the blinds tight, so to speak. But in a dialectical twist identified by Benjamin and his followers, 'even when artworks divest themselves of every atmospheric element – a development inaugurated by Baudelaire – it is conserved in them as a negated and shunned element'.[27] In Baudelaire's 'Landscape', the atmosphere of the night street can still be sensed, through the drawn blinds, within the warm atmosphere of poetic creation. Its opening atmospheric obser-vations of the lighting of the lamps and the moon against the city smoke are themselves already displaced into the realm of poetic fiction: 'How sweet to watch . . . ' If in Baudelaire 'aura in the sense of "atmosphere" is taboo', we still hear, within that act of silencing, the 'crackling noise' with which meanings atmospherically exceed the empirical realities to which they refer.[28]

Atmosphere in these accounts provided the medium through which modernist poetry reflexively defined its purposes and strategies. In such a 'textual atmospherics', it is not simply that 'the weather described in texts can function as a metaphor for textual relations themselves'.[29] Thanks to its complex structures of double troping, literary atmosphere functioned equally as 'a major mode by which texts can indicate their own relation to social formations' – and indeed, their relation to relations between society and nature.[30] This paradoxical dynamic of Baudelaire's atmospheres, which are legible as filled with allegorical meaning precisely in virtue of their depoeticised literalism, would be further elaborated in French poetry through the twentieth century: see, for instance, Guillaume Apollinaire's 1918 calligram 'Il pleut' ('It's raining'), in which the lines of the poem are set as lines of rain falling down the space of the page.

Similar dynamics, in which poetic atmosphere is made to bear symbolic freight by being radically literalised and iconicised, can be traced in other national traditions too. It can be found in the American modernism of Ezra Pound, H. D. (Hilda Dolittle), T. S. Eliot, William Carlos Williams, Louis Zukofksy, and Charles Olson, for example. The atmospheric definition given in 1912 to the 'image' by Pound – of an 'intellectual and emotional complex in an instant of time' – would be one prominent instance.[31] Another would be the breath line of Olson's projective verse of 1950, in which the space of the page is used to measure the poem's respiratory rhythms.[32] In her long poem 'The Walls Do Not Fall', H. D. writes of atmosphere as the medium of an indelibly creative writing:

> the indicated flute or lyre-notes
> on papyrus or parchment
> are magic, indelibly stamped
> on the atmosphere somewhere,
> forever.[33]

In poem after poem from the twentieth century, we are presented with complex recodings of atmospheric experience and transfigured samples of the air around us. 'Poetry', the Romanian-born German-language Jewish poet Paul Celan would state in 1960, 'is perhaps this: an *Atemwende*, a turning of our breath.'[34] These were poetic structures open to registering in atmospheric qualities and changes historical processes that might otherwise resist perception and conceptualisation. As Margaret Ronda has shown of John Ashbery's poetry of the 1970s, postmodern atmospheres continued to communicate the 'incipient problem' of the 'historical present, one that is not yet recognizable but somehow borne on the air'.[35] Ashbery's atmospheres, Ronda writes, then present an affective repository for histories that are as 'powerfully resistant to comprehension' as our own uneven experience of ecological crisis and climate change.[36]

Atmosphere was likewise critical to the modern history of the novel. Taylor has linked the atmospherics of Victorian fiction to the Crystal Palace and other Victorian glasshouses. Glasshouses 'created a space that was fictive not merely in its artifice but also in its visibility, in the sense that everything that occurred within it was staged, in the manner of a scientific experiment'.[37] Climate models of a similarly fictive order can be found in the atmospheres of Victorian novels – those of Dickens, for example – which frequently presented moods and settings in which 'air's material and metaphorical qualities' were 'intimately interconnected'.[38] As Taylor shows, these textual atmospheres did more than merely model an atmospheric system that was at once meteorological and moodily affective. He points out that the example Roland Barthes uses to illustrate his notion of 'the reality effect' is the barometer from Gustave Flaubert's 1877 story 'A Simple Heart'. The reality effect involves the appearance of an ostensibly unmotivated detail, one inconsequential to the novel's plot. This detail atmospherically evokes the idea of a larger reality by virtue of its sheer irrelevance, suggesting that the world of the fiction continues on past the literal limit of the textual signs that comprise it. But, as Taylor remarks, realist novels are themselves a kind of barometer. Both novels and barometers are objects that decorate bourgeois interiors; both also function to register atmospheric pressures and the intangible forces of what is in the air. Flaubert's barometer is at once a meteorological instrument, an instance of the reality effect, and a moment of literary self-reference, suggesting that in modelling atmospheric conditions, literary realism also models its act of modelling. In the modern novel, both the reality and the fictionality of its fictions are rendered, as it were, barometrically legible. For Taylor, realist fiction thereby offers a peculiarly 'performative model of climatic phenomenology', which makes available an 'explicitly mediated, vicarious knowledge' of the atmosphere.[39]

Comparable atmospheric techniques can be found in modernist experimental fiction from James Joyce to Katherine Mansfield and Virginia Woolf to Franz Kafka. For W. B. Yeats, Joyce's 1914 *Dubliners* was 'all atmosphere'; in her 1922 story 'The Garden Party', Mansfield poses the question, in free indirect discourse: 'But the air! If you stopped to notice it, was the air always like this?'; in 1926, Woolf advises readers to 'remind ourselves there is such a thing as atmosphere'.[40] In the detranscendentalised allegory of Kafka's *The Trial*, published posthumously in 1925, Josef K. finds the atmosphere in the vicinity of the court to be literally stifling. Suspicion, nameless dread, the law: these for Kafka were modern atmospheric conditions experienced as difficulty in breathing.

The opening page of Robert Musil's *The Man without Qualities*, from 1930, presents three very different atmospheric reports. The first is meteorological: 'A barometric low hung over the Atlantic.'[41] The second performatively recodes this scientific observation in everyday language: 'In a word that characterizes the facts fairly accurately, even if it is a bit old-fashioned: It was a fine day in August 1913.'[42] And the third recodes the statement once again in a virtuosic modernist set-piece that describes the soundscape of pre-war Vienna as a thick metaphoric interlacing of impressions and rhythms: 'Hundreds of noises wove themselves into a wiry texture of sound with barbs protruding here and there, smart edges running along it and subsiding again, with clear notes splintering off and dissipating.'[43] Literary atmosphere in these pages cannot be identified with any single one of these reports. It resides instead in the movements between them – and in the way these movements are themselves figured in the novel's interweaving of 'hundreds of noises' to communicate 'a special quality' that 'cannot be captured in words'.[44] A comparable trick is played in the opening page of Michel Tournier's *Gemini* (in the original French: *Les Météores*) of 1975. Tournier's novel begins: 'On the twenty-fifth of September 1937, a depression moving from Newfoundland to the Baltic sent masses of warm, moist oceanic air into the corridor of the English Channel.' This meteorological event opens out into a series of local atmospheric instances that includes a gust of wind metafictionally turning over 'eight pages of Aristotle's *Meteorologica*, which Michel Tournier was reading on the beach at Saint-Jacut'.[45] The novel lies open to the history of the atmospheric realism it re-enacts, its pages ruffling in an intertextual breeze.

In Ursula Le Guin's *The Lathe of Heaven*, from 1971, we find a similarly metafictional awareness of literary atmosphere as at once an imaginative model and a model of that model. We also find one of the first explicit references in fiction to anthropogenic global warming: '"Come on up with me," he said. "It's raining already." In fact it was, the endless drizzle of spring – the ice of Antarctica, raining on the heads of the children of those responsible for melting it.'[46] The speaker of these words – 'It's raining already' – is George Orr, who resembles a novelist in that his dreams take on the force of reality. He is also like a novelist in that he is not wholly in control of the real fictions he creates. For even as the alternative worlds he dreams into being are of purely human construction – realised figments of the human spirit of imagination – they nonetheless remain materially burdened by the injustices of the world as it was before Orr first closed his eyes to dream. Climate change here marks within the novel the material inescapability of the practices that underwrite the novel's own imaginative creations, just as Orr's dreams communicate into ever more distant imaginative frames the future climatic consequences of the everyday actions of Le Guin's own readers. When Le Guin confronts us with this human climate – an atmosphere at once figuratively and literally anthropogenic – we are no longer facing the pathetic fallacy of Ruskin: of the imaginative but insecure projection of human meaningfulness beyond its modern epistemological warrant. Instead, the double troping of literary atmosphere now registers a profound transformation in the epistemological and semantic relations within which modern literature had been reflexively framed. Climate change changes literary atmospheres: both how they are being written and how they might be read.

Technical Atmosphere

Literal atmosphere was always a technical construction. It was a product of emergent modern sciences of air, including materialist philology. It required innovative techniques for tracking and notating atmospheric processes and states, and the introduction of specialised terminology from cirrus and cumulus to oxygen and carbon dioxide. It was achieved through the invention and standardisation of technological instruments like the barometer. And it involved new rhetorical modes of scientific self-presentation and of public claims to authority. But even as these concepts, instruments, and rhetorics helped to transform air understood as locally eventful and providentially meaningful into atmosphere understood as a deconsecrated and global theatre of knowable processes and lawlike regularities, their own mediating role in that transformation tended to fall from view. The fundamental reconstitution of aerial knowledge they effected shifted emphasis from the act of knowing onto the thing known. In so doing, they helped to establish a new sense of literalness as non-textual, unmediated, and objective.

So although literal atmosphere was constructed through technological and figurative means, it was also often a figure of technical self-erasure. Robert Boyle's 'spring of the air' is a case in point. As Wendy Beth Hyman has shown, Boyle's self-fashioning 'as the champion of non-figurative and univalent language' involved a 'simultaneous reliance on and disavowal of metaphoricity'.[47] Jan Golinski has similarly observed that 'for all Boyle's criticisms of the influences of rhetoricity and literary traditions in natural philosophy, his project can be shown to depend on the persuasive power of particular narrative and representational techniques, which were themselves literary in form and rhetorical in intention and in effect'.[48] Climate change now reconfigures the discursive and semantic relations within which atmosphere was elaborated as a medium of literary self-reflection through the nineteenth and twentieth centuries. It does this because it likewise reconfigures the underlying rhetorical technicity of literal atmospheres. The literal facts of our globally changing climate are underwritten entirely by the technical and rhetorical instruments, agencies, and figures that allow us to know them. In this sense, climate change imposes a new rhetorical situation.

As John Frow has noted, the technical meaning of *climate* shifted in the late 1970s 'from describing the average of the weather over a period of time to describing an integrated global system of great complexity'.[49] The shift was driven largely by the computational power of climate models capable of simulating atmospheric and other major ecosystem processes on planetary scales. In these models, atmosphere is typically treated as if it were composed of discrete layers, and carved up analytically into a three-dimensional grid.[50] Values at node points in this imaginary grid rarely correspond to any observed measurements because node points rarely coincide with instrument sites. So most values are imputed to nodes by extrapolation from smoothed observational data. These constructed values are then used to calibrate and re-adjust the observational data on which they were originally based. And these are only some of the counterfactual assumptions and strange loops of self-reference commonly employed in climate models. Climate change, literally, refers not out to a nature understood as already there but instead to an assemblage or construction that can exist only within institutional and social frameworks.[51] And this sense in which climate change is technically figured and technologically constructed, rather than marking some instability or uncertainty in our knowledge, is instead the basis of its very considerable epistemic strength.

Literature is not where one would usually look for knowledge of this nature. But the emergence of climate change and the urgency of its present claims are legible nonetheless in the literary atmospheres of the present, and of the past. The atmosphere of a novel or poem registers a particular historical configuration of the semantic and discursive dimensions of the literal, the figurative, and the technical. As a literary atmosphere, it refigures these intersections fluidly and reflexively. Its ambiguities in consequence reach deep into the structural fault-lines of meaning that have shaped our modern organisation of knowledge. Words on a page may be airless, but so, increasingly, is the atmosphere itself. There is smoke in the air again today. If you are outside too long it becomes hard to breathe. It is there – a high orange tinge to the light – even if you can't smell it.

Notes

1 J. O. Taylor, *The Sky of Our Manufacture: The London Fog in British Fiction from Dickens to Woolf* (Charlottesville: University of Virginia Press, 2016), 6.
2 T. Ingold, 'The Atmosphere', *Chiasmi International* 14 (2012), 79.

3 L. Irigaray, *The Forgetting of Air in Martin Heidegger* (London: Athlone Press, 1999).

4 G. Böhme, *The Aesthetics of Atmospheres* (Abingdon: Routledge, 2016); T. Brennan, *The Transmission of Affect* (Ithaca, NY: Cornell University Press, 2004).

5 J. O. Taylor, 'Atmosphere as Setting, or, "Wuthering" the Anthropocene', in A. Johns-Putra (ed.), *Climate and Literature* (Cambridge University Press, 2019), 31.

6 C. Martin, 'The Invention of Atmosphere', *Studies in History and Philosophy of Science Part A* 52 (2015), 44–54.

7 J. Wilkins, *The Discoverie of a World in the Moone* (London: Michael Sparl and Edward Forrest, 1638), 138.

8 S. Shapin and S. Schaffer, *Leviathan and the Air-Pump: Hobbes, Boyle, and the Experimental Life* (Princeton University Press, 1985); F. Engels, 'Preface', in K. Marx, *Capital*, vol. 2 (New York: International Publishers, 1972), 14–15; T. Kuhn, *The Structure of Scientific Revolutions* (University of Chicago Press, 2012), 53–7.

9 2 Corinthians 3:6.

10 B. Cummings, 'Literally Speaking, or, the Literal Sense from Augustine to Lacan', *Paragraph* 21 (1998), 200–26.

11 S. Johnson, *A Dictionary of the English Language* (London: W. Strahan, 1755), s. v. 'Spirit'.

12 Johnson, s.v. 'Air'.

13 M. Gamper, 'Rätsel der Atmosphäre: Umrisse einer "literarischen Meteorologie"', *Zeitschrift für Germanistik* 24 (2014), 238.

14 T. Menely, '"The Present Obfuscation": Cowper's *Task* and the Time of Climate Change', *PMLA* 127 (2012), 481.

15 M. H. Abrams, 'The Correspondent Breeze', *Kenyon Review* 19 (1957), 128.

16 S. T. Coleridge, *Biographia Literaria*, vol. 2 (Princeton University Press, 1984), 70.

17 J. Ruskin, *Modern Painters*, vol. 3 (London: George Allen, 1904), 318

18 S. Mentz, 'Hurricanes, Tempests, and the Meteorological Globe', in H. Marchitello and E. Tribble (eds.), *The Palgrave Handbook of Early Modern Literature and Science* (London: Palgrave Macmillan, 2017), 257.

19 R. Markley, '"Casualties and Disasters": Defoe and the Interpretation of Climatic Instability', *Journal of Early Modern Cultural Studies* 8 (2008), 109.

20 Ruskin, *Modern Painters*, 318.

21 Ruskin, *Modern Painters*, 201–20.

22 A. Somaini, 'The Atmospheric Screen: Turner, Hazlitt, Ruskin', in C. Buckley et al. (eds.), *Screen Genealogies: From Optical Device to Environmental Medium* (Amsterdam University Press, 2019) 174.

23 C. Baudelaire, 'Philosophical Art', in *The Painter of Modern Life, And Other Essays* (London: Phaidon, 1964), 205.

24 Baudelaire, 'The Salon of 1846', in *Selected Writings on Art and Artists* (Cambridge University Press, 1981), 107.

25 R. Chambers, *An Atmospherics of the City: Baudelaire and the Poetics of Noise* (New York: Fordham University Press, 2015), 19.

26 Baudelaire, 'Paysage', trans. J. Ashbery, *A Wave: Poems* (New York: Penguin, 1985), 7.

27 T. W. Adorno, *Aesthetic Theory* (Minneapolis: University of Minnesota Press, 1998), 274.

28 Adorno, *Aesthetic Theory*, 79.

29 Chambers, 'Nervalian Mist and Baudelairean Fog: An Essay in Textual Atmospherics', in E. J. Mickel (ed.), *The Shaping of Text: Style, Imagery and Structure in French Literature* (Lewisburg, PA: Bucknell University Press, 1993), 90.

30 Chambers, 'Nervalian Mist', 90.

31 E. Pound, 'A Few Don'ts by an Imagiste', in Lawrence Rainey (ed.), *Modernism: An Anthology* (Oxford: Blackwell, 2005), 95.

32 C. Olson, 'Projective Verse' in *Collected Prose* (Berkeley: University of California Press, 1997).

33 H. D[oolittle], 'The Walls Do Not Fall', in *Trilogy* (New York: New Directions, 1998), 10.

34 P. Celan, *Collected Prose*, trans. Rosmarie Waldrop (New York: Routledge, 2003), 47.

35 M. Ronda, *Remainders: American Poetry at Nature's End* (Stanford University Press, 2018), 62.

36 Ronda, *Remainders*, 80, 44.

37 Taylor, *Sky of Our Manufacture*, 23.

38 G. Yeats, '"Dirty Air": *Little Dorrit*'s Atmosphere', *Nineteenth-Century Literature* 66 (2011), 329.

39 Taylor, *Sky of Our Manufacture*, 29.

40 W. B. Yeats, 'W. B. Yeats on Joyce, 1915', in R. H. Deming (ed.), *James Joyce: The Critical Heritage Volume 1 1907–1927* (New York: Routledge, 1997), 79; K. Mansfield, *The Garden Party, and Other Stories* (New York: Alfred A. Knopf, 1922), 64; V. Woolf, *On Being Ill* (Ashfield, MA: Paris Press, 2006), 26.

41 R. Musil, *The Man without Qualities I* (New York: Vintage, 1996), 3.

42 Musil, *Man without Qualities*, 3.

43 Musil, *Man without Qualities*, 3.

44 Musil, *Man without Qualities*, 3.

45 M. Tournier, *Gemini* (London: Collins, 1981), 9.

46 U. K. Le Guin, *The Lathe of Heaven* (New York: Scribner, 2008), 160.

47 W. B. Hyman, '"Deductions from Metaphors": Figurative Truth, Poetical Language, and Early Modern Science', in H. Marchitello and E. Tribble (eds.), *The Palgrave Handbook of Early Modern Literature and Science* (London: Palgrave Macmillan, 2017), 32.

48 J. Golinski, 'Robert Boyle: Scepticism and Authority in Seventeenth-Century Chemical Discourse', in A. E. Benjamin *et al.* (eds.), *The Figural and the Literal: Problems of Language in the History of Science and Philosophy, 1630–1800* (Manchester University Press, 1987), 59.

49 J. Frow, *On Interpretative Conflict* (University of Chicago Press, 2019), 183.

50 P. N. Edwards, *A Vast Machine: Computer Models, Climate Data, and the Politics of Global Warming* (Cambridge, MA: MIT Press, 2010).

51 Frow, *On Interpretative Conflict*, 176.

3

JENNIFER MAE HAMILTON

Weathers of Body and World
Reading Difference in Literary Atmospheres before Climate Change

Climate and weather are distinct ways of describing the skies, but they are also terms that enable the contemporary study of the Earth's atmosphere in the language and methods of science. Climate and weather are related terms, but they are neither analogies nor synonyms. Their difference is primarily one of spatio-temporal scale, a distinction nurtured by several centuries of Western scientism.[1] Now, their shifting significance and relation is at the heart of transdisciplinary debates about the cultural impacts of climate change.[2] The latter definitional struggle has come about because weather averages are now so consistently broken in the short term (extreme weather), we are quite probably witnessing long-term atmospheric alteration before our eyes (climate change). Although the base spatio-temporal distinction between climate and weather is teetering on the edge of collapse in the world, the distinction remains conceptually and rhetorically important. Hence, this chapter examines the question: if the terms 'climate' and 'weather' are valuable for undertaking contemporary literary studies in a time of climate change, how can we engage the distinction to shape new environmental literary histories as well?

The answer is not straightforward because climate and weather have epistemologies that intersect in complex ways with phenomenological human experience. On one hand, 'the Western concept of climate', Thomas H. Ford argues, 'is entwined in quite complex ways with the concept of meaning'.[3] In other words, like meaning itself, 'climate' is not historically or politically neutral. On the contrary, climate relates to the assumptions brought to a text regarding elements of the world (both literal and metaphorical) that are taken for granted. For example, the town slogan of Grants Pass in Oregon is 'It's the Climate', which presumably relates to an atmospheric pleasantness locals cherish and take for granted, but it is also amusingly vague for travellers not familiar with those ambient conditions. While the 2020 novel coronavirus pandemic has demonstrated that what is taken for granted can change rapidly, the basic claim holds steady: understanding

55

global climate change is an epistemological challenge. Mike Hulme catalogues the different historical meanings of climate, from the 'delicate' and 'sweet' climate of Sicily in Shakespeare's *The Winter's Tale* to the El Niño-Southern Oscillation as a measurable pattern. But Hulme also unearths a base phenomenological claim about climate that directly corresponds with Ford's observation, that climate is 'the ordinary man's [*sic*] expectation of weather ... there is a limit to the indignities that the weather can put upon him, and he can predict what clothes he will need for each month of the year'.[4] Defining climate as that which frames the assumptions of 'ordinary man' – a white patriarch, for example – links the epistemology and phenomenology of climate to other hegemonic norms; climate is the status quo and both an ideological and ecological state. Such a notion of climate is, like universalism itself, fundamentally challenged by knowledge and recognition of human difference. It is in this context that Christina Sharpe defines the 'total climate' of the planet as its pervasive 'anti-blackness'.[5] Thus, if a stable climate is both epistemologically and phenomenologically representative of a paradigm, climate change is some kind of paradigm shift. While for environmentalists, climate change is generally characterised as bad and something that must be stopped, for those who suffered the stable climate of patriarchal anti-blackness, changes to the status quo are urgent for different reasons. A major critical challenge of our time is thus how to parse the good and bad aspects of eco-social climate change.

Weather, on the other hand, is specific, stochastic, localised, and individualised, but, like climate, it also has phenomenological and epistemological significance. In other words, a storm is experienced in the body while also signifying cultural ideas and emotions. In fact, the desire to forecast weather, possibly to mitigate anxieties about both change and the future, set the experimental standards for modern meteorology.[6] Moreover, in contrast to Ford's claim about climate's relation with meaning, the weather in the modernised and secularised West was frequently associated with existential meaninglessness or banal polite conversation. So, what is going on at a given moment or on a particular day is weather; how weather is forecast and scientifically measured is determined by the structures and methods of meteorology. In terms of its aggregate significance, weather represents radical plurality, multiplicity, and difference. Weather is the specific and the localised; it is the particular within the universal. Despite its specificity, weather can operate in a range of poetic modes. Claudia Rankine's 'The Weather' (2020) uses weather as a euphemism: 'I say weather but I mean / a form of governing that deals out death / and names it living'.[7] Like climate, interpreting the weather involves attending to its material and historical specificity, and also how the two complicate each other at every turn. Atop this general sketch of the complexities of both climate and weather, literary historians are interested in textuality and meaning. So if climate is related to worldly meanings that *were* taken for granted and are now changing, and weather is taking on newly rich and diverse significances with each puff of wind, the cultural and textual dimensions of climate are also changing. In literary works that predate climate change's mid-twentieth-century acceleration, though, climate and weather still had literal and poetic functions. The present chapter proposes climatological and meteorological reading as distinct, albeit related, methods for interpreting textual atmospheres. It brings knowledge of the textual operation of climate and weather now emerging in a time of climate change to bear on literary close reading of texts from before climate change.

Climate as Structure, Not Theme

The distinction between climate and weather bears similarities with some other conceptual distinctions that were used in literary studies before climate change. From history, we inherit the idea of the *longue durée* as distinct from the microhistory; from philosophy, we receive considerations of the universal in relation to the particular. Both invoke a distinction between a big process or concept and a small, localised event or example. From structural linguistics, diachronic and synchronic studies of language, and the distinction between language as a system (*langue*) and acts of speaking (*parole*), inform our thinking about sign systems across time and in a given instance of its use.[8] In these examples, the *longue durée*, the universal, diachrony, and *langue* invoke a bigger system, much like climate. Meanwhile, a microhistory, the particular, synchrony, and *parole* refer to a shorter-term event, something specific, or even a single speech act, analogous with weather. These analogies are, at least in the first instance, metaphors. That is, *langue* and *parole* do not *literally* map onto climate and weather in a straightforward way; rather the comparison invokes the spatio-temporal distinction between weather and climate in order to offer a structure for guiding distinctive methods of atmospheric reading. In all examples, the distinctions are not binary oppositions; rather, they are different ways of framing the same thing: history, philosophy, linguistics, and atmospherics as either big and durational or small and discrete. Just as *parole* enables us to see a speech act as individual expression, but situates it in relation also to the history of a language as a whole, weather can be seen as the atmospheric version of a speech act, only possible within a particular climate.

The development of methods for literary close reading of atmospheres is part of the bigger scholarly project of rewriting history to include non-human nature as a significant actor across time. Dipesh Chakrabarty argues that contemporary knowledge of anthropogenic environmental change requires the complete rewriting of history on a range of fronts, and the same is true for literary history, but the questions that follow are how and why?[9] In explicitly distinguishing climate and weather in close reading, this chapter approaches this anachronistic task of rewriting Western literary histories differently. I want neither to dismiss nor to unnecessarily solidify the similarities and differences between now (wherever you are and whenever you are reading a book, a poem, or a play) and then (when and where the text you are reading was written). Instead, the chapter works from three assumptions. First, the historical significance of climate and weather is as varied, complex, and ideologically fraught as it is today. Second, despite Chakrabarty's claim that climate is absent in earlier histories, a relatively stable climate that is conducive to human life is necessarily present *as an absence* in the pre-climate -change archive.[10] Third, the weather has always punctuated the long-term stability of climate, both predictably and unpredictably making and taking life, while stirring up big existential and political questions.[11] In this context weather, climate, body, and world are rarely in neatly aligned or analogical relation, but are nonetheless always related in material and meaningful ways.

When it comes to the appraisal of climate's significance in history, there remains a focus on climate *change* rather than stability. The most well-known examples are instances of general periods of tumult like Brian Fagan's work on the Little Ice Age and Gillen Wood's investigations of the eruption of Mount Tambora.[12] Here the ambient conditions or the texture or the background of the archive changes, and the archive is reinterpreted, highlighting the substantial social impact of a temporary climate change. Of course, making temporary alternations to climate visible as a historical event that predates anthropogenic climate change of the present era is not the endgame of such scholarship; Fagan and Wood are re-reading the archive to show us that climate change influences culture, politics, trade, and that it is legible as such in the cultural record. I use these examples to establish a point of contrast with the distinctive reading methods offered in this chapter.

Stemming from the distinction between climate and weather, the work of the rest of this chapter is threefold: it outlines methods for climatological and meteorological readings of texts, demonstrates this method via two canoni-cal examples – *Wuthering Heights* (1847) and *King Lear* (1606) – and considers the concept of 'weathering' as a theoretical lens for close reading climate and weather in a time of climate change. The next section on climate and climatological reading is more closely related to integrating atmo-spherics into understanding genre and ideology (including race and gender). In the section that follows, weather and meteorological reading are directly related to discrete plot points, motifs, characters' interactions, and the representation of events and emotions. Finally, a section on 'weathering' examines reading atmospheres in a time of climate collapse. Overall, the chapter develops methods for reading climate and weather in texts that predate climate change while attending to historical specificity and human difference.

Climatological Reading

Climate is a way of describing an all-encompassing atmosphere, an ambience, or dominant state. In examining the quest in writing and criticism to create or name the genre that can adequately represent climate change, Stephanie LeMenager observes that this quest is not just an isolated academic pursuit but rather something that transcends the academy and enters mainstream culture: 'People outside of academia, people who might not be expected to care about genre, are looking hard for Anthropocene genres – for patterns of expectation in narrative form with which to combat this unsettling era of climate shift and social inquiry.'[13] LeMenager is not alone in critically examining this reckoning. Axel Goodbody and Adeline Johns-Putra show that the emergence of climate change fiction is 'probably the first time the birth of a literary genre actually made the news'.[14] While the scramble to define a genre or genres in and for the Anthropocene and climate change is of critical concern for contemporary literary studies, it also tells us something about extant forms – Holocene genres – that occupy the attentions of literary historians and represent the climate as a relatively stable background that contains human conflict. That climate change generates a crisis in literary genres suggests a correspondence between genre conventions and a stable climate. Indeed, in writing about genre and climate change, Johns-Putra argues that 'any given genre resembles in itself an environment as those codes and expectations interact with each other and are exchanged amongst writers and readers'.[15] Building on these observations, this section theorises a mode of climatological reading that can bring out the affinities between a stable climate and literary genres, and what Jesse Oak Taylor calls 'literal' and 'literary' textual atmospheres.[16]

Literary genres set expectations for readers in ways analogous to how a general knowledge of a stable climate once set expectations for a suite of human affairs. How we understand climate and genre then and now is nuanced. For example, Lucy Burnett seeks more and faster 'climate change' in contemporary literary genres to counter what she identifies as a logic in the emerging canon of climate change literature that 'continues reproducing versions of the established patterns of thought'.[17] At the same time, LeMenager's overarching claim is that extant genres are struggling to adequately represent a changing climate. But these contemporary critical concerns mask stranger historical questions: is global climate change difficult to represent in extant literary forms because what we now know as a 'stable climate' is represented in literature before climate change? And/or is a planetary climate in literature prior to anthropogenic climate change present or a structuring or foundational absence? John Frow's work describing the role of genre as implicit in meaning-making processes is useful here. He argues that 'to speak of genre is to speak of what need not be said because it is already so forcefully *presupposed* ... genres frame the world as a certain kind of thing, and we notice this framing only at its intersection with other subcultures of meaning'.[18] In other words, Frow posits genre as the frame that gives rise to the conditions of possibility of a text. Hence, likening a stable climate to the presuppositions of genre is neither to say that climate is absent from texts because invisible nor is it to assert that representations of climate exist in one-to-one relation with genre, but rather it is to say that a global climate before climate change is, like genre, active in a text as an absence that structures and informs how we read it: spring, summer, autumn, winter are a set of Eurocentric seasonal patterns and climatological averages that can or at least once could be 'presupposed', like the rise and fall of a hero in tragedy. Thus, a stable global climate is represented in a text but often *not* actually represented; in other words, a stable climate is neither completely absent (because it underpins the conditions of possibility for life on Earth as it underpins the conditions of possibility of a text) nor it is fully present. In literature, then, a stable climate is tangled in the set of norms tacitly constitutive of textuality itself. In historical literary texts, a stable global climate is always already a ghost, an anachronism, and a basic formal principle.

To illustrate the process of climatological reading, consider the blustery and weather-worn novel *Wuthering Heights*. The text is thoroughly wind-swept; at times it feels as if Wuthering Heights (the house) is actually an outgrowth of that hillside, and correspondence between the persistent emotional intensity of the novel and the severity of the ambient weather conditions repeatedly blurs the line between human and non-human environment. Taylor's careful reading of the novel's atmospherics makes a strong case for 'the ultimate impossibility of distinguishing between either climate and atmosphere in their nominally literal ... and historical', or what he calls 'literary', senses.[19] In other words, to read the literary climate, Taylor argues not simply that the atmospheric tumult of the novel is metaphorical (in the sense that metaphor's chief poetic operation is to add to meaning via comparison with that which is not *literally* applicable to the circumstances at hand), rather, that the atmospheric dimension of the novel is best understood as the imbrication of the *literal* and the *literary* tumult. In one sense, then, climatological readings of the literal and the literary ambient climates are inseparable.

The question is, though, how do we understand the literal and the literary? For many literary historians, meaning in literary texts is derived from examining the interaction between what is tacit (presupposed, assumed) and what is explicit (represented). And the significance of the interaction between the tacit and the explicit and the conclusions that can be drawn about meaning as a result are arguably at the heart of literary studies. While Frow suggests that 'generic framework constitutes the unsaid of texts, information which lies latent in a shadowy region from which we draw it as we need it', there are other ways of understanding omission, absence, or the unsaid.[20] In this regard, rather than climatological reading being an entirely *new* practice, it is best understood as the addition of a new atmospheric dimension to established critical reading practices that aim to bring the unsaid or the presupposed to light.

Drawing from explicitly *feminist* scholarship, I suggest two well-established strategies for making visible the invisible or making meaning out of what is not said. First, instead of writing a new explicitly gendered literary criticism, feminist deconstructionist Barbara Johnson makes gender visible where it is seemingly absent.[21] She argues that it would be 'easy to accuse ... male theorists of having avoided the issue of gender entirely'.[22] But she contends instead that they are actually always writing about gender. For Johnson, the law of gender works in the same way as the law of genre: they structure assumptions that prefigure hermeneutic practices.[23] Climatological reading can operate similarly by attending to powerful presuppositions that accompany a stable climate, such as normative genres of gender. Second, seeking to take in the complete textual climate, including its constitutive absences, requires attention to what antiracist feminist Christina Sharpe calls the 'total climate' of anti-blackness.[24] For Sharpe, the planet's total climate is its literal atmospherics (including the ocean and its depths) and the pervasive political climate of anti-blackness. Given the similarities between climatological reading and reading against the absences in the feminist archive, the primary challenge of climatological reading is not how to make the climate visible *as such*, but how to do it without disappearing all the other historical absences, silences, and omissions scholars have worked for generations to bring to light.

Although the setting of *Wuthering Heights* is overrun by a seemingly hybrid climate–weather atmosphere that is enduringly extreme and tumultuous, climatological reading is not interested in discrete weather events; rather, it calls attention to ambient atmospheric and socio-political conditions. In this regard, both Johnson's and Sharpe's framings of gendered and racialised presuppositions can inform climatological reading too. What is both interesting and vexing about *Wuthering Heights* is that, despite the intensity of the microclime and the isolation of the two houses from the rest of the world, the whole novel is completely subsumed by bigger logics – an even bigger climate – that troubles the story. The conventions of romance narratives and Victorian regulation around heterosexual desire in relation to marriage, the logics of white patriarchal inheritance, and hierarchical race, gender, and class norms. These norms have shaped the characters' worlds, as much as the reliably tumultuous microclimate has shaped the Heights's windows. An iconic moment in *Wuthering Heights* is not directly experienced by the narrator but recounted second-hand: during Cathy's convalescence at Thrushcross Grange for five weeks after her escape with Heathcliff and attack by a dog. The reader discovers later, twice removed from the act itself, via Cathy to Nelly Dean and Dean's recounting to Lockwood, that Cathy has chosen a life dictated by the aspiration for class mobility and convention over the excitement and freedom she seemed to feel with Heathcliff. What makes Cathy's choice *plausible* (if no less distressing) in the context is her gender and the need to marry for power and wealth, and Heathcliff's marginal status as a black orphan.[25] As a result, the household itself is as much afflicted by the intensity of the microclimate, and the individual emotions of the characters, as it is by the emotional fallout of bigger socio-historical climates. Indeed, the intensity with which the characters in the novel subscribe to social conventions, in spite or perhaps because of both the isolation and the weather, constitute the novel. In other words, there is no way of reading the climate of *Wuthering Heights* without combining thinking about the narrow windows designed to keep the persistently cold weather out and the Victorian social hierarchy that dooms the central romance before it ever really begins. At the same time, though, there are discrete weather events in the novel that have an important bearing on plot, character, motivation, and plausibility that are important to see as distinct from the generally hybrid ideological-material atmosphere of the climate. It is to the weather's discrete specificity that this chapter now turns.

Meteorological Reading

Meteorological reading is different to climatological reading. Rather than seeking to understand the atmospheric logic of a whole form, either as a stable or changing climate, reading the weather deals more specifically with what is explicitly represented in a text – a stanza, an act, a scene, a chapter, a line, a sentence, a motif, a metaphor, or even a character. Meteorological reading involves focusing on where the weather (good or bad) becomes noteworthy in relation to the particular story being told or the specific idea being examined. Meteorological reading is more explicitly concerned with a logic of presence. A different hermeneutic pragmatism is required here. The enabling constraint of a focused climatological reading is the limited number of genres/forms and presuppositions, and thus the limited number of correspondences between a given form (for example: a Gothic novel, a tragedy) and the total climate of a particular text (for example: the literal and literary location of *Wuthering Heights* in both time and space; the particular patriarchal structure of the world in *King Lear* and the emotional and territorial battle waged in those terms). The constraints on reading weather are different. Meteorological reading is constrained because there are limited kinds of weathers (hot, cold, wet, dry) and such events can occur at any time and any place in a text (more often features of plot than genre). The meaning of the weather depends on the placement of the meteorological event within the wider context or its position in a particular literal/literary climate. Meaning emerges not in general as it might in a dream dictionary where snow or wind could assume a generalisable significance, but instead in particularities (the kind of weather, the duration of the event, its relation to characters, their relative exposure or shelter, and particular relationship with the conventions of the wider textual genre or climate).

There are many different kinds of literary storm, for example. Some texts have storms as climactic events, while others have no storms at all; meanwhile, sometimes storms are imbricated in the conditions of a text's possibility and plausibility, and others are critical plot points. Poetry can represent a single weather state throughout the text, or invoke it briefly as a metaphor for love. The snowstorm that traps Lockwood at the Heights and accelerates his curiosity about the history of the place and its various residents is an example of a storm that is constitutive of a premise. This storm is as much about narrative plausibility as it is about its presence as storm. In *King Lear*, the storm comes at a key dramatic turning point, approximately halfway through the play; once Lear has refused to dismiss the knights, and his daughters have refused the knights a lodging, thunder rumbles. Meteorological reading is interested in the particularities of these events, in these stories, at these points in the plot, and in relation to the particular characters.

One aspect of meteorological reading that is important in this sense is to see the weather neither as discretely holding significance in relation to a single human character (Lockwood or Lear) alone, nor merely as indicator of the textual climate, but as always and already both. Just as a speech act (*parole*) draws on the entire history of language (*langue*) for its meaning and performative force, so too a weather event both refers to the local conditions at the same time as referencing the text's total climate. In other words, far from signifying nothingness or boredom,[26] literary weather is almost always overdetermined.

As with climatological reading, though, there is much work to be done to restore the significance of the weather in its own right. The first wave of ecocritical readings of *Lear*'s storm emphasised its literal presence in the play. Of *King Lear*'s iconic storm, Steve Mentz argued that the 'storm scenes literalise the play's crisis of authority' because the storm does not respond to the king.[27] Gwilym Jones argues that 'the storm is consistent ... and consistently *just a storm*'.[28] Laurie Shannon describes the storm scenes as a representation of the 'literal problem of weather on skin'.[29] These interpretations systematically respond to an anthropocentric Western scholarly tradition that diminishes the significance of weather's material importance in the play. The ecocritical move to emphasise the literal is an important step in taking the weather more seriously in a time of climate change, but we can take this even further. If you pay close attention to the several scenes of mayhem on the heath during *Lear*, the storm is more than a metaphor for his madness and is a literal event present within the reality of the world that all the characters have to respond to, but it is also evidently *more than just a storm*.

Thus, meteorological reading brings together the ecocritical turn towards the literal with the bigger social, philosophical, ideological reckoning that is enabled by the reading of the storm as metaphoric: again, the literal and the literary. First, it is both a theorisation of the poetics of the literal and mundane by interrogating weather as metonymy, as a part for a whole and a link in a chain. In this regard, it is also a method for understanding how these dimensions of the literal and mundane are historically circumscribed. Second, meteorological reading aims to view strictly metaphoric interpretations as products of a particular historical context. By strictly metaphoric, I mean instances when the meaning of 'storm' emerges only insofar as it is not literally applicable to Lear's situation, where the weather is ferried in to decorate our reading of the human condition, or interhuman relation or to symbolise the political tumult, but its own atmospherics are not considered part of it. Third, meteorological reading situates analysis within the text's total climate, as even the most randomly stormy *deus ex machina* is in some ways related to the broader textual atmosphere.

When thinking about discrete events or motifs, one finds that reading the weather in literary and literal terms is similar to examining the metaphoric and metonymic poles of signification. Paul Ricoeur observes that 'association by contiguity and association by resemblance ... define metonymy and metaphor' respectively.[30] Metonymy, then, is a rhetorical term for meaningful relations that are proximate or nearby, while the similarity that makes a metaphor viable is based on separation. Roman Jakobson placed metaphoric and metonymic language on a rhetorical continuum along which all meaning takes shape: 'In normal verbal behaviour both processes are continually operative, but careful observation will reveal that under the influence of a cultural pattern, personality, and verbal style, preference is given to one of the two processes over the other.'[31] The key point is that the significance of a term is never an either/or equation, but contingent and changeable. In readings of *King Lear*, the cultural pressure, or deep and abiding interest, in understanding the human mind in the twentieth century has given rise to the focus on reading the storm as a metaphor for Lear's madness, for example.[32] The metaphoric reading has become dominant because of wider contextual pressures. But weather events in texts will usually operate at both metaphoric and metonymic levels. In *Lear*, the storm evidently invokes an emotional state, as distinct from the storm itself, but the weather is also an intensely literal part of the dramatic situation. A meteorological reading, then, is interested in first historicising the metonymic because it advances an ecocritical argument for literal reading. If storm as metonymy is a literal part of something that represents a whole, even if the meaning of the part is self-evident or brute (cold, wet, windy, thunderous), to what *whole* does storm refer? Is it the king, the kingdom, the play, or something else? At the same time, however, literal reading cannot be an endgame; the return to the focus on the literal is in itself under the influence of a particular cultural pattern: a rise in extreme weather events, a changing climate, and rising cultural and political anxiety about the literal alterations in the Earth's atmosphere. Thus, what ultimately separates a meteorological reading from a literal reading is the task of bringing together the weather itself with the total climate of the text, to read it in both literal and literary ways.

Conclusions, Weathering

While the weather report may be useful for determining what clothes one might wear on a given day, love poetry would be boring if it were obliged to be literally calibrated to a thermometer. This is an opinion, but literary historians ought to agree with me as if their profession depended on it: better still, the literal and the literary remain in contradiction with one another, and the day be freezing cold while my heart is aflame. What I mean here is that literary analysis does not always have to perfectly align with scientific truths or promote accurate understandings of materiality to have something to contribute to the current crisis. The struggle for genre, as LeMenager calls it, is a struggle for meaning in and of a changing climate. The struggle is bigger than a 'fact versus fiction' binary, being about the changing meaning of life, experience, and consciousness on Earth. To conclude, then, I proffer a concept for atmospherically attuned reading (and possibly writing) in a time of extreme weather and climate change, where the distinction between climate and weather or climatological reading and meteorological reading is unstable and *in media res*.

Carefully and closely reading strange representations of climates, extreme weathers, and anxious poems is a form of *weathering* the present catastrophe in literary terms, as proposed by Astrida Neimanis and Rachel Loewen Walker. They suggest that climate is carried in human bodies in, through, and as the cumulative impacts and durational experience of being alive and in the weather world.[33] The gerund of *weathering* summons the duration that enables weathers to accumulate. While bodily responses to short-term weather phenomena such as sweat and goose bumps may be obvious responses to ambient conditions, Neimanis and Loewen Walker contend that climate, usually understood as beyond human perception, is embodied too. Weathering – similar to ageing, enduring, and surviving – names the accumulation of the world (human and non-) in the body. Their initial conceptualisation of weathering, largely focused on the possible archiving of non-human atmospheres into the body, has more recently expanded to take on accumulative cultural weatherings too: racism, misogyny, and the suite socioeconomic oppressions manifest as body burdens.[34] Weathering can be the felt experience of coming up against worldly climates, hierarchical genres of being, and resistance to such models of subjection; weathering is the tumult of a life not quite fitting its presupposed genre.

Weathering is also a concept that can be used to read back into history, where a particular life, event, or creature takes on a climatic duration, and accumulates its own calculable averages. Nearing death, Simone de Beauvoir imagines the measure of her life as the accumulation of everything that she has ever done and everywhere she has ever been. She 'loathes the thought' of her own dying: not the death of her body as such, but rather the end of the singular constellation of experiences that are archived in and as her living body:

> that unique sum of things, the experience that I lived, with all its order and all its randomness – the Opera of Peking, the arena of Huelva, the candomblé in Bahia, the dunes of El-Oued, Wabansia Avenue, the dawns in Provence, Tiryns, Castro talking to five thousand Cubans, a sulphur sky over a sea of clouds, the purple holly, the white nights of Leningrad, the bells of the Liberation, an orange moon over Piraeus, a red sun rising over the desert, Torcello, Rome, all the things I've talked about, others I have left unspoken – there is no place where it will all live again.[35]

An accumulation of particulars makes Beauvoir's universe just as an accumulation of weathers constructs a climate. This concluding invocation of Beauvoir proposes weathering as a way of knowing the archive of weathers (literal and literary) embedded in a total climate (literal and literary) across a life or a text. Beauvoir's listing of all the things she has done, and the ad hoc nature of the list (places, atmospheres, vistas, art events, political watersheds), provide the sense of one's life as accumulation. A life as a microclimate of accumulated weathers can thus always be read *both* meteorologically, focusing on discrete events, sunsets, moments in time, *and* climatologically, as a selfhood operating within the mutable and immutable climates of patriarchy, heteronormativity, existentialism, the literal and political climates of France, mechanised war. In sum, while the distinction between climatological and meteorological reading proposed in this chapter has been maintained for pragmatic purposes, it must be kept in mind that literary close reading will mostly demand both methods be used at the same time.

Notes

1 See G. A. Fine, *Authors of the Storm: Meteorologists and the Culture of Prediction* (University of Chicago Press, 2007); J. Golinski, *British Weather and the Climate of Enlightenment* (University of Chicago Press, 2007).

2 In cultural studies, gender studies and human geography, see B. Szerszynski, 'Reading and Writing the Weather', *Theory, Culture and Society* 27.2–3 (2010), 9–30; A. Neimanis and R. Loewen Walker, 'Weathering: Climate Change and the "Thick Time" of Transcorporeality', *Hypatia*, 29.3 (2014), 558–75; K. Yusoff and J. Gabrys, 'Climate Change and the Imagination', *WIREs Climate Change* 2.4 (2011), 516–34. In climatology, see W. Steffen *et al.*, *Cranking up the Intensity: Climate Change and Extreme Weather Events* (Canberra: Climate Council of Australia, 2017).

3 T. H. Ford, 'Climate Change and Literary History', in T. Bristow and Ford (eds.), *A Cultural History of Climate Change* (Abingdon: Routledge, 2016), 157.

4 M. Hulme, *Weathered: Cultures of Climate* (London: Sage, 2017), 4, citing K. Hare, 'The Concept of Climate', *Geography* 51 (1966), 99–100.

5 C. Sharpe, *In the Wake: On Blackness and Being* (Durham, NC: Duke University Press, 2016), 21.

6 K. Anderson, *Predicting the Weather: Victorians and the Science of Meteorology* (University of Chicago Press, 2005).

7 C. Rankine, 'Weather', *The New York Times Sunday Book Review* (21 June 2020), 1.

8 F. de Saussure, *Course in General Linguistics* (1916), in P. Rice and P. Waugh (eds.) *Modern Literary Theory: A Reader* (New York: St. Martin's Press, 1996), 3rd ed.

9 D. Chakrabarty, 'The Climate of History: Four Theses', *Critical Inquiry* 35.2 (2009), 197–222.

10 See Chapter 2 of '"What Is the Cause of Thunder?": The Storm's Three Ambiguities', in J. M. Hamilton, *This Contentious Storm: An Ecocritical and Performance History of King Lear* (London: Bloomsbury Academic, 2017), 31–64.

11 For a study of the diverse cosmological and ecclesiastical significance of historical weathers, see A. Walsham, *Providence in Early Modern England* (Oxford University Press, 1999).

12 B. M. Fagan, *The Little Ice Age: How Climate Made History 1300–1850* (New York: Basic Books, 2002); G. D. Wood, *Tambora: The Eruption That Changed the World* (Princeton University Press, 2015).

13 S. LeMenager, 'Climate Change and the Struggle for Genre', in T. Menely and J. O. Taylor (eds.), *Anthropocene Reading: Literary History in Geologic Times* (University Park: Pennsylvania State University Press, 2017), 220.

14 A. Goodbody and A. Johns-Putra, 'The Rise of the Climate Change Novel', in Johns-Putra (ed.), *Climate and Literature* (Cambridge University Press, 2019), 230.

15 Johns-Putra, 'Ecocriticism, Genre, and Climate Change: Reading the Utopian Vision of Kim Stanley Robinson's Science in the Capital Trilogy', *English Studies*, 91.7 (2010), 748.

16 J. O. Taylor, 'Atmosphere as Setting, or, "Wuthering" in the Anthropocene', in Johns-Putra (ed.), *Climate and Literature*, 31–44.

17 L. Burnett, 'Firing the Climate Canon: A Literary Critique of the Genre of Climate Change', *Green Letters* 22.2 (2018), 164.

18 J. Frow, 'Genre Worlds: The Discursive Shaping of Knowledge', *Arena Journal* 23 (2005), 140.

19 Taylor, 'Atmosphere as Setting', 31.

20 Frow, 'Genre Worlds', 132.

21 B. Johnson, 'Gender Theory and the Yale School' (1985), in Rice and Waugh (eds.), 215.

22 Johnson, 'Gender Theory and the Yale School', 215.

23 Johnson, 'Gender Theory and the Yale School', 216.

24 Sharpe, *In the Wake*, 21.

25 A. L. Cory, '"Out of My Brother's Power": Gender, Class and Rebellion in *Wuthering Heights*', *Women's Studies* 34.1 (2004), 1–26; C. Fowler, 'Was Heathcliff Black?' *The Conversation* (26 October 2017).

26 R. Barthes, 'Where to Begin?', in *New Critical Essays*, trans. R. Howard (Los Angeles: University of California Press, 1990), 81; W. Benjamin, 'Convolute D: Boredom, Eternal Return', in R. Tiedemann (ed.), *The Arcades Project*, trans. H. Eiland and K. McLaughlin (Cambridge, MA: Belknap, 1999), 101.

27 S. Mentz, 'Strange Weather in *King Lear*'. *Shakespeare* 6.2 (2010), 143.

28 G. Jones, *Shakespeare's Storms* (Manchester University Press, 2015), 74.

29 L. Shannon, *The Accommodated Animal: Cosmopolity in Shakespearean Locales* (University of Chicago Press, 2013), 141.

30 P. Ricoeur, *The Rule of Metaphor: The Creation of Meaning in Language*, trans. R. Czerny (1977; London: Routledge, 2003), 136.

31 R. Jakobson, 'Two Aspects of Language and Types of Aphasic Disturbances', in Jakobsen, *On Language*, edited by Linda R. Waugh and Monique Monville-Burston (1990; Cambridge, MA: Harvard University Press, 1995): 115–33, 129.

32 See Hamilton, *This Contentious Storm*.

33 Neimanis and Loewen Walker, 'Weathering', 558–75.

34 A. Neimanis and J. M. Hamilton, 'Weathering', *Feminist Review* 118.1 (2018), 80–4.

35 S. de Beauvoir, qtd. in J. Biggs, 'The Earth Had Need of Me', *London Review of Books* 42.8 (16 April 2020).

PART II

Current Issues in Climate Change Criticism

4

DEREK WOODS

Scales
Climate versus Embodiment

King Lear's famous speech to the storm is an encounter between the scale of embodiment and the scale of climate:

> Blow, winds, and crack your cheeks! rage! blow!
> . . .
> Vaunt couriers to oak-cleaving thunderbolts
> Singe my white head! And thou, all-shaking thunder,
> Strike flat the thick rotundity o' the world!
> Crack nature's moulds, an germens spill at once,
> That make ingrateful man![1]

Betrayed by his family, Lear throws impotent words at the storm. Stripped of sovereignty, he courts apocalypse, commanding the flood to 'drown the cocks' and drench 'our steeples' – to foreclose both morning and salvation. He evokes his own embodiment by referring to his 'white head'. The speech makes it easy for readers to imagine a human body, ranting at the weather, surrounded by objects that give the scene its sense of scale. But by evoking 'the rotundity of the world' (from Latin *rota*, wheel), Lear shifts reference to the planetary, a spherical form that marks the proper scale of 'climate'. This jump from weather to the scale of Earth leaves the immediacy of the storm behind. Similarly, but zooming in the opposite direction, 'All germens spill at once / That make ingrateful man' shifts the soliloquy's spatial reference from the globe, down past the human, and down still further to a microworld of 'germens' alien to direct human experience. Lear wants the storm to make time for both the coarse-grained and the fine-grained work of apocalypse, to both smite our habitat and squish every germ of potential humanity.[2]

The futility of trying to command a storm exemplifies the scalar binary that guides this chapter: the distinction between climate and embodiment. As biologist D'Arcy Wentworth Thompson wrote in his underappreciated book *On Growth and Form* (1917), the 'scale of human observation and experience lies within the narrow bounds of inches, feet, or miles, all measured in terms drawn from our own selves and our own doings'.³ Timothy Clark associates this 'given dimensionality' with the weather and so with the distinction between weather and climate.⁴ In this chapter, terms like *body*, *weather*, *sensory world*, *lifeworld*, and *phenomenology* all refer to anthropo-scalar norms of embodiment. With these constraints, planetary climate can only be mediated by data, concepts, narratives, and so on that re-present it at our scale.⁵ But there are exceptions to this scalar binary. Like Shakespeare's 'germens', such exceptions offer third scales and excluded middles from which to perform the cherished critical activity of deconstructing paired opposites.

Lear's desire to command the storm evokes twenty-first-century debates about the (in)ability of literary forms such as novels, plays, and poetry to represent the overwhelming spatial and temporal scales of climate.⁶ But core critical questions about the relation between literature and climate are relevant both before and after the rise of environmentalism and today's climate politics. How does literature write the encounter between bodies and climate? What trends in literary form and content do critics track when they study climate change? What concepts have they then created or rethought? To answer these questions, we need to look outside the contemporary moment and compare historical periods. This chapter looks at four topics: the 'superorganism', the climate theory of race, the concepts of 'hyperobject' and 'trans-corporeality', and the novel as climate model.

Superorganism

At times, in both literature and science, the scale of climate is *itself* embodied as an enormous organism. Consider a second literary storm from the British Renaissance, this time in John Milton's *Paradise Lost* (1667). In an epic simile, the speaker compares Satan, floating in a sea of fire after God has cast him down from heaven, with a giant sea creature, the Leviathan. Extending the simile, Milton imagines a lost sailor, who, mistaking the Leviathan for an island, 'Moors by his side under the lee'.⁷ Such (mis)recognition is fundamental to narratives of *organicism*: the habit of thought that treats large-scale things or processes as organisms in their own right.

This is true of two great superorganism narratives, Octavia Butler's *Xenogenesis Trilogy* (1987–9) and N. K. Jemisin's *Broken Earth* (2015–17). In Butler's trilogy, an alien spacecraft turns out to be an enormous spherical organism; in Jemisin's novels, 'father Earth' is malevolently animate, punishing humans for what they did to the moon.⁸ In both novels, characters only gradually become aware that they are living inside, or on, a vast spherical living being. A shorter example is Ursula K. Le Guin's story 'Vaster than

Empires and More Slow'. Le Guin's title alludes to Andrew Marvell's 'To His Coy Mistress' (1681), a poem of erotic persuasion that likens humans to plants.[9]

In the story, a group of explorers from Earth arrive at a planet inhabited only by plants. With its lack of animals, it presents us with a kind of 'incomplete' trophic web, a world in which evolution turned out differently. The central character is an 'empath' who experiences the emotions of others directly. He needs isolation by the time the crew reach the plant-planet. But even in the forest he is not alone. He can sense the 'fear' of the plants: what turns out to be a vague 'sentience . . . like a draft in a closed room', a mental ambience that pervades the forests despite the fact that there are no animals to emit affects like fear.[10]

On this plant-planet that embodies the perennial organicism and holism of ecological thought, 'all the biosphere' turns out to be 'one network of communications', one great organism rather than a collective of individual bodies.[11] Le Guin's metaphors of networks and communication match those of many science writers concerned with ecological questions after the rise of cybernetics, information theory, and computing, writers who are often willing to write of the superorganism as an information technology.[12] The same language ties the story to James Cameron's popular film *Avatar* (2009), which borrows from both 'Vaster' and Le Guin's novel, *The Word for World Is Forest* (1972). Finally, the story's planetary plant mind evokes debates about plant 'thinking' and communication that have seen serious scientific and critical attention in recent years.[13]

The best thing about the story is how Le Guin writes the first-person experience of this botanical superorganism: she imagines the scale of climate as though it were not just experienced at the scale of embodiment but identical with it. For a moment, the empath feels the plant mind's perspective: 'To know the whole daylight, after all, and the whole night. All the winds and lulls together. The winter stars and the summer stars at the same time . . . To be whole . . . '.[14] With this fiction of a planetary plant's phenomenology, Le Guin crosses the gap between weather and climate with a knowledge that occurs only at the specific scale and geometry of a planetary sphere. As Jesse Oak Taylor puts it, 'the encounter with climate' is the encounter with 'an abstraction that cannot be experienced firsthand'.[15] But Le Guin imagines this barrier transcended without technological mediation. Her superorganism's phenomenological lifeworld is less like a concave dome bounded by horizons, more like a convex kaleidoscope of seasons, skies, and temperatures. Embodiment absorbs the scale of climate, with no gap between first-person experience and the materiality of the planetary climate.

As a trope, the superorganism – the plant as biosphere – is a *synecdoche* in which a part stands for a whole. In recent decades, this trope has become a controversial one in biology and Earth science, where it unites the super-organism with climate as a modern, planetary, scientific object of study. According to James Lovelock's 'Gaia' theory, life interacts with the geochemistry of Earth in such a way that it 'regulates' key variables such as the concentration of oxygen and carbon dioxide in the atmosphere.[16] Lovelock took the word *regulate* from its cybernetic context, where it initially referred to organisms and machines. In extending self-regulation to chemical flows among the biosphere, atmosphere, and lithosphere, he drew on the ability of organisms to maintain their own body temperatures.

Commentators often forget that microbiologist Lynn Margulis was one of Lovelock's co-authors, and that she continued to contribute to Gaia theory throughout her career. Her emphasis was always on the role of microorgan-isms in life's regulation of Earth's climate.[17] In the context of the super-organism, we might think of Gaia's microbiome, like Shakespeare's germens, as an exception to the scalar binary embodiment/climate. Taking it into consideration means routing the climate through single cells roughly 2 million times shorter than a two-metre human body. The Earth micro-biome thus complicates the tropological dynamics by which an organism stands for the planetary scale by adding a third term to distinctions between tenor and vehicle, micro and macro.

The Climate Theory of Race

In an argument relevant to the superorganism, Mark McGurl suggests that the rise of the novel correlates with the decline of giants – a historical shift in the aesthetics of scale. As the English realist novel emerged in the eighteenth century, with its interest in lower classes, fantastic giants and monsters began to disappear, sidelined to self-consciously unreal genres such as Gothic, horror, and fantasy. They disappeared not just because they were imaginary, or non-realist, but because realism is a scale-dependent form. The disappearance of giants is a symptom of how the novel normalised a particular scale, the lifeworld or the scale of embodiment, as *the* world of reality during the same historical period when telescopes and microscopes were showing that much of reality, like the planetary climate, is inaccessible to our senses.[18] The new novelistic realism was less modernity learning to read stories about monsters and gods with a grain of salt and more so compensation for the dislocation of humans in the hierarchy of being.

This new explosion of scales in its relation to human self-understanding led to what McGurl calls 'posthuman comedy', a literary mode in which humans mock their own centrality. The mode stretches from early modernity to the climate change era. But the word *climate* did not always refer to the planetary, and while race is often forgotten in climate change discourse about species, to see the relation between race and *climate* in the word's early modern sense is to explore an exception to the modern binary between embodiment and climate that still shapes worlds today. For early modern Europeans, the word *climate* and its cognates referred to the conditions of a region or a continent: the climate of northern Europe compared to that of the Mediterranean, or the climate of the new world compared to the old.[19] One dominant theory of racial difference held that a region's climate determines the appearance, even the intelligence, of its inhabitants. As Fabian Lorcher and Jean-Baptiste Fressoz argue, to avoid projecting the present onto this early modern colonial worldview we have to 'think our way into a now defunct epistemological realm' in which 'technique, political form, environment, and bodies all overlapped'.[20] In the Anthropocene, it should be more difficult than it is to talk about species without race and race without species. This is no less true when Anthropocene writing puts forward a new kind of giant, the human understood as a species-subject that has evolved to become a geological force pushing the Earth's climate into a new state.

Alongside microscopic and telescopic expansions, modernity's encounter with the colonial other threatened to dislocate Europeans from their presumptive position near the top of the great chain of being. New global relations of human life both caused and challenged the superiority of their racial self-descriptions. Realism compensates for this state of affairs by diverting 'the problem of scale to children's literature and science fiction' and by presenting 'a serious, human-scaled world as the norm', so that, 'whether pitched at the level of small-scale intimacies or straining toward a grasp of the entire social system, the limits of the novel are defined by the limits of the human' – which are never simply the limits of the species as a whole.[21] In this context, Daniel Defoe's *Robinson Crusoe* (1719) and Jonathan Swift's *Gulliver's Travels* (1726) offer cross-sections of scale aesthetics in transition.

In *Robinson Crusoe*, the story of a man stranded on a 'primitive' island, the scalar norms of realism are evident in Defoe's 'avoidance of traditional romance plots in favor of a quasi-autobiographical', practical, and 'individualist form'.[22] When Robinson sees a large footprint in the sand after years of solitude, he measures it against his own to reassure himself that it is not the sign of a giant. Realism's *compression*, here illustrated through the trace of a body part, compensates for the dizzying proliferation of scales and peoples revealed to Europe by 'scientific and colonial adventures'.[23] Conversely, rather than forcing the other into the mould of the human, McGurl's mode of 'posthuman comedy' widens the gap between these footprints on the beach of scalar modernity. Published only seven years after *Robinson Crusoe*, *Gulliver's Travels* shows the 'hidden strangeness in the nature of ordinary physical reality'.

Swift's novel is a counter-anthropocentric satire of colonial and scientific optimism because it sees the question of scale 'in *dynamically relative* terms'.[24] The 'people' Gulliver meets oscillate wildly in scale, form, and species. First come the tiny Lilliputians, ant-like in comparison to Gulliver. Next come the giant Brobdingnagians, who make Gulliver look like an ant. Such examples are about race as much as species. The derangement of scale is as much colonial as cosmic and geological. Swift's invented 'races' vary as Gulliver moves from one climate to another. *Gulliver's Travels* narrates 'climates', or local weather, geography, flora, and fauna, that match the morphologies of his fictional races and species. For example, soon after he sees his first Brobdingnagian giant, Gulliver encounters a country 'fully cultivated', in which 'the length of the grass was about twenty foot high'.[25]

Yet the funniest satire of such climate determinism comes not in Lilliput or Brobdingnag but in the relation between the Balnibarbians and their rich Laputan overlords. The Laputans live on an island that floats in the air above a continent populated by their Balnibarbian subjects. The faces of the intellectual Laputan race are distorted: one eye turns inward and one looks straight up; they are so absent-minded that their servants must remind them to listen and speak during conversation. But on the continent of Balnibarbi, Gulliver finds the people 'wild, their eyes fixed', and 'generally in rags'.[26] Their ragged appearance reflects the land. Gulliver sees hardly an 'ear of corn or blade of grass'. His host explains that the problem is how the locals have modified the climate and been modified by it in turn. Forty years before, a group ascended to Laputa, returning with 'volatile spirits acquired in that airy region'. The sky island's knowledge and climate transformed the Balnibarbians. Back on the continent, they decided to apply their knowledge to climate control: 'all the fruits of the earth shall come to maturity at whatever season we think fit to choose'.[27] But the project failed. They transformed their climate badly, and it fed back to alter their appearance. The fate of the Balnibarbians reflects the prejudice of naturalists like Buffon that, in Kyla Schuller's words, 'condemned residents of the Americas as unfailingly degenerate on account of a humid and otherwise unfavourable climate', or Hegel's idea, as Zakiyyah Iman Jackson puts it, that 'the African character … springs from a geographical climate hostile to the achievement of the spirit'.[28]

The climate theory was a false explanation of racial difference. But in narratives of the Anthropocene, the directional arrow of environmental determinism seems reversed, re-scaled, and displaced from nature to artifice.[29] 'The human species', or colonialism and racial capitalism, have realised this fantasy of environmental determinism by creating geographies where the poor and people of colour suffer far more from climate change and pollution, while contributing far less to them.[30] What started as a colonial fiction about racial hierarchy now takes the form of hierarchies inscribed in the land, air, and water, not by nature but by differential exposure to artificial environments. Modern environmental racism has materialised the climate theory of race. What species-based universalism hides is that 'the human' exists simply as a differential between the 'superhuman' that produces Earth's climate and the 'subhuman' that suffers the effects.[31] If McGurl is right that realism has shaped spurious limits of the human, and if 'science fiction is the realism of our time', then fantastical works like Swift's satire take on a certain verisimilitude keyed to scales where the human is too excessive or too diminutive to fit the mould of humanism.[32] In literary history, the realism that gets closest to reality might not seem real at all.

Hyperobjects and Trans-Corporeality

So many people have had the following conversations. First, one makes small talk about the weather. But the conversation suddenly turns to climate change – or it threatens to, or you hope it will. 'Talking about the weather' is no longer a reliably 'phatic' and apolitical way of being social for sociality's sake because global warming has reached a certain threshold of awareness. Second, some consumer object enters your social world – especially food. At first it seems like safe and nourishing enjoyment. But then your companion worries that the food could be mildly toxic, containing some carcinogenic ingredient. You remember that pollution is intimately corporeal and that we live in a society of invisible, uncertain risks.[33] The first conversation expresses Timothy Morton's concept of the *hyperobject*, or 'things that are massively distributed in time and space relative to humans', like nuclear waste or the climate system or the world wide web.[34] The second conversation expresses Stacy Alaimo's concept of *trans-corporeality*, a feminist approach to embodiment that stresses the 'material interchanges between bodies (both human and nonhuman) and the wider environment'.[35] Contrasting these two concepts is another way to think the scalar encounter between climate and embodiment.

The hyperobject comes from the tradition of phenomenology, the philosophy of how things appear, which stretches from Kant to Heidegger to the 'object-oriented ontology' (OOO) embraced by Morton. One way to illustrate the hyperobject is via Kant's notion of the *mathematical sublime*. Kant characterises the sublime with a narrative of embodiment versus large-scale objects. First, he asks the reader to imagine standing before a mountain range, whose vastness makes them feel small. But what, he asks, does it mean to assert 'that anything is great, or small, or of medium size?'[36] It means comparing one thing with another, such as King Lear with the 'the rotundity o' the world'. Kant offers a chain of comparisons: a tree, a mountain, and the Earth. The list extends to the solar system, the Milky Way, the 'immeasurable host of such systems', which may 'themselves form such a system', and so on, with 'no prospect of a limit'.[37] Humiliation before the magnitude of nature is the first moment of the mathematical sublime.

In the second moment, the tiny embodied human grasps that the massive becomes small because scale is relative: the mountain is hardly visible from space, and the Earth quickly vanishes in cosmic expanses. Human *embodiment* sinks 'into insignificance' given this mathematical relativity – but so do things of all sizes. What keeps high status, however, are the '*ideas* of reason', here the idea of infinity. 'The *mere ability even to think* the given infinite' means that the thinker has a faculty beyond senses, empiricism, and embodiment.[38] Only reason possessed of this idea can place the chain of scales on an infinite continuum where the big can be small and the small can be big. Reason, more universal than objects such as bodies and planets, offers a compensation similar to the realism of McGurl's 'great compression'. The conflict between embodiment and climate creates no absolute limit to knowledge.

The radical gap between 'supersensible' and sensible, transcendental and material, or the phenomenon and the thing in itself is a key for Morton's hyperobject. Their reading of phenomenology makes hyperobjects more than just *really big things*. Hyperobjects are indeed big relative to humans, and last far longer. Humans live inside them, 'like Jonah in the Whale'.[39] But a rift separates 'us' – the human scalar norm – from hyperobjects such as the climate. This rift is just as deep as Kant's rift between the experience of relative sizes and the idea of infinity. For Kant, this rift dualistically separates the transcendental realm of pure reason from the messy empirical world. For Morton, ontological rifts exist among *all* objects because their essences withdraw from relation with one another. No relation can grasp their essence.

With global warming, weather 'turns out to have been a false immediacy' or 'pseudo-reality'. Weather 'can't stand up against the looming presence of an invisible yet far more real global climate. Weather ... has ceased to exist, and along with it, the cozy concept of *lifeworld* itself. *Lifeworld* was just a story we were telling ourselves inside of a vast, massively distributed hyperobject called climate.'[40] With this argument, Morton arrives at the core of the hyperobject. Hyperobjects have 'ruined' the conversation about the weather. Such conversations are about a 'cozy' (but was it?) shared world that no longer exists because of the giants looming outside the snow globe. Morton makes an ontological choice: the larger scale is more real and the lifeworld is a vestigial effect of how sensory experience translates hyperobjects, like the illusory island in the mind of Milton's sailor.

Readers familiar with new materialist theory will be able to see how the hyperobject conflicts with trans-corporeality. The clearest difference is scale. Even if both thinkers ultimately make their concepts relevant to all scales, Morton emphasises gigantic objects and terrifyingly long durations, while Alaimo looks to the invisible micro-materialities where 'the figure/ground relation between the human and the environment dissolves'.[41] This is why the conversation about toxic substances expresses trans-corporeality. Hyperobjects deal with the big and the sublime, trans-corporeality with the small and the intimate – with feeling your 'own' body traversed by 'other' materialities to the extent that you begin to question the assumption of a distinction between self and other. Indeed, Alaimo's focus on the body's constant decomposition and recomposition out of its molecular environment leads her to treat the notion of an *individual* body as oxymoronic.

Another difference between the hyperobject and trans-corporeality is the status of the transcendental. Grounded as it ultimately is in Kant's transcendental phenomenology, OOO's case for non-relation is incompatible with the far more fluid and relational thought of trans-corporeality. New materialist thinkers such as Alaimo often treat relations as prior to relata, echoing the work of Gilles Deleuze and his influence Gilbert Simondon. In this way, the differences between Alaimo and Morton replay to some extent the incommensurabilities between 'Deleuzeans' and phenomenologists.[42] But the idea most relevant for understanding Alaimo's position on the transcendental is that bodies and the material flows that pass through them allow no gap between the 'false immediacy' of the lifeworld and the scale of climate. With trans-corporeality, matter sutures together what seems to distance us from climate, making even the planetary scale immediate, intimate, and corporeal. There is no transcendental gap between our embodied selves and the climate. Nor is there racialised climate determinism. Instead, there is plasticity and reciprocal production, and Alaimo is closer than Morton to the embrace of connectedness that, for better or worse, forms the 'principle of principles' of ecological thought.[43]

Alaimo grounds her approach to transcendence and objectivity in feminist theory, including the 'science studies' of Donna Haraway and the claim that all knowledge is situated in relation to the histories and identities of the collectives that produce it. For Alaimo, 'thinking as the stuff of the world has a long feminist history, due to the way women, along with racially marked and disabled peoples, have grappled with being subjects often categorized and systematically treated as objects'.[44] Briefly, feminist new materialism is wary of how objectivity and objectification enable each other. This raises the spectre of philosophical debates about truth in science. More than truth, however, Alaimo attends to a messy reality of artistic and activist practices where philosophy is far from the most important thing at stake. For example, she argues that mediations of the climate suffer from a 'view from above', view from nowhere, or 'god trick' of 'disembodied perspective' that derives from how patriarchy shapes scientific representation.[45] The scale of climate is important, but trans-corporeality is wary of the 'rotundity o' the world'. We do not need the planetary scale to see how climate is enmeshed with our bodies, from Lear's 'white head' down to his microscopic 'germens'. Trans-corporeality is thus another exception to the binary between climate and embodiment, whereas the hyperobject depends on a rift between two scales.

The Novel as Climate Model

The idea that the novel can represent and/or anticipate the effects of climate change is central to the new genre of 'climate fiction'. Here too there are precursors and exceptions to the opposition of climate and embodiment. Jesse Oak Taylor looks back to Charles Dickens's *Bleak House* (1853) to show how the novel sets up its (dis)junction between weather and climate in the contextual smog of Victorian London: 'the novel performs a kind of fictional "greenhouse effect" in which the real is severed from its stabilizing lifeline to the natural'.[46] By 1901, the greenhouse became an analogy for global warming in the work of Swedish meteorologist Nils Ekholm; by 1908, Svante Arrhenius used it as a figure of climate engineering. The figure appeared in the context of the rise of 'greenhouses', 'glasshouses', and 'hot-houses' in nineteenth-century Europe. Such artificial microclimates made the metropole into a space that 'compressed' the Earth's multiplicity of climates within its own, for science or exoticist enjoyment. In this it shares something with McGurl's theory of realism as compensation for scalar derangement.

Taylor's work on the 'The Novel as Climate Model' favours a realism that does not *represent* the lifeworld like *Robinson Crusoe* but uses *metonymy* to simulate the operational logic of artificial climates such as Victorian London.[47] For example, the trope 'greenhouse effect' is metonymic. Different from synecdoches like the superorganism, metonymy works by making *x* stand for *y* because two things have a close spatial relation such as cause and effect. The greenhouse is the cause, and the effect, trapped heat, is analogous to climate change. The 'cause', in this model, stands for an effect beyond direct human experience: the planetary effect of global warming. As a theory of the novel, this argument comes close to saying that the environment determines the narrative world from the outside.

For Taylor, another example of metonymy is the famous barometer singled out by literary theorist Roland Barthes as an example of 'the reality effect' in the nineteenth-century French novel. For Barthes, the barometer is one of the 'pointless' details that aid realism by saying 'nothing but this: *we are the real*', this scene takes place in the everyday world.[48] The barometer is metonymic and causal because it is an *indexical sign*. Like a foot causes a footprint, ambient atmospheric pressure causes the barometer to signify. Taylor wonders why critics have not taken literary atmospheres more literally, as metonymic models rather than vehicles of mood. The fog in *Bleak House* is the imprint of an industrial climate too vast to see all at once. The greenhouse is less a microcosm, more a refraction of that larger-scale reality.

By the twenty-first century, climate fiction takes on a realism with both similarities and differences compared to Taylor's account of atmospheric form. The metonymic butterflies at the centre of Barbara Kingsolver's novel *Flight Behaviour* (2012) are a good example. The novel's focal character is a rural woman who lives in the mountains of Appalachia. One day, on a walk in the woods near her farm, she discovers a massive swarm of orange insects. Scientists arrive to study this strange discovery, which turns out to be a colony of migrating monarchs. Global warming has made the Appalachian winter hospitable; in the past, they overwintered in Mexico, but in Kingsolver's diegetic world, unlike our own, the climate has shifted just enough to create a *slight* difference from the norm. So this narrative is technically speculative fiction despite its apparent realism and twenty-first-century setting. As an *effect* of climate change that *figures* climate change, the swarm's presence in Appalachia constitutes a tropological version of the 'climate proxy'.[49] The idea has often arisen that swarming social insects are superorganisms in their own right, an organic whole at a larger scale. Unlike this synecdoche – unlike Le Guin's vegetal superorganism – Kingsolver's swarm is an effect that figures climate change at the scale of her protagonist's lifeworld. Like Margulis's Gaian microbiome, the swarm is another exception to the binary between climate and embodiment.

In *Flight Behaviour*, the vivid orange butterflies also lead, via the scientist who studies them, to the protagonist's education about global warming – a telling plot in a moment when, as Nicole Seymour argues, didacticism has taken on a new life in environmental literature and culture.[50] Didactic literature makes teaching as important as entertainment or pleasure. Early modern science often took the form of long poems. Today, the urgent need to teach the public in ways that lead to climate action has made didacticism central to climate fiction as a genre. By subjecting art to a purpose, many writers, journalists, and scholars embrace a level of instrumentalism that would previously have been dismissed.[51]

One example is novelist Sarah Holding's article 'What Is Cli-Fi? And Why I Write It', where she stresses that climate fiction can help restore the climate to 'equilibrium'.[52] Like Amitav Ghosh, Holding thinks that the form of climate fiction best able to achieve this goal is an extrapolative realism similar to the form of Kingsolver's *Flight Behaviour*.[53] Accordingly, fantastical aliens and science-fiction apocalypses lack the scientific grounding to represent climate change. Political purpose and realism are inversely proportional.[54] The more climate fiction succeeds in stabilising the climate, the less its extrapolative realism will have been accurate; but the more accurate its extrapolation, the less successful it will have been at accomplishing its purpose.

Perhaps the atmotechnical device that best suits this theory of climate fiction is not the barometer but the thermostat. Thermostats register the temperature of a room through indexical signs. By feeding this data back to a furnace or an air conditioner, by turning it on or off, they also change the temperature by keeping it balanced around a set point. Such is the unreachable limit case of climate fiction as a genre of action, which resonates with texts on climate engineering that imagine adjusting the thermostat of planet Earth.[55] Metonymic realism is a two-way process. Literature aspires to the same agency demanded by King Lear – though with the opposite, placating effect.

This realism and Taylor's are more complex than mimesis, but as we work to understand and critique the relation between the scale of embodiment and the scale of climate, realism should not become a normative form. In much cli-fi discourse, as Rebecca Evans argues, extrapolative plausibility has become just that.[56] If this norm were followed, it would deem irrelevant all giants, aliens, and other imaginary beings. The norm of realism and didacticism would force critics to turn away from some of the most pleasurable, popular, and intricate works of climate fiction.

Le Guin's *The Lathe of Heaven* (1971) tells the story of a character who lives in a near future when the 'greenhouse effect had been quite gradual'.[57] In the misty atmosphere of the narrative present, we have 'the endless warm drizzle of spring – the ice of Antarctica falling softly on the heads of those responsible for melting it'.[58] This sounds like realist extrapolation, but it gives way to Le Guin's characteristic use of fantasy. The protagonist is able to completely remake the world with his dreams. This is no slight alteration as in Kingsolver's novel, but a total shift in the diegetic conditions of the story-world. The character dreams pink dogs and benevolent turtle-like aliens; when he awakes, they become real.

Far from irrelevant to understanding climate fiction's coupling of purpose and form, *The Lathe of Heaven* seems to satirise the cli-fi thermostat. When the protagonist's psychiatrist learns of his powers, the psychiatrist devises a machine that lets him capture and direct the protagonist's dreams. The psychiatrist uses the machine to create a utilitarian, eugenic, eco-authoritarian society in which the population is carefully managed and the 'ecological balance of the planet' has been restored.[59] The protagonist's dreams become a tool to balance the climate. The scale of embodiment controls the scale of climate through the medium of a prosthetic mind. In retrospect, Le Guin's novel seems to have been a work of meta cli-fi. The novel thematises its genre's tendency to instrumentalise climate fiction's imaginary worlds, as though their chief value were to serve as the cultural wing of geoengineering.

*

The synecdoche of the superorganism, race determined by climate, material relations versus ontological 'gaps' between lifeworld and climate, and the novel as climate model have been my examples of the encounter between climate and embodiment. Each example unfolds, in its way, the idea that climate change creates a problem of scale that literature does or does not overcome – a problem added to that of writing a 'reality' that, even at the scale of the lifeworld, is never the same reality that a text presents to its reader's imagination. The Anthropocene has certainly created new configurations of climate and embodiment coupled to changes in literary form, including what sort of narrative worlds seem real to their readers. Yet present configurations of embodiment, climate, and form are still constrained by those of the past. It's clear across periods of literary study that the play of causality, figuration, and distinction between body and climate has become essential to narratives of the artificial Earth.

Notes

1 W. Shakespeare, *King Lear* (London: Cassell, 1888), 160.
2 Sophie Chiari notes that '"seeds," "grains," and "germens" in Shakespeare are sometimes half-veiled allusions to the atomist doctrine', in *Shakespeare's Representation of Weather, Climate, and Environment: The Early Modern 'Fated Sky'* (Edinburgh University Press, 2019), 191.
3 D. W. Thompson, *On Growth and Form* (Cambridge University Press, 1992), 17.
4 T. Clark, 'What on World Is the Earth? The Anthropocene and Fictions of the World', *The Oxford Literary Review* 35.1 (2013), 9.

5 See U. K. Heise, *Sense of Place and Sense of Planet: The Environmental Imagination of the Global* (New York: Oxford University Press, 2008) and J. Gabrys, *Program Earth: Environmental Sensing Technology and the Making of a Computational Planet* (Minneapolis: University of Minnesota Press, 2016).

6 See T. Clark, *Ecocriticism at the Edge: The Anthropocene as a Threshold Concept* (London: Bloomsbury Academic, 2015); T. Menely and J. O. Taylor (eds.), *Anthropocene Reading: Literary History in Geologic Times* (College Park: Penn State University Press, 2017); S. Craps and R. Crownshaw, 'Introduction: The Rising Tide of Climate Fiction', *Studies in the Novel* 50.1 (2018), 1–8; and A. Johns-Putra, *Climate Change and the Contemporary Novel* (Cambridge University Press, 2019), 30–40.

7 J. Milton, *The Complete Poems* (London: Penguin, 1998), 126.

8 O. Butler, *Dawn* (New York: Grand Central, 1987); N. K. Jemisin, *The Fifth Season* (London: Orbit, 2015).

9 Andrew Marvell, *The Complete Poems* (London: Penguin 2005), 50–2.

10 U. K. Le Guin, 'Vaster Than Empires and More Slow', in R. Silverberg (ed.), *New Dimensions 1: Fourteen Original Science Fiction Stories* (New York: Doubleday, 1971), 123.

11 Le Guin, 'Vaster', 128.

12 S. Kingsland, *The Evolution of American Ecology, 1890–2000* (Baltimore, MD: Johns Hopkins University Press, 2005), 209–13.

13 See M. Marder, *Plant Thinking: A Philosophy of Vegetal Life* (New York: Columbia University Press, 2013); J. T. Nealon, *Plant Theory: Biopower and Vegetal Life* (Stanford University Press, 2015), and for a focus on speculative fiction in print and film, N. Meeker and A. Szabari, *Radical Botany: Plants and Speculative Fiction* (New York: Fordham University Press, 2020) and M. Gagliano *et al.*, *The Language of Plants: Science, Philosophy, Literature* (Minneapolis: University of Minnesota Press, 2017).

14 Le Guin, 'Vaster', 129.

15 J. O. Taylor, *The Sky of Our Manufacture: The London Fog in British Fiction from Dickens to Woolf* (Charlottesville: University of Virginia Press, 2016), 27. Dipesh Chakrabarty agrees in 'Postcolonial Studies and the Challenge of Climate Change', *New Literary History* 43.1 (2012), 1–18.

16 In ancient Greek origin myth, Gaia is a primordial deity, the personification of Earth and the mother of the Titans. Melissa K. Nelson notes that 'Gaia' evokes, and displaces, 'pre-industrial Earth-honoring traditions shared by many Indigenous peoples', in 'Indigenous Science and Traditional Ecological Knowledge: Persistence in Place', in R. Warrior (ed.), *The World of Indigenous North America* (New York: Routledge, 2015), 204.

17 For Margulis and Gaia, see B. Clarke, *Gaian Systems: Lynn Margulis, Neocybernetics, and the End of the Anthropocene* (Minneapolis: University of Minnesota Press, 2020). For Gaia and science fiction, see Clarke, 'The Planetary Imaginary', in Clarke (ed.), *Earth, Life, and System: Evolution and Ecology on a Gaian Planet* (New York: Fordham University Press, 2015), 171–4.

18 M. McGurl, 'Gigantic Realism: The Rise of the Novel and the Comedy of Scale', *Critical Inquiry* 43 (2017), 420.

19 P. S. Langeslag, 'Weathering the Storm: Adverse Climates in Medieval Literature', in A. Johns-Putra (ed.), *Climate and Literature* (Cambridge University Press, 2019), 76–91.

20 F. Lorcher and J. B. Fressoz, 'Modernity's Frail Climate: A Climate History of Environmental Reflexivity', *Critical Inquiry* 38.3 (2012), 579–98.

21 McGurl, 'Gigantic Realism', 420.

22 McGurl, 'Gigantic Realism', 409.

23 McGurl, 'Gigantic Realism', 403.

24 McGurl, 'Gigantic Realism', 415.

25 J. Swift, *Gulliver's Travels* (New York: Signet, 1960), 97.

26 Swift, *Gulliver's Travels*, 190.

27 Swift, *Gulliver's Travels*, 193

28 K. Schuller, *The Biopolitics of Feeling: Race, Sex, and Science in the Nineteenth Century* (Durham, NC: Duke University Press, 2018), 165; Z. I. Jackson, *On Becoming Human* (New York University Press, 2020), 29. See also N. Hudson, 'From "Nation" to "Race": The Origin of Racial Classification in Eighteenth-Century Thought', *Eighteenth-Century Studies* 29.3 (1996), 247–64, and R. Bernasconi, 'Who Invented the Concept of Race? Kant's Role in the Enlightenment Construction of Race', in Bernasconi (ed.), *Race* (London: Blackwell, 2001), 11–37. Kant was a hinge in the turn away from the climate theory represented by Buffon and others. Kant understood races as a hereditary sub-species, breaking the link between climate (in the regional sense) and the human body, but shifting the source of European superiority to heredity.

29 For precursors of the Anthropocene concept that challenge its novelty, see C. Bonneuil and J. B. Fressoz, *The Shock of the Anthropocene* (London: Verso, 2017) and N. Heringman, 'Deep Time at the Dawn of the Anthropocene', *Representations* 129.1 (2015), 58.

30 See R. Nixon, *Slow Violence and the Environmentalism of the Poor* (Cambridge, MA: Harvard University Press, 2011). Climate determinism may have reappeared in the twenty-first century; see E. DeLoughrey, *Allegories of the Anthropocene* (Durham, NC: Duke University Press, 2019), 191–5.

31 For a critique of the Anthropocene's concept of the human that addresses poetics, science fiction, myth, and origin stories, see K. Yusoff's *A Billion Black Anthropocenes or None* (Minneapolis: University of Minnesota Press, 2018). See also A. Karera, 'Blackness and the Pitfalls of Anthropocene Ethics', *Critical Philosophy of Race* 7.1 (2019), 32–56.

32 K. S. Robinson, 'Science Fiction When the Future Is Now', *Nature* 552 (2017), 330.

33 See U. Beck, *Risk Society: Toward a New Modernity* (London: Sage, 1992). For environmental risk and literature, see Heise, *Sense of Place*, 119–60, and Nixon, *Slow Violence*.

34 T. Morton, *Hyperobjects: Philosophy and Ecology after the End of the World* (Minneapolis: University of Minnesota Press, 2013), 1.

35 S. Alaimo, *Bodily Natures: Science, Environment, and the Material Self* (Bloomington: Indiana University Press, 2010), 16.

36 I. Kant, *Critique of Judgement* (Oxford University Press, 2007), 78.

37 Kant, *Critique of Judgement*, 87.

38 Kant, *Critique of Judgement*, 85–6.

39 Morton, *Hyperobjects*, 20.

40 Morton, *Hyperobjects*, 103. The 'lifeworld' (*Umwelt*) derives from the Kantian biologist Jakob von Uexküll. See his *Forays into the Worlds of Animals and Humans, with a Theory of Meaning*, trans. J. D. O'Neill (Minneapolis: University of Minnesota Press, 2010).

41 S. Alaimo, 'Trans-corporeality', in R. Braidotti and M. Hlavajova (eds.), *The Posthuman Glossary* (London: Bloomsbury Academic, 2018), 435.

42 See K. A. Pearson, *Germinal Life: The Difference and Repetition of Deleuze* (Abingdon: Routledge, 1999), 70–1.

43 F. Neyrat, 'Elements for an Ecology of Separation: Beyond Ecological Constructivism', in E. Hörl and J. Burton (eds.), *General Ecology: The New Ecological Paradigm* (London: Bloomsbury Academic, 2017), 101.

44 Alaimo, 'Trans-corporeality', 436.

45 S. Alaimo, *Exposed: Environmental Politics and Pleasures in Posthuman Times* (Minneapolis: University of Minnesota Press, 2016), 7–8, 108, 153–7.

46 Taylor, *Sky of Our Manufacture*, 20.

47 Taylor, *Sky of Our Manufacture*, 19.

48 R. Barthes, *The Rustle of Language*, trans. R. Howard (Berkeley: University of California Press, 1986), 148. Emphasis in original.

49 T. P. Pringle, 'The Climate Proxy: Digital Cultures of Global Warming', PhD dissertation, Brown University, 2020; W. H. K. Chun, 'On Patterns and Proxies, or the Peril of Reconstructing the Unknown' *e-flux architecture* (25 September 2018).

50 N. Seymour, *Bad Environmentalism: Irony and Irreverence in the Ecological Age* (Minneapolis: University of Minnesota Press, 2018), 27.

51 See M. Schneider-Mayerson, 'The Influence of Climate Fiction: An Empirical Survey of Readers', *Environmental Humanities* 10.2 (2018), 473–500.

52 S. Holding, 'What Is Cli-Fi? And Why I Write It', *The Guardian* (6 February 2015).

53 A. Ghosh, *The Great Derangement: Climate Change and the Unthinkable* (University of Chicago Press, 2016), 27.

54 I elaborate in 'Genre at Earth Magnitude: A Theory of Climate Fiction' (forthcoming).

55 Aspiring climate engineer David Keith asks, 'whose hand will be on the thermostat?' in *A Case for Climate Engineering* (Cambridge, MA: MIT Press, 2013), 153

56 R. Evans, 'Fantastic Futures: Climate Fiction, Climate Justice, and Queer Futurity', *Resilience: A Journal of the Environmental Humanities* 4.2–3 (2017), 94–110.

57 Le Guin, *The Lathe of Heaven* (1971; New York: Scribner, 2008), 7.

58 Le Guin, *Lathe*, 160.

59 Le Guin, *Lathe*, 146.

5

ELIZABETH MAZZOLINI

Capitalist Cultures
The Taste of Oil

Labour and class remain stubbornly neglected concepts within ecocriticism, despite significant scholarly contributions on related topics such as poverty and capitalism, activism, and popular entertainment.[1] The preservationist history of American environmentalism, along with critique-oriented practices of humanist scholarship, and the general American disinclination to confront class, are all among the major factors that obscure labour and class from the direct view of ecocritics.[2] This essay traces some material environmental effects of labour to symbolic trappings of class and back again, in order to show how ecocriticism might expand its interventional power.

Except among the most doctrinaire Marxists, popular understandings of environmentalism's relation to class have been reduced to a function of symbolic consumption – what kind of car/food/clothing/TV programming do you purchase and consume and how does this express your relation to climate change? – and these impoverished senses of class and environmentalism respectively, I will argue, emerge from oil culture, or petroculture. Petroculture capitalises on flowing oil and the symbols of consumerism, with labour and material circumstances rendered all but invisible.

Petroculture's effects, and maybe its vulnerabilities, are particularly apparent in the production, reception and content of one very popular genre – the boom narrative. Boom narratives are written in a variety of media for a variety of audiences, but their core idea, of a common person striking it rich, is written indelibly into the American imagination. Boom narratives hold wide appeal, as with various oil and gold histories, songs, and legends entering the American storytelling pantheon over past decades and centuries. Boom narratives are built around the labour, economics, and aesthetics of class. The form and content of various boom narratives, and popular and critical responses to them, make plain the stakes and effects of petrologic, and moreover may suggest modes for interrupting petroculture's flow.

North Dakota Went Boom

The narratives around North Dakota's recent natural gas booms are cases in point. From around 2006 until around 2014, North Dakota's economy underwent tectonic changes. With natural gas having been discovered in the Baaken shale formation beneath the state, by 2010 North Dakota had gone from ninth among US fossil-fuel-producing states to fourth, and then in 2012 to second, behind only Texas. In response to crude oil prices going down, the natural gas boom has since settled down a bit, but the economies of the town of Williston and the Fort Berthold Indian Reservation, the two municipalities most powerfully affected by the Baaken discovery, remain boosted as of this writing. Coverage of North Dakota's natural gas boom has run the gamut of salacious and serious, speculative and journalistic, and everything in between. Those rendering the North Dakota boom into newspaper accounts and documentary films draw on well-established elements of boom narratives, such as transient labour in search of a quick buck, and associated social effects. These storytelling conventions foreground relations between labour and class under conditions of radically cycling scarcity and abundance.

Newspaper reports of North Dakota's natural gas boom read like pop-culture treatments of battles over such cycles, such as HBO's *Deadwood* (2004–6), about a town built around a gold rush,[3] and the 1974 film *Chinatown*, about the politics surrounding a water shortage. For example, a 2014 *New York Times* story about North Dakota, titled 'In North Dakota, a Tale of Oil, Corruption and Death', tells a darkly compelling story of corruption surrounding control of a resource – the news story is about a hit man, murders, corruption and intergenerational affairs, on the Fort Berthold Indian Reservation. Other *New York Times* stories track 'the downside of the boom', and 'where oil and politics mix', making sure to tell the story of debauchery that follows fast money.[4]

Besides the stories in the *New York Times*, the North Dakota boom featured in television journalism, too. Some of this journalism uses hyperbolic means to portray the Wild West. The National Geographic series *Underworld, Inc.* (2015–16) indulges a *Deadwood*-esque fantasy in its account of Williston, North Dakota, entitled 'Fracking Hell'.[5] The *Underworld, Inc.* series overall is devoted to interviewing people who make their living illegally in a variety of pursuits from sex work, to card sharking, to racketeering. 'Fracking Hell' features people with bandanas and masks covering their faces to protect their identity, but also to titillate their audience and emphasise that what they are seeing is truly clandestine. The piece describes a Wild West town with bar fights, extortion, prostitution, and robbery as a way of life, all parts of a modern Western fantasy (such as in another HBO show, *Westworld* [2016–]) and all leaning toward the 'vice' style of documentary that the series appears to be going for.[6] Notably, the producers of the show were later accused of exaggeration and outright lies, which seems in keeping with tall tales about resource booms.[7] Also notably, almost nothing actually happens during the course of that documentary, making the reports about its producers lying or exaggerating almost beside the point; for example, we are told repeatedly that biker gangs control an extortion business in town, but we are never shown evidence of it beyond shots of a motorcycle cruising down a street, among other anticlimactic features. As with many boom-related promises, this show doesn't really pan out (pun intended).

Other filmic and televisual treatments of the North Dakota oil boom confront the tension introduced by sudden abundance and stark scarcity in close proximity to each other; for example, the critically acclaimed documentary *The Overnighters* (2014).[8] This film eschews lurid storytelling in favour of documenting the everyday life of Pastor Jay Reinke, who allows the transient men looking for work in Williston to sleep in his church or in their cars in the church parking lot. Within boom narrative conventions, this film explores the push-and-pull between extravagant generosity and parsimonious accumulation. For example, as Pastor Jay is confronted by his parishioners and the community about his 'overnighters' programme, he doubles down on the Christian values of giving and welcoming, while Williston citizens are concerned about safety, appearances, and sanctioning the Earth's exploitation. As the oil gushes, Pastor Jay's hospitality flows unimpeded, and the people around him work to stall both. It is difficult to categorise people in *The Overnighters* into heroes and villains – and indeed this same moral ambiguity is sometimes noted as a feature of late capitalism, or postmodernism, or even post-postmodernism, with its lack of grand narratives or moral centres, in which many people seem to benefit a great deal, but not without trade-offs, and financial logic pervades and absorbs moral contradictions.[9] *The Overnighters* also reflects how petroculture creates impossible scenarios of choice between putting food on the table and conserving finite resources in order to protect the Earth. This impossible choice is one of the ways that environmentalist interests get pitted against those of the poor, in the framework of the strategically invoked contradiction between abundance and scarcity. This contradiction exceeds the smoothing capacities of financial logic, a logic which, for example, extends welfare to corporations but not individuals.[10] *The Overnighters* stands out as a boom narrative that questions boom narrative logic.

89

One-off documentaries such as 'Fracking Hell' and *The Overnighters*, whether salacious or serious, reach fairly limited audiences, though, and while coverage of the North Dakota natural gas boom may have been national, and drew on the deep well of boom narrative conventions, the boom narrative as such has not reached the scale and influence referenced by ecocritical scholars when they theorise relationships between literature and petroculture. Recent and already influential ecocritical scholarship relates resource extraction to literature via petroculture's ideological effects on narrative writ large, and The Novel. For example, Stephanie LeMenager's book *Living Oil* seeks a 'coherent narrative' for oil in journalism, museums, and literature.[11] Likewise, in *The Great Derangement*, Amitav Ghosh has addressed climate change via the concept of modernity.[12]

LeMenager and Ghosh locate modern literary traditions in the same historical trajectory as fossil-fuel consumption. For example, LeMenager delineates the ways that oil physically and philosophically underwrites so many aspects of life, art, and imagination, making petroculture seem inescapable. The very moment you consider breaking free from oil is a moment already underwritten by oil, in that the very notion of freedom is predicated on the kind of mobility that oil enables. In her search for a coherent narrative for oil, LeMenager locates sites where petroculture permeates American identity. In extended readings of Vladimir Nabokov's *Lolita* (1955) and Jack Kerouac's *On the Road* (1957), for example, LeMenager points out that these canonical works seen as prototypically 'American' are road novels whose characters' literal itineraries and so therefore also their narrative arcs are predicated on the use of fossil fuels. Similarly, Ghosh situates the domestic bourgeois novel genre alongside oil consumption within the economic and philosophical traditions of modernity. Ghosh notes that the novel's development has precisely paralleled that of industrialisation. For Ghosh, privatisation and anthropocentrism bind the novel's form to oil's infrastructure. The politics and epistemologies enacted by the bourgeois novel correspond to the politics and epistemologies of late capitalism, in which relations are governed by ubiquitous consumerism. This is why, for Ghosh, the novel cannot be adequate to climate change – the novel's capacities are dictated by the very source of the problem.

As *The Overnighters* suggests, boom narratives are built upon an individualistic fallacy of abundance versus scarcity, and so could be marshalled to infuse ecocriticism with class interests in resources, and to poke holes in that fallacy. For their displays of class symbolism and their erasure of labour, along with the figuration of energy as property in excess or absence, boom narratives offer to ecocriticism the chance to be abundantly generous, without cost, toward stories and media that otherwise might not warrant consideration as serious, artistic or influential, let alone canonical.

Ecocriticism's DNA derives partly from cultural studies, a discipline with a history of theorising popular culture and the very concept of popularity alongside class.[13] Some ecocritics have already begun to embrace popular culture and explore class consciousness.[14] These scholars help forward popular entertainment, class, and climate change criticism together. Harkening back to scholarly work in cultural studies in the 1980s, the link between popularity and resource use – and the link's relative obscurity – can be squarely identified as an effect of petroculture. Within cultural studies in the 1980s, media scholars turned to lowbrow television forms for insight into everyday politics. In considering popularity versus artistry, Ien Ang examined structures of feeling and politics in symbolic hierarchies. Reflecting on that era, Ang writes that, among scholars who turned up their noses at the idea of a scholarship of television, 'what tended to be snubbed was a politics of pleasure', and notes that these critics ridiculed fans as stupid masses and also feminised them, thereby denigrating women along the way of policing class through taste.[15] Television scholars who took popular media and its fans seriously combined, as Ang puts it, a 'formal study of texts (genres, aesthetics, forms) and their embedding within anthropological and sociological contexts (viewer subjectivities, audiences, social and cultural formations and conditions of reception)'.

Ang's reflective words here address television studies in the 1980s generally, but are also more pointedly about her influential book, *Watching Dallas*, about the widely watched television show (and boom narrative), *Dallas*.[16] *Dallas* is one of the most successful and influential treatments of petroculture in the United States, one whose influence continues today, affecting how we narrate oil in any form, though it has yet to be addressed (until now) by ecocritics. *Dallas* originally aired from 1978 to 1991, encompassing the decade of the 1980s, and perhaps even defining 'the long 1980s'.[17] In form and content, the show is the epitome of extravagance and abundance, and it is easy to speculate that it was primed to take off by the energy shortages of the 1970s, after which once again the energy and money flowed. The show's excesses matched many of the excesses of the 1980s (excesses, I should point out, that did not extend to everyone, with the 1980s providing myriad case studies in strategically invoked abundance and scarcity). The show was also wildly successful, so successful that even Ang's *Watching Dallas*, esoteric cultural theory written about the show, was translated into English in 1985, three years after it first appeared in Dutch – extraordinary popularity for academic writing. In the book, Ang notes that:

> In over ninety countries, ranging from Turkey to Australia, from Hong Kong to Great Britain, *Dallas* has become a national craze, with the proverbial empty

streets and a dramatic drop in water consumption when an episode of the serial is going out. In the Netherlands, for example, over half the population watched *Dallas* every week in the spring of 1982, when its popularity reached its peak. No other fictional programme, foreign or domestic, has ever achieved such high viewing figures.[18]

Dallas's excessive viewership matched its excessive story line. Ang writes that that story line could, 'in principle, go on *ad infinitum*'.[19] Her descriptions of the overarching story line and of individual story lines show that the soap opera's structure works something like a perpetual motion machine. A number of Ang's sentences and paragraphs summarising plot points end with 'and so on', such as 'Pamela finds her mother Rebecca again, who appears to be very well-to-do and is the head of Wentworth Industries, which are brought in by Cliff Barnes as a new weapon against J.R. And so on and so on.' She also notes that every episode is structured in the same way, that the 'number of locations of the action is limited', that 'nearly all the scenes consist of conversation', and that 'physical violence, and even milder forms of action, play a marginal part in *Dallas*'. She writes, 'And this continues endlessly, in one episode after another. When one problem is still unsolved, another looms on the horizon.'[20] In other words, although the show did ultimately end, there existed no narrative structure that indicated it would. It was all boom, with no bust in sight – all abundance and immanence; no scarcity or pausing.

As a theoretically never-ending show about very rich people with almost no physical action, and that was consumed nearly universally, *Dallas* represents one version of adequacy to climate change. 'Adequacy' is the term Ghosh uses regarding the ability of literature to meet (and potentially interfere in) the rhythms and movements of capital. The show's extreme popularity represents oil's permeation of culture. Via *Dallas* we can see petroculture's emphasis on symbolic consumption, displaced engagements with labour, and the strategic depiction of abundance for private consumption of resources rather than for the public good. The smoothness, continuity, abstractions, and self-perpetuation of *Dallas* recall those oil derricks that look like the 'drinking bird' desk trinket novelty, which constantly dips up and down, unimpeded and fluid, well lubricated and continuous. *Dallas* may not have been positioned to interfere in petroculture, but a critical look at it now highlights some of petroculture's effects, including widespread pleasure in watching the drama of socioeconomic hierarchies.

Another enormously popular boom narrative that contributed to aestheticising class (and perhaps *an*esthetising viewers to class) is the television programme *The Beverly Hillbillies*, which aired from 1962 to 1971.[21]

Despite some scepticism that preceded its production, this boom narrative turned out to be popular beyond anyone's expectation.[22] According to historian Tony Harkins, 'By redefining the hillbilly stereotype, the show also offered an often overlooked and at times trenchant critique of postwar American culture and values. ... [T]he program's astounding success reshaped network television, as the show became a catalyst for the wave of rural sitcoms that swept over the airwaves in the 1960s.'[23]

The show's plot, around an Ozark family who discover oil on their land and move to Beverly Hills with their newfound riches, is just as nonsensical as that of *Dallas*. *The Beverly Hillbillies* also made clear that when it comes to getting rich, hillbillies have only dumb luck to rely on (whereas people such as the Ewings, who hail from major metropolitan areas and do not have regional accents, can rely on wise investments and family connections). The plot of *The Beverly Hillbillies* trafficked entirely on the rural and uneducated goofiness of the Clampetts, with the show's creator, Paul Henning, 'redefin[ing] the meaning and image of the hillbilly, making it more broadly appealing and innocuous'.[24] *The Beverly Hillbillies* provided a narrative space where social prejudices against poor rural mountain whites could be exercised while the cares of the world could be ignored. For example, at the time of its airing, an 8 January 1964 episode of the show (two months after the assassination of JFK), in which Granny mistakes a kangaroo for a jackrabbit, attracted 44 per cent of all possible television viewers and garnered the highest ratings of any half-hour of television in history.[25] The politics of pleasure are broad.

The Beverly Hillbillies' popularity went a long way toward rendering socioeconomic class a matter of symbolic consumption. Since the Clampetts wanted for nothing, they did not work and had plenty of money to support a lifestyle the viewing audience was meant to see as ridiculous. For example, Granny's moonshining ways did not change as a result of her riches, and the whole Clampett family's ignorance and innocence was not cured by having a lot of money all of a sudden. *The Beverly Hillbillies* propagates the idea that class inheres in consumption and ethnic and geographical origins, rather than in relations to and between labour and production. It also showed that boom narratives are immensely popular escapism. Regarding fossil fuels, the show also showed that, unlike coal, oil represented easy and labour-free money.

Critical response to *The Beverly Hillbillies* highlights relations between critical judgement and popularity. According to Harkins, press reaction was overwhelmingly negative, in stark contrast to the show's very high ratings. Harkins quotes one critic calling it 'an esthetic regression, mindless, stupid, a striking demonstration of cultural Neanderthalism'.[26] Comments such as these, as well as any snobbery around *Dallas* or other cultural practices (such as making certain purchasing choices), whether on aesthetic or political grounds, reinforce class as a matter of symbolic consumerism. When ecocritical scholars address only a canon of works blessed by critics, they miss the opportunity to address ways that petroculture has been written into everyday life and rendered invisibly pernicious. They also miss the ways that criticism and judgement of taste are themselves implicated in petroculture. In the case of *The Beverly Hillbillies*, petroculture dictates that work doesn't matter when it comes to either acquiring resources or navigating culture. Petroculture dictates that white people from certain locations are dumb and unsalvageable, and you can tell who they are from the booze they drink and the cars they drive. That doesn't sound so different from now, fifty years after *The Beverly Hillbillies*, though the food eaten and the cars driven can now also be read as symbolically related to climate moralism.

Logics of Television

Television scholars from cultural studies have understood their object of study to be embedded in intertwined epistemic and financial regimes. For example, Patricia Mellencamp, in her introduction to *The Logics of Television*, argues that the rhythms of sitcoms from the 1980s reproduce the political and narrative formations of the 1950s.[27] Ang, in her reflections on *Watching Dallas*, notes that the intimacy of television drama is not just personal, but cultural. This intimacy emerges from an epistemic material regime, in which people watch television in the privacy of their own homes, and in which, as was the case during the decades of *Dallas* and *The Beverly Hillbillies*, a few television networks dominated the airwaves. In other words, such an epistemic material regime emphasises private property and corporate control. Narratives within the regime adopt oil's underwriting aestheticised lifestyle choices. Critics oblige by being active judgemental consumers – critique is another form of consumerism, after all.

Media scholars since the 1980s make similar points about epistemic and financial regimes around contemporary television shows. One example is Morgan Fritz's analysis of *Breaking Bad* (2008–13), in which Fritz likens the narrative content of that show (an everyman being compelled by circumstances to create artisan methamphetamine while cut off from the rest of the world in a 'superlab') to the conditions of the show's production and reception – niche television studios working on 'peak TV' artistic programmes, meant to be bingeable to a population told to be authors of their own fate in an economy defined by rapidly multiplying gigs and side hustles – all conducted from within the privacy of the home.[28] Fritz's attention to conditions of work, both the work depicted in the pro-gramme and also the work of producing and marketing that programme, suggests one direction ecocriticism could take, in which stories are embedded in production and reception networks that have material envir-onmental effects.

Because critique may not be enough. As Ang reflects on the rise of irony in television since *Dallas*: the shifting terrain of emotional narrative content and expected audience affect can appear to subvert the production mechanisms, since irony appears to be subversive; however, even these seeming subversions are absorbed, such is the capacity of petroculture to resolve contradictions. For example, in the case of 1980s night-time soap operas, *Dallas*'s main rival *Dynasty* (1981–9) made tongue-in-cheek self-conscious references and cri-tiques of the night-time soap opera genre.[29] However, this novel emotional content did not really challenge the privatised network-driven culture of night-time soap opera watching, but rather extended it into a greater range of private feelings. Capitalistic compulsions to market everything, including criticism of itself, show that artistic or analytic judgement, no matter whether it comes from the inside or outside, is not adequate to intervening in petroculture. Petroculture can accommodate all consumers' opinions, no problem.

Class and Taste

Perhaps more productive would be an account of how class, understood socioeconomically and aesthetically, relates to climate change. Class expressed in consumer choices is what Pierre Bourdieu, founding theorist of taste and class, would call the 'stylization of life', or the 'aesthetic disposition'.[30] Bourdieu's stylisation of life is enacted by the rhythms and textures of the literary novel as described by LeMenager and Ghosh. Indeed, a symbolic relationship to climate change is a standout option people in the twenty-first-century Western world have for expressing an aesthetic disposition. Given the education and time required to understand global or national environmental issues, and given the level of abstraction necessitated by the term 'climate change', the feeling that one wants to do something about climate change and being able to do it is a luxury. Globally minded environmentalism is both expression and creator of class stratifica-tion, much like the appreciation of literature.

Theorists have noted that class systems produce the very rules they purport to use as the basis for judgement. With regard to taste reflecting class, Bourdieu, in 'The Aristocracy of Culture', writes that 'upper-class propriety ... cannot conceive of referring taste to anything other than itself'.[31] Taste, like other systems that maintain social hierarchies, is rigged, though unfortunately not conspiratorially; otherwise, its heart could be struck. Hierarchies like taste are rigged across the board because the judges of winners and losers benefit from the same system to which they refer. Modernity treats its modes of reference and organising as eternal, even though they are actually built and used simultaneously. Such is the case with class and with taste, and the same goes for entrenched and common-sensical practices that create knowledge regimes, like academic disciplines, which are built to perpetuate themselves. There are winners and losers not because of an external or innocent measuring stick but because winners and losers are what help a system justify its existence.[32]

Many of these points are illustrated in Jennifer Haigh's novel *Heat and Light* (2016), which could (along with books like Richard Powers' recent *The Overstory* [2018]) be treated as argumentative writing in a genre that extends beyond the boundaries implied (and reinforced) by Ghosh's treatment of The Novel. Perhaps ecocritical scholars could push past the bourgeois and industrial genre delimitations to treat these works as practices or theories, methods of reorientation, or even as forms of work that could alter everyday common sense via the imagination. Perhaps curriculum designers, when not valuing literature for its own sake, may value such prose for its contributions to solving climate crisis.

In any case, *Heat and Light* addresses fossil-fuel production in Pennsylvania, a state literally built on coal (and more figuratively on coal's associated labour unions), and which has recently seen an upsurge in fracking for its likewise abundant natural gas. *Heat and Light* demonstrates boom-and-bust cycles on a number of time and space scales, and also demonstrates the boom-and-bust narrative's false choices of abundance versus scarcity. *Heat and Light* engages a variety of forms of work, including bodily and machinic labour, as well as symbolic production and the relations between matter and ideology. A character named Trexler is a member of the intelligentsia – a college professor and activist – and Haigh uses Trexler to explore the most judgemental and self-centred urges in such a figure. In a scene that takes place in the late 1980s (when *Dallas* was at its peak of popularity), Trexler loathes the base tastes of the college students in his charge, and disparages their cultural milieu:

> Trexler despairs of these students, he weeps for them – at once spoiled and neglected, raised on TV so bad he can't believe it exists, even worse than the dreck he watched as a child: the broad comedies and sentimental morality plays; the old cowboys, heroes of genocide, trapped in the terrible immortality of eternal syndication in spectral monochrome. Today's television is at once emptier and more malignant. There are many shows – an entire genre of TV

drama – concerned mainly with real estate. The characters, ruthless tycoons and their conniving offspring, are incidental. The true protagonists are the vast and ostentatious houses of the rich, a crass American fantasy of elegance.[33]

If Haigh's novel lends itself to treatment outside the bounds of its genres, Trexler's representation is a perfect example of what Ang and Mellencamp have argued regarding the denigration of popular taste. Trexler's story is an argument within an argument, and Trexler is the consummate critical consumer, who believes he is working against fossil-fuel consumption, but is instead fulfilling some of fossil fuel's most extravagant potential, of continuity through contradiction.

To put this in the context of the current argument, climate change criticism (even when it comes from a fictional character), when focusing on oil and other resource extraction, treats labour as an afterthought, in its smoothly continuous analysis of literature and other media without interrupting commonsensical practices of critique and judgement of aesthetic quality. Ecocriticism already goes a long way in valuing varieties of genre and approach. It could go even further by directly addressing work. Generalised avoidance of the topic by what should be interested parties is illustrated by the Google Scholar citation index of another essay that came perhaps before its time, Richard White's 'Are You an Environmentalist or Do You Work for a Living?', an incisive article published in 1996 whose citation count twenty-four years later numbers a low 575, especially considering the essay's capacity to produce an entire subfield.[34] White's essay and its as yet unrealised potential are an appropriate note to end on, because the question in his title, a reference to a bumper sticker used to make fun of effete environmentalists in the northwest United States during controversies about jobs versus species protection (once again, environmentalism being pitted against the needs of working people, and the logic of zero sum derived from strategically mobilised abundance and scarcity), is just the type of wedge I hope ecocritics will use regularly, with climate change front and centre, and with the logic of globalised consumerism thicker than ever. White closes his essay by writing:

> If environmentalism could focus on our work rather than on our leisure, then a whole series of fruitful new angles on the world might be possible. ... It unites issues as diverse as workplace safety and grazing on public lands; it unites toxic sites and wilderness areas. ... [I]n unmasking the connections of our labor and nature's labor, in giving up our hopeless fixation on purity, we may ultimately find a way to break the borders that imprison nature as much as ourselves.[35]

Putting work first, and, just as importantly, aesthetic judgement last, would reconnect class to labour rather than consumerism, could make ecocriticism's most incisive knowledge accessible to those who can foment change, would reinvigorate the activist power of genres, and position ecocriticism to intervene in widespread (that is, popular and environmentally impactful) practices. The balloon of class, now bloated with oil-based consumeristic judgement, could deflate and, instead of critique-based knowledge, ecocritical scholars, in all their undisciplined glory, could alter the flow of petroculture.

Notes

1 J. B. Foster *et al.*, *The Ecological Rift: Capitalism's War on the Earth* (New York: Monthly Review Press, 2010); R. Nixon, *Slow Violence and the Environmentalism of the Poor* (Cambridge, MA: Harvard University Press, 2013); P. Pezzulo, *Toxic Tourism: Rhetorics of Pollution, Travel and Environmental Justice* (Tuscaloosa: University of Alabama Press, 2007).

2 E. Mazzolini, 'Materialism's Affective Appeal', *The Goose* 17.1 (2018); R. White, 'Are You an Environmentalist or Do You Work for a Living?' in W. Cronon (ed.), *Uncommon Ground: Rethinking the Human Place in Nature* (New York: W.W. Norton, 1996), 171–85.

3 *Deadwood*, created by D. Milch (HBO, 2004–6).

4 D. Sontag and B. McDonald, 'In North Dakota, a Tale of Oil, Corruption and Death', *New York Times* (28 December 2014); see also Sontag and R. Gebeloff, 'The Downside of the Boom', *New York Times* (22 November 2014) and Sontag, 'Where Oil and Politics Mix', *New York Times* (24 November 2014).

5 'Fracking Hell', dir. A. Lee-Jones, *Underworld, Inc.*, Wall to Wall and National Geographic (14 October 2015).

6 *Westworld*, created by L. Joy and J. Nolan (HBO, 2016–).

7 E. Hackenberg, 'Local Uproar over Nat Geo's "Fracking Hell"', *Williston Herald* (19 October 2015).

8 *The Overnighters*, dir. J. Moss (Mile End Films, 2014).

9 F. Jameson, *Postmodernism, or, the Cultural Logic of Late Capitalism* (Durham, NC: Duke University Press, 1991); J. T. Nealon, *Post-Postmodernism, or, the Cultural Logic of Just-in-Time Capitalism* (Stanford University Press, 2012).

10 We might think here too about, for example, the thousands and thousands of plastic water bottles that have been put to use in Flint, Michigan (and other places) so that families do not ingest lead.

11 S. LeMenager, *Living Oil: Petroleum Culture in the American Century* (Oxford University Press, 2014).

12 A. Ghosh, *The Great Derangement: Climate Change and the Unthinkable* (University of Chicago Press, 2017).

13 L. Buell, 'Toxic Discourse', *Critical Inquiry* 24.3 (1998), 639–65.

14 A. O. Bares, 'Representations of the White Working Class and Environmental Consciousness in Petrophilic Culture' and C. Galentine, 'Dust's "Disrupting Darkness" and the Formation of Multi-Racial Class Consciousness in Sanora

Babb's *Whose Names are Unknown*', Association for the Study of Literature and Environment Biennial Conference, University of California, Davis, 27 June 2019, presentations; D. J. Rosenthal, 'Climate-Change Fiction and Poverty Studies: Kingsolver's *Flight Behavior*, Diaz's "Monstro", and Bacigalupi's "The Tamarisk Hunter"', *ISLE: Interdisciplinary Studies in Literature and Environment* 27.2 (2020), 268–86.

15 I. Ang, 'Television Fictions around the World: Melodrama and Irony in Global Perspective'," *Critical Studies in Television* 2.2 (2007), 18–30. I'd submit that collateral damage here included willed ignorance of all that resource use and economic activity, an especial shame for a discipline that considers itself essentially Marxist.

16 *Dallas*, created by D. Jacobs (CBS, 1978–91).

17 A reboot that aired on TNT from 2012 to 2015 was, by all accounts, a critical and commercial flop.

18 I. Ang, *Watching Dallas: Soap Opera and the Melodramatic Imagination* (New York: Routledge, 1985), 1.

19 Ang, *Watching Dallas*, 6.

20 Ang, *Watching Dallas*, 8–9.

21 *The Beverly Hillbillies*, created by P. Henning (CBS, 1962–71).

22 A. Harkins, 'The Hillbilly in the Living Room: Television Representations of Southern Mountaineers in Situation Comedies, 1952–1971', *Appalachian Journal* 29.1/2 (2001–2), 110.

23 Harkins, 'Hillbilly in the Living Room', 109.

24 Harkins, 'Hillbilly in the Living Room', 113.

25 Harkins, 'Hillbilly in the Living Room', 114.

26 Harkins, 'Hillbilly in the Living Room', 112.

27 P. Mellencamp, 'Prologue', in Mellencamp (ed.), *Logics of Television: Essays in Cultural Criticism* (Bloomington: Indiana University Press, 1990), 1–13.

28 M. Fritz, 'Television from the Superlab: The Postmodern Serial Drama and the New Petty Bourgeoisie in *Breaking* Bad', *Journal of American Studies* 50.1 (2016), 167–83; *Breaking Bad*, created by V. Gilligan (AMC, 2008–13).

29 *Dynasty*, created by R. and E. Shapiro (ABC, 1980–9).

30 P. Bourdieu, 'The Aristocracy of Culture', trans. R. Nice, *Media, Culture and Society* 2 (1980), 234.

31 Bourdieu, 'Aristocracy of Culture', 225.

32 E. Watkins, *Everyday Exchanges: Marketwork and Capitalist Common Sense* (Stanford University Press, 1998), 128–59.

33 J. Haigh, *Heat and Light* (New York: Ecco, 2016), 277.

34 White, 'Are You an Environmentalist', 171–85.

35 White, 'Are You an Environmentalist', 185.

6

FIONA PROBYN-RAPSEY

Animals and Extinction

As I write this chapter, the east coast of Australia, where I live, has just experienced its heaviest rainfalls in three decades, extinguishing bushfires that have burnt through approximately 12 million hectares (roughly the size of Ireland), killing an estimated 3 billion non-human animals, including remnant populations of koalas, macropods, birds, lizards, insects and fish affected by ash run-off into depleted river systems.[1] The death count does not include non-evacuated domesticated animals, such as chickens, sheep, and cattle, whose deaths are often hidden as 'losses' to agricultural businesses. Australia is currently a poster child for climate-changed emergencies and, though political leadership fails to account for the *nature-culture* of climate change, the animals have declared the emergency regardless.[2] Koalas in the midst of fire were heard screaming and those recorded screams travelled long distances through social media networks. Magpies (whom Descartes believed to 'have no thoughts' but only passions like 'fear, hope and joy') started to sing emergency sirens, much like the lyrebirds who called out the Anthropocene when they began to incorporate the sound of chainsaws in their song.[3] Yet another 'zooflu' (Covid-19) intensifies the proximities of industrial animal agriculture and concomitant habitat/biodiversity loss. In contemporary cli-fi featuring animals (let's call it 'zoo cli-fi' for short), the animals have already called it. They are 'soothsaying creatures' speaking a 'new internationally dimensional language about global warming' in Alexis Wright's *The Swan Book* (2013).[4] The stranding of giant cuttlefish and beaching of fish and other sea creatures is 'a warning' in Jennifer Mills' *Dyschronia* (2018), while in Charlie Jane Anders' *All the Birds in the Sky* (2016), the birds shout, 'Too late! Too late'.[5] In Laura Jean McKay's *The Animals in that Country* (2020), a 'zooflu' pandemic is unleashed, bringing with it new capabilities to hear and sense other animals' soothsaying and thinking.[6] As the narrator of *Dyschronia* says, how 'can anyone keep track of all the portents?'.[7]

The *natureculture* of the climate crisis, its scale and ripple effects, exceed national borders, apparently defy perspectives born of singular intellectual approaches (Chakrabarty, Giddens, Morton, Ghosh), and, as Claire Colebrook puts it, 'we come up against a complex multiplicity of diverging forces and timelines that exceed any manageable point of view'.[8] Points of view are crucial for literature; they create orientations of temporality, subjectivity, and landscape, all dependent on there being a, or some, point(s) of view through which worlds can be imagined. Zoo cli-fi is necessarily attentive to the question of 'point of view' because at its best it signals that the animal herself has a 'point of view' from the outset. That is, the animal is not merely a negative foil or a crucible from which modernity emerges (as Philip Armstrong explores and critiques), but it might also be the only one left standing to proclaim the 'aftermath' of the sixth mass extinction event.[9] The zoo cli-fi I am interested in here includes literature that does not necessarily mourn 'our' extinction, and may wean us off the idea that we are central to planetary survival. Zoo cli-fi that follows the broader 'animal turn' attributes greater significance to animals as beings-in-themselves and illustrates a powerful 'point of view' often missing: animals have their own 'point of view' that may or may not include 'us' in it.

Points of View

Laline Paull's novel *The Bees* (2015) takes us into the hive mind and self of a single bee, Flora 717, a bee born in a colony that has lived through 'two winters' in a climate-changed landscape.[10] Bees are the proverbial planetary 'canary in the coalmine' and are under significant pressure in the current global climate emergency. Paull's novel localises and individualises the experience of these threats. The hive exists in an orchard, a tiny island of trees between 'a dullard's patchwork' of monoculture crops and an industrial zone where insecticide is sprayed and insecticide is practised.[11] The novel portrays hive life from Flora's more-than-human point of view and it is one that is also 'many' in the sense of being distributed across her body (eyes, antennae, feet, wings) and distributed to her and with her from the affects of bee energies: dance, scent and sound producing 'kin sensitive scent-locks' and 'story fragrances'.[12] The farming of honey is represented from the bee's perspective as a ransacking of home, knowledge, supplies, and life itself. The reader is drawn into the intimacy of the hive, as both place and architecture of sensations. One of the effects of the narrative point of view is to make 'us' the strangers, remind us that we are the giants who farm, pollute, and destroy and that animals have a point of view about us that is not necessarily reassuring. As Patricia in *All the Birds in the Sky* says, 'humans don't have any natural predators left, so nature has to find other ways to handle us'.[13] In much of the literature that features extinction, the animals are indeed looking for ways to handle us, avoid us, or even kill us.

McKay's novel, *The Animals in That Country*, rewrites the zookeeping fantasy of wildlife parks that presume loving relations between keepers and captives, where 'talking to the animals' implies a promise to tourists of multispecies friendly encounters. As 'zooflu' sweeps the country, one of its symptoms is the ability to hear, feel, and think with animals, a symptom that is at first very attractive to two of the novel's protagonists, Jean and her granddaughter Kim. Their desire to be afflicted with animal communication is based on the presumption that they can *already* talk with the animals and that their friendship and love is mutual and reciprocated across species boundaries. But Ange, the park's manager, warns that when communication starts to flow, 'everything we knew about animals is going to change'.[14] One of the first to contract the disease, Lee, says: 'I thought it'd be great, but they're all institutionalized. Messed up in the head.'[15] When she contracts 'zooflu', Jean is able to hear the lab mice, bred as food for the zoo animals: 'They scream bloody murder, the death of everyone, death in the cages and death in the walls. All the little kids in the whole world die . . . Disease eats my face.'[16] When Ange contracts the disease, she is suddenly able to understand birds and also experiences a kind of empathy overload.[17] Panic-stricken, she is told by Jean to simply 'Tell them you're their friend.' Instead, Ange informs her that the birds have already made it very clear that 'I'm not their friend. I'm their predator. I'm their prey. They're hunting me back.'[18] When the conditions under which animals are kept are factored into multispecies relations, and when it is made clear that it is humans who manage those relations through various forms of dominance and control (fences, drugs, poisons, food), then the dream of multispecies communities based on friendly encounters premised on love and 'protection' is turned on its head. The animals talk in terms of horror and fear in the hands of human torturers: '"He can taste me. I'm like deadly salt. I'm poison. He says . . . he . . . " She gets back to staring.'[19] Interestingly, human speech is depicted as incapable of representing human cruelty in words fit for our ears; we cannot hear or see the cruelty we have inflicted. Infected with new powers of listening, the human characters are forced to hear that they are predators, not 'friends' with 'happy' animals under their 'protection'.

Literature written with the point of view of animals in mind, and *with* minds, shifts and destabilises anthropocentrism.[20] As the work of McKay and Paull explores, animals are capable of cognitive feats that often *exceed* human capacities and our anthropocentric attempts to measure them. While animals have routinely been enlisted to give ideological shape to the human form, they have also troubled and pushed at any certainty regarding our uniqueness and our sovereign right to dominate them.[21] The tragic irony of extinction narratives, however, is that they suffer from what seems like poor timing: 'our growing awareness and documentation of this mass extinction event coincides with a dawning recognition of animals' own cognitive and cultural abilities'.[22] Or perhaps the timing tells us something about the nature of recognition and awareness: that it flourishes when little is at risk, when the animals are already gone, or that the cost of knowing them is akin to the death of us, or certain kinds of knowledge that define 'us'. Not the least of these forms of knowledge is that of the 'rational man'. It is no coincidence that it is women with various kinds of 'dis-ease' who feature prominently in these narratives of 'undoing'.[23] This is rich literary and philosophical territory, and while animals who are being protected from extinction are *good to think human hubris with* (to paraphrase and take liberties with Claude Lévi-Strauss), animals who are already extinct may be even better (to put it in morbid stark terms).[24]

'The Logic of Elimination'

Louis Nowra's novel *Into That Forest* (2012) features two thylacines (or 'Tasmanian tigers' as they were also called) as significant characters.[25] The eradication of the thylacine in Australia is probably Australia's best-known animal extinction story, in part because of the charismatic and beautiful animal captured on film before 'extinction', and in part as a result of the apocryphal stories of threat and settler anxiety that laid the foundations for their eradication.[26] Their story is a good reminder that species do not just 'become extinct'; rather, they are actively and deliberately eradicated by acts of violence that are orchestrated by cultural politics well before any shots are fired. Much of this cultural politics relies on naturalising domesticated animals into the colonised landscapes (including sheep and cattle) and naturalising human (rather than tiger) predation as a form of pastoral care and protection.[27] *Into That Forest* is narrated from the point of view of an older woman looking back at her childhood spent in the company of thylacines, where she forgets her own name and how to speak English, and wonders if she is just one of the tigers. The two girls, Hannah and Becky, survive a wreck that leaves them stranded in remote wilderness in Tasmania, Australia. They are rescued by two thylacines, whom Hannah names Dave and Corinna. The girls are fed by Dave and Corinna, communicate with barks, growls and whimpers, and hunt running on all fours. As part of the 'wild child' genre that has fascinated generations of writers (because it troubles the human/animal divide and generates debate about nature/nurture), *Into That Forest* also fractures the 'tiger' narrative that made thylacines eradicable in the eyes of white settlers.[28] As Carol Freeman has shown, thylacines were subjected to an intense eradication scheme, with farmers and hunters encouraged to collect bounties for scalps, because they were represented as ruthless sheepkillers.[29] In Nowra's novel, the 'tigers' are not interested in sheep but instead teach the girls to hunt wallabies, birds, and seal. It is one of the young girls (Becky) who comes up with the idea to predate on sheep during a particularly harsh winter, a perspective on sheep that she brings with her as a settler.[30] It is settlers, after all, who are the 'sheepkillers', the predator pastoralists. Hannah loves the hunt: 'the sense of the four of us being at one with our purpose and the sheer, juicy thrill of the chase, our thumping hearts, the way we knew without words what to do ... Oh it felt good to see a fresh dead animal ... and my nerves tingled cos the blood and meat were so fresh that it were like we were tasting life even though the prey were just dead.'[31] Towards the end of the novel, Becky is accidentally shot dead by her father when she leaps to protect her tiger mother from his gunfire. In her old age, Hannah lives alone because 'How could I explain to them what I have been through? Who would understand?', and she sees the tigers in the bush less and less frequently but wants to believe they have survived the eradications: 'I want to believe that, I got to, cos tigers saved me life and Becky's.'[32]

The idea that there must be a thylacine still out there, that extinction is not the final fate of the thylacine, plays an important role in the narrative, seemingly energised by the horror of hunting violence and the hope that maybe the eradication schemes weren't so bad if one or two persist. Doubt about the extinction of the thylacine persists in projects to find traces of them, a phenomenon that fits with Ursula Heise's *Imagining Extinction*, where she posits that the way extinctions are currently imagined tends towards overwhelming narratives of decline and nostalgia for losses brought about by modernity and colonialism.[33] For Heise, animals in extinction literatures feature largely as 'cultural tools and agents in human's thinking about themselves'.[34]

Julia Leigh's *The Hunter* (1999) features a misanthropic hunter tracking down the 'last' tiger for a biotech company that wants her tissue, in order to 'de-extinct' her kind.[35] Like many of those 'last of her kind', she is what Rick De Vos has described as an 'endling', individuals who are 'singular in body and in time, holding together the notions of species and specimen'.[36] When the 'endling' is found, the hunter cuts out her uterus and takes part of her body for samples. Her death is supposed to 'undo' the violence of eradication, but this endling (now 'startling'?) returns us to human hubris and violence yet again; '"reinvented" by the same logic that "deinvented" it', as Kylie Crane writes.[37] The logistical enclosure, mythological corralling and instrumentalist use of the 'tiger' continues. In the novel, the logic of elimination the tiger is subjected to is linked to the attempts to eradicate Aboriginal people (Palawa) from Tasmania:

> One day his attention is caught by a ring of blackened stones and he imagines they might have been laid by the local Aboriginal people, in the years before they, the full-bloods, were almost driven to extinction. He remembers reading that the government had once tried to make another island, De Witt, an Aboriginal sanctuary, anything to redress their embarrassing demise. It was a tiny and forbidding rock of a place, shunned by all. And, naturally, the experiment failed. Then in 1936, the year the last thylacine died in captivity at Mrs Mary Roberts's private Beaumaris Zoo, it was again suggested that De Witt island could be put to use for any tigers to be rounded up and sent away.[38]

The passage draws together a 'logic of elimination' that settlers applied to Palawa and the thylacine under colonisation, a twinning that has been observed by Nicholas Smith in the following: 'Eco-narratives of extinction deny and express the nightmare of the colonists' dispossession and murder of Palawa.'[39]

The relationship between animal eradications and settler colonialism is a complex one and is explored at length by Susan McHugh in *Love in a Time of Slaughters* (2019).[40] From the outset, she notes that biodiversity is highest where Indigenous people retain occupation and sovereignty over country. This fact alone should inspire a form of 'epistemological humility' for westerners who may have held the 'long-standing colonial narrative … that Western cultures are superior when it comes to animal treatment'.[41] Or, in the words of Australian writer Tony Birch: 'we must listen to those who have lived with country for thousands of years without killing it'.[42] McHugh's study focuses on narratives that draw stories of animal eradications into parallel with attempted genocides committed against Indigenous people (in Libya, the Marshall Islands, Canada, and the USA). One example is the 'systematic campaign in the mid-twentieth century to exterminate Inuit via their sled dogs',[43] experienced as 'a special form of terrorism that exploits the unique relationship shared between Inuit (in Inuktitut, literally 'people') and their *quimmit* ('many dogs')'.[44] This attempted eradication of the dogs rendered Inuit immobile and unable to hunt, drastically altered their world and practices, and became entangled with relocations, child removal, and other state interventions. Reading sources from the Inuit-initiated Quiiqtani Truth Commission, McHugh follows the ways in which the retelling of their human–animal bond is a form of resurgence and resistance to the 'extinctionist ideologies' that were applied to both people and dogs, to people *via and with* their dogs.[45] McHugh's particular interest in the book is to engage with 'alternative perspectives that are grounded in traditions with different metaphysical assumptions' and that do not share a Western logic of dualisms that situate animals and humans as mutually opposed and separable.[46] The loss of animal species that constitute a worldview and a complex weave of human–non-human kinship is part of the removal of Indigenous people from their land.[47] Relatedly, the attempts to eradicate the human and animal may share an instrumentalist and eugenicist logic kept in circulation between the human and 'animal sciences'.[48] McHugh shows that animal extinctions and attempts at genocide are entangled not as 'mere metaphors' for each other, but as mechanisms of the same destructive agency. Audra Mitchell puts it even more boldly: '"extinction" is not a metaphor for genocide or other forms of large-scale violence: it is a distinct manifestation of genocide'.[49] Inspired by Eve Tuck and Wayne Yang's argument that 'decolonization is not a metaphor', Mitchell tells us that extinction is (like illness, woman, and animal) also not (only) a metaphor.[50] When critics call a halt to metaphor they mean: *don't appropriate or falsely compare in a way that reduces and collapses vital differences*. They are also saying *don't use distancing mechanisms that create space for not speaking of things that need to be spoken of*. But metaphors are, for writers, about as easy to avoid as breathing air. Metaphors, allegories, and analogues are implicated in strategies of avoidance precisely because they rely on juxtapositions, and while they can, as Tyson Yunkaporta describes, 'create frameworks for powerful transformation processes', he points out that if the metaphor lacks 'integrity' it 'only damages connectedness'.[51] Yunkaporta's example helps illustrate the point: an Aboriginal school in the Northern Territory was 'using the metaphor of Aboriginal fishing nets as an education framework', a metaphor that lacked integrity because it depicted 'the school as an entity that captures children and takes them away to be consumed'.[52] Other examples of metaphors without integrity include depicting women as 'sexy meat', which, in Carol Adams' work, identifies the animal whose body the meat comes from as the 'absent referent' and the woman as someone inviting violence.[53] Another metaphor that lacks integrity is the situation of animal extinction as the same as genocide, rather than, as Mitchell has it, as a 'distinct manifestation of genocide'. The broader implication of this is to say that while eradications are linked and interconnected, they are not interchangeable, and political context is key. When it comes to zoo cli-fi in Australia, for example, settler colonialism and its ongoing structural violence of occupation is a crucial factor in how genocide and extinctions manifest, or do not manifest, as the case may be.

The narrator in Wright's *The Swan Book* tells us that Australia was built on not saying things about genocide: 'genocide, or mass murder, which were crimes thought to be so morally un-Australian, it was officially denied that anything like it ever happened'.[54] As a consequence of this denial, the only words of English that remain in the song of the birds, the ones who create a 'new internationally dimensional language about global warming' are 'just short words, like *Not true*'.[55] These words are 'the most commonly used words you would have heard to try to defeat lies in this part of the world'.[56] The birds of the future speak these words 'not true' and thereby remember the terms through which extinctions and genocide, the mass killings of animals and people, were denied. We are left with denial itself as the evidence of historical truths. In the epilogue the narrator instructs us: 'Really listen hard to what they [the birds] were saying.'[57]

Animal Agriculture

When it comes to animals, extinction and climate change, animal agriculture is a major driving factor, and not seeing animal agriculture for what it is in terms of climate change means we fail to reckon with it. Anthropocentrism dictates that we not think of cattle, sheep, and chickens (the most commonly instrumentalised animals in the livestock sector) as having had 'lives' or 'species life' in the first place; they are commodities kept largely out of sight and beyond categories of 'nature' and the discourse of 'protection'.[58] This poses a problem for reckoning with the threat the livestock sector poses. In 2006, the United Nations Food and Agriculture Organization (FAO) declared that the livestock sector may be the leading driver in the reduction of biodiversity due primarily to habitat loss, and that it contributes 'significantly' to climate change.[59] Reports from the IPCC (2014, 2018) since then have confirmed this. The significance of this problem is that it runs headlong into cultural barriers: cultures of meat-eating that obscure the violence meted upon millions of animals whose over-reproduction/massification contributes to climate change. Zoo cli-fi should, ideally, to warrant the 'cli' in its name, reach beyond the generic claims of pastoralism (its woolly denialism) and beyond the charismatic species (the 'endlings'), and reckon with animal agriculture as a broader project of extinction.

While it is economically and politically dominant in Australia, pastoralism in its literary form also tends towards the romantic and the off-staging of the unpalatable horrors of animal agriculture: incarceration, forced breeding, and slaughter on the outskirts of our urban cities and regional centres.[60] Pastoralism remains protected by a foundational set of seductive national myths and typologies (the drover, shearer, farmer, bushman and his wives and dogs) that accompany the 'animal industrial complex', something which conservation biologists work with and around when it comes to garnering support for extinction-prevention work.[61] Extinction-prevention work happens in a cultural landscape that is replete with Aboriginal stories and pastoral myths that are characterised by erasure or an uneasy form of recognition. In literature and conservation biology as well, where denial and uneasy recognition of settler-colonial violence also play a role in determining whose lives are extended, who is exterminated, and who is ignored as merely part of the industrialised landscape.[62]

And so, rather like the puzzle of industrial-scale killing of animals in 'meat processing' factories, where the act of killing is itself wilfully concealed by a complex and distributed politics of sight, it is possible to conclude that, just as in the abattoir, so too in agricultural land, and the pastoral literary form, it is *as if* there is no 'actual killing'.[63] So too, with extinctions brought about by something so vast and concealed 'in plain sight' like animal agriculture (rarely positioned as the problem, but since the FAO's report it is now under greater scrutiny as a leading factor in climate change), the act of killing animals seems not to happen at all.[64] If we do not notice, or pause upon, the mass deaths of livestock (the suppressed violence also at the heart of the pastoral literary form), then it's hardly surprising that 'collateral' deaths of animals in deforested land are also framed out of the picture.

While the novels that I have cited so far focus on what might be called 'charismatic' animal species (thylacines, dingoes, 'wild' birds), they are charismatic precisely because they are not subjected to *direct* human violence associated with animal agriculture; they are not made mute and invisible by instrumentalist discourses. By and large, the sheep and the cattle whose captivity in animal agriculture implicates them in climate change, environmental degradation and therefore extinction do not 'speak' in literary texts; indeed, it is as if they barely exist at all beyond the palatable myths of pastoralism. Alex Lockwood also observes this trend in 'new nature writing', which he finds also excludes agricultural animals from considerations of 'nature' and romanticises the rare and the comparatively free-living.[65] This literary absence extends to other fields, including those that explicitly focus on animals and human encounters in the everyday life of our cities.[66] Given this generalised 'off-staging' of agricultural animals (the ones at the dead centre of the industries that drive climate change and species extinctions), it is hardly surprising that animal extinctions also slip into the background all too easily. We are already so well versed in forms of denial and anthropocentric exclusions when it comes to reckoning with mass animal death.

*

Eileen Crist and Helen Kopnina highlight the 'public invisibility of the mass extinction that humanity has instigated'.[67] Crist and Kopnina argue that not only are we seemingly unmoved by species extinctions but we are also unmoved by the decimation of worldviews that might have provided an alternative: 'Indigenous ways and languages also became and are becoming extinct. None of these events – if perceived at all – has been perceived as existentially or ethically problematic.'[68] This rather grim view of 'us' is one that I am quite sympathetic to, but it makes me also wonder how it is fostered by the term 'extinction' itself – something that re-inscribes the hopelessness it laments. Sometimes the word 'extinction' seems to evacuate human agency at the very same time that it is supposed to summon it into political and ethical action. The word extinction is taxonomic, working at the scale of population, and describes a condition of species death rather than the conditions under which death comes about. The distinction is important in a political and ethical sense because, as many Animal Studies scholars have shown, how animal deaths are represented greatly influences how attached or distanced we are from the problem. The word extinction and the phrase 'they became extinct' does little to bring home how humans are connected to what can seem a mere 'biological' process that occurs somehow outside of a cultural political context. Extinctions are cultural processes, not just biological events that happen offstage; indeed, they may represent a 'choice', to quote Margaret Atwood on a recent visit to Australia.[69] This point is perhaps more powerfully brought home when we consider the phrase 'Indigenous ways and languages also became and are becoming extinct', an observation that might be better served in the active sense of 'were subjected to attempted eradication', a switch that puts the spotlight back on settler-colonial culture as actively pursuing what Patrick Wolfe has called a 'logic of elimination'.[70] That Aboriginal people not only resisted successive waves of plans for their eradication but also continually work to have their persistence remembered and recognised shows that the logic of elimination fails, though it continues to circulate whenever the logic is conflated with Aboriginal people's actual existence – that is, whenever they are represented as becoming or going 'extinct'.[71] Clearly the words that accompany 'extinct', whether it's *becoming*, or *going*, or *making* extinct, are lively predictors of political action and cultural impact.

Animal extinctions are, as Heise points out, felt differently by different communities, troubling a universal subject organised around mourning specific animals. Dingoes, for example, are exterminable in some states of Australia and protected as a native species in others. Feral animals may be thought of as refugees by advocates but also seen as a 'plague on the face of the country', *'feral-ing* up the place'.[72] Animal advocates may not mourn the extinction of broiler chickens or sheep or cattle, massively over-reproduced as they are. Indeed, some extinctions may be welcome if they signal the end of animal exploitation. Heise's example of competing perceptions of endangered animal value includes the polar bear as an icon of decline and loss, with images of skinny polar bears on melting ice a feature of consciousness-raising campaigns in *An Inconvenient Truth* (2006) and car commercials selling electric vehicles. Heise contrasts this image with a documentary featuring Inuit community members who are concerned about the polar bears' *high* population numbers, their encroachment on towns, and the disruptions caused by wildlife biologists who keep tracking the bears. While one perspective might be *I'm with the Bears* (the title of a collection of short stories edited by Bill McKibben), the other points out the realities of what being with actual bears might look and feel like, including fear and a sense of needing to carry a gun.[73] Heise uses this example to highlight that 'divergent cultural meanings are the stuff of living in multispecies communities'.[74] But just how 'multispecies' is this community if the polar bears are not also granted a 'point of view'? Heise focuses on the 'human stories that frame our perception and relations with endangered animals' because this is the most effective way to get people to care in the first place.[75] While it might be difficult to imagine capturing polar bears' perspectives, there are ways in which the lives of animals can be brought into view more prominently within narratives. Such attention to animals offers the possibility that the animal's preferences will be included; it offers greater potential for the 'sympathetic imagination' to be extended beyond the human and our charismatic animal others.[76] It pushes us to 'really listen hard' because doing so might just change 'everything'.[77] Otherwise it might just be, as the birds say, 'Too late. Too late', for us to act on the extinctions we make.

Notes

1 'Non-human animals' is used in the field of Animal Studies to signal that the human is also an 'animal'. For the sake of brevity I will refer to 'animals' as 'they', 'he', 'she'. Macropods refers to a group of animals that includes, but is not limited to, kangaroos and wallabies. The figure of 3 billion comes from a report by World Wide Fund for Nature (WWF), see G. Readfern and A. Morton, 'Almost 3 Billion Animals Affected by Australian Bushfires, Report Shows', *The Guardian* (28 July 2020).

2 'Natureculture' is a concept that expresses the inextricable ties of nature with culture, coined by Donna Haraway, *Companion Species Manifesto: Dogs, People, and Significant Otherness* (University of Chicago Press, 2003).

3 R. Descartes, 'From the Letters of 1646 and 1649', in L. Kalof and A. Fitzgerald (eds.), *The Animals Reader: The Essential Classic and Contemporary Writings* (Oxford: Berg, 2007), 59–62.

4 A. Wright, *The Swan Book* (Sydney: Giramondo, 2013), 329.

5 J. Mills, *Dyschronia* (Sydney: PanMacmillan, 2018), 83; C. J. Anders, *All the Birds in the Sky* (London: Titan Books, 2016), 370.

6 L. J. McKay, *The Animals in That Country* (Brunswick, Vic.: Scribe Publications, 2020).

7 Mills, *Dyschronia*, 83.

8 D. Chakrabarty, 'The Climate of History: Four Theses', *Critical Inquiry* 35 (2009), 197–222; A. Giddens, *The Politics of Climate Change* (Cambridge: Polity Press, 2009); T. Morton, *The Ecological Thought* (Cambridge, MA: Harvard University Press, 2010); A. Ghosh, *The Great Derangement: Climate Change and the Unthinkable* (University of Chicago Press, 2016); C. Colebrook, *Death of the Posthuman: Essays on Extinction* (Ann Arbor, MI: Open Humanities Press, 2014), 11.

9 P. Armstrong, *What Animals Mean in the Fiction of Modernity* (London: Routledge, 2008).

10 L. Paull, *The Bees* (London: Fourth Estate, 2014).

11 Paull, *The Bees*, 1.

12 Paull, *The Bees*, 39, 80.

13 Anders, *All the Birds*, 196.

14 McKay, *Animals in That Country*, 51.

15 McKay, *Animals in That Country*, 66.

16 McKay, *Animals in That Country*, 75–6.

17 L. Gruen 'Empathy' in Gruen (ed.), *Critical Terms for Animal Studies* (University of Chicago Press, 2018), 141–53.

18 McKay, *Animals in That Country*, 87.

19 McKay, *Animals in That Country*, 73.

20 Anthropocentrism is understood here as much more than a mere 'perspective' or a human 'standpoint', it is a pernicious form of human arrogance towards other species; see F. Probyn-Rapsey, 'Anthropocentrism', in L. Gruen (ed.), *Critical Terms for Animal Studies*, 47–63.

21 See Armstrong, *What Animals Mean*; G. Huggan and H. Tiffin, *Postcolonial Ecocriticism: Literature, Animals, Environment*, 2nd ed. (London: Routledge, 2015); C. Wolfe, *Animal Rites: American Culture, the Discourse of Species, and Posthumanist Theory* (University of Chicago Press, 2003).

22 M. Chrulew and R. De Vos, 'Extinction: Stories of Unravelling and Reworlding', *Cultural Studies Review* 25.1 (2019), 24.

23 On the topic of gender, species, madness and other forms of dis-ease regarding human/animal relations, see L. Gruen and F. Probyn-Rapsey (eds.), *Animaladies: Gender, Species, Madness* (New York: Bloomsbury Academic, 2018).

24 Anthropologist Claude Lévi-Strauss argued that animals are 'good to think with', meaning that animals have been enlisted by human societies to symbolise human differences; *Totemism*, trans. R. Needham (Boston, MA: Beacon Press, 1963), 89.

25 L. Nowra, *Into That Forest* (Sydney: Allen & Unwin, 2012).

26 See C. Freeman, *Paper Tiger: How Pictures Shaped the Thylacine* (Hobart: Forty South Publishing, 2014).

27 J. R. Fischer, *Cattle Colonialism: An Environmental History of the Conquest of California and Hawaii* (Chapel Hill: University of North Carolina Press, 2015).

28 G. Melson, *Why the Wild Things Are: Animals in the Lives of Children* (Cambridge, MA: Harvard University Press, 2001).

29 Freeman, *Paper Tiger*.

30 Nowra, *Into That Forest*, 60.

31 Nowra *Into That Forest*, 159.

32 Nowra *Into That Forest*, 172.

33 U. K. Heise, *Imagining Extinction: The Cultural Meanings of Endangered Species* (University of Chicago Press, 2016).

34 Heise, *Imagining Extinction*, 6.

35 J. Leigh, *The Hunter* (London: Faber, 1999).

36 De Vos, 'Extinction Stories: Performing Absence(s)', in L. Simmons and P. Armstrong (eds.), *Knowing Non-Human Animals* (Leiden: Brill, 2007), 185.

37 K. Crane, 'Tracking the Tassie Tiger: Extinction and Ethics in Julia Leigh's *The Hunter*', in L. Volkmann *et al.* (eds.), *Local Natures, Global Responsibilities: Ecocritical Perspectives on the New English Literatures* (Amsterdam: Rodopi, 2010) 107.

38 Leigh, *The Hunter*, 57.

39 The phrase 'logic of elimination' belongs to Patrick Wolfe, elaborated across his scholarship; see P. Wolfe, 'Settler Colonialism and the Elimination of the Native', *Journal of Genocide Research* 8.4 (2006), 387–409. N. Smith, 'The Return of the Living Dead: Unsettlement and the Tasmanian Tiger', *Journal of Australian Studies* 36.3 (2012), 283.

40 S. McHugh, *Love in a Time of Slaughters: Human Animal Stories Against Genocide and Extinction* (University Park: Pennsylvania State University Press, 2019).

41 M. Deckha, 'Postcolonial', in L. Gruen (ed.), *Critical Terms for Animal Studies*, 288.

42 T. Birch, 'Friday Essay: Recovering a Narrative of Place-Stories in the Time of Climate Change', *The Conversation*, 27 April 2018.

43 McHugh, *Love in a Time of Slaughters*, 124.

44 McHugh, *Love in a Time of Slaughters*, 123.

45 McHugh, *Love in a Time of Slaughters*, 131.

46 McHugh, *Love in a Time of Slaughters*, 14.

47 D. B. Rose, *Wild Dog Dreaming: Love and Extinction* (Charlottesville: University of Virginia Press, 2011).

48 F. Probyn-Rapsey, 'Dingoes and Dog Whistling: A Cultural Politics of Race and Species in Australia', in K. Struthers-Montford and C. Taylor (eds.), *Colonialism and Non-Human Animality: Anti-Colonial Perspectives in Critical Non-Human Animal Studies* (London: Routledge, 2020), 181–200.

49 A. Mitchell, 'Extinction Is Not a Metaphor – It Is Literally Genocide', *Worldly*, 27 September 2017, https://worldlyir.wordpress.com/category/extinction/.

50 E. Tuck and K. W. Yang, 'Decolonization Is Not a Metaphor', *Decolonization: Indigeneity, Education and Society* 1.1 (2012), 1–40; S. Sontag, *Illness as Metaphor* (New York: Farrar, Straus and Giroux, 1978); E. F. Kittay, 'Woman as Metaphor', *Hypatia* 3.2 (1988), 63–86.

51 T. Yunkaporta, *Sand Talk: How Indigenous Thinking Can Save the World* (Melbourne: Text Publishing, 2019), 119.

52 Yunkaporta, *Sand Talk*, 119.

53 C. Adams, *The Sexual Politics of Meat: A Feminist Vegetarian Critical Theory* (New York: Bloomsbury Academic, 2016).

54 Wright, *The Swan Book*, 309.
55 Wright, *The Swan Book*, 329–30.
56 Wright, *The Swan Book*, 330.
57 Wright, *The Swan Book*, 329.
58 Probyn-Rapsey, 'Anthropocentrism', 47–63; A. Lockwood, 'H Is for Hypocrite: Reading "New Nature Writing" through the Lens of Vegan Theory', in L. Wright (ed.), *Through a Vegan Studies Lens: Textual Ethics and Lived Activism* (Reno: University of Nevada Press, 2019), 205–22.
59 H. Steinfeld *et al.*, *Livestock's Long Shadow: Environmental Issues and Options* (Rome: Food and Agriculture Organization of the United Nations, 2006), xxiii.
60 P. Arcari *et al.*, 'Where Species Don't Meet: Invisibilized Animals, Urban Nature and City Limits', *Environment and Planning E* 3.3 (2020).
61 'Animal industrial complex' is a term used by B. Noske, *Beyond Boundaries: Humans and Animals* (Montreal: Black Rose Books, 1997) and developed further in R. Twine, 'Revealing the "Animal Industrial Complex": Concept and Method for Critical Animal Studies' *Journal for Critical Animal Studies* 10.1 (2012), 12–39.
62 See Huggan and Tiffin, *Postcolonial Ecocriticism*.
63 T. Pachirat, *Every Twelve Seconds* (Ithaca, NH: Yale University Press, 2011); N. Vialles, *Animal to Edible*, trans. J. A. Underwood (Cambridge University Press, 1994), 32.
64 Livestock are 'one of the major drivers of habitat change (deforestation, destruction of riparian forests, drainage of wetlands), be it for livestock production itself or for feed production'; Steinfeld *et al.*, *Livestock's Long Shadow*, 186–7.
65 Lockwood, 'H Is for Hypocrite', 205–22.
66 Arcari *et al.*, 'Where Species Don't Meet'.
67 E. Crist and H. Kopnina, 'Unsettling Anthropocentrism', *Dialectical Anthropology* 38 (2014), 391.
68 Crist and Kopnina, 'Unsettling Anthropocentrism', 390.
69 A. Morton, 'Extinction Is a Choice: Margaret Atwood on Tasmania's Forests and Saving the Swift Parrot', *The Guardian* (29 February 2020).
70 Crist and Kopnina, 'Unsettling Anthropocentrism', 390; Wolfe, 'Settler Colonialism', 402.
71 W. E. H. Stanner, *The Dreaming and Other Essays* (1968; Black Inc Books, Melbourne, 2009), 224; I. Watson, 'Sovereign Spaces, Caring for Country, and the Homeless Position of Aboriginal Peoples', *South Atlantic Quarterly* 108.1 (2009), 30.
72 D. Celermajer and A. Wallach, 'The Fate of the Illegible Animal: The Case of the Australian Wild Donkey', *Animal Studies Journal* 8.2 (2019), 229–58; Wright, *The Swan Book*, 316, 325.
73 B. McKibben (ed.), *I'm with the Bears: Short Stories from a Damaged Planet* (London: Verso, 2011).
74 Heise, *Imagining Extinction*, 243.
75 Heise, *Imagining Extinction*, 5.
76 J. M. Coetzee, *The Lives of Animals* (Princeton University Press, 1999), 35.
77 Wright, *The Swan Book*, 329; McKay, *Animals in That Country*, 51.

7

CHITRA SANKARAN

Climate Justice and Literatures of the Global South

The term 'climate justice' links environmental problems surrounding global warming and its manifold consequences with ethical and political considerations. It connects the impact of climate change to concepts of justice that incorporate environmental and social justice, involving the investigation of individual and collective human rights, equality, and historical responsibility. Climate justice affirms the rights of communities, dependent on natural resources for their livelihood and cultures, to own and manage these resources in a sustainable manner. It is opposed to the commodification of nature and its resources.[1] One of the central ironies of climate justice is that those who are *least* responsible for climate change suffer its gravest consequences. Kofi Annan, the seventh secretary-general of the United Nations, remarks:

> Climate change is the greatest humanitarian challenge facing mankind today. And it is a challenge that has a grave injustice at its heart. It is the major developed economies of the world which contribute the overwhelming majority of global greenhouse emissions. But it is the poorer and least developed nations that are hit hardest by its impact.[2]

Annan's view is endorsed by scholars like Elizabeth DeLoughrey, Jill Didur, and Anthony Carrigan, who observe that 'In the last decade ... experiences of environmental violence, rupture and displacement are central ecological challenges across the Global South.'[3] Indeed, the issue of climate justice and its complexities have come under increased scrutiny and one outcome that stands out is refugeeism, which also includes internal displacements.

In 1994, 'The Almeria Statement' estimated that the number of migrants in the world would continue to increase by about 3 million each year.[4] The environmentalist Norman Myers forewarned the world of this emerging crisis.[5] In 2005, he projected up to 200 million in estimated refugee numbers. He was talking about both political and environmental refugees.[6] It is often the case that the lines between the two are blurred. Essam El Hinnawi defines environmental refugees as people 'forced to leave their traditional habitat, temporarily or permanently, because of marked environmental disruption (natural or triggered by people) that jeopardized their existence and/or seriously affected their quality of life'.[7] Bram Büscher and Veronica Davidov expand on this idea of 'environmental disruption', which they identify as *environmentally induced displacements* or EIDs, 'whereby specific populations find their use of land irrevocably altered, whether as a living space, as a livelihood resource, as a cultural site, or on any number of other claims to territory due to some form of environmental change'.[8] However, the plight of internal refugees is not surfaced even in international discussions on refugee aid. Stranded *within* their countries and largely ignored by the media, these refugees are the world's forgotten people. A Christian Aid report claims that almost all the countries in the developing world have large numbers of internal refugees.[9] The untold hardship of these populations goes unnoticed.

Laura Westra argues for the term 'ecological refugees', which encompasses those displaced by both environmental and climate catastrophes, since, whether due to industrial hazards or natural disasters, in all instances, local ecologies have been destroyed and are no longer habitable.[10] Furthermore, environmental disruptions are not always the result of spectacular catastrophes. Indeed, Rob Nixon advocates for a more nuanced view of environmental violence as not just a 'highly visible act' that is 'event focused, time bound, and body bound', but also as dispersed through time and affecting the poor, who form the most vulnerable group.[11] He argues that what he labels 'slow violence' can fuel 'long-term, proliferating conflicts in situations where the conditions for sustaining life become increasingly but gradually degraded'.[12] Nixon identifies 'petro-imperialism, the mega-dam industry, out-sourced toxicity, neocolonial tourism, antihuman conservation practices and the militarization of commerce' as some of the problems that create 'the environmentalism of the poor', making them the 'principal casualties' of slow violence.[13]

Through an analysis of texts from the Global South that provide a much-needed perspective from the ground on the grey areas of climate justice, this chapter negotiates a complex set of concerns that a simple definition of 'justice' will not adequately address with regard to the most vulnerable populations. Timothy Clark, in a chapter on 'Post-colonial Ecojustice', points to the complex questions involved, which are 'fraught with political, ethical and religious overtones'.[14] He discusses how social complexities render climate justice issues difficult to resolve. These views are germane to the texts I examine from the Philippines, Pakistan, India, and Sri Lanka that yield insights into climate justice problems. The first set of texts – several poems about Typhoon Yolanda and a children's novella about floods in Pakistan – depicts the problem of refugeeism, here, 'internal displacements' of the poor. The ensuing three texts from Sri Lanka and India together reveal another aspect of climate justice, namely, the challenges involved in attempting to balance the innate precarity between social and environmental justice.

I examine texts across a range of genres: poetry, fiction, and a children's novella. This range is essential for it not only reveals the ubiquitous presence of the theme of climate justice across all genres in the Global South, but it also demonstrates its pertinence to all age groups. Moreover, texts in each of these genres assert an important aspect of the multi-pronged problem and facilitate readers' understanding of it as 'glocal' experience. Thus, while the poems effectively convey the trauma in compacted words, in the children's novella, the inner resilience of the survivors is emphasised. The novels enable a more layered and expansive exploration of the complex issues at stake. In these ways, the diverse genres are useful, indeed essential, in providing distinct insights into a complex problem.

First, I consider a set of poems that describe Typhoon Yolanda (with the international codename 'Haiyan') which barrelled through the Visayan Islands of the Philippines on 8 November 2013. It was one of the strongest tropical cyclones in history. Entire provinces and cities in Samar and Leyte were massively destroyed and flattened. Over 6,300 people in Central Philippines were killed and 4.1 million were displaced. Nearly 1,600 are still reported missing. Even as news of the immense catastrophe was being broadcast to the world, many writers and artists gathered online and began recording their emotional responses to the tragedy. An anthology was launched: *Outpouring: Typhoon Yolanda Relief Anthology* (2014), edited by Dean Francis Alfar and his team.[15] Others followed, such as *Verses Typhoon Yolanda: A Storm of Filipino Poets* (2014), edited by Eileen Tabios.[16] The poems I examine on Typhoon Yolanda are available both from within and outside these collections, which describe the trials and tribulations of the people of the Visayas during and in the aftermath of the typhoon, connecting these to climate justice issues.

Next, I examine a children's novella based on the 2010 floods in Pakistan, caused by unprecedented rains during the monsoons in the Khyber Pakhtunkhwa, Sindh, Punjab, and Baluchistan regions of Pakistan. Approximately one-fifth of Pakistan's total land area was affected. The Khyber Pakhtunkhwa province was the worst affected. According to official sources, there was a death toll of around 2,000, and a further 20 million people suffered loss of land and damage to property, among whom around 8.6 million were children. *Rani in Search of a Rainbow* (2014) by Shaila Abdullah – an award-winning, Pakistani-American writer based in Austin,

Texas – is about a little girl and her family who become victims of extreme weather.[17] Displaced from their homes by torrential rain, they flee to a refugee camp.

The Sri Lankan writer Jean Arasanayagam is a Burgher married to a Tamil. Arasanayagam's short-story collection, *All Is Burning* (2014), which describes various aspects of the Sri Lankan civil war, is remarkable for its non-partisan presentation.[18] 'I Am an Innocent Man' becomes relevant in the way it presents the injustices that occur when 'global capitalism pits itself directly against traditional land use' or commercialises 'the commons', creating climate injustices of a different order from those discussed above.[19] Meanwhile, Arundhati Roy has established herself as an environmental activist. In her novel *The God of Small Things*, which won the Booker Prize in 1997,[20] she shows how even well-meaning Western efforts to help with environmental crises in the Global South can, in fact, lead to climate injustices. Finally, I discuss Amitav Ghosh's *The Hungry Tide* (2004) to spotlight a problem that is not unusual in developing nations, where human rights questions clash with ecojustice protocols.[21] Ghosh, an internationally acclaimed novelist, identifies some intricate socio-environmental issues in his novel.

In examining these texts emerging from the Global South, I also make a bid for the usefulness of imaginative literatures that focus on environmental catastrophes and probe the ways in which they add value. If one way to mitigate the disproportionate impact of these disasters to achieve climate justice is to involve disenfranchised and marginalised groups in the planning and policy-making process, so that these individuals have a say in their own futures, then imaginative literatures emerging from situated locations that give voice to their troubles become equally pertinent. They also depict the overwhelming emotions that accompany such disasters, which statistical studies cannot convey. In their book *Numbers and Nerves: Information, Emotion and Meaning in a World of Data*, Paul and Scott Slovic argue that humans are unable to process numerical data in holistic ways. They remark that 'Perhaps the first thing to realize ... is that we are all, to some degree, "innumerate". Even the most mathematically gifted human beings are psychologically limited when it comes to attaching feelings to numerical information.'[22] The authors draw attention to the importance of *imagination* and the power of *narrative* to augment the abstract with the specific, as the only means available for galvanising common humanity to action in times of risk. For climate change as a macro-environmental issue meets the criteria of 'super wicked problems'.[23] These are problems characterised by 'uncertainty over consequences, diverse and multiple engaged interests, conflicting knowledge, and high stakes'.[24] Jakob Arnoldi believes that 'Culture affects how humans understand the world, because we make sense of the world by cultural means.'[25] Peter Berger and Thomas Luckmann famously present how our reality is the result of social construction, a collective effort to make sense of the world as we see it.[26] The way we construct this reality by means of social communication has been subject to a wide range of sociological research. Jennifer Helgeson, Sander van der Linden, and Ilan Chabay stress the role of cognitive structures in the concept of a mental model, which is 'a person's internal, personalized, intuitive, and contextual understanding of how something works'.[27] Erving Goffman introduces *framing* as a means to read and understand situations and activities in social life.[28] All these scholars stress the importance of cultural narratives, not only to communicate and educate humans about action in relation to environmental catastrophes, but to stress the idea of humanity as a community that needs to bond in order to survive, thus underscoring the need to engage with imaginative literature.

Narratives of Internal Displacement

In 'Typhoon, Typhoon, an Appeal', Elizabeth Padillo Olesen points out the relentlessness of natural disasters: 'Typhoon, typhoon, you clothed yourself / as Yolanda or Haiyan or Koppu / or Lando'.[29] Olesen laments:

> Many times in a year you come,
> visit this land with your own rage;
> Each raging visit you make
> makes people homeless,
> hungry, naked and restless.

She petitions: 'please, can you give us a long break / from your constant visits?'. Olesen's remonstrance is against what Westra terms the loss of 'the resource base, the integrity of the lands where a community resides'. As Westra points out, when this is destroyed, 'it can no longer support human life'.[30] Invariably, the speed and suddenness of these extreme weather catastrophes take the communities by surprise, well illustrated in *Rani in Search of a Rainbow*, which describes the rapid escalation of weather conditions and the lack of preparedness of the communities. It all begins with fun and play: 'A few weeks ago, the rain had started innocently in their village in Pakistan. Pitter patter, dancing droplets were a signal to the young children that it was time to celebrate by dancing. And dance they did.'[31] Soon, however, the celebration turns to mourning: 'But the rain did not stop … Rivers and creeks overflowed, but the rain did not stop … Rain, the adults warned, was not a friend anymore. That is when the dancing stopped.'[32] The narrative emphasises the vulnerability of marginal communities and their lack of protection against extreme weather. The families are forced to leave behind their few precious possessions carefully collected over a lifetime of labour. They face the total destruction of their homes and all they have painstakingly hoarded over the years. The texts highlight the poverty and desperation of the refugees. The scenes describe the 'internal displacements' that repeatedly occur in the Global South as a consequence of extreme weather.

It is impossible to overestimate the extent of the problems caused by extreme weather. Christian Aid predicts that, 'given current trends, 1 billion people will be forced from their homes between now and 2050'.[33] The report estimates that around 250 million people will be permanently displaced by climate change-related phenomena, such as floods, droughts, famines, and hurricanes by 2050. These privations, however bravely confronted, take their toll. 'This year, the thirty days of Ramadan had been a time of great changes in their lives. There had been neither feasts nor treats', Rani ruminates despondently.[34] The bathos of her innocent worry, that even though it was Eid she had nothing special to wear, not only contrasts the scale of the catastrophe with her childish anxieties, but also shines a light on the millions of children in the Global South who routinely fall ill or die in climate catastrophes. Their lives, bereft of even basic necessities, reflect the deep economic chasm that divides the rich and the poor. Olesen reaffirms this 'environmentalism of the poor' by pointing to the complete breakdown of life during climate catastrophes:

> After the storm, hunger and thirst scream
> for attention; shelter from rain and sun is gone
> Food and clean water are scarcely to be found
> And people weep to find help in desperation.[35]

Ulrich Beck, the German sociologist, explains that transitioning from industrial society to 'second modernity' or a 'risk society' occurs as the new and unintended side effects of industrial society (such as radioactive emissions) end up creating unprecedented risks.[36] Olesen's descriptions reveal some rather paradoxical aspects of climate upheavals that the British scholar, Anthony Giddens, characterises in 'post-scarcity' societies, wherein the problems we face need not be the result of backwardness or ignorance but of technology and industrialisation: a result of the 'advancement of knowledge'.[37] Also, as Giddens reminds us, 'no one can be completely free' from 'the diffusion of circumstances of manufactured risk'; this is all the more the case with 'natural risk'.[38]

In a risk society, the differences of class hierarchies appear to be erased since everyone is exposed to the same risks. What is noteworthy, though, is that, despite the ubiquitous nature of risk and indeed of the catastrophes caused by extreme weather, it remains a contradiction that the *consequences* of these catastrophes are never evenly distributed. Though everyone is affected in various measure, it is the poor and the sub-dominant classes that are the most vulnerable in the aftermath and suffer the gravest consequences. Thus, climate disasters disproportionately affect the poorest people in the world as they have no infrastructure or social networks to protect them or to mitigate the effects. The novella and the poems uncover the suffering of the disenfranchised of the world and describe their extreme privation and material loss: For poor Rani, 'Good meals were so few these days. Her stomach growled.'[39] For Ric Bastasa:

> the typhoon last night
> was devastating
> it was strong and prolonged
> the roof almost gave way
> the windows about to be flown away
> the floors shook
> and walls broke[40]

Olesen, too, graphically invokes this image of total loss in 'After the Super Typhoon': 'After the storm, people move and walk / on flooded streets and roads, treading on the / debris of ruined houses, trees and memories … '. Olesen's reference to not just 'ruined houses' and 'trees' but also to 'memories' is significant because it touches on the intangible factors that climate justice implicitly invokes: the subjective feelings of the disenfranchised, a perspective that is usually not the focus of 'evacuation summaries' and 'Aid Reports'. Aside from the loss of material belongings, these narratives show that the very core of human identities changes irrevocably, leaving a feeling of *unheimlich*. The uncanny effect produced by 'effacing the distinction between imagination and reality', where one's worst nightmare becomes reality, resonates with catastrophe survivor accounts.[41] Abdullah's text captures just such an uncanny moment. As the families in Rani's and the surrounding villages are evacuated by helicopters, to young Rani, her 'home looked like a helpless boat as the water surrounded it'.[42] This moment, when her familiar home becomes unrecognisable, scares the little girl.

The logic of Westra's preference for the term 'ecological refugees' becomes plain since it is not just refugees' environment that is destroyed but the very ecology of their subsistence that is ravaged and transformed to such an extent that they can no longer successfully re-bond as a community there. They are not only physically and materially affected, but the psychological dysfunction caused by the climate catastrophe remains with them, sometimes for the rest of their lives, as trauma. Westra believes that if ecological integrity is central to human health and survival, as well as to the normal functioning of ecosystems, then its absence represents an attack on all of these.[43]

Literary writers responding imaginatively to climate disasters are invested in recreating this sense of trauma that overtakes the affected. But, remarkably, even as these texts add value by making visible the 'affect' of the catastrophe on the communities, they are as important for the different emphasis that they offer, not on the extensive damages alone but on human resilience. In 'The Typhoon Last Night', even as Bastasa describes how Yolanda tears their houses, roads, schools, and possessions apart, his emphasis is determinedly on the close emotional bonds that lend strength to the community:

> we hug for comfort
> we prayed together
> and curled together
> we intertwined like vines
> on the tree
>
> that morning after
> I am thinking about our intimacy
> tested by storm and darkness[44]

He is proud to be part of this indomitable humanity that stands together against the elements.

Similarly, in surviving the Pakhtunkhwa floods, though the dire problems faced by the dispossessed community are laid bare, the focus is on demonstrating an alternative set of values. Rani's sense of adventure and feeling of joy, unmarred by circumstances that might be traumatic to the adults, presents the idea that the potential for joy is not dependent on possessions. The capitalistic insistence on ownership and consumerism as core to comfort and even identity is turned on its head. Rani leaves home with the barest essentials, and yet, despite the many privations in the refugee camp, these people, used to living with the bare minimum, are not unhappy. The narrative foregrounds the view that possessions are not what bring pleasure or sorrow, challenging capitalism's basic premise. In the refugee camp, the sense of community and reciprocity is given prominence. Rani's mother, well versed in midwifery, assists in the birth of Beeni's baby. *Daadi* (grandmother) helps with cooking for the multitude of refugees, while Rani's father volunteers with carrying the supplies that are brought by helicopter to the camp. Rani learns important life-lessons from her *Daadi*. Through her interactions with her grandmother, her family, and others in the community, Rani gradually realises a fundamental truth: that human communities can only survive through mutual help and selfless acts of service. The narrative speaks directly to Al Gore's views, when he remarks: 'Human civilization is now so complex and diverse, so sprawling and massive, that it is difficult to see how we can respond in a coordinated, collective way to the global environmental crisis. But circumstances are forcing just such a response.'[45] Similarly, Mary Robinson, former Irish President and UN Climate Envoy, observes that climate justice links human rights and development to achieve a human-centred approach, safeguarding the rights of the most vulnerable and sharing the burdens and benefits of climate change and its resolution equitably and fairly.[46] This is made essential due to the vast gulf in resources between nations of the Global North and South, and within those, between the rich and the poor, making this rift one of the starkest injustices of our age.

The incapacity of global systems to provide for an equitable distribution of resources, leading to a lack of resource-fairness, has caused billions of humans to suffer. These literatures from the Global South on climate change expose this chasm between the haves and the have-nots. They reveal the vulnerability of the human race as a whole, accentuating the need for human interdependence and the necessity for humanity to work together. Texts such as these emphasise human values. Rani's refugee camp then becomes a microcosm of planet Earth. This children's novella serves to underscore the idea that great efforts by global organisations will come to nought unless each member of every small and big community acts responsibly and selflessly. A noteworthy incident in the book occurs when Rani meets her neighbour, a little boy called Juju, who lives in the tent next to hers. Rani and Juju queue up for blankets. But, when it is their turn, there is only one left and, as they both grab it, it is ripped in half.[47] The blanket tellingly becomes a metaphor for social cohesion. Each child initially refuses to give up his or her half. However, when Rani learns that Juju is very ill and that his half of the blanket is not sufficient to cover him, she quietly sews both halves together and hands over the whole to Juju. This selfless act, and the joy and relief it brings to the feverish Juju, form an evocative textual moment. 'Juju's eyes flew open. "Is it ... ? Yes, it is our blanket," ... "I fixed it for you." "For tonight?" Juju asked. "No silly, forever," Rani answered. "It's a gift from me." Juju's eyes twinkled like the shiniest star in the night sky.'[48] The idea of communal sharing rather than personal possession is key here. The importance of communing with nature and being attuned to it is also gently emphasised. This marks humanity's place in a larger design, what Ursula Heise terms a 'sense of place, sense of planet'.[49] Rani 'stared at the twinkling star in the night sky ... its brilliance made her happy'.[50]

The Typhoon Yolanda poems and *Rani in Search of a Rainbow* are important as crisis narratives. They reveal the importance and usefulness of imaginative literature in opening up a dialogue about alternative values necessary to take humanity forward on this imperilled planet. They provide object-lessons about the necessity of joint human effort needed to save our species through portraying abstract emotion alongside disaster statistics. The eminent anthropologist Arjun Appadurai discusses the significance of imagination as a social practice:

> The image, the imagined, the imagery – these are all terms which direct us to something critical and new in global cultural processes: the imagination as a social practice. No longer mere fantasy ... no longer simple escape ... no longer elite pastime ... and no longer mere contemplation ... the imagination has become an organized field of social practices, a form of work ... and a form of negotiation between sites of agency ('individuals') and globally defined fields of possibility.[51]

Appadurai's definition is especially apposite when it is applied to fictional texts that become equivalent to (imaginative) testaments that illustrate the more abstract aspects of climate justice problems.

Environmental versus Social Justice

In most global discussions, environmental and social justice issues are examined in tandem. Paradoxically, an underexamined problem in the Global South is that, often, environmental and social justice issues are at odds with each other. The texts I examine in this section present this composite association and its problems. Arasanayagam's 'I Am an Innocent Man', set in a small village in civil-war-riven Sri Lanka, is a first-person narrative by the village schoolteacher, Das. The complex narrative centres on the idea of guilt. Das, who begins his tale rather self-righteously, elaborately discoursing on the reasons as to why he is innocent of guilt in the goings-on between the two factions, very soon falters in his narrative as it gradually dawns on him that no human is untouched by guilt or untainted by war.

It is particularly telling that this short story begins with the narration of an ecojustice issue, as if to highlight the parallels between environmental (in)justice and civil war: that, in both cases, ideas relating to innocence and guilt, regrettably, can often become a matter of perspective, and no human can be completely exonerated. The text opens with what can be identified as 'slow violence': the acquisitive role of global capital and its contribution to inequitable resource management. As Das cycles through the village, he sees newly mushrooming prawn farms. He experiences a moment of cognitive dissonance, 'this feeling that the ponds were seething, alive, and that the prawns were trapped in their aquatic prisons from which they could not escape until they grew large enough to be trapped, netted, packed and sent away to titillate the appetites of the wealthy gourmets who could afford them'.[52] However, he is so inured to injustices of all kinds that his comments are tinged with resignation, lacking anger or malice: 'To me, the prawns appeared to have an even greater price than that placed on human life. They were being reared for profit.'[53] The commodification of humans, especially in the Global South by global capital, has had a long history beginning with early colonisation and the slave trade. But what concerns me here are the neocolonial forms of such depredations. Before the prawn farms appeared, these lands had belonged to no one. Now they have become private property, 'enclosed and fenced in', a graphic description of how an 'environmentalism of the poor' is created and nurtured by global, predatory capitalism.[54] Hence, the villagers become trespassers in what was once their 'commons'. The hapless villagers, deprived of their sustenance, resort to stealing. The security team employed by the investors beats up the villagers, even going so far as to 'hang' repeated offenders. One villager complains and the army moves in. The ramifications are overwhelming, destroying the village, the fields, and the community. What therefore begins as an environmental problem instigates a whole set of socio-political issues leading to civil war, underlining the impossibility of neatly compartmentalising these issues. The rights of the people to their 'commons' are overturned, their civil liberties decimated. They are left without means of survival. Such texts open our eyes to pervasive practices that are in direct contravention to stated climate justice principles. Contrary to the 'legal' narrative which 'proves' that the villagers have stolen prawns from a private property, the larger truth that emerges is that elite members of the capitalist-patriarchy have stolen from the poor people land that should rightfully be theirs.

In neocolonial regimes, often, corrupt governments are complicit in these nefarious transactions. This is quite against the universally agreed principles enshrined in Robinson's climate justice document, which insists that the 'The opportunity to participate in decision-making processes which are fair, accountable, open and corruption-free is essential to the growth of a culture of climate justice.'[55] Capitalist-patriarchy, we see, plays with the lives of the subalterns in the Global South.

Ironically, though, in some cases, even if the environmental interventions are not capital-driven but initiated by well-intentioned international bodies like the World Bank, the results may be equally disastrous. This is revealed in Roy's novel, *The God of Small Things*. Broadly invested in challenging the hierarchies of dualism that legitimise patriarchal oppression of women and hegemonic oppression of the subalterns, the novel describes an environmental catastrophe in Ayemenam, a village in the Indian state of Kerala, where the story unfolds. It focuses on how, contrarily, countries in the Global South suffer environmental catastrophes as the unintended side effect of 'developmental projects' that are funded by global initiatives, for example, World Bank-funded agricultural development in India in the 1960s, leading to what came to be known as the 'Green Revolution'. Agricultural production was greatly boosted with new, hybridised, high-yield varieties of paddy and wheat, supplemented by the application of large amounts of chemical fertilisers that had the unfortunate effect of introducing toxins into these food products and also damaging the environment. The World Bank offered large loans to support such intensive agriculture, but mismanagement by local governments and lack of proper follow-up by the World Bank officials meant that both local governmental bodies and lofty Western institutions were culpable for the toxic side effects. Thus, in Roy's novel, we are informed that Estha, one of the characters, 'walked along the banks of the river that smelled of shit and pesticides bought with World Bank loans'. The river itself is described as 'thick and toxic'.[56] As Clark remarks, this kind of 'colonial and neocolonial exploitation offers little space for an ecocriticism that has sometimes looked like the professional hobby of a western leisure class'.[57] The novel spotlights the fact that, between centralised initiatives and localised applications, many things can go wrong, and the result is a deep distrust of institutions. In these cases, attributing blame and finger-pointing by various interest groups becomes more the issue than tackling climate justice concerns to safeguard communities. When establishments disavow responsibility, they also distance themselves from the disastrous repercussions of the mismanaged projects. This is vividly demonstrated by Roy's narrative.

The Hungry Tide by Ghosh surfaces another unusual but increasingly acknowledged climate justice problem in the Global South, namely the question of whose rights should take precedence when subaltern human rights and animal rights are in conflict. In the novel, the Bengali-American Piya comes to the Sundarbans, the rich backwaters of Bengal, to study dolphins, and teams up with a local fisherman, Fokir. The two, though unable to communicate through a common language, discover a deep bond due to their mutual love for the dolphins. While highlighting the problems surrounding dolphins, the novel draws our attention to another parallel conservation issue, namely, the Morichjhanpi problem.

In 1978, around 30,000 Bangladeshi refugees broke out of their camp in central India due to harsh treatment by the Indian government and sailed to Morichjhanpi, an island in the Sundarbans. Within weeks, the refugees had cleared the forest and created a settlement. However, Morichjhanpi was located within the National Reserve Forest meant to protect Bengal Tigers; therefore, it was against the law for anybody to settle there. The Indian government was determined to remove the new inhabitants from the island, and, in 1979, set up a blockade around Morichjhanpi. When the blockade began, media were denied access to the island and were banned from reporting. According to the Udbastu Unnayanshil Samiti (the Refugee Development Association), within the first month of the blockade, nearly 700 people died due to police firings, starvation, and a lack of medical supplies. Also, more than a thousand huts were burned down and nearly two hundred boats were confiscated by the authorities. In the end, all of the remaining refugees were forcibly removed from Morichjhanpi by the police.[58] This becomes a problematic case in that tiger conservationists and human rights activists were at loggerheads debating the superior rights of the respective groups to the land. These circumstances, where human rights and animal rights directly confront each other, become so complex to manage that an amicable resolution appears impossible. It is no wonder that, aside from presenting the problem, *The Hungry Tide* does not presume to take a position or indeed offer solutions.

*

Thus, these fictions from the Global South reveal the complicated nature of climate justice problems and how it becomes important to understand the diverse issues before we attempt to pass judgement or suggest solutions. In such instances, the simplistic polarisation of the concerned North and the hapless South gets obfuscated. Pablo Mukherjee pinpoints the historical interconnections between environmentalism and postcolonialism as being a 'comprehensive critique of European modernity, in particular its core components of capitalism, colonialism, imperialism and patriarchy'.[59] In short, what emerges is that climate justice involves a range of stakeholders, both local and global, Western and Eastern, from the Global North and South. The texts emphasise the idea that unless there is a uniform understanding of the problems involved and a common resolve to address them, climate justice remains a distant dream.

Notes

1 'Bali Principles of Climate Justice', 29 August 2002, EJnet.org.
2 'Kofi Annan Launches "Beds Are Burning" Global Musical Petition to Demand Climate Justice', *Kofi Annan Foundation* (1 October 2009), kofiannanfoundation.org.
3 E. DeLoughrey *et al.*, 'Introduction: A Postcolonial Environmental Humanities', in DeLoughrey *et al.* (eds.), *Global Ecologies and the Environmental Humanities*, (London: Routledge, 2015) 2.
4 'The Almeria Statement on Desertification and Migration', *Environmental Conservation* 21.2 (1994), 179–81.

5 N. Myers, 'Environmental Refugees in a Globally Warmed World', *Bioscience* 43.11 (1993), 752.

6 N. Myers, 'Environmental Refugees: An Emergent Security Issue', 13th Meeting of the OSCE Economic Forum, Prague, 22 May 2005.

7 E. El Hinnawi, *Environmental Refugees* (Nairobi: United Nations Environment Programme, 1985), 4.

8 B. Büscher and V. Davidov, 'Environmentally Induced Displacements in the Ecotourism–Extraction Nexus', *Area* 48.2 (2016), 161–7.

9 Christian Aid, 'Human Tide: The Real Migration Crisis' (May 2007), www .christianaid.org.uk/sites/default/files/2017-08/human-tide-the-real-migration-crisis-may-2007.pdf.

10 L. Westra, *Environmental Justice and the Rights of Ecological Refugees* (London: Earthscan, 2009), xviii.

11 R. Nixon, *Slow Violence: The Environmentalism of the Poor* (Cambridge, MA: Harvard University Press, 2011), 3.

12 Nixon, *Slow Violence*, 3–4.

13 Nixon, *Slow Violence*, 5.

14 T. Clark, *The Cambridge Introduction to Literature and the Environment* (Cambridge University Press, 2011), 120.

15 D. F. Alfar *et al.*, ed. *Typhoon Yolanda Relief Anthology* (Manila: Kestrel DDM and Flipside Publishing, 2014).

16 E. R. Tabios, ed., *Verses Typhoon Yolanda: A Storm of Filipino Poets* (San Francisco: Meritage Press, 2014).

17 S. Abdullah, *Rani in Search of a Rainbow* (Ann Arbor, MI: Living Healing Press, 2014), Kindle edition.

18 J. Arasanayagam, 'I Am an Innocent Man', in Arasanayagam, *All Is Burning* (New Delhi: Penguin, 1995), 22–42. Burghers are an ethnic minority in Sri Lanka of mixed Dutch and/or Portuguese and Sri Lankan descent.

19 Clark, *Cambridge Introduction to Literature and the Environment*, 120.

20 A. Roy, *The God of Small Things* (New York: Random House, 1997).

21 A. Ghosh, *The Hungry Tide* (New York: Harper Collins, 2004).

22 S. Slovic and P. Slovic, 'Introduction: The Psychophysics of Brightness and the Value of a Life', in Slovic and Slovic (eds.), *Numbers and Nerves: Information, Emotion and Meaning in a World of Data* (Corvallis: Oregon State University Press, 2015) 7.

23 R. J. Lazarus, 'Super Wicked Problems and Climate Change: Restraining the Present to Liberate the Future', *Cornell Law Review* 94 (2009), 1153.

24 I. Lorenzoni *et al.*, 'Climate Change, Human Genetics, and Post-Normality in the UK', *Futures* 39 (2007), 65–82.

25 J. Arnoldi, *Risk: An Introduction* (Cambridge: Polity Press, 2009), 107.

26 P. L. Berger and T. Luckmann, *The Social Construction of Reality: A Treatise in the Sociology of Knowledge* (1966. New York: Anchor Books, 1990).

27 J. Helgeson *et al.*, 'The Role of Knowledge, Learning and Mental Models in Public Perceptions of Climate Change Related Risks', in A. E. J. Wals and P. B. Corcoran (eds.), *Learning for Sustainability in Times of Accelerating Change* (Wageningen: Wageningen Academic Publishers, 2012), 331.

28 E. Goffman, *Frame Analysis. An Essay on the Organization of Experience* (Boston, MA: Northeastern University Press, 2010).

29 E. P. Olesen, 'Typhoon, Typhoon, an Appeal', *Poem Hunter* (21 October 2015).
30 Westra, *Environmental Justice*, 3
31 Abdullah, *Rani in Search of a Rainbow*, Kindle Loc. 26.
32 Abdullah, *Rani in Search of a Rainbow*, Kindle Loc. 28.
33 Christian Aid, 'Human Tide'.
34 Abdullah, *Rani in Search of a Rainbow*, Kindle Loc. 90.
35 Olesen, 'After the Super Typhoon', *Poem Hunter* (11 November 2013).
36 U. Beck, *Risk Society: Towards a New Modernity*, trans. M. Ritter (London: Sage, 1992), 19–50.
37 A. Giddens, *Affluence, Poverty and the Idea of a Post-Scarcity Society* (Geneva: United Nations Research Institute for Social Development, 1995), 3.
38 Giddens, *Affluence*, 6.
39 Abdullah, *Rani in Search of a Rainbow*, Kindle Loc. 82.
40 R. Bastasa, 'The Typhoon Last Night', *Poem Hunter* (17 April 2009), also available in Tabios (ed.), *Verses Typhoon Yolanda*, 21.
41 S. Freud, 'The Uncanny', *The Standard Edition of the Complete Psychological Works of Sigmund Freud, Volume XVII (1917–1919): An Infantile Neurosis and Other Works* (London: Hogarth Press, 1953–77), 229.
42 Abdullah, *Rani in Search of a Rainbow*, Kindle Loc. 35.
43 Westra, *Environmental Justice*, 5.
44 Bastasa, 'The Typhoon Last Night'.
45 A. Gore, *Earth in the Balance: Forging a New Common Purpose* (London: Earthscan, 1992), 385.
46 'Principles of Climate Justice', *Mary Robinson Foundation – Climate Justice*, 2011, www.mrfcj.org/wp-content/uploads/2015/09/Principles-of-Climate-Justice.pdf.
47 Abdullah, *Rani in Search of a Rainbow*, Kindle, Loc. 66.
48 Abdullah, *Rani in Search of a Rainbow*, Kindle, Loc. 159.
49 U. K. Heise, *Sense of Place and Sense of Planet: The Environmental Imagination of the Global* (New York: Oxford University Press, 2008).
50 Abdullah, *Rani in Search of a Rainbow*, Kindle, Loc. 151.
51 A. Appadurai, *Modernity at Large: Cultural Dimensions of Globalization* (Minneapolis: University of Minnesota Press, 1996), 31.
52 Arasanayagam, 'I Am an Innocent Man', 22–3.
53 Arasanayagam, 'I Am an Innocent Man', 23.
54 Arasanayagam, 'I Am an Innocent Man', 25.
55 'Principles of Climate Justice', 2
56 Roy, *God of Small Things*, 119
57 Clark, *Cambridge Introduction to Literature and the Environment*, 120.
58 'Massacre in Morichjhanpi', *Life in the Sundarbans Mangrove Forest: Cultural Beliefs, Religious Practices, and Environmental Degradation*, uddin.digital.con-ncoll.edu.
59 U. P. Mukherjee, *Postcolonial Environments: Nature, Culture and the Contemporary Indian Novel in English* (Basingstoke: Palgrave Macmillan, 2010), 145.

PART III

Ways of Telling Climate Stories

8

THERESA J. MAY

Climate Theatre
Enacting Possible Futures

In 2005, Bill McKibben, founder of 350.org – an organisation dedicated to generating the political and public will to respond proactively to prevent continued climate change – mused that 'what the warming world needs now is art, sweet art'.[1] The arts, he argued, must translate the facts of climate change into felt experience. '[T]hough we know about it, we don't *know* about it. It hasn't registered in our gut; it isn't part of our culture. Where are the books? The poems? The plays? The goddamn operas?' McKibben asked. Climate denial, entrenched in cultural patterning, is as real (and perhaps as dangerous) as climate change itself. Scientific information, political rhetoric, as well as increasingly frequent catastrophic climate-related events have all been at a loss to reverse it. Sociologist Kari Marie Norgaard explains how collective denial is socially constructed: 'society teaches us what to pay attention to and what to ignore', and when new information is inconsistent with long ingrained 'cognitive traditions' we fail to 'integrate this knowledge into everyday life or to transform it into social action'.[2] Even when confronted with overwhelming evidence, Norgaard argues, large cultural matrixes of shared understandings rooted in shared histories, beliefs, and memories – or *stories* – maintain the social norms and cultural values that hold denial in place. Because they govern the very cognitive space in which to imagine a future, these stories in turn fuel and rationalise social (in)action.[3]

As a site of culture-making in which stories are already manifested as action, albeit dramatic action, theatre is uniquely positioned to bear witness in this ecological moment, serving as a form and a site to enact what Norgaard calls a 'revolution of our shared imagination'.[4] Theatre can both amplify the voices of those most impacted by climate change and generate possible futures. We must, Norgaard argues, 'imagine the reality of what is happening to the natural world ... imagine how those ecological changes are translating into social, political, and economic outcomes, and ... imagine how to change course'.[5] As the realities of climate transform the daily configurations of our lives, they also make demands on our collective imagination, reshaping understandings of what it means to be human in the span of geologic time. Climate theatre aims to reimagine and revitalise the relationships between and among communities (human and otherwise) and places (material and imagined) even as they continue to be at risk.

Observing a theatrical performance requires a different kind of engagement than the act of reading might for the relatively passive reader of fiction. Theatre is a living art form, one in which people gather together in a material time and place to enact shared stories. While actors and audience have discrete roles in this event, both participate in conjuring the fictional world of the play. This imaginative partnership, together with theatre's requisite present time and space, makes it a species apart from literature. While dramatic literature like poetry, or forms of fiction, may be enjoyed by a reader in isolation, a play is nevertheless always also a blueprint for a performance and must be understood not as literature but as action. Aristotle's *Poetics* identifies action, or plot, as the central and most significant aspect of theatre.[6] Plot is the pattern of events in a play, which unfold over time and are caused by human reactions, responses, and choices in the face of given circumstances. But understanding theatre as action involves more than mapping the plot of the play; it requires appreciating how the liveness of theatre, the present time and place in which *the event* of theatrical performance necessarily occurs, enriches and activates civil society and civic discourse. It is this embodied, present, immediate, and communal nature of theatre that makes it an apt site for exploring the confounding realities of climate change, and gives theatre a unique capacity to engender empathy and exercise democratic values. What follows explores the unique capacity of theatre as an artistic force to leverage social change, and examines how emergent theatrical forms and strategies might be employed as innovative artistic responses to the climate crisis.

Theatre as a Way-of-Knowing

Plays are blueprints for live performance that require collective co-imagining by people who have come together in time and place. Theatre's very form begins with an invitation to ask/imagine *What if?* Through this willing suspension of disbelief, audiences and actors set aside rigidly guarded world views about self, world, and other. As characters, places, and temporalities are brought to life on stage, a give-and-take occurs between the imaginations, sensibilities, and embodied experiences of the performers and the audience. This alchemy of embodied communal feeling, visceral response, and shared risk reminds us that, no matter how abstract or virtual our interactions may be outside the theatre space, we nonetheless inhabit the world as embodied organisms. In 'Performance, Utopia, and the "Utopian Performative"', Jill Dolan describes theatre's primary function as not to formulate the new organisational structures (laws, policies, and programmes), but rather to provide a forum in which people might engage the magical 'what if' in order to *feel into* experience not their own.[7] Theatre allows us to feel into worlds, realities, and events that expand the very sense and sensibility of being human. By feeling into the past, theatre can increase awareness of the ongoing-ness of exploitation manifesting in patterns of climate injustice in everyday life. As such, theatre's 'way-of-knowing' involves an inherent embodied reciprocity that is foundational to eco-consciousness, as it expands our capacity to empathise with the experience of others (including non-human others).

The nexus between theatre's way-of-knowing and the burgeoning arena of climate theatre finds expression in the term 'ecodramaturgy', which describes a theatre praxis that puts ecological relations at the centre of dramatic action.[8] Foregrounding as permeable and fluid the socially constructed boundaries between nature and culture, human and non-human, and individual and community, ecodramaturgy includes three interwoven endeavours:

> (1) examining the often invisible environmental message of a play or production, making its ecological ideologies and implications visible; (2) using theater as a methodology to approach contemporary environmental problems (writing, devising and producing new plays that engage environmental issues and themes); and (3) examining how theater as a material craft creates its own ecological footprint and works to both reduce waste and invent new approaches to material practice.[9]

This chapter understands climate theatre broadly as the response of dramatists to the changes and injustices resulting from anthropogenic climate change. The plays discussed below wrestle with the implications, including moral implications, of these changes, while giving voice to those who are most affected. As theatre attempts to represent a climate discourse steeped in scientific data and longitudinal measurement, innovations have included: rejecting singular climactic plot structure in favour of episodic, multivocal, and/or multitemporal narrative weavings; expanding the role of the actor's body and voice in ways that blur the boundaries between species of matter; moving away from the theatre as site set apart from the world in favour of integrating performances with environments; and/or emphasising theatre-making as a process of democratisation through community-engagement and coalition-building that involves communities directly in the development and performance of stories that represent them and their lived experience of the climate crisis. Each of these varied strategies has political, and indeed ecological, implications; in what follows I unpack these formal elements for the future of climate theatre.

Plot: The Structure of Stories

In 1994, theorist Una Chaudhuri called on theatre artists and critics to recognise that, as the very epitome of cultural artifice, theatre was deeply allied with the ideologies of modernity, including industrialisation and Western European humanism. Chaudhuri claimed that theatre is 'programmatically anti-ecological', resulting in a long-standing tendency for artists, critics, and audiences to interpret *any* representation of ecological circumstances as the mere backstory to human action, or as metaphors for human struggles.[10] Ironically, metaphors that originate in lived experience can become, in the theatre, mechanisms that erase the living, palpable world around us. This euro-humanist habit-of-mind means that audiences and critics have tended to miss environmental themes and ecological circumstances even when a play makes direct reference to them. Thus, Chaudhuri argued for 'a new materialist-ecological theater practice that refuses the universalization of metaphorization of nature'; she encouraged theatre artists not only to take up ecological themes, but also to use theatrical *forms* in ways that resist humanist interpretation.[11] Since then, dramatists working with ecological themes have actively resisted the humanist habit of using nature as a metaphor or backdrop for human action, and instead many have worked to represent the intractable interdependence of communities, families, workers, and the environments in which they live, work, play, and worship. This shift in focus from the singular, universal human story to stories of collective experience also required new story structures that eschew the Aristotelian (and Hollywood) climactic plot in favour of episodic, multivocal, and trans-temporal story structures.

Climate theatre pushes back against the Western tradition that has defined dramatic action as a sequence of causal events that unfold chronologically. Instead, dramatists engaging climate perspectives have employed episodic and ceremonial plot structures that may have multiple protagonists or parallel plots, and that may scramble logical time sequences in favour of wide historic scope and/or non-human timelines. These structures create meaning through the juxtaposition of images and events and invite contemplative reflection on the ways in which each one of us is implicated in the realities of climate change.

Episodic innovations strive to grapple with the agency of weather, land, and animals in an effort to represent geologic forces beyond the human, and they recognise that communities rather than individuals may be central characters. In Chantal Bilodeau's *Sila* (2015), for example, three parallel plots – an Inuit family, a polar bear family, and a Canadian Coast Guard crew – all form part of the community that is struggling to cope with the effects and losses of a shifting climate.[12] In *Fairly Traceable* (2015), Mary Kathryn Nagle asks the audience to ask 'what if' the catastrophic 2005 Hurricane Katrina and the devastating 2011 tornado in Joplin, Missouri, occurred at the same time?[13] As events affect two culturally and geographically distanced families connected through a love affair, the play demonstrates that the singular events of front-page news are ongoing conditions of life for those who live with and through them. In *Burning Vision* (2003), Marie Clements brings temporal and geographic realities together to overlay a kaleidoscope of experiences related to the development and detonation of the first atomic bomb in order to illuminate the interconnectivity across time and space of human actions.[14] The characters and their communities – one Japanese, one Indigenous North American – are connected by their shared experience of radiation exposure. As a victim of the atomic blast in Hiroshima finds his way through the magic of theatre into the life of a Dene ore carrier at Great Bear Lake in Canada where the uranium for the bomb was mined, a sense of community is forged that resists the human cognitive tendency to see another's pain as separate from one's own. In each of these plays, meaning accumulates not through the mounting sequence of dramatic actions, but through the relationship and interconnection between and among experiences and emotions. Such episodic plot structures can call attention to the vast timescales of climate as well as the transnational, transcultural, and trans-species impacts and implications of climate change.

In 'Climate Change as the Work of Mourning', Ashlee Cunsolo Willox posits that 'grief and mourning have the unique potential to expand and transform the discursive spaces around climate change to include not only the lives of people who are grieving because of the changes, but also to value what is being altered, degraded, and harmed as something mournable'.[15] How might theatre and performance help us stay present to the loss that has continued, is continuing, and will continue in the face of climate change? Part of theatre's function in the age of climate change is grief work, which is served and expressed in ceremonial plot structures. Laguna Pueblo poet and theorist Paula Gunn Allen describes 'ceremonial time' as 'achronological' and representing the 'tribal concept of time [that is] timelessness', in which both time and space are multidimensional. In this Indigenous perspective, which is consistent with theories of relativity in contemporary physics, the self is conceived 'as a moving event within a moving universe'.[16] On stage, this concept shapes a plot that does not move linearly through time but rather moves in outwardly expanding circles of relation. In *Burning Vision,* time literally stops short, as each scene folds back on itself to that singular moment of detonation. For example, a scene in which the widow of a Dene ore carrier grieves and talks to the fire she keeps burning for her husband's return is followed by one in which a Japanese grandmother tells her grandson to wait by the cherry tree if he gets lost; this is followed by a scene in which the lost uranium rock, personified as a child, is trying to find his way home. These scenes link the characters and the land as one family across geographic and temporal space. *Burning Vision* thus asks the audience to contemplate *the relationship* between events by invoking a sense of time that is neither past nor present, but palpably here and now on stage. In this hyper-present, audience members might contemplate the way that human and non-human life are part of a single ecological fabric. In this way, *Burning Vision* uses ceremonial plot structure to cause the audience to stop, to think, to rethink, and to reflect on the impact that one human decision can have.

Plot structure is the foremost tool that dramatists use to render the trans-local, transnational, and trans-temporal impacts of the global economic forces that have caused climate disruptions. Instead of offering linear narratives that neatly peak and resolve, authors of climate plays accumulate associative meanings so that audience members might be helped to acknowledge the multiple and multiplying ways each and every one of us are implicated in patterns of ecological and cultural destruction. Moreover, by formally interweaving the ecological, economic, social, and spiritual impact of environmental loss, their plays challenge theatre's long-standing tradition of positioning nature as a metaphor and instead reveal humanity as a geologic force and highlight the reciprocity between human and the non-human forces. Episodic forms also serve to represent and amplify the voices and experiences of peoples and communities that have been and continue to be disproportionally affected by the climate crisis, such as the Inuit communities at the centre of *Sila,* or the Dene ore carriers in *Burning Vision.* Using episodic and ceremonial forms to tell multivocal, multitemporal, transnational, and trans-species stories, climate plays personalise ecological issues even as they inspire collective responsibility in ways that move beyond apocalyptic visions and despair.[17]

Character: Towards an Ecological Self

Through the strategic use of character, dramatists can consciously and directly engage the complex economic, scientific, and cultural challenges of climate change and climate justice, (re)imagining what it means to be human in the age of the Anthropocene. The impacts of global climate change are profoundly localised, personal, and intimate. The emergence of environmental justice discourse as a prominent aspect of environmental thought and activism has inspired many theatre artists to explore the ways in which person and place are permeable. Theatre can powerfully connect the dots between climate change, racism, sexism, and economic injustice through stories that resist environmental and cultural imperialism by amplifying the voices of those most affected by environmental risk.

Some plays, such as Anne Galjour's *Alligator Tales* (1996), utilise the simplest of theatricalities – the body of the actor – as a means to explore the ways in which our bodies and our homelands are intertwined and interdependent, sharing both aliveness and vulnerability.[18] As Galjour uses her corporeal body to presence human and non-human within a dynamically alive and indeterminate world living in the onslaught of a hurricane, she conjures a visage of what Stacy Alaimo calls 'trans-corporeality, in which the human is always intermeshed with the more-than-human world ... the substance of the human is ultimately inseparable from "the environment"'.[19] As the singular performer, Galjour plays all these roles – from human to animal to weather itself – as she narrates the story. As she does, it becomes clear that she (and all of us) is not an individual, but a collective – a neighbourhood, an inter-tidal world in which forms and forces (ecological, economic, and social) intermingle. In a similar vein, Cherríe Moraga theatricalises the reciprocity between bodies and land by writing ecological injustice into the body of her main character in *Heroes and Saints* (1994), a woman born with unimaginable birth defects as a result of pesticide exposure.[20] Though her mother would want her to stay indoors, out of sight, Moraga's Cerezita becomes a spokesperson for her community and a visible embodiment of the often-invisible harm done to farmworkers and their families. In works like these, character becomes the site where the slow violence of environmental and economic policy becomes visible and palpable.

Many dramatists writing on ecological themes have taken on the task of representing characters who are non-human others. Performance artist Rachel Rosenthal, for example, infuses feminism and ecological consciousness into a character that gives voice to the outrage of the Earth itself. In *Gaia, Mon Amor* (2001), Rosenthal takes on the persona of the Earth itself, crying out in a more-than-human rage for humans to come to her aid, to resist forces of environmental degradation lest they too perish.[21] Through her own body and voice, Rosenthal personifies the suffering of the planet.[22] Through its uniquely embodied, immediate, and communal qualities, theatre can strategically animate the ecological world so that the very boundaries between nature and culture, self and other, begin to dissolve. Exploding the

Western tradition of agency as solely human, climate theatre's embodied exploration of trans-corporealities leads to compassion and perhaps inter-species solidarity. As actors put their bodies to the wheel of what it might be like to be a polar bear, or an avalanche of mud, audiences have opportunities to feel into the non-human through human forms. Chaudhuri has described this effort as 'theater of species ... remind[ing] us that we humans are one species among many, among multitudes, all equally contingent and threa-tened'; the theatre-of-species 'brings the resources of performance to bear on what is arguably the most urgent task facing our species: to understand, so as to transform, our modes of habitation in a world we share intimately with millions of other species'.[23] Representing non-human others on stage carries ethical responsibilities: Alaimo observes that, in light of the very real suffer-ing – both human and non-human – exacted by environmental degradation, we must proceed with caution in representation. Meaning-making has become a 'swirling landscape of uncertainty where practices and actions that were once not even remotely ethical or political matters suddenly become so'.[24] Plays like Bilodeau's *Sila* and Colleen Murphy's *The Breathing Hole* (2017) offer audience members an opportunity to explore and embrace this ethical responsibility by empathising with non-human animals as they would their own family.[25] But the challenge of theatre-of-species asks more from theatre-makers as well, demanding an approach to representation that fore-grounds not the 'object' of the animal but rather the interweaving of human and animal lives in a way that calls attention to their biological and ecological interdependence.

In Bilodeau's *Sila*, for example, the director and designer must make decisions about who to represent the character of Mama polar bear and her daughter, Paniapik. They might consider giant puppets that risk confusion with the iconic Coca-Cola bear so ubiquitous in media, or they might con-sider masks reminiscent of Inuit art, taking care not to appropriate Indigenous forms without credit and consultation. Or they might use projec-tions, film footage of actual Arctic polar bears, but in this they betray the dramatist's conception of the bears as characters with agency, autonomous beings in their own right. Or they might use the bodies of actors working through movement to suggest the character of the bear as a choreography rather than a singular persona. Whatever their choices, the artists have an ethical responsibility that can either re-inscribe ideas that audience members may already have regarding the polar bears, or challenge those assumptions by provoking new realisations and curiosities. Climate theatre thus resists the tendency of Western traditions to read animals as allegorical humans, stand-ins for human experience, and discursively silent.[26] In climate thea-tre, animals-as-kin are important signifiers of the complex ways that ecologies and culture are enmeshed, intertwined, and indivisible. Climate theatre demonstrates this larger set of community relations and kinship between human and environment best when animals are integral to the Indigenous traditions and/or ecological fluidity between animal, human, and the vitality of the land itself.[27]

In the shared live space of the theatre, the representation of non-human animals through human bodies can be a collective contemplation on *both* the socially constructed animal and the ecological animal. The community of bodies – actors and audience – forms an ecological system in which they affirm, merely through the act of breathing together, the interweaving of body and environment. In live theatre, the actor's body is an ecological system in present time: bodies burn fuel, exchange oxygen and carbon molecules, and otherwise carry on their aliveness. Philosophical arguments alone, Matthew Calarco maintains, will not 'suffice to transform our thinking about what we call animals'. He suggests that 'any genuine encounter with what we call animals will occur only from within the space of surrender'.[28] Theatre, when understood as a way-of-knowing that is at once dynamic, emergent, and embodied, can become this *space of surrender* in which we might conceive of the unknown Other. Through their kinaesthetic engagement as a community of bodies, performers not only open a space of contemplation regarding the kinship between non-humans and humans, but also commit mind and muscle, like a practice, to coming into trans-corporeal relation with all that they know and do not know about what lies beyond their (s)kin.

Diction and Song: Ways of Speaking

Much in the way that climate theatre revises the idea of character and agency to include forces beyond the solely human, dramatists also approach language and song in new ways. Dramatists have been sensitive to the ways in which language and rhetorical mode can help communicate not only the scientific realities of climate change but also the ways of knowing beyond the human that human values and policies must include. In *Sila*, characters speak in three languages – Inuktitut, French, and English – effectively de-centring Euro-colonial privilege. In *Burning Vision*, the character of Fat Man/the bomb speaks in a rhetoric reminiscent of 1950s cowboy westerns, while the character of Tokyo Rose embodies the sexualised rhetoric of Cold-War paranoia. Shonni Enelow's *Carla and Lewis* (2011) turns disassociated word patterns that echo GIFs and social media acronyms into hyper-hip mutated characters.[29] Steve Waters's *Contingency Plan* (2009) contrasts political policy rhetoric with scientific speak to show that neither really expresses the connection people feel to their home-places.[30] In *Contingency Plan* and Ellen Lewis's *Magellanica* (2017), formal scientific and geopolitical policy-speak contrast with intimate expressions of grief and fears associated with catastrophic loss.[31]

Aristotle might have recognised spoken dialogue between characters, soliloquy, or choral odes, but climate dramatists have made use of a spectrum of *ways of speaking* that not only include spoken-word poetry, litanies of scientific facts, and protest rants, but also Indigenous storytelling and what Okanagan poet and novelist Jeanette Armstrong calls 'land speaking': 'It is said in Okanagan that the land constantly speaks. It is constantly communicating', she writes.[32] The 'land as language surrounds us completely, just like the physical reality of it surrounds us. Within that vast speaking, both externally and internally, we as human beings are an inextricable part.'[33] In *Sila*, Mama 'reads' the surface of the water and ice moans its messages underfoot; in *Burning Vision*, the land speaks through the pounding hooves of caribou; in *Carla and Lewis*, the onrush of mud and floodwaters penetrates the imagined boundary between privileged North American and impacted African home-places.

This vast vocabulary of expression or ways of speaking in *Sila*, for example, calls into question the primacy of human language itself, suggesting instead that language is part of our fluid enmeshment in the world, no more distinctly human than bodies themselves. *Sila* asks its audience to consider themselves creatures who are part of a complex and dynamic web of relationships, reciprocal in their interdependence, a trans-corporeal world in which we are enmeshed, entangled with all matter, and implicated in the ethical complications that such a perspective carries.[34] The character of Tulugaq, for example, invites Jean, a Quebecois climatologist, to listen to the ice and the wind. Knowledge of such speakings is part of Tulugaq's Indigenous traditional ecological knowledge. He also enjoins Jean to trust stories as well as science, and challenges Jean to speak with Nuliajuk, an Inuit goddess of the undersea world, to find out what she wants of him.

Spectacle, Scenography, and Site: Envisioning Possible Futures

Theatre is a visual art form, and for Aristotle the idea of spectacle – literally, that which can be seen – was central to how a play delivers its thematic message. Yet, while the classical stage employed a variety of visual effects, the physicality of ancient theatres, set as they were in the outdoor rugged terrain of Greece, open to the land, sky, and sea, was perhaps their most spectacular aspect. Ironically, climate theatre, which strives to re-engage our connection to that larger fabric of the Earth and cosmos, is steeped in a modern tradition in which plays are performed indoors with the benefit of advanced and lavish technologies. But for dramatists who see theatre as a place to envision possible futures in light of climate change, the stage is a flexible, mutable palette of opportunity. First and foremost, climate theatre has addressed the irony implicit in theatre's artifice head-on by employing 'green' material practice and minimalist scenography.[35] Some artists have left the theatre building altogether in favour of site-specific and place-based staging echoing back to the theatre of classical Greece, and other cultural traditions in which stories and storytelling are linked to the land.

The idea of visual elements that depict a realistic setting for the action of a play is often exploded in climate theatre, which must frequently strive to represent multitemporal locations and hyper-geographies. In *Carla and Lewis*, for example, the mud from a flood affecting Bangladesh soaks through into the apartment walls of a New York art curator. In *Fairly Traceable*, a category 6 hurricane on the US Gulf Coast crashes together on stage with a killer tornado in the Midwest in a braided indictment of negligent resource extraction; in *Burning Vision*, Hiroshima, Japan, and Dene territorial homelands of northern Canada are superimposed upon one another in the split-seconds of the atomic blast; *Sila* calls for a location that is under the ice of the Arctic Sea. Each of these trans-temporal worlds give on-stage presence to the lie that we are safe and separate, and scenographers must find visual ways to represent these liminalities. Sense-of-place realism, however, is sometimes used in climate plays when those locations can underscore a sense of urgency. In *Contingency Plan*, an ageing scientist and his wife at home on the coast of Britain are poised for the impact of a storm that will wipe that home away. In *Magellanica*, a team of eight international scientists wintering over in Antarctica share a capsule-like accommodation in an inhospitable environment, housed within a thin layer of shelter powered by generators, and where all supplies – everything they will eat, wear, use, burn, or break – have come with them. The play conjures the very visage of what Buckminster Fuller called the Spaceship Earth.[36]

Cultural Competency and the Means of Production

Theatre linked to communities or connected to ongoing social justice movements has long engaged powerfully with environmental concerns, revealing the interlocking systems of racism, sexism, and environmental imperialism. This 'grassroots theatre', as Downing Cless argues, has been infused with environmental themes because it reflected the voices of people and communities who were experiencing the loss, injury, and struggle of the disproportionate impact of environmental destruction.[37] For example, dramatists like

Moraga, Octavio Solís and Josí Cruz González have amplified the call for environmental justice by representing the concerns and challenges still facing the migrant labour force – both immigrant and US-born – in the industrial agriculture of California and the Southwest. Kyle Powys Whyte points out that the kinds of apocalyptic, dystopian futures that arise in the popular imagination in relation to climate change are ones that Indigenous peoples of the Americas have already lived through: 'Sometimes I see settler environmental movements as seeking to avoid some dystopian environmental future or planetary apocalypse. These visions are replete with species extinctions, irreversible loss of ecosystems, and severe rationing. ... Yet for many Indigenous people in North America, we are already living in what our ancestors would have understood as dystopian or post-apocalyptic times.'[38] Many Indigenous theatre artists such as Clements and Nagle have also worked to call attention to the interweaving of land and identity and to explore the ways loss of land due to ongoing settler colonialism is coupled with loss of culture, language, and often health. These dramatists use theatre to reclaim the places and assert the sovereignty of diverse Indigenous peoples of the North American continent.

Playwrights working in the arena of climate theatre must take care not to replicate the structures of oppression their work seeks to address. The critical questions that researchers and artists alike must ask are: 'Whose research is it? Who owns it? Whose interests does it serve? Who will benefit from it? Who has designed its questions and framed its scope? Who will carry it out? Who will write it up? How will its results be disseminated?'[39] Often climate plays that tell stories that belong to oppressed or colonised peoples are written by members of those communities, like Clements and Nagle, who have access to both the traditions of storytelling and 'the kind of creativity that Indigenous peoples have [already] used to survive some of the most oppressive forms of capitalist, industrial, and colonial domination'.[40] In other cases, playwrights have productively partnered with artists and scholars from such communities to make sure their stories are told with care and respect, as was the case when Murphy collaborated with the Qaggiavuut performing arts society on her play *The Breathing Hole*.

Performing Possible Worlds into Being

Our historical moment requires theatre to rise to the ecological occasion, envisioning nothing short of a reimagined human animal in kinship with our world. As the ecological effects of human agency – once so central to the very definition of drama – circle back to dwarf human history, climate change theatre has opened up new dramaturgical questions that challenge theatre's traditional focus on human-scale narratives. As a way-of-knowing that is at once imaginative, affective, immediate, embodied, and communal, theatre can become a place to cope with shifting realities and to envision ways of being that preserve humane democracy. At a time when the master narratives of empire have induced a global ecological crisis, with implications for human and animal suffering of catastrophic proportion, the critical role of the performing arts as a site of counter-discourse, resistance, and reimagining can hardly be more apparent. The task of dismantling the stories that have sanctioned destruction must proceed apace with the task of generating new stories that help flesh out the possibilities of a just, humane, and sustainable world. Theatre is a site of confluence in which ecological relationships might be (re)imagined, explored, articulated, and, if not healed, at least brought to consciousness in ways that might sustain us on the path ahead. Surely the world needs theatre's 'what if?' now more than ever.

Notes

1 B. McKibben, 'What the Warming World Needs Now Is Art, Sweet Art', *Grist* (22 April 2005).

2 K. M. Norgaard, *Living in Denial: Climate Change, Emotions, and Everyday Life* (Cambridge, MA: MIT Press, 2011), 5–6, 11.

3 I am grateful to Wendy Arons for her close reading and strategic suggestions in thinking through the scope of this chapter. This chapter also draws significantly on ideas and illustrations discussed in T. May, *Earth Matters on Stage: Ecology, Environment and American Theater* (London: Routledge, 2020); see particularly 1–17 and 238–75.

4 K. M. Norgaard, 'Climate Change Is a Social Issue', *The Chronicle of Higher Education* (17 January 2016).

5 Norgaard, 'Climate Change'.

6 See Aristotle, 'Critical Contexts: From *The Poetics*', trans. G. E. Else, in W. B. Worthen (ed.), *The Wadsworth Anthology of Drama*, 5th ed. (Boston: Wadsworth, 2007), 123–4. For the full work, see Aristotle, *Aristotle's Poetics* (New York: Hill & Wang, 1961).

7 J. Dolan, 'Performance, Utopia, and the "Utopian Performative"', *Theatre Journal* 53.3 (2001), 455–79.

8 In recent decades, the ecodramaturgy lens has gone by various names, including green dramaturgy, environmental dramaturgy, and ecological theatre. Now, artists and theorists embrace what Una Chaudhuri has called an 'ecological theater' in '"There Must Be a Lot of Fish in that Lake": Toward an Ecological Theater', *Theater* 25.1 (1994), 23. See also W. Arons and T. May, 'Queer Ecology/Contemporary Plays', *Theatre Journal* 64.4 (2012), 562–82; D. Cless 'Eco-Theatre, USA: The Grassroots Is Greener', *TDR* 40.2 (1996), 79–102; C. Lavery, *Performance and Ecology: What Can Theatre Do?* (Abingdon: Routledge, 2018); May, *Earth Matters*, and 'Beyond Bambi: Toward a Dangerous Ecocriticism in Theatre Studies', *Theatre Topics* 17.2

(2007), 95–110; and L. Woynarki, *Ecodramaturgies: Theatre, Performance and Climate Change* (London: Palgrave Macmillan 2021).

9 May, *Earth Matters*, 4.

10 Chaudhuri, 'There Must Be a Lot of Fish', 24.

11 Chaudhuri, 'There Must Be a Lot of Fish', 24.

12 C. Bilodeau, *Sila: The Arctic Cycle* (Vancouver: Talonbooks, 2015).

13 M. K. Nagle, *Fairly Traceable* (Los Angeles: Native Voices at the Autry, 2015), unpublished.

14 M. Clements, *Burning Vision* (Vancouver: Talonbooks, 2003).

15 A. Cunsolo Willox, 'Climate Change as the Work of Mourning', *Ethics and Environment* 17.2 (2012), 141.

16 P. G. Allen, 'The Ceremonial Motion of Indian Time: Long Ago, So Far', in H. Geiogamah and J. T. Darby (eds.), *American Indian Theater in Performance: A Reader* (Los Angeles: UCLA American Indian Studies Center, 2000), 69–70.

17 Similar themes of transnational effects of environmental injustice are evident in *Ruined* by Lynn Nottage (New York: Theatre Communications Group, 2009) and *Bhopal* by Rahul Varma (Toronto: Playwrights Canada Press, 2005).

18 A. Galjour, *Alligator Tales*, 1997, manuscript, courtesy of Joyce Ketay Agency.

19 S. Alaimo, *Bodily Natures: Science, Environment and the Material Self* (Bloomington: Indiana University Press, 2019), 16–17.

20 C. Moraga, *Heroes and Saints*, in *Heroes and Saints and Other Plays* (Albuquerque, NM: West End Press, 1994), 85–149.

21 R. Rosenthal, 'Gaia, Mon Amor', in Chaudhuri (Ed.), *Rachel's Brain and Other Storms: The Performance Scripts of Rachel Rosenthal* (New York: Bloomsbury, 2001); see also Chaudhuri's introduction, 1–13.

22 Ecofeminist theatre and performance art have captured, critiqued, and ritualised the ways in which the desecration of the earth and women's bodies were aspects of the same patriarchal social values; see, for example, Arons and May, 'Queer Ecology/Contemporary Plays'.

23 U. Chaudhuri, 'The Silence of the Polar Bears', in Arons and May (eds.), *Readings in Performance and Ecology* (New York: Palgrave Macmillan, 2012) 50.

24 S. Alaimo, 'States of Suspension: Trans-corporeality at Sea', *ISLE: Interdisciplinary Studies in Literature and Environment* 19.3 (2012), 476.

25 C. Murphy, *The Breathing Hole* (Toronto: Playwrights Canada Press, 2020).

26 For an in-depth discussion of the way cultural representation *of* animals operates as a discourse *about* animals, see C. Wolfe, *Animal Rites: American Culture, the Discourse of Species, and Posthumanist Theory* (University of Chicago Press, 2003) and M. Calarco, *Zoographies: The Question of the Animal* (New York: Columbia University Press, 2008). For how these theories translate into dramatic criticism, see Chaudhuri, 'The Silence of the Polar Bears'.

27 While *Sila* is not a Native play (the playwright is French-Canadian), Bilodeau has drawn on strategies employed by many Native playwrights, which Christy Stanlake describes in more detail; C. Stanlake, *Native American Drama: A Critical Perspective* (Cambridge University Press, 2009). Scholarship in Native and First Nations drama and performance and ecocriticism shares much common ground, and what I have elsewhere called 'ecodramaturgy' would benefit from the example of the traditions, models, and methods of Native and First

Nations theatre as example of effective eco-centred theatre-making; see, N. Gray and S. Rabillard, 'Theatre in an Age of Ecocrisis', *Canadian Theatre Review* 144 (2010), 3–4.

28 Calarco, *Zoographies*, 4.

29 S. Enelow, *Carla and Lewis*, in U. Chaudhuri and S. Enelow, *Research Theatre, Climate Change, and the Ecocide Project: A Casebook* (New York: Palgrave Pivot, 2014), 87–116.

30 S. Waters, *The Contingency Plan: On the Beach* and *Resilience* (London: Bush Theatre, 2009).

31 E. M. Lewis, *Magellanica* (Portland, OH: Actors Repertory Theatre, 2017), unpublished.

32 J. Armstrong, 'Land Speaking', in S. Ortiz (ed.), *Speaking for Generations* (Tucson: University of Arizona Press, 1998), 176. Armstrong writes in detail about her Okanagan tradition; I urge others who wish to deploy her terminology of 'land speaking' to credit her directly and not to assume that this is theory-jargon that can be appropriated. See also Stanlake, *Native American Drama*, 23 and 39–42. For the ceremonial structure of indigenous plays, see Allen, 'The Ceremonial Motion' and *The Sacred Hoop: Recovering the Feminine in American Indian Traditions* (Boston, MA: Beacon Press, 2000).

33 Armstrong, 'Land Speaking', 178.

34 In this, *Sila* refers to what one might call the web of life, Gaia, or 'the mesh'; see T. Morton, 'Guest Column: Queer Ecology', *PMLA* 125.2 (2010), 273–82.

35 The ecological footprint of the material craft of theatre is the third strand of ecodramaturgy. See, for example, I. Garret, 'Theatrical Production's Carbon Footprint', in Arons and May (eds.), *Readings*, 201–10; L. K. Fried and May, *Greening Up Our Houses: A Guide to a More Ecologically Sound Theatre* (New York: Drama Book, 1994). See also the *Center for Sustainable Practice in the Arts* (CSPA), www.sustainablepractice.org; the Broadway Green Alliance, www.broadwaygreen.com, and Julie's Bicycle, www.juliesbicycle.com.

36 R. B. Fuller, *Operating Manual for Spaceship Earth* (New York: Simon & Schuster, 1969).

37 Cless, 'Eco-Theatre, USA', 79–102.

38 K. P. Whyte, 'Let's Be Honest, White Allies', *Yes* 85 (2018), 47–8.

39 L. T. Smith, *Decolonizing Methodologies: Research and Indigenous Peoples* (London: Zed Books, 1999), 10.

40 Whyte, 'Let's Be Honest', 47–8.

9

JOHN PARHAM

Digital Cli-Fi
Human Stories of Climate in Online and Social Media

Climate is multifaceted. It defies understanding, interpretation, or narration because climate disperses through differing dimensions of our lives. It is both day-to-day expectation and scientific 'big data'. Climate change is extreme weather events, an urgent socio-political issue, and, as John Ruskin prophesied in the nineteenth century, a looming existential 'storm-cloud'.[1]

Climate and climate change compel different scales of time and space to speak to each other. The 'experiential or embodied' timescale of individual lives is confronted with the long 'climatological' time of the Earth; daily life is reworked by changes at macro and microscopic levels.[2] While the enormous hyperobject of planetary climate change plays out graphically in extreme weather events (flash floods or, at the time of writing, horrific bush fires in Australia), it also registers as virtually imperceptible, microscopic change: fewer uncountable caterpillars; incrementally warming seas; marginally more yielding ice on local rinks. Such 'scale variance' is why critics have suggested that some prominent forms of literature, the novel or play, are ill-equipped to address climate change.[3] They allege that such forms are too focused on individual human lives and concerns, privilege humanly rewarding or meaningful conclusions, and are structured to the scale of experiential time.

For Stephanie LeMenager, conventional forms of literature help maintain the 'emotional and social infrastructure' underpinning a damaging, narrow, human perspective when actually it is crucial that we focus on the wider contexts – ecosystems, the Earth, the atmosphere – in which we live. We need to dismantle existing literary genres and establish new ones. LeMenager advocates 'cli-fi' and specifically identifies 'digital climate change media' as a form that might speak to entangled 'multiple scales of space and time involved in global climate change'.[4]

Advocating for digital media in this context may seem peculiar. Andrew Kalaidjian has written that:

> humans have a more direct influence on the environment than ever before. At
> the same time, never have humans engaged with the world in such an indirect

and mediated fashion. This is the paradox at the heart of the Spectacular Anthropocene. To make sense of this contradiction is the central task for establishing a viable environmental aesthetics in the twenty-first century.[5]

At the heart of Kalaidjian's challenge sits digital media, certainly when stereotyped as individuals facing downwards, often in the auditory seclusion of headphones and earphones, scrolling down a smartphone screen. Even worse is the 'direct' impact of digital technologies on global warming and the depletion of finite matter.[6] As Rachel Rochester concedes about podcasting, the use of ecologically destructive media to encourage users to live more responsibly 'is nothing if not paradoxical'. Yet what choice do we have? Given the ubiquity of digital media, and the absolute imperative of countering the hyperobject of climate change by engaging an equivalent mass population, perhaps the best way of managing we have, she continues, is to try to use finite media to stimulate the kinds of long-term changes – in how people think and act towards climate change – that might eventually lead us to eliminate damaging technologies.[7]

And maybe the relationship between the Earth system and digital media is not as paradoxical as it seems. In Richard Powers' *The Overstory* (2018), the multimillionaire programmer Neelay becomes wheelchair-bound as a child falling out of an oak tree. Staring from the ground, he sees 'networks of conjoined' branches, tubes, pipes, and cells 'pulsing with energy' – sunlight, water, minerals – a 'spreading metropolis', and 'the most perfect piece of self-writing code'.[8] Correspondingly, looking up from a 'code-filled' computer screen, five hundred pages later, Neelay perceives a world, which he himself has helped create, where 'tendrils of data' swell, merge, and stream.[9] Spreading (in his case) through the towns, cities, and suburbs of California, data fuses and merges, as does all 'living code'.[10] With such consonance in mind, by absorbing, sorting, matching, and exchanging data, 'learners' could 'form small communities', figure out how to translate between human language and 'the language of green things', even, ultimately, learn 'what life wants from people'.[11] Data unites the macro and micro perspectives through which we have to see climate. It expands human vision to read 'vast boreal forests from space' but also 'species-teeming tropics from eye level'.[12] Ultimately, scepticism appears to infuse Powers' correlation of trees with digital data as it will colour all considerations of digital cli-fi. Nonetheless, it makes sense to explore the possibilities of a cultural form typified by movement across and between scales: the microscopic level of tweets or data; a macroscopic digital sphere that ranges from debilitating 'infowhelm' to the possibilities of mass, global, networked, resistant communities; and middle-ground, human experiences of climate carried in, for example, blogs or cross-platform storytelling.

The most productive environmentalism insinuates itself in everyday life. Examples include campaigns against plastic and fast fashion, and veganism. The most profitable niche that cultural or media forms can occupy in terms of 'raising awareness' is, therefore, to translate ecological aspirations or values so as to be integrated in everyday lives: people's attitudes or behaviours.[13] This exploratory survey won't so much privilege the macro-accumulated data and networked and resistant communities, as emphasise how changes in climate are being recorded and registered in the quotidian dimensions of digital and online media. In three sections, I will explore: how effectively citizen science can stream data from ground-level to a macro-level understanding of global climate change and its impact; whether digital forums – tweets or blogs – might swell 'inconvenient' findings, opinions, or experiences of climate change into a global environmental public sphere; and how, through deeper, qualitative storytelling formats, often adapted from or in dialogue with old media, might cross-platform storytelling, self-published creative writing, or online diaries supplement data with lived stories of climate which, at a human level, might affect the rest of us to change? LeMenager writes, 'Were I to imagine cli fi in terms of formal innovation, my focus would be on how new media expand the possibilities of interactive and multi-sited authorship'.[14] Those are the criteria by which each form might just allow users to assuage the paralysing dimensions of climate change and manoeuvre digital media into self-writing code for a cooler green world.

Citizen Science

For those fortunate enough (so far) to have evaded extreme weather events, climate change exists as a dark, barely perceptible shadow brought to light only by digital data and its visualisation in statistics, graphs, or infographics. Data is plentiful but its ubiquity threatens to 'infowhelm' us into distraction, terror, resignation, or paralysis, a denialism of 'fake news', or a distrust of experts. Looking at the United States' National Oceanic and Atmospheric Administration's (NOAA) visualisation models for climate predictions, Heather Houser argues that, even where the aim is for people to experience data through computer modelling, colour graphics, and animation, the actual impact is to 'overwhelm rather than enlighten'.[15] Our senses become bombarded by vivid, disconcerting reds and oranges; we are overwhelmed by 'overt emotional appeals' which only show 'that we humans have already succumbed to our own emissions', and by a performance of infrastructure, expertise, and authority that we ourselves lack.[16]

As Derek Woods points out, however, 'infowhelm' is an 'imprecise' term. Visually bewildering graphics and cascading 'tendrils of data' do overwhelm, but these are just one type of information. Woods distinguishes between 'information as a statistical quantity' and information as meaning, a 'semantic affect that arises for readers of signs'. The tendency now is to 'offload' (as Bruce Clarke writes) the latter for the former.[17] So for climate information to be useful, quantitative data must co-exist with qualitative meaning. Katherine Bode and Paul Longley Arthur argue in *Advancing Digital Humanities* that, while the strength of data-rich analysis lies in seeing culture from a 'distance', and in observing 'patterns and conjunctions that could not otherwise be perceived', the gathering of information should, methodologically speaking, be integrated with empirical observation on the ground.[18] This is also true socially. For Robin Wagner-Pacifici, John Mohr, and Ronald Breiger, a comprehensive understanding of 'social life' – which would encompass how people, collectively, experience climate – requires measuring statistical data against lived experience to form a 'phenomenology of the social'.[19] Accordingly, Houser suggests, infowhelm can be managed and reworked into meaning via innovative forms of art and literature that work with data. Rather than simply translating or relaying climate science, such work transforms information by entangling data and observation with embodiment and feeling.[20] It is also true, therefore, in terms of agency. We may better internalise the realities of climate change, and be willing to act upon it, when information (including data) emerges from the circumstances of everyday life.

Caterpillars Count!, funded by the National Science Foundation and University of North Carolina, invites the public to collect data on caterpillars, beetles, and spiders that researchers then map against bird populations. The website explains that climate change incrementally affects when leaves come out in spring, insect activity, and bird migration and breeding, each of which has an economic and environmental impact on forests and crops. Participants are taught to identify arthropods, establish survey sites, and how to survey leaves, branches, and arthropods. There is a quiz, classroom activities, and a resources page.[21] The Smartfin Project was created by Lost Bird, a non-profit artists' group, with researchers at the Scripps Institution of Oceanography and the Surfrider Foundation, a group that actively defends sand and sea habitats. Its website explains that since oceans have absorbed 90 per cent of the excess heat and 50 per cent of excess CO_2 since the Industrial Revolution, how the ocean handles continued increases 'will largely determine how Earth responds to climate change'. Via specially adapted, research-grade surfboard fins, the project commissions surfers to collect and submit data on temperature and CO_2 from nearshore coastal zones. Such zones are rich in biodiversity and human activity, but are 'challenging and expensive' to collect information from because they are 'dynamic'.[22] *Rinkwatch* is an initiative by Wilfrid Laurier University. Encompassing (so far) 1,400-plus outdoor rinks and ponds, mainly in Canada and the United States, participants monitor skating conditions so as to gather evidence about the impact of long-term climate change. The website explains that 'skateability' deteriorates rapidly as temperatures rise to approach $-5°C$. Consequently, there is a real danger that skating will decline markedly because of climate change. Participants enter information through the website. Researchers monitor the current effect of warming while projecting impacts up until the end of the twenty-first century.[23]

Both *Caterpillars Count!* and *RinkWatch* are hosted on SciStarter.org, a platform designed to encourage public participation in science and offer a shared space 'where scientists can talk with citizens'.[24] The aspirations of citizen science around climate change might be summarised as: disseminating information and education; creating a community; encouraging people to integrate the monitoring of climate change into everyday life; and ultimately, to encourage people to share their experiences and stories of climate. However, on *Caterpillars Count!*, participation appears a largely one-way process – supplying the data. Thereafter, there seems limited further involvement (and even less conversation) beyond a 'Leaderboard' that displays where and from whom the most data has been collected. Evidence accumulates but findings are not clearly communicated. Instead, statistics, graphs, and curious (but somewhat abstract) site photographs display the scientific authority and graphical wizardry that Houser describes. *Smartfin.org*, likewise, presents its findings via an impenetrable maze of perplexing maps, data specifications, abstract imagery, and statistics.[25] Data is transformed by, but then seemingly detached from, citizen scientists.

Smartfin is described as 'a community science initiative focused on collecting coastal water quality data and communicating critical ocean health issues' and as providing 'opportunities for members to engage others, learn and be heard'.[26] Yet the website epitomises how ostensibly participatory and shared initiatives can preclude citizens from telling their own climate stories. Beyond sharing data, communication is largely dominated by 'old media' – news features on the BBC, NBC, CNN – or a blog largely comprising corporate, scientific, or technical material (not least 'On Data Visualization').[27] The other notable forms of communication are requests for donations and an invitation to engage speakers. The site stresses 'open dialogue between experts, scholars and engaged, empowered citizens' as a means to 'large-scale, meaningful change'. It encourages 'members to be vocal about their Smartfin participation, ocean health and climate change'.[28] Yet this seemingly narrow alliance of professional infrastructure and scientific experts – performing, as Mike Hulme has written, 'epistemic authority'[29] – with the corresponding (and likewise closely guarded) '(sub) cultural capital' of surfing communities[30] indicates that this is less a community of two-way learning than the top-down authority of engaged, empowered advocates and leaders.

Smartfin does, nonetheless, elicit a valuable narrative about climate change out of everyday life. And, in the other examples, integration goes further. The *Caterpillars Count!* data, for example, is collected from local shrubs, trees, habitats, and backyards. The project encourages the participation of community groups and schools and its website includes school materials. Participants can print data sheets on paper (they don't need access to apps or a smartphone) and can even learn to rear caterpillars indoors. *Rink Watch*, likewise, aligns scientific education with people's own experiences of climate. Research results can be readily accessed via a link to a scholarly article in *Canadian Geographer* and so can supplementary research (for example, a paper on the impact of warming on skating marathons in the Netherlands). The visualisation of the data is more user-friendly with findings clearly comprehensible.[31] For example, correlating their own citizen scientists' data to IPCC computer simulations, the researchers project 'the number of skating days by the year 2090 to decline on average by 34 percent in Toronto and Montreal, and 19 percent in Calgary'.[32] There is tangible educational benefit – for example, resources developed from rink data for teaching maths and science to nine- to eleven-year-olds – and genuine, two-way engagement. And *Rink Watch* builds a community around the goal of protecting outdoor skating for future generations to 'prevent rinklessness'. As a result, it engages people involved in a mass-participation but locally grounded sport in climate. The website encompasses practical advice for making ice and maintaining rinks; a *Rink Talk* podcast series covers science but also the importance of backyard rinks to families;[33] more personal stories appear in discussions and photos on the *Rink Watch* Facebook page. Though not always the case, in citizen science, individuals' experiences can accumulate and build into grassroots stories of climate and climate change.

Social Media and Online Communities

Those climate stories could, theoretically, be swelled by social media, where numerous blogs and microblogs integrate climate, climate change, and everyday life. The aspiration of bringing climate science to the general population is supported, for example, by scientists' personal stories. Kaitlin Naughten, an ocean modeller working at the British Antarctic Survey in Cambridge, created the *ClimateSight* blog when just sixteen. It now intersperses reports about her research – for example, on Arctic and Antarctic meltwater disrupting deep ocean currents and therefore climate patterns – with stories of life as a climate scientist. Naughten also narrates her career choice as inspired by the organisational elegance of the periodic table and by comprehending climate change as 'a fascinating math problem, a symphony unfolding both slowly and quickly before our very eyes'. Describing climate change 'compassion fatigue', she writes insightfully about the value of compartmentalising. Cycling home in the mist to 'eat Cornish pasties on the couch with my husband' enables the intensive bouts of work by which Naughten gets on with her 'piece of the fight'.[34]

Other bloggers communicate their personal investment in climate. LeMenager cites Emily Ferguson's *Line 9 Communities* blog.[35] In 2013, Ferguson attended a public meeting in which the Enbridge energy company explained plans to reverse the direction of flow, increase the capacity, and begin carrying heavy crude oil from the Alberta Oil Sands along the Sarnia-Montreal pipeline (originally constructed in 1976). Angered by a refusal of company representatives to give her a copy of the 'extra info packages they held in their hands', Ferguson began mapping the pipeline. The maps are documented on her website. Moreover, by blogging the information, she built a community online and along the pipeline itself.[36] Enbridge's website boasts of supplying nearly two-thirds of Canada's crude oil exports to the United States, transporting almost 20 per cent of the natural gas consumed in the United States, and operating 'North America's third-largest natural gas utility by consumer count'.[37] From Ferguson's below-the-line responses it is clear that local residents' concerns – people moving into the area, raising children, or just fearful for the 'delicate terrain' – mirror Ferguson's own motivations. She tells two autobiographical stories: of discovering that the pipeline lay less than two hundred metres away from her old elementary school playground; and of losing both her grandmothers during the project and her own desire, consequently, to 'work toward a brighter future for my own grandchildren'. A contrasting example is the *Trees, Fish, and Dreams Climateblog* created by Scott T. Starbuck, a college tutor, fisherman and poet.[38] It combines media posts (Keira Knightley's video for Extinction Rebellion) with news stories, scientific reports, and his own reports from climate events. However, Starbuck also writes about his dreams (one describes koalas with human voices asking for a seat at the United Nations!), posts family photos, provides updates on marital relations with his wife 'Suz', and describes his fishing trips. If idiosyncratic, the blog's homespun nature offers, to its audience, an effective, comprehensive, and multifaceted picture of the personal impact of diminished fish stocks in American rivers.

In microblogging too, interactive communities now proliferate around climate. #ClimateChangeIsReal was, originally, an initiative that reached 265 million people across five continents on Earth Day 2015. A website aggregated general content; a Tumblr account gathered original work by artists, musicians, filmmakers, and so on.[39] The hashtag's 'slight bite' and 'subtle dig at deniers' gave the campaign, it is claimed, greater clout and facilitated more 'organic activity than other, more bland frames'. Nonetheless, its spectacular global reach neither embodied grassroots inter-activity nor generated alternative or autonomous climate narratives. Rather, it was a campaign founded upon influencers and prominently supported by celebrities, public figures, and consumer brands: Barack Obama, Virgin, Paul McCartney, Nike, Russell Brand, Unilever. More fundamentally, a playful tone ('in contrast to typical sober and gloomy communications on the issue') was actually designed to celebrate 'positive progress being made on clean energy and climate solutions'. In other words, #ClimateChangeIsReal tapped an irreverence associated with 'cool capitalism' to steer our faith towards technological solutions framed firmly by the domineering narrative of the global market.[40]

Jutta Haider has noted the slippage of environmental and climate social media towards such narratives. Social media has become central, she writes, to how information on environmentally friendly living 'is articulated, shaped, and filled with meaning', a meaning 'rooted in the conditions of the Web'.[41] Haider argues: first, that an increasingly pervasive formation of identity through online communication and interaction has played a key role in normalising practices of green living; secondly, that much environmental information circulating on social media emanates from government, NGOs, campaign groups, and businesses; and, thirdly, that social media affords opportunities for greener living but only via what Michel Foucault called 'governmentality'.[42] Practices of self-discipline (that is, self-governance) demanded within neoliberal society take the form on social media, suggests Haider, of 'self-writing'. This is 'specific to the ways in which in today's neoliberal society people are expected to control their own conduct, to improve and work on themselves, and to also perform their accomplishments and failures in public according to internalised rules. This perspective shifts the focus from the staging of identities to the formation of selves on social network sites'.[43] Accordingly, while one could deploy community-detection algorithms or aggregate retweets, shares, followers, and so on to highlight vast and interactive networks,[44] closer analysis might actually identify a narrative in which individuals' self-regulation of environmental lifestyles, including actions around climate, is framed by neoliberalism and narrowed by discourses of consumerism such as self-reward or freedom of choice: 'Oh dear ... seems that the implications of Electric Vehicles hasn't actually been thought through ... but there again, maybe it has & independent means of transportation is to [be] removed from the masses?'[45]

The picture, however, is complicated: 'When we were poor, we couldn't afford a car, or to go anywhere, so yeah, pretty green. Would I like to go back to that? Not really. But unless we all do, the planet's fucked'.[46] Dhiraj Murthy argues that a less statistical approach to, for example, coding tweets might identify 'movements of history' and 'anthropological transformations of subjectivity'.[47] A cursory analysis reveals that, beyond the original campaign, #ClimateChangeIsReal has interestingly evolved into an active grassroots global community. A scroll down on a given day (31 January 2020) detects varied and numerous tweets describing local experiences of climate change: Australian bushfires; an invasion of desert locusts in Kenya; plastic-filled rivers in Indonesia; seasonally early cherry blossom in Stockholm; flooding and a loss of drinking water in Bukavu, Democratic Republic of Congo; a campaign to save oak trees in Manchester. The format and the richness of the information may be limited, but there's space enough to register despair, fear, humour, fact, or to trigger empathy, even when cataclysmic scenarios trickle out of somewhat matter-of-fact posts. From New South Wales, Michael Oud tweets an image from *weather.com* of the temperature at 5am, 73°F, and the day's predicted optimum temperature, 109°F: 'Not looking forward to another one of these days. It wasn't that long ago that we would get only a handful of these super hot days over summer. Now it feels like they come around every couple of weeks. Everyone stay safe'.[48] In these brief, localised stories of climate change, one discerns, through both aggregation and overlapping narratives, an 'anthropological transformation'. Dominant narratives of economic progress, the unstoppable expansion of oil, are met by the swell of a digitally enabled culture – a quiet communal resistance; counter-stories of people's attachment to other people and animals; stories from cherished places where climate matters.

Digital Storytelling

Digital stories can potentially do three things. They can help transcend the segregation into 'like-minded' communities that sometimes occurs in citizen science or social media.[49] Secondly, websites and apps for online publishing or podcasting, for example, allow narratives describing climate and especially climate change to disperse and accumulate in the spaces of individual life, meeting, as Walter Benjamin once wrote of reproducible media, 'the beholder or listener in his own particular situation', who themselves can be reactivated by that encounter.[50] Likewise, argues Erin James, 'storyworlds can cultivate greater environmental awareness by fostering emotional connections between readers and narrators/characters'.[51] This distinctive, intimate character to digital storytelling can stimulate, thirdly therefore, empathy, a mode of affect integral to both the potency of narrative and the imperative of converting climate information into meaning. Here I will consider three forms of digital storytelling: self-published climate fiction, podcasting, and autobiographical online 'climate stories'.

Story 'tagging' is not always reliable and 'climate' is a multifaceted word, yet platforms such as *Wattpad.com* and *FanFiction.net* host many cli-fi stories (almost five thousand on *Wattpad* alone). The fiction is heavily generic – mainly science fiction, adventure or fantasy – and conventional: dystopian, post-apocalyptic societies where society has broken down and individuals and families struggle to survive; quests to save the Earth; the habitual appearance of mythical creatures (the water dragon of *Guangzhou Future Tense*) or aliens. Online cli-fi describes, in both senses, a 'future tense'. For example, *Wattpad*'s cli-fi stories are repeatedly set in the 'near future' (that is, the twenty-first century). Such stories both describe the plausible impacts of climate change – flooding, desertification, cooling or warming temperatures, poisoned seas – and place the blame on humans. By far *Wattpad*'s most popular cli-fi story, Jule Owen's *The Boy Who Fell from the Sky* (47,500 readers) describes 'a future where climate change *and* technology have transformed the world'.[52] A short story suggests that our 'battle to live in sync with nature may not be with the planet' (*A Human's Approach to Adaptation*); another (*They Watched*) addresses 'how little we are actually doing to stop it'.[53] Consequently, as typifies speculative or science fiction, several stories, projecting forward, question how our all-consuming present might change the future.

Wattpad and *FanFiction* also operate as social networks, potentially enhancing the significance of online publishing as climate fiction. *Wattpad* registers 'Reads' of each book in hundreds and sometimes thousands. Its tagline is 'where stories live'. Whether this profuse data nurtures feelings, beliefs, or actions, however, is less certain. Feedback tends to be technical, fixated on the accuracy and originality of the characters or storyline, the quality of the writing, or the adaptation. While online readers are drawn into storyworlds, and are frequently impatient to know what happens next, they rarely seem to reflect on the narrative's meaning, a character's actions, or their own lives or experiences of environment or climate.

If readers are not, then, internalising these climate stories into their own lives, the social network in online self-publishing nevertheless remains significant. The sheer volume of original online cli-fi, its immense readership and popularity in many countries (for example, China), and the fervour with which *FanFiction.net* authors adapt (say) *Frozen*, *Transformers*, or *Alien vs. Predator*, does suggest a potential to extend the storyworld of each novel into a 'meta-world' of writers and readers engaging with climate. Perhaps this needs, for now, a more prominent medium. *Forest 404* is a 2019 BBC Radio 4 drama that utilises the considerable reach (broadcast) and resources of old media.[54] It offers more extensive cross-platform storytelling, deeper, more qualitative storytelling formats, and more sensory, immersive media, qualities Rochester attributes to audio drama.[55] The series is set in the twenty-fourth century. Forests, and even the memory of them, have disappeared, as has most nature. Following 'The Cataclysm', a data crash, Pan is tasked with sorting and deleting any surviving sound files. She discovers recordings of the Sumatran rainforest and, haunted by what she hears, tries to find out how they died. She is pursued by government agents. Each of the nine episodes is supported by both an accompanying talk exploring the themes raised and a short 'soundscape'. The broadcasts feed into 'The Forest 404 Experiment' (led by the University of Exeter and the Open University), which assesses the impact of natural sounds on mental health and well-being.

Sound is a disregarded but central part of digital media central to music streaming, audio messaging, podcasting, and so on. Correspondingly, Rochester argues, sound has a neglected potency 'as a medium through which to encourage listeners to internalize some of the unpalatable issues surrounding ... climate change'.[56] That potency lies in its immersive, affective properties and auditory collapse of the boundary between the listener's space and the storyworld. On a continuous feed of episode, talk, soundscape, *Forest 404* immerses listeners (especially if using headphones) in a world of depletion, much as Rochester describes about her example, the American podcast series *We're Alive*.[57] The drama elicits empathy, via sound effects, narrative, and character: the evocative impact when Pan hears the Sumatran rainforest recording for the first time; the affective pull of the quest narrative and thriller genre; and the emotional connections kindled by recognisable cultural reference points and (sympathetic) characters' down-to-earth London accents. For, while the dialect could imply a particular resonance for a British audience, I'd argue that this relatively recognisable accent adds a sheen of authentic place-based experience comparable to Starbuck's Oregon fishing stories or the globally diverse regional voices populating

#ClimateChangeIsReal. Drawn in, we are more likely to engage intellectually with themes, presented across the platform, which resonate with our own anxieties: of an artificial humanity primarily constituted by data; of the twenty-fourth century putting into perspective what the show calls our current 'slow times'; or of how sound assists us in thinking about climate. *Forest 404*'s second talk, for example, describes how climate change would prevent animals communicating by sound.

Some elements of *Forest 404* are less successful. The drama is a little generic. The quest narrative and specific tropes – for example, separating the future world on two levels, with the lower level 'Fumetown' deprived of direct sunlight – are overly familiar from Japanese anime and derivative of H. G. Wells' *The Time Machine* (1895). The show can be didactic, notably towards the middle when Pan learns about how the 'old world' came to end. The experiment connects the lives of its audience (7,600 of whom participated) to a meta-textual, real-life narrative about climate. A form of citizen science, it seemingly highlights similar limitations in agency. Participants listened to natural sounds and, like Pan, selected which to keep and which to delete. Curiously, though, the data feeds not a study of climate but of whether virtual natural environments boost well-being for those facing barriers in gaining access to actual landscapes.[58] Nonetheless, *Forest 404* does demonstrate both the communicative value of aural drama, a medium reinvigorated by podcasting, and that digital multi-platform media can offer complex multifaceted climate narratives. In *The Time Machine*, a 'lifeless' world ruined by human intervention is signified by aural absence: 'the sounds of man, the bleating of sheep, the cries of birds, the hum of insects, the stir that makes the background of our lives'.[59] Movingly, this is recreated in the final episode of *Forest 404*. Pan recites a litany of extinct species and then plays a sequence of recordings of natural sounds now only audible as catalogued digital files: 'seashore, 271; pack-ice, 1199'; 'horses galloping, 761'; 'domestic cat, 4578'; 'Forest, 404'.

The deficit of agency which bedevils new as much as it does old media might perhaps be addressed by individual stories of climate. The online *Climate Stories Project* focuses on 'oral histories'. It seeks to move climate change discussion beyond 'the impersonal perspective of science or the contentious realm of politics', to bring 'immediacy to the sometimes abstract nature of climate change communication' and highlight how 'more and more of us are feeling the effects of climate change on a personal and community level'.[60] People record their experiences of dramatic weather, untimely seasonal changes, and climate disruption, stories of communities adapting to climate change, and hopeful narratives of protest and action. The allegiance to letting people speak for themselves is supported by webpages on how to tell your story and 'documents' explaining how to run a workshop, conduct an interview, or do audio editing.

In a personal profile on the website, project manager Berenice Tompkins describes how people told stories on 2014's Great March for Climate Action across the United States. She hazards that people are 'much more willing to talk about climate change when they had a human face to connect it to'. Climate Stories recognises that the same is true of listening. The project hitches storytelling to digital online media's unprecedented ability to connect people globally.[61] Like #ClimateChangeIsReal, multifaceted stories of flooding (Malawi), coastal erosion (Senegal), deforestation (Mali), ocean warming (Japan), or seasonal shift in India ultimately inscribe a greater narrative which demarcates the all-encompassing impacts and experience of climate change. James argues that in postcolonial literature, narrative techniques such as focalisation and free indirect discourse transport audiences' empathy across continents.[62] Here, the unsettling accumulation of information is supplemented by experience and acquires enhanced potency through the even more direct form of first-person testimony. We hear, watch, and feel the Kyoto fishmonger Ishino Akihiro's nervous bafflement at warming seas reducing stock and altering the seasonal availability of fish, or the distinct Alabaman voice of Karrie Quirin, frustrated by people dismissing unusual weather patterns, vexed by a pipeline 500 feet adjacent to her local school, but resolute as she narrates her own community action. A 'Climate Music' page, moreover, amplifies the stories via music, song, or montages of sound. In the moving 'Ice Is What I Remember', New Yorker Joseph Dumoulin recollects, from childhood, 'reliable' winter ice and mass-participation ice hockey. Represented online by an evocative black-and-white image, Dumoulin's memories are juxtaposed with a visceral digital recording of skates scouring ice (recalling *Forest 404*'s archiving of natural sound) and bass-playing, by Jason Davis, that portends sparser, emptier space.

Conclusion

Conclusions are not always reassuring. Nor can they be if we are to face up to today's changing climate. Each mode of digital/online storytelling nonetheless helps us address climate, extending the narrative capacity of stories to cultivate awareness by fostering emotional connections. Online self-published fiction builds social networks; podcast audio drama deepens empathy by eliciting immersive, sensory responses; biographical storytelling extends this further, offering direct, real-life communication. Moreover, as the *Climate Stories Project* insists, 'There is no "right" way to talk about climate change as it is a vast topic that is increasingly touching every corner of our lives'. For the fullest possible story, we need the most inclusive picture.

Timothy Clark writes that 'Global environmental issues such as climate change entail the implication of the broadest effects in the smallest day-to-day phenomena, juxtaposing the trivial and the catastrophic in ways that can be deranging or paralyzing – for what can *I* do?'[63] Far from perfect, digital and online media offers, nevertheless, an added dimension to cli-fi. Interactive and first-person platforms such as social media, blogging, and online testimonies democratise and expand the repertoire of climate stories. Audio drama, blogs, and online self-publishing give evidence of the continued value of much maligned human modes of narrative and storytelling. Citizen science's blend of data with everyday life helps create a more comprehensive body of 'information' about climate. These forms also embody the scale variance by which we have to learn how to see climate. 'Hyperobjects' largely form out of microscopic levels of activity (for example, individual carbon emissions). The shared, repeated interaction by which multi-sited digital media engender micro-stories of climate – of warming seas, pipelines, melting ice rinks, or localised protest – mirrors this. In amassing digital information perhaps a greater overstory may yet emerge.

Notes

1 J. Ruskin, 'The Storm-Cloud of the Nineteenth Century (1884)', in E. T. Cook and A. Wedderburn (eds.), *The Complete Works of John Ruskin*, vol. 34 (London: George Allen, 1908), 7–80.

2 R. Markley, 'Climate Science', in B. Clarke and M. Rossini (eds.), *The Routledge Companion to Literature and Science* (New York: Routledge, 2010), 65.

3 T. Clark, *Ecocriticism on the Edge: The Anthropocene as a Threshold Concept* (London: Bloomsbury Academic, 2015).

4 S. LeMenager, 'The Humanities after the Anthropocene', in U. K. Heise *et al.* (eds.), *The Routledge Companion to the Environmental Humanities* (London: Routledge, 2016), 475–7.

5 A. Kalaidjian, 'The Spectacular Anthropocene', *Angelaki* 22.4 (2017), 20.

6 See S. Cubitt, *Finite Media: Environmental Implications of Digital Technologies* (Durham, NC: Duke University Press, 2016).

7 R. Rochester, 'We're Alive: The Resurrection of the Audio Drama in the Anthropocene', *Philological Quarterly*, 93.3 (2014), 374.

8 R. Powers, *The Overstory* (London: Vintage, 2018), 129.

9 Powers, *Overstory*, 605–6.

10 Powers, *Overstory*, 614.

11 Powers, *Overstory*, 614, 616–17.

12 Powers, *Overstory*, 614.

13 J. Parham, *Green Media and Popular Culture: An Introduction* (London: Palgrave Macmillan, 2015), 1, 29.

14 LeMenager, 'Humanities after the Anthropocene', 477.

15 H. Houser, 'Climate Visualizations: Making Data Experiential', in Heise *et al.* (eds.), *The Routledge Companion to the Environmental Humanities* (London: Routledge, 2016), 362.

16 Houser, 'Climate Visualizations', 366, 362.

17 D. Woods, 'Accelerated Reading: Fossil Fuels, Infowhelm, and Archival Life', in T. Menely and J. O. Taylor (eds.), *Anthropocene Reading: Literary History in Geologic Times* (University Park: Pennsylvania State University Press, 2017), 205.

18 K. Bode and P. L. Arthur, 'Collecting Ourselves', in Bode and Arthur (eds.), *Advancing Digital Humanities: Research, Methods, Theories* (Basingstoke: Palgrave Macmillan, 2014), 5.

19 R. Wagner-Pacifici, J. Mohr, and R. Breiger, 'Ontologies, Methodologies, and New Uses of Big Data in the Social and Cultural Sciences' *Big Data & Society* 2.2 (2015), 2–3, 9.

20 H. Houser, *Infowhelm: Environmental Art and Literature in an Age of Data* (New York: Columbia University Press, 2020).

21 *Caterpillars Count!*, https://caterpillarscount.unc.edu.

22 'About', *Smartfin*, https://smartfin.org.

23 *RinkWatch*, www.rinkwatch.org/rink_map.html.

24 SciStarter.org, http://edutechwiki.unige.ch/en/Scistarter.

25 See 'Smartfin Surf Fin Sea Water Monitoring Project', *Smartfin*, https://smartfin .org.

26 'About', *Smartfin*, https://smartfin.org.

27 'On Data Visualization', *Smartfin*, https://smartfin.org.

28 'About', *Smartfin*, https://smartfin.org.

29 M. Hulme, 'How Climate Models Gain and Exercise Authority', in K. Hastrup and M. Skrydstrup (eds.), *The Social Life of Climate Change Models: Anticipating Nature* (New York: Routledge, 2013), 39, quoted in Houser, 'Climate Visualizations', 362.

30 For a broadly equivalent example, see T. Langseth, 'Liquid Ice Surfers: The Construction of Surfer Identities in Norway', *Journal of Adventure Education and Outdoor Learning Ontologies* 12.1 (2012), 3–23.

31 See 'Activities: Science', *RinkWatch*, www.rinkwatch.org/activities_science .html.

32 C. Robertson *et al.*, 'Winters Too Warm to Skate? Citizen-Science Reported Variability in Availability of Outdoor Skating in Canada', *Canadian Geographer/Le Géographe canadien* 59.4 (2015).

33 'Rinks of Hope', *RinkTalk*, podcast, www.rinktalk.org/133551/606021-rinks-of -hope.

34 K. Naughten, *ClimateSight: Climate Science from the Inside*, https://climatesight .org/. See also *Kate Has Things to Say*, www.marvelclimate.blogspot.com.

35 LeMenager, 'Humanities after the Anthropocene', 479.

36 E. Ferguson, 'My Story', *Line 9 Communities*, https://line9communities.com/my-story/.

37 'About Us', *Enbridge*, www.enbridge.com/about-us.

38 S. T. Starbuck, *Trees, Fish, and Dreams Climateblog*, www.riverseek.blogspot.com.

39 For the information in this and the next paragraph, see '#ClimateChangeIsReal', *Shorty Awards*, https://shortyawards.com/8th/climatechangeisreal-2. The Tumblr page is now inactive.

40 Parham, *Green Media*, 131.

41 J. Haider, 'The Shaping of Environmental Information in Social Media', *Environmental Communication* 10.4 (2016), 473.

42 Haider, Shaping of Environmental Information, 473–4, 477.

43 Haider, Shaping of Environmental Information, 485.

44 See H. T. P. Williams *et. al.*, 'Network Analysis Reveals Open Forums and Echo Chambers in Social Media Discussions of Climate Change', *Global Environmental Change* 32 (2015), 130.

45 @IanRCrane, *Twitter*, 7 February 2020, 7:58 pm https://twitter.com/IanRCrane/status/1225508973174050822.

46 @xomebody, *Twitter*, 29 July 2019, 9:08 am, https://twitter.com/xomebody/status/1155736941998104577.

47 D. Murthy, 'The Ontology of Tweets: Mixed-Method Approaches to the Study of Twitter', in L. Sloan and A. Quan-Haase (eds.), *The SAGE Handbook of Social Media Research Methods* (Los Angeles: Sage, 2016), 560.

48 @michael_oud, *Twitter*, 1 Feb 2020, 5:34 am, https://twitter.com/michael_oud/status/1223313526350966785.

49 Williams *et. al.*, 'Network Analysis', 135.

50 W. Benjamin, 'The Work of Art in the Age of Mechanical Reproduction', in H. Arendt (ed.), *Illuminations*, trans. H. Zohn (New York: Schocken Books, 1969), 221.

51 E. James, *The Storyworld Accord*: Econarratology and Postcolonial Narratives (Lincoln: University of Nebraska Press, 2015), 209.

52 J. Owen, *The Boy Who Fell from the Sky*, *Wattpad*, www.wattpad.com/story/46949633-the-boy-who-fell-from-the-sky (emphasis added).

53 G. C. Huxley, *A Human's Approach to Adaptation*, *Wattpad*, www.wattpad.com/112090524-a-human%27s-approach-to-adaptation; Kiwifruitini, *They Watched*, *Wattpad*, www.wattpad.com/630764661-they-watched.

54 *Forest 404*, dir. B. Ripley, written by T. X. Atack, BBC Radio 4, 2019. See 'What is *Forest 404*?', *BBC Radio 4*, www.bbc.co.uk/programmes/articles/5yXQydgzYhZchzTs1km4vxT/what-is-forest-404.

55 Rochester, 'We're Alive', 361.

56 Rochester, 'We're Alive', 364.

57 Rochester, 'We're Alive', 365.

58 'The Forest 404 Experiment', *nQuire: Explore your World*, https://nquire.org.uk/mission/forest-experiment.

59 H. G. Wells, *The Time Machine*, J. Lawton (ed.). (London: Everyman, 1995), 74–5.

60 'About', *Climate Stories Project*, www.climatestoriesproject.org/about.html.

61 See 'Climate Stories Map', *Climate Stories Project*, www.climatestoriesproject.org/climate-stories-map.html.

62 James, *Storyworld Accord*, 209.

63. Clark, *Ecocriticism on the Edge*, 14.

10

ALEXA WEIK VON MOSSNER

Climate on Screen
From Doom and Disaster to Ecotopian Visions

While most of the literary texts discussed in this companion rely on words to help readers imagine climate change, film relies on a somewhat – if not entirely – different narrative toolset. Most obviously, it uses images, motion, and sound, pre-packaging our perception to some degree, if not our affective response. In the case of climate change cinema, such pre-packaging has tended towards the dark and disastrous as filmmakers are torn between the desire to forewarn and the need to entertain and make money. It has thus become a critical commonplace that cinematic depictions of climate change offer a spectacle-driven, apocalyptic vision that is at odds with the diffuse experience of climate and the slow violence of climate change.[1] Some critics fear that such dark and disastrous visions might prove detrimental to our capacity to address the issue properly because people end up disengaging from it entirely.[2] Watching disastrous but entertaining depictions of climate-changed future worlds, the logic goes, will either lead us to not take the issue seriously enough, or to be so overwhelmed by negative emotions that we fall into apathy and become incapable of doing anything at all.

There are at least two problems with this assessment. The first problem results from what is often a relatively narrow focus on blockbuster fiction films, such as Roland Emmerich's *The Day After Tomorrow* (2004), Bong Joon-ho's *Snowpiercer* (2013), and George Miller's *Mad Max Fury Road* (2015), and a handful of documentaries that offer less spectacular but similarly apocalyptic views of the future in support of their dire calls for action.[3] Typical examples include Davis Guggenheim's *An Inconvenient Truth* (2006), Franny Armstrong's *The Age of Stupid* (2009), Jeff Orlowski's *Chasing Ice* (2012), and Fisher Stevens's *Before the Flood* (2017). Often overlooked are films that are more concretely utopian in outlook and that deal in more nuanced and/or less pessimistic ways with the ecological, economic, and social repercussions of climate change, some of which I will discuss in this chapter.

Secondly, and just as importantly, we need to develop a better understanding of how exactly films – including climate change films – engage
viewer emotions and what effects such engagements might have. A related
aim of this chapter is therefore to explore the ethical and affective dimensions of depictions of climate change in fiction and documentary film. It
will consider the empathetic relationships and calls to action that cinema
might be capable of effecting in ways that partially draw from but perhaps
also elude literary strategies. And it will argue that both negative and
positive emotions are important for how climate change films engage
viewers. The first part of the chapter will dig deeper into the concerns
that critics and scholars have voiced about the cueing of negative emotions through the depiction of (future) climate doom and disaster.
The second part will then turn to films that have tried an entirely different
affective approach by presenting possible solutions to the climate crisis
along with desirable ecotopian futures in a mode that is often humorous,
witty, and uplifting. Both narrative strategies, I will suggest, have their
place in climate change cinema, and both can be effective with some
audiences.

A Cinematic History of Climate Doom and Disaster

Many cli-fi authors, notes Matthew Schneider-Mayerson, write 'with an
activist bent, hoping to alert their audiences to the gravity of the threat and
the need to take immediate action'.[4] By contrast, there are very few cli-fi films
that one might call activist by any stretch of the imagination. In his 2016
overview of 'Cli-Fi on the Screen(s)', Michael Svoboda lists more than sixty
films that, in some capacity, include an element of climate change, but the list
includes only a few films that are concerned with the scientific side of the
issue, let alone show any interest in communicating causes or possible solutions. As Svoboda notes, filmmakers have instead 'focused on extreme
weather events and the possibility of Earth slipping into a new ice age',
choices that 'reflect filmmakers' predispositions more than any scientific
consensus'.[5] At the same time, the very nature of those global phenomena
causes problems for cinematic representation. As Richard Lawson has
pointed out, it can be 'hard to locate a singular hero in such a global
narrative; what grizzled hunk or butt-kicking babe is going to singlehandedly
stop the rise of the oceans, reorder our weather, and repair the sky?'[6] Even
though at their root they are anthropogenic, the massive environmental
changes brought about by a changing climate dwarf individual human
agency to such a degree that even Hollywood seems to have trouble coming
up with a plausible hero's journey.

This does not mean that no filmmaker has ever tried. One of the first and by many counts still the most influential and successful of cli-fi movies was Roland Emmerich's sci-fi disaster film *The Day After Tomorrow*. Like no other filmmaker to date, Emmerich uses the representational power of film to translate abstract scientific notions about our changing climate into spectacular images of a hostile nature and a melodramatic story about a paleo-climatologist and his teenage son who get separated in the cataclysmic events that follow the stalling of the Atlantic Meridional Overturning Circulation. As is typical for Hollywood action movies, both father and son are idealised heroes who must overcome seemingly unsurmountable obstacles before they can be reunited in the end. Quaid's Cassandra-like scientist tries everything he can to warn the world of the coming climate catastrophe. And when that fails, he tries to save as many people as he can, including his son. Those who believe him – like his son – have a chance to survive the abrupt and drastic climate shift, and those who doubt him – like the American government – are doomed. At the end of the film, the new US President (and former Vice President) is forced to admit that he 'was wrong' to ignore scientific insights in the reckless pursuit of economic growth. He has learned that by way of an onslaught of natural catastrophes that are only vaguely related to actual scientific projections but highly effective in engaging audiences on the visceral level in an entertaining cinematic spectacle of doom and disaster. While the central cause of the chain of disasters depicted in the film – the stalling of the Atlantic Meridional Overturning Circulation – is an actual scientific scenario that in recent years has received renewed attention due to the so-called 'cold blob' in the North Atlantic, the spectacular tornados, tidal wave, and sub-zero storms freezing everything on contact are not part of that scenario.[7]

The film thus perfectly fits Schneider-Mayerson's description of 'a typical example of American climate fiction: a cautionary tale of a quasi-apocalyptic climate-changed near-future, intended to dramatize what might happen if readers [or viewers] do not intervene in the present to slow climate change'.[8] And much to the surprise of those who criticised the film, that tale was actually quite effective. Empirical research has shown that *The Day After Tomorrow* 'had a significant impact on the climate change risk perceptions, conceptual models, behavioral intentions, policy priorities, and even voting intentions of moviegoers' in the United States and elsewhere in the world.[9] These unexpected results led researchers and science communicators to rethink the role of popular culture in climate change communication for the very reason that it engages people's emotions in ways that traditional science communication cannot tap into.[10] And so it is perhaps not surprising Emmerich's film was still used by science communicators ten years after its release as a means to engage and connect with the general public, precisely because it is so drastic in its depiction of climate change and so entertaining.[11] Ecocritics have analysed its narrative strategies, drawing attention to the way it uses visual spectacle and a melodramatic family-reunion narrative to engage viewer emotions.[12] And it is important to note that many of those emotions are positive even though the underlying scenario is catastrophic. In fact, the enticing combination of excitement, awe, admiration, and curiosity is one of the reasons why viewers enjoy the dark worlds of action-driven cli-fi films like *The Day After Tomorrow*.[13]

However, few other films fit Schneider-Mayerson's definition of climate fiction to the same degree. Movies like *Snowpiercer, Mad Max Fury Road*, and *Interstellar* (2014) all feature 'quasi-apocalyptic climate-changed near-future[s]', but whether they understand themselves as 'cautionary tales' or are read that way by viewers is a different question.[14] Unfortunately, we still do not know enough about what exactly audiences take away from watching cli-fi films, but a recent study by Helena Bilandzic and Freya Sukalla suggests that even movies that are less openly moralising than *The Day After Tomorrow* can have an impact on intentions for pro-environmental behaviour.[15] The study focuses on Tim Fehlbaum's near-future science fiction film *Hell* (2011), which imagines the cannibalistic consequences of a dysfunctional biosphere in ways that are reminiscent of John Hillcoat's *The Road* (2009), only in this case it is not the lack of sunlight that causes the problem, but an overabundance of it.[16] Even though climate change is front and centre in this German-Swiss film, it remains unclear whether the drastic conditions it depicts were caused by human activities. All we learn is that solar radiation has increased to a point where it is dangerous to go outside and that water has become as scarce as food in this future world. The lethal power of the sun is made visceral for viewers through the overexposed, dusty look of the images, the actors' physical performances of suffering, and the desiccated worlds around them. But as in *The Road*, the worst enemies in this hostile world are other humans who are so starved that they have taken to slaughtering humans like animals. And, as in *The Road*, viewers are cued to empathise with the film's protagonists, who try to escape the cannibals and hope to get to a place on Earth that is still somewhat more liveable.[17]

Unlike *The Day After Tomorrow*, then, *Hell* does not make any overt link between scientific scenarios regarding CO_2 emissions and global warming, and the nightmarish future world it depicts. Bilandzic and Sukalla's study shows that the film nevertheless had an 'indirect effect on behavioral intentions by raising the personal norm (a sense of personal obligation to act)'.[18] Moreover, narrative engagement in the film also had an indirect effect on such intentions by increasing guilt, which the researchers were able to link directly to their subjects' narrative engagement. 'The more the audience was cognitively and emotionally involved with the narrative', observe Bilandzic and Sukalla, 'the more they experienced the moral emotion of guilt that results in stronger intentions to act'.[19] Cognitive and emotional involvement – involving a sense of immersion or transportation into the cinematic storyworld – was an important driver for attitude and potential behaviour change, a result that is consistent with other research in social psychology and media communication.[20] One lesson, then, that we can learn from the empirical studies of *The Day After Tomorrow* and *Hell* is that climate fiction does not have to be scientifically accurate or even explicit about the cause of the climate change it depicts in order to have an impact. Secondly, as I have argued elsewhere, it seems to be misguided to assume that the cueing of negative or even painful emotions (such as guilt) is necessarily problematic or leads to an apathetic disengagement from the issue, in particular if such emotions are cued in conjunction with more positive emotions such as curiosity, hope, admiration, and amusement, as is the case in most fiction films.[21]

Precisely this argument has been made repeatedly, however, by journalists and climatologists alike, who complain about the tendency to frame climate change narratives in negative, dystopian or even (post-)apocalyptic terms.[22] Ecocritics such as Nicole Seymour have argued that a more playful and ironical stance may be more effective than the overly 'serious affective modes' we find in many environmentally oriented films.[23] 'Even when leavened by a dose of humour', writes Seymour, these films 'tend to be underwritten by earnest beliefs' and thus 'solicit serious affective responses from viewers, such as reverence, guilt, dread, and conviction'.[24] As Bilandzic and Sukalla have shown, such serious affective responses may not be ineffective, but Seymour nevertheless urges critics and filmmakers to embrace more irreverent approaches, arguing that they 'can foster a self-critical attitude that does not hinder but in fact enables environmentalist work'.[25] Her examples of films that employ irony include Daniel Gold and Judith Helfand's climate change documentary *Everything's Cool* (2007), to which we could add Laura Gabbert and Justin Schein's *No Impact Man* (2009), Simon Lamb's *Thin Ice* (2011), and Kip Andersen and Keegan Kuhn's *Cowspiracy* (2014).[26] But in the end, these films, too, remain 'underwritten by earnest beliefs' and a serious desire to move viewers to become more climate-conscious and, ideally, adopt a more sustainable lifestyle.

True irreverence, or 'bad environmentalism', as Seymour has called it in her recent book, may indeed be hard to find among filmmakers who invest time, effort, and money to make a film about climate change.[27] But in recent years there have been a string of documentaries that are a little more radical in their affective approach without sacrificing sincerity. Instead of just throwing in some irony to cut the edge off their dire message, these films aim to provide what everyone seems to be waiting for these days: positive, utopian visions of the future. Such visions, the argument goes, can cut through apathy and fear by instilling in us both the hope for a better and more sustainable future and the belief that such a development is realistic and achievable. Pessimists might argue that the very combination of those two attributes – hope and realism – makes the creation of such visions an impossibility because climate change has already advanced too far. But a number of documentary filmmakers have nevertheless embraced what the German philosopher Ernst Bloch called concrete utopianism – 'the unfinished forward dream' – and employed it in their cinematic visions for the future.[28] And as it turns out, such visions can even be funny and (self-)ironic.

Looking on the Bright Side: From Intentional Communities to Ecotopian Visions

When looking at the utopianism of recent climate change films, it is important to keep in mind Bloch's differentiation between 'abstract' and 'concrete' utopias. While the former is a form of escapism and has compensatory functions, Bloch understands the latter as a form of social dreaming that has 'the power of anticipation' and serves as a potentially transformative 'methodical organ for the New, an objective aggregate state for what is coming up'.[29] As such, it is entwined with hope rather than just with the desire for a better way of being. Diana Fritz Cates reminds us that 'we hope only in what we regard as possible', meaning that our utopian projects are always circumscribed by 'limits of knowledge and imagination, partial perspectives, self-interest biases, [and] the consequences of previous, poor choices'.[30] It also means, however, that in order to truly hope rather than just desire, we need to believe that something might actually happen. And so a climate change film that wants to instil not only the desire for a better future but also the hope that it can be attained needs to convey that there are realistic ways of achieving this goal by anchoring itself in the realities of the present.

An incomplete list of films that aim to do this includes Josh Fox's *How to Let Go of the World* (2016), Cyril Dion and Mélanie Laurent's *Demain* (*Tomorrow*, 2016), Damon Gameau's *2040* (2019), and the 2019 HBO documentary *Ice on Fire*, directed by Leila Conners.[31] Instead of dwelling on the potential horrors of the upcoming climate disaster with only the last few minutes focusing on possible solutions to the crisis, as many other climate change documentaries have done, these recent films try out a different approach. In a way, they turn that narrative strategy on its head by dedicating most of their running time to exploring possible solutions and featuring people who are *already* working on these solutions.

The French film *Demain* is a particularly interesting example. The filmmakers – the actress Mélanie Laurent and the civic activist Cyril Dion – take their viewers, for example, to the urban gardens of Detroit and Todmorden; to San Francisco to take a look at the city's advanced recycling and composting programme; to an organic permaculture farm in Normandy; to an envelope factory in Lille which reinvests its profits to make the company more ecologically sustainable; and to Copenhagen, which boasts an admirable renewable energy model and pervasive cycling culture. While the filmmakers are present in their film and – as young parents of a small child – serve as identification figures for viewers who are worried about the prospects of the next generation, it is the people whom they visit during their global quest for solutions that invite hope and admiration. Most of them are 'normal' citizens who have been able to make a difference at the local level, not only in their own lives but also in their communities. In their conversations with Laurent and Dion, they make clear that it takes guts, tenacity, and often also a healthy dose of humour to start doing things differently from the way they were previously done and convince others to follow in your footsteps. The other lesson that can be learned from the featured projects is that they build a sense of community and instil feelings of hope, pride, and confidence in participants.

The uplifting affective dimension of *Demain* has been of central importance to its warm reception. The focus on concrete solutions is 'refreshing', writes Nicole Herrington in her review for the *New York Times*, but the film's 'real triumph is its pervasive feeling of hope'.[32] It is a feeling that indeed seems to have been 'infectious', as Herrington predicted.[33] *Demain* has earned over 11 million dollars at the box office – which is quite remarkable for a crowdfunded documentary film – and was screened at places like COP 21, the European Parliament, and the United Nations.[34] Even more remarkable in terms of tangible impact, however, is the fact that it encouraged so many viewers to start working on small-scale solutions themselves that Dion ended up shooting a sequel, entitled *Après-Demain* (2018), which showcased some of the more than 1,000 projects directly inspired by the film.[35] While this is not a peer-reviewed scientific study of narrative impact, it is an impressive practical demonstration of what a film can do if it manages to inspire individuals and communities to take action.

A more recent and equally remarkable example of this new trend in climate change cinema is the Australian film *2040*, which deftly combines fact and fiction in a way that is reminiscent of *The Age of Stupid*.[36] Unlike

Armstrong's film, however, *2040* is unabashedly optimistic in outlook. As Damon Gameau explained in an interview at the 2019 Berlin Film Festival, he conceived *2040* as:

> an antidote to all the doom-and-gloom, dystopian narratives about the future that we find at the moment ... I just felt like ... there is another option. We don't have to just march blindly into that future. That it's important to throw up different visions of the future and especially around the climate, which feels a bit helpless at the moment and people don't know what to do. That there are solutions and there are great people doing amazing things around the world. So can we shift that spotlight away from the fear and the doom-and-gloom and put it onto promoting these people who are doing the right things?[37]

Just like *Demain*, then, *2040* focuses on individuals and communities who are *already* engaged in activities that – if adopted by more people around the world – would significantly curb CO_2 emissions and make communities more resilient to climate change. In indirect reference to Bloch, Gameau's film calls such activities 'fact-based dreaming' which, just like Bloch's idea of concrete utopianism, is not based on the purely hypothetical but on an 'extrapolation of what people already do now'.[38] Where *2040* differs somewhat from *Demain* is in its tone and in the overall presentation of the climate-friendly lifestyles it portrays.

Like Laurent, Gameau is an actor-turned-documentary-filmmaker. The success of his first documentary, *That Sugar Film* (2015), taught him that a more humorous and playful approach can work well when dealing with serious issues (in this case, the detrimental effects of sugar on human health), which is why *2040*, too, relies on humour to loosen up its environmental message.[39] Following a conviction that seems to resonate with Seymour's call for a more 'irreverent' ecocinema, Gameau suggests that 'if we really want to engage a family and get the conversation going then ... it's important to have elements of fun and playful[ness]' because 'people are more open to learning and listening when they are engaged and there is something new to look at' since 'you're activating a different part of your brain'.[40] This implicit reliance on the insights of cognitive psychology shows that documentary filmmakers have begun to consider human 'hardware' – a.k.a. the ways in which our brains are wired – when they conceptualise films to not only entertain but also teach. In another interview, Gameau explains that he learned from an environmental psychologist that getting constantly bombarded with fear-inducing messages will lead us to 'shut down parts of our brain that are problem-solving areas or creative thinking areas' and that this in turn makes it 'very hard getting people to act on this topic'.[41] His documentary tries to avoid such cerebral shutdowns not only by avoiding fear-inducing messages but also by extrapolating current experiments in sustainable living into the future, using acting and animation to showcase what life in 2040 might look like if everyone would embrace them.

The use of animation is nothing new in the genre of climate change documentaries. *An Inconvenient Truth*, *The Age of Stupid*, and *Cowspiracy* are all examples of earlier films that include animation to help viewers envision future states of the world. However, instead of flooded coastlines, drowning polar bears, and burning cities, 2040 shows what places could look like if we did the *right* thing. In addition to allowing viewers (and Paul Hawken) to enjoy the pastoral view from the top of a wind turbine, it presents them with time-lapse animations that show urban freeways converted to pedestrian-filled linear parks and tar sand oil fields growing thousands of trees until they are covered in lush green. While these enticing visions of the future are designed to cue desire in viewers, the concrete portrayals of current efforts in that direction are meant to show that these optimistic future states are, in fact, achievable. 'The key purpose of 2040', says Gameau, 'was to install hope in people' in the Blochian sense.[42]

That perhaps explains the film's explicit focus on children.[43] Not only was 2040 conceptualised as a family film, but it also puts children at the centre of its narrative. This is most obvious in the ostensible addressee of the film, which is framed as a letter to Gameau's four-year-old daughter Velvet. Not only is the real Velvet frequently featured in the film, but so is the actress that plays Velvet as a 25-year-old in the film's version of the year 2040. There, she emerges as a contented young woman who enjoys the advantages of an ecologically sustainable way of life and, when learning about the lifestyle of the 2010s, incredulously asks her middle-aged parents, 'What were you thinking?'. That Gameau and his wife – who is also an actor – play their own aged, future selves with the help of make-up and animation demonstrates his unorthodox and extremely hybrid approach to climate change storytelling. It is an approach that invites viewer identification from at least two age groups. The parental generation might identify with Gameau and his wife, who are desperate to find out about ways to secure a sustainable future for their daughter. In this way, the film very much mirrors the narrative strategies of *Demain*. In addition, however, 2040 also invites younger viewers to identify – if not with the four-year-old Velvet then with her twenty-five-year-old alter ego, who lives a 'normal' life in an attractive-looking future instead of the catastrophic one that many of them fear, in part because of the dystopian media representations with which they have grown up.[44] That the ecological awareness of this generation is much higher than that of any generation before them at their age is demonstrated in the short statements from young children that are interspersed throughout the film, which are often thoughtful and sometimes funny. They are all shot in close-up before a neutral grey background, allowing viewers to fully focus their attention on the face of the respective child and their personal visions for 2040. And, as the critical and commercial success of Benh Zeitlin's brilliant low-budget film *Beats of the Southern Wild* (2012) has demonstrated, putting the emotions of children at the heart of a story about climate change and environmental injustice can be emotionally powerful also for older audiences.[45]

Even though *2040* has not enjoyed the extraordinary global success of *Beasts of the Southern Wild* or that of *Demain*, Gameau's film was well received in Australia and has won several awards. Perhaps unsurprisingly, its unabashedly optimistic display of an ecotopian future has also been criticised for being wilfully ignorant and somewhat naïve. 'It's understandable why the film-maker didn't want to get bogged down in tackling those awfully adult, awfully sobering ideas of vested interests', writes Luke Buckmaster in his review for *The Guardian*, thus making clear that the utopian world seen in the film is unlikely to take shape within the foreseeable future.[46] Buckmaster's critique is justified, but it is also true, as Claudia Lenssen has observed, that *2040* provides viewers with vivid images of things they might have heard about but not have been able to picture in their minds, things such as decentralised energy generation, communalised electric transport systems, CO_2 sequestration, or the restoration of devastated marine environments.[47] And so it is telling that even Buckmaster's verdict is positive in the end. 'In *2040*', he writes, 'Gameau defaults to the position of inspiring people rather than alarming or overwhelming them. You leave the film wanting more, not less, of these sorts of productions'.[48]

The use of humour and ecotopian visions of the future is, of course, not limited to documentaries, but it is still a rare combination in fiction film. One of the few examples is Alexander Payne's science fiction comedy *Downsizing* (2017), starring Matt Damon, Christoph Waltz, and Kristen Wiig.[49] Rather than providing viewers with another doomsday scenario, *Downsizing* imagines a future world where people can choose to be shrunk to a height of five inches, thereby minimising their ecological footprint while maximising the housing and consumer goods they can afford. A light-hearted social satire with occasional (mis)steps towards the decidedly weird, the film checks many of the boxes that Seymour considers definitive of a new, irreverent form of environmental storytelling. Despite its major star power, however, it flopped at the box office.[50] Reviewers have speculated that its poor showing was related precisely to the fact that instead of the usual dramatic dystopian fare, it provides viewers with a vaguely utopian vision that, in the end, is boring.[51] However, one could also make the argument that – as long as we have not figured out how to shrink people to the height of five inches – the film envisions an abstract rather than a concrete utopia and thus at best qualifies as escapism instead of harnessing 'the power of anticipation' as *Demain* and *2040* aim to do.[52] If it is true that people are desperate for actual solutions to the climate crisis, then *Downsizing* does not qualify as a film that imagines such solutions for them. This might have contributed to the mediocre reviews and poor box office of the film.

Conclusion

A closer look at how climate has been featured on cinema screens shows that the situation is not nearly as bad as journalists and scholars seem to assume when complaining about the overly serious and/or apocalyptic tone of climate change cinema. The affective registers of such films have diversified much more in recent years than is often acknowledged. What is arguably still missing is a greater diversity in terms of both the filmmakers themselves and the communities they portray. While both *Demain* and *2040* showcase sustainable practices in communities around the world, these films are firmly anchored in Western worldviews. And even documentaries that focus exclusively on non-Western and non-white communities, such as Briar March's *There Once Was an Island* (2010), John Shenk's *The Island President* (2011), and Matthieu Rytz's *Anote's Ark* (2018), were made by filmmakers who are outsiders to these communities. There are exceptions to this rule, such as Zacharias Kunuk's *Inuit Knowledge and Climate Change* (2010), but, aside from film festivals, they rarely make it to the big screen.[53] This is unfortunate, since not only can such films provide alternative perspectives on the social and ecological repercussions of climate change, they also use different narrative techniques that might engage viewers differently on the emotional level.

This also means that we should not jump to conclusions about which affective registers are most effective or assume that one such register fits all audiences. As David Roberts has pointed out, we do not even know yet whether hope inspires more action on climate change than fear, since the scientific evidence on this matter is still inconclusive.[54] But what seems to be certain is that different affective approaches can speak to different audiences or even to the very same spectator at different times of their life journey. Those who still believe that climate change does not exist, or that it will not ever affect them and their loved ones personally, might be shocked into awareness by more dystopian modes of narration, be it in fiction or non-fiction film. Others might be so saturated with the doom and gloom that what they need to move forward is a glimmer of hope and concrete information about how they can personally make a change in their life and inspire others to do the same. It is thus a sign of hope that climate change cinema is increasingly diversifying to offer a wide range of approaches on how to represent, communicate, and possibly tackle, climate change.

Acknowledgements

Research carried out with support from the project 'Cinema and Environment: Affective Ecologies in the Anthropocene' (Reference PID2019-110068GA-I00 / AEI / 10.13039/501100011033).

Notes

1 R. Nixon, *Slow Violence and the Environmentalism of the Poor* (Cambridge, MA: Harvard University Press, 2013).
2 See, for example, P. Willoquet-Maricondi, 'Shifting Paradigms: From Environmentalist Films to Ecocinema', in Willoquet-Maricondi (ed.), *Framing the World: Explorations in Ecocriticism and Film* (Charlottesville: University of Virginia Press, 2010), 43–60.
3 *The Day After Tomorrow*, dir. R. Emmerich (Twentieth-Century Fox, 2004); *Snowpiercer*, dir. Bong Joon-ho (Weinstein Company, 2013); *Mad Max Fury Road*, dir. by G. Miller (Roadshow Films, 2015).
4 M. Schneider-Mayerson, 'Climate Change Fiction', in R. Greenwald Smith (ed.), *American Literature in Transition: 2000–2010* (Cambridge University Press, 2017), 309.
5 M. Svoboda, 'Cli-Fi on the Screen(s): Patterns in the Representations of Climate Change in Fictional Films', *WIREs Climate Change* 7.1 (2016), 43–64.
6 R. Lawson, 'When Will Hollywood Actually Tackle Climate Change?', *Vanity Fair* (19 September 2019).
7 S. Rahmstorf *et al.*, 'Exceptional Twentieth-Century Slowdown in Atlantic Ocean Overturning Circulation', *Nature Climate Change* 5 (2015), 475–80.
8 M. Schneider-Mayerson, '"Just as in the Book"? The Influence of Literature on Readers' Awareness of Climate Justice and Perception of Climate Migrants', *ISLE: Interdisciplinary Studies in Literature and Environment* 27.2 (2020), 327–64.
9 A. Leiserowitz, 'Before and after *The Day After Tomorrow*: A U.S. Study of Climate Risk Perception', *Environment* 46.9 (2004), 34; see also F. Reusswig, 'The International Impact of *The Day After Tomorrow*', *Environment* 46.9 (2004), 43.
10 D. R. Abbasi, 'Americans and Climate Change: Closing the Gap between Science and Action', *Forestry & and Environmental Publication Series* 3 (2006).
11 M. Svoboda, 'The Long Melt: The Lingering Influence of *The Day After Tomorrow*', *Yale Climate Connections* (5 November 2014).
12 For detailed ecocritical analyses of *The Day After Tomorrow*, see D. Ingram, 'Hollywood Cinema and Climate Change: *The Day After Tomorrow*', in M. Devine and C. Grewe-Volpp (eds.), *Words on Water: Literary and Cultural Representations* (Wissenschaftlicher Verlag Trier, 2005), 53–63; R. L. Murray and J. K. Heumann, *Ecology and Popular Film: Cinema on the Edge* (Albany: State University of New York Press, 2009); A. Weik von Mossner, *Affective Ecologies:*

Empathy, Emotion, and Environmental Narrative (Columbus: Ohio State University Press, 2017).

13 Weik von Mossner, *Affective Ecologies*, 158.

14 Schneider-Mayerson, 'Climate Change Fiction', 309.

15 H. Bilandzic and F. Sukalla, 'The Role of Fictional Film Exposure and Narrative Engagement for Personal Norms, Guilt and Intentions to Protect the Climate', *Environmental Communication* 13.8 (2019), 1.

16 *Hell*, dir. T. Fehlbaum (Paramount Pictures, 2011); *The Road*, dir. J. Hillcoat (Dimension Films, 2009).

17 For a detailed analysis of the film's narrative and emotionalizing strategies, see Weik von Mossner, 'Visceralizing Ecocide in Science Fiction Films: *The Road* and *Hell*', *Ecozon@: European Journal of Literature, Culture, and Environment* 3.2 (2012), 42–56.

18 Bilandzic and Sukalla, 'Role of Fictional Film Exposure', 1.

19 Bilandzic and Sukalla, 'Role of Fictional Film Exposure', 1.

20 See, for example, M. C. Green and T. C. Brock, 'The Role of Transportation in the Persuasiveness of Public Narratives', *Journal of Personality and Social Psychology* 79 (2000), 701–21; P. J. Mazzocco *et al.*, 'This Story Is Not for Everyone: Transportability and Narrative Persuasion', *Social Psychology and Personality Science* 1.4 (2010), 361–8.

21 These positive emotions can be cued by a number of elements in the film, be it dramatic tension or viewers' empathic relationship to the protagonists of the film; Weik von Mossner, 'Climate Change and the Dark Side of Translating Science into Popular Culture', in F. Italiano (ed.), *The Dark Side of Translation* (London: Routledge, 2020), 111–25. On the mix of negative and positive emotions in fiction films, see also C. Plantinga, 'Trauma, Pleasure, and Emotion in the Viewing of *Titanic*: A Cognitive Approach', in W. Buckland (ed.), *Film Theory and Contemporary Hollywood Movies* (London: Routledge, 2009), 237–56.

22 Such arguments abounded in the media response to David Wallace-Wells's 2017 article 'The Uninhabitable Earth', *New York Magazine* (9 July 2017).

23 N. Seymour, 'Irony and Contemporary Ecocinema: Theorizing a New Affective Paradigm', in A. Weik von Mossner (ed.), *Moving Environments: Affect, Emotion, Ecology, and Film* (Waterloo, ON: Wilfrid Laurier University Press, 2014), 61.

24 Seymour, 'Irony and Contemporary Ecocinema', 61.

25 Seymour, 'Irony and Contemporary Ecocinema', 62.

26 *Everything's Cool*, dir. J. Helfand and D. B. Gold (City Lights Pictures, 2007); *No Impact Man*, dir. L. Gabbert and J. Schein (Eden Wurmfeld Films, 2009): *Thin Ice*, dir. S. Lamb and D. Sington (Green Planet Films, 2013); *Cowspiracy: The Sustainability Secret*, dir. K. Andersen and K. Kuhn (Appian Way Productions, 2014).

27 N. Seymour, *Bad Environmentalism: Irony and Irreverence in the Ecological Age* (Minneapolis: University of Minnesota Press, 2018).

28 E. Bloch, *The Principle of Hope*, trans. N. Plaice *et al.* (Cambridge, MA: MIT Press, 1986), 157.

29 Bloch, *Principle of Hope*, 157.

30 D. F. Cates. 'Hope, Hatred and the Ambiguities of Utopic Longing', in D. Boscaljon (ed.), *Hope and the Longing for Utopia: Futures and Illusions in Theology and Narrative* (Cambridge: James Clarke, 2015), 25.

31 *How to Let Go of the World and Love the Things the Climate Can't Change*, dir. J. Fox (HBO, 2016); *Demain (Tomorrow)*, dir. C. Dion and M. Laurent (Mars Films, 2015); *An Inconvenient Sequel: Truth to Power*, dir. B. Cohen and J. Shenk (Paramount, 2017); *Ice on Fire*, dir. L. Conners (HBO, 2019).

32 N. Herrington, 'Review: Worried about a Sustainable Tomorrow? There's Hope', *New York Times* (19 April 2017).

33 Herrington, 'Worried'.

34 For the film's box office record, see Box Office Mojo: www.boxofficemojo.com /release/rl3053487617/.

35 *Après-Demain*, dir. C. Dion (Mars Films, 2018).

36 *2040*, dir. D. Gameau (Madman Entertainment, 2019).

37 'Damon Gameau Interview: *2040* at Berlin Film Festival 2019', *The Upcoming* (24 February 2016), www.youtube.com/watch?v=zlqmNNKMj4Y.

38 'Damon Gameau Interview'.

39 *That Sugar Film*, dir. D. Gameau (Madman Entertainment, 2015).

40 'Damon Gameau Interview'.

41 'Interview: Damon Gameau', *Cinema Australia* (29 April 2019), www.youtube .com/watch?v=ngcNZb4cOh4.

42 'Interview: Damon Gameau'.

43 '*2040*: Behind the Scenes', *Screen News* (21 May 2019), www.youtube.com /watch?v=iATxyo-NQK8.

44 J. Plautz, 'The Environmental Burden of Generation Z: Kids Are Terrified, Anxious and Depressed about Climate Change. Whose Fault Is That?', *Washington Post* (3 February 2020).

45 *Beasts of the Southern Wild*, dir. B. Zeitlin (Fox Searchlight, 2012).

46 L. Buckmaster, '*2040* Review – An Idealist's Vision of a Healthy Earth', *The Guardian* (4 April 2019).

47 C. Lenssen, 'Kritik zu *2040* – Wir Retten die Welt', *EPD Film* (25 October 2019).

48 Buckmaster, '*2040* Review'.

49 *Downsizing*, dir. A. Payne (Paramount, 2017).

50 *Downsizing* had a budget of $68,000,000 and earned $55,003,890 worldwide, '*Downsizing*', *Box Office Mojo*, www.boxofficemojo.com/release/rl628917761/.

51 D. Sims, 'Downsizing Has Big Ambitions but Little Payoff', *The Atlantic* (December 22, 2017), www.theatlantic.com/entertainment/archive/2017/12/ downsizing-review/548966/.

52 Bloch, *Principle of Hope*, 157.

53 *There Once Was an Island*, dir. B. March (Roadshow, 2010); *The Island President*, dir. J. Shenk (Samuel Goldwyn Films, 2011); *Anote's Ark*, dir. M. Rytz (Eyesteel Film, 2018); *Inuit Knowledge and Climate Change*, dir. Z. Kunuk and I. Mauro (Isuma, 2010).

54 D. Roberts, 'Does Hope Inspire More Action on Climate Change than Fear? We Don't Know', *Vox* (5 December 2017).

PART IV

Dialogic Perspectives on Emerging Questions

Science Fiction and Future Fantasies

II

GERRY CANAVAN

Ice-Sheet Collapse and the Consensus Apocalypse in the Science Fiction of Kim Stanley Robinson

In his 1970 book *The Universe Makers: Science Fiction Today*, long-time science fiction editor Donald A. Wollheim identifies what he calls the consensus cosmogony of Golden Age science fiction: the story of an inexorable march of progress that leads human beings off Earth to settle the surrounding planets of our solar system, then the neighbouring stars, and then the entire future across the Golden Age.[1] Such narratives range from Isaac Asimov's *Foundation* (original stories, 1942–1950) to Frank Herbert's *Dune* (1965), but Gene Roddenberry's film and television franchise *Star Trek* (1966–) may well be the most influential, as it combines technological progress with an ethos of liberal-humanist social progress to imagine a utopian Federation of Planets, a sort of Galactic Republic instead of a militaristic or autocratic Galactic Empire.[2] For many years the consensus future was assumed by those both inside and outside the science fiction genre to be the inevitable future of the human race, with only the possibility of global atomic war threatening to pre-empt our rightful colonisation of the stars; prognosticators frequently put the dates of early interplanetary missions within the projected lifespans of their audiences, à la Stanley Kubrick and Arthur C. Clarke's *2001: A Space Odyssey* (1968), or Philip K. Dick's *Do Androids Dream of Electric Sheep?* (1968), the inspiration for *Blade Runner*, set in 1992 in the original novel and in 2019 in the film, both dates now safely in the past with no off-world colonies yet in sight.

Now, the consensus future was by no means unreservedly optimistic, and indeed became less so as the post-war period went on and the techno-optimism of the Golden Age gave way to the much more dyspeptic and cynical 'New Wave' in the late 1960s and 1970s. Even an extremely utopian storyworld like *Star Trek*'s includes a devastating thermonuclear war in the early twenty-first century as one significant road bump on the path to utopia, while the much bleaker *Do Androids Dream of Electric Sheep?* includes not only a nuclear war but the mass extinction of nearly all non-human life on Earth as a consequence. Even earlier Golden Age works, like Asimov's, contain sour notes of pessimism and doubt. Wollheim identifies an eight-stage cycle for extraplanetary expansion that includes the collapse of the first Galactic Empire (stage five), a lengthy, perhaps millennia-long dark age of backslide and collapse (stage six), followed by the renewal of intergalactic community in the founding of a Second Empire, imagined to be freed of the flaws that doomed the first one (stage seven). It is this seventh stage, along with the eighth stage, 'The Challenge to God . . . the effort to match Creation and solve the last secrets of the universe', that establishes the consensus cosmogony as finally optimistic, despite the possibility of an uneven path for progress along the way; in the consensus future of the Golden Age, there is literally nothing outside humankind's grasp, no achievement our creative ingenuity can't realise, and no problem that our amazing technological acumen ultimately can't solve.[3]

The nagging doubts about the consensus future, always present but becoming louder and louder towards the end of the 1960s, become all-encompassing in the New Wave period and after, as the failure of the space programme to inaugurate a cycle of permanent human settlement of outer space and the environmental movement's recognition of the severe damage being done to the environment by the forces of technological modernity combine to show us a future that seems permanently confined to a single planet that appears to be dying at our hands. Climate change – the rapid escalation, in geological terms, of average global temperatures as a consequence of widespread fossil-fuel use – is only the most urgent contemporary marker of the global ecological crisis that has become our negative version of the consensus future; posited as early as the mid 1800s, and formally quantified by the Swedish scientist Svante Arrhenius in 1896, the reality of the greenhouse effect has been a matter of scientific consensus since the 1970s, with the evidence becoming only more undeniable since then.

In this way, the consensus future has given way to something that might be called the *consensus apocalypse*: where the old consensus future seemed to promise unlimited possibilities for humankind, the future now appears to us to be a site of ever-worsening catastrophe and collapse. Even something as closely tied to the optimism of the original consensus future as *Star Trek* has succumbed to this spirit of ecological pessimism. Since the 1990s the series has revealed that warp drive tears holes in spacetime (*The Next Generation*: 'Forces of Nature', 1993), while the so-called spore drive on *Star Trek: Discovery* (2017–) causes damage to the mycelial network on which it depends; then, while other entries have seen planetary catastrophes destroy the Klingon, Romulan, and Vulcan homeworlds in short succession, on *Picard* (2020–) an increasingly bedraggled Federation seems to be rapidly heading towards that stage-five moment of fracture and final collapse, an era of deflation and failure we see dramatised in *Discovery*'s third season (also 2020).[4]

A survey of science fiction since the 1970s likewise sees a similar ongoing revision of the optimism of the consensus future, in terms that only grow more jaundiced and more deflationary as time goes on. The terms of this consensus apocalypse can be allegorical – one need think only of the many nightmare futures of robot rebellion, from *Terminator* (1984) to *The Matrix* (1999) – or they can be quite literalised, as in the familiar ruined planetary ecologies of *Soylent Green* (1973), *WALL-E* (2008), the *Blade Runner* duology (1982 and 2017), *Interstellar* (2014) or the Mad Max series (1979–2015) (to focus only on blockbuster films, and to only begin to name them). Even Asimov – whose Foundation series Wollheim so closely identifies with the optimism of the consensus cosmogony that he suggests it, along with Olaf Stapledon's *Star Maker* (1937), as its originary ur-text – ultimately revises the terms of the series away from the wild technological optimism of the Golden Age 'Galactic Empire' to something much more environmentally minded. In *Foundation's Edge* (1982), a return to the series written more than thirty years after the original Foundation stories, the main character chooses to inaugurate a galactic-level communal superorganism called Galaxia, with a single collective consciousness, as a radically posthuman future for the human race, rather than pursue the establishment of the Second Empire whose 'Encyclopaedia Galactica' is quoted in the other books in the series – an internal plot contradiction left unresolved by Asimov's death in 1992. In *Robots and Empire* (1985), we even discover that the Galactic Empire only came into existence in the first place because robots, sensing that humankind would never permanently settle the cosmos of its own free will, deliberately poisoned the Earth's crust with radioactive poison to force us to leave. The robots take this extreme action because they are hardwired to protect us, and want to insure species immortality by spreading us across many worlds – at the cost of abandoning the one place in all the universe where we most belong. In this way, the old consensus future and ecological consciousness of the environmental movement can be seen to be locked in fundamental, irresolvable conflict in post-60s science fiction – with the ecological mode, however panicked and apocalyptic, typically winning out.

One place where we can strongly see this collision of the old consensus future with the new consensus apocalypse is in the work of Kim Stanley

Robinson, long regarded (somewhat paradoxically) as one of the most utopian thinkers in contemporary science fiction as well as one of the most ecologically minded. This paradox between the utopian and the ecological is by no means superficial: Robinson's fiction posits that revolutionary social change could transform the conditions of life on Planet Earth, while recognising first that the possibilities for this social change are deeply inflected by physical law and environmental realism and second that the ongoing deterioration of the planetary ecology due to relentless capitalist expansion is constraining the sorts of changes we yet might make, while at the same time making the need for those changes much more urgent by the year. The long arc of Robinson's works traces this dialectical relationship with political hope; while his earliest works (*Icehenge* [1984] and *The Memory of Whiteness* [1985]) depict comparatively old-style techno-optimistic expansions of human civilisation into the larger solar system, and the Mars trilogy (1992–96) for which he is still best known perfects this vision of outer-space colonisation going hand-in-hand with social progress, his most recent works exhibit a much more halting relationship with the future, with both the environmental situation and the prospects for political revolution subject to unhappy reversal and collapse. The remainder of this chapter explores how deeply the intensifying prospect of ecological collapse informs the (increasingly retreating) possibilities for utopian social revolution in Robinson's fiction, with particular attention to an especially important recurring motif in his fiction, the spectre of ice-sheet collapse.

'A Lot of People Lived on the Coast': Robinson and Rising Sea Levels

For a global society in which 40 percent of the population lives within 100 kilometres of the ocean, with commerce on all continents deeply dependent on the presence of megacities on the coasts, ice-sheet collapse – the prospect of rapid, significant sea-level rise as a result of the displacement of frozen water from landlocked polar glaciers into the oceans – would augur a major catastrophe from which industrial civilisation might never fully recover. It may be a bit surprising, then, that, in Robinson's Mars trilogy, ice-sheet collapse is, from the perspective of the Martian colonists at least, an opportunity for them to break away from Earth's control and establish true political independence. In *Green Mars* (1993), this phenomenon is not even primarily the result of climate change; instead, a series of dormant volcanoes under Antarctica suddenly regains activity and destroys the ice sheet, flooding coastal cities and sending Earth into chaos, destabilising the planetary situation to such a degree that its inhabitants can no longer maintain their stranglehold on Martian politics. 'This catastrophic break will raise sea levels about two or three meters, in a matter of weeks', one scientist tells another in a rare Earthbound chapter appropriately called 'Phase Change': 'What's left of the sheet will be afloat in a matter of months, or a few years at most, and that will add another three meters'.[5]

Here, we see the possibility of climate apocalypse multiplied and displaced psychologically: the climate apocalypse becomes instead a geological event entirely out of human control, and even has salutary political effects despite the larger loss of life and the destruction of the economy (a displacement further exacerbated by the fact that all our point-of-view characters in the series are Martian colonists with few social ties to their home planet). For them, at a remove of 150 million miles, it is an opportunity for liberation. But the actual human cost to Earthlings is catastrophic:

> Bangladesh would have to be entirely evacuated; that was three hundred million people, not to mention the other coastal cities of India, like Calcutta, Madras, Bombay. Then London, Copenhagen, Istanbul, Amsterdam, New York, Los Angeles, New Orleans, Miami, Rio, Buenos Aires, Sydney, Melbourne, Singapore, Hong Kong, Manila, Djakarta, Tokyo ... and those were only the big ones. A lot of people lived on the coast, in a world already severely stressed by overpopulation and declining resources. And now all kinds of basic necessities were being drowned by salt water.[6]

In *Green Mars*, then, the apocalypse can thus still retain, however oxymoronically, some of that utopian kernel identified by Robinson's former dissertation advisor, Fredric Jameson, who has noted that, not only is it 'easier to imagine the end of the world than to imagine the end of capitalism', but also that 'We can now revise that and witness the attempt to imagine capitalism by way of imagining the end of the world'[7] – while safely inoculated from confronting the actual human toll. Indeed, the safety of our Martian heroes, removed as they are from the disaster by tens of millions of miles, becomes the justification for their inaction, much like the wealth and prosperity of the industrialised nations does in our own era:

> 'Sax,' she said, 'we should be helping them. Not just ... '
> 'There is not much that we can do. And we can do that best if we're free. First one, then the other.'
> 'You promise?'
> 'Yes,' he said, looking surprised. 'I mean – I'll do what I can.'[8]

The explosive crisis of ice-sheet collapse, while deeply terrible to people who are mostly offstage, retains an unexpected sense of disruptive utopian potentiality for the novel's protagonists, as the divine violence powerful enough to actually shake the foundations of power, control, and unfreedom that deform human society and poison its future.[9]

As I have suggested elsewhere, much of Robinson's post-Mars-trilogy career can be understood as an attempt to think through, and test, the implications of the Mars books by remixing different elements of their narratives and storyworlds. The ice-sheet collapse of *Green Mars* becomes one such topos, taking new forms again and again in the post-Mars novels. Robinson's next major long-form work of science fiction,[10] the 'Science in the Capital' trilogy (2004–07), eventually condensed and published as a single novel, *Green Earth* (2015), is a climate change story without the hopeful 'release valve' of extraplanetary colonisation; shifting the cause of potential ice-sheet collapse back to climate change, the trilogy posits a 'rapid' (but not outside the bounds of possibility) worst-case scenario in which climatological changes that are currently predicted to take decades or centuries happen instead over the course of just a few years. The detachment of the Antarctic Ice Sheet once again happens in the trilogy, deeply imperilling the world's coasts in an incredibly short period of time. But this remains the opportunity for a union of democratic institutions, finance capital, and scientific and engineering know-how to unite to save the planet – almost a kind of wake-up call allowing society to so completely transform itself that, as no less a figure than its fictional President of the United States Phil Chase prophesies, *'taking care of the Earth and its miraculous biological splendor will then become the long-term work of our species ... an ongoing project that will never end'*.[11]

In the next major phase of Robinson's career, this hope of miraculous, just-in-time reversal has become all the slimmer – and ice-sheet collapse accordingly becomes less and less the impetus for social revolution and more and more the major obstacle to it. By *2312* (2012) and *Aurora* (2015), the Mars books are even more explicitly being rewritten; whereas in the Mars trilogy, Mars was first settled by careful scientists who debate the proper level of environmental impact for quite literally hundreds of pages, ultimately settling on a compromise between total preservation and total human exploitation of the Red Planet, in *2312* Mars is maximally terraformed, resulting in an eighth of the planet being destroyed and the rest being made inhabitable by humans without spacesuit or any assistive device. Humans in *2312* live everywhere in the solar system, from Mercury to Pluto to the interiors of asteroids retrofitted into luxurious orbital mansions. In a sort of perverse confirmation of the fantasies of space-obsessed contemporary billionaires like Jeff Bezos and Elon Musk – a wider scale version of the sort of class divide depicted in Neill Blomkamp's 2013 film *Elysium* – outer space is a paradisal playground only for the rich. Earth, meanwhile, is a wreck – 'the planet of sadness'; the bulk of human population, its teeming, starving billions, lives on an increasingly impoverished and ecologically devastated homeworld:

> Clean tech came too late to save earth from the catastrophes of the early Anthropocene. It was one of the ironies of their time that they could radically change the surfaces of the other planets, but not Earth. The methods they employed in space were almost all too crude and violent. Only with the utmost caution could they tinker with anything on Earth.[12]

Here again we find Robinson preoccupied by ice-sheet collapse, with the 'inundation of the coasts ... one of the main drivers of the human disaster on Earth'. The terraforming techniques that made it possible to colonise the planets are too destructive to work on an inhabited world, leaving humans unable to fix the ecology of their home planet through the geoengineering that opened up the solar system to them – and yet despite its problems, Earth was 'still the center of the story. It had to be dealt with ... or nothing done in space was real'.[13]

The film 2312 thus depicts space colonisation as having occurred just when 'late capitalism writhed in its internal decision concerning whether to destroy Earth's biosphere or change its rules', with many arguing for the destruction of the planet as 'the lesser of two evils'.[14] Thus, the struggle of the protagonists of 2312 is in some sense to take a version of the old consensus future and take it back down to Earth to undo the consensus apocalypse, and to find some way that both might be true (if only so, the good future still has some time to fix the bad one).

In *Aurora* even *that* slender hope seems to recede into the distance. *Aurora* depicts interstellar colonists launched from Earth on a generational spaceship, in yet another version of the techno-optimistic 'Accelerando' that has characterised his vision of the future since the Mars trilogy. This intergenerational starship left the solar system in 2545; now, over 150 years later, the 2,122 descendants of the original explorers approach Tau Ceti, where probes have indicated Earth-like planets that can support terrestrial plant and animal life. The spaceship has always been an attractive metaphor for ecological thinking, a formulation Robinson perfects in the early sections of the novel, showing how the fantasy of outer-space colonisation is not some suspension of ecological rationality but instead requires total, absolute commitment to it.[15] Everything on the ship in *Aurora* is part of a tightly controlled biological-ecological machine that has been constructed inside a space that is simply too small and too overdetermined, with essentially zero external inputs, to ever work reliably; it functions, but only just barely, requiring constant correction and intervention from its human caretakers.

Their arrival on Tau Ceti offers a potential new horizon for exploration, but it is ultimately not a significant escape from these constraints: there's no reason to expect any extrasolar planet to be especially hospitable to terrestrial life, which evolved precisely *here*, on Earth, at precisely this distance from the sun, at this precise moment between ice ages.[16] The surface of another planet won't look like a California studio backlot or the Vasquez Rock formations where the original *Star Trek* was shot so often on location – it will look to us more like Antarctica, or the pock-marked surface of the moon, or the Mariana Trench, or Hell. The Tau Ceti colonists have been launched from Earth to undertake a task that would be almost unthinkably, unfathomably difficult, doomed to certain failure – a lunatic task, which Western civilisation has not only convinced itself is its destiny but which has been used to justify all manner of short-sighted, anti-ecological behaviours in the meantime.

Thus the twist that rocks *Aurora*, and that so upset many space opera partisans in the science-fictional fan community when it was published. Not only is the population of the intergenerational starship not especially happy that their great-grandparents launched them on this wild endeavour without their consent, and without considering what it would be like for them to grow up, live, and die, in such incredibly artificial conditions, unlike those any human has ever endured – but when they reach Tau Ceti they find out it is actually uninhabitable, compromised by prions (pre-bacteria lifeforms) that interfere with human biology and kill anyone who sets foot on the planet. A rump group of the colonists presses on, trying to continue their mission and find some place in the galaxy other than Earth that humans might call home, but the majority of the colonists choose to simply turn around and go back to Earth, concluding that the entire consensus future was itself just a fantasy, and that there will never be any place for us in the universe other than the place we already live. The narrative logic of the book seems to confirm this grim prognosis; the point of view of the novel follows the returners, and absolutely nothing is ever heard from the rump group again. The consensus future was a fantasy; the only future for humanity is here on Earth.

Manhattan as New Venice: *New York 2140*

It is perhaps fitting, then, that Robinson's next novel, *New York 2140* (2017), re-enacts the same narrative detachment from extraplanetary colonisation that the 'Science in the Capital' books did after the Mars trilogy. Here again we are exploring a terrestrial future without extraplanetary settlement, once again dominated by the prospect of ice-sheet collapse; with no one from outer space to save us, the question becomes whether we can save ourselves. *2140's* sardonic narrative voice gives us a history of the future in miniature:

> . . . the floods of the twenty-first century revealed a salient fact that wasn't very important before: lower Manhattan is indeed much lower than upper Manhattan, like by about fifty vertical feet on average. . . . The floods inundated New York harbour and every other coastal city around the world, mainly in two big surges that shoved the ocean up fifty feet, and in that flooding lower Manhattan went under, and upper Manhattan did not. Incredible that this could happen! So much ice off Antarctica and Greenland! Could there be that much ice, to make that much water? Yes, there could.[17]

In short, once again, ice-sheet collapse becomes the skeleton key to understanding both the transformative potential of history and the nightmarish terms of our own likely near-term future, flooding coastal cities like New York and forcing a radical revision of the ordinary terms of capitalism (though here on a timetable nearly a century longer than the 'rapid climate change' of the 'Science in the Capital' books, with all the attendant misery, suffering, and exploitation that delay would itself entail). The basic terms of the prediction of ice-sheet collapse, remarkably stable across Robinson's career, more or less hold: one-eighth of the world's population wind up displaced and impoverished, 'a refugee crisis rated at ten thousand katrinas'.[18]

New York in *New York 2140* is a new Venice, simultaneously an object of revulsion and desire; the city is a thriving ruin, a glorious wreck. While climate change has transformed the city, and made some elements of living in it significantly worse, its inhabitants have not given up or fallen into despair, and, indeed, by the end of the novel they have cleverly laid the foundations for a social revolution that may, we hope, save the tiny utopia of squatters, refugees, the homeless, and the undocumented that they have built for themselves out of what was once the financial capital of the planet (and that is still always at risk for reclamation by its billionaire former owners, who have safely relocated to Denver). Remarkably, even after everything that has happened to human society and to the natural world, it is *still* not too late for hope, or revolution, or even for utopia.

Their achievement may be small comfort, though, to those of us whose projected lifespans do not quite reach 2140. In the storyworld of the novel, at least, our fate is far less happy; our lives cover instead the Pulses, the megafloods, a period of prolonged and ever-worsening disaster the narrator describes as 'Apocalyptic, Armageddonesque, pick your adjective of choice. Anthropogenic could be one. Extinctional another. Anthropogenic mass extinction event, the term often used. End of an era'.[19] *New York 2140* dates the start of the First Pulse to 2052, when I will be a spry seventy-three, and my oldest child will be the age that I am now, forty. If the readers of Golden Age science fiction were once unhappy to discover that their happy sci-fi fantasies of easy interstellar travel did not come true within their lifetimes – how much more unhappy will we be when we confirm the consensus apocalypse did instead?

Conclusion: Utopia as Memory

The development of Robinson's work since the Mars books registers, as we have seen, intensifying anxiety about the future of the environment, as the climate situation grows more and more dire (and the time we have left to take action becomes ever shorter) without sufficient response from any of our governmental institutions. It is, after all, hard to follow contemporary climate science, or contemporary climate politics, without succumbing to a very deep and abiding pessimism. But this is not the same thing as hopelessness, or surrender. In 'Theses on the Concept of History', Walter Benjamin describes the work of historical materialism as an attempt 'to seize hold of a memory as it flashes up at a moment of danger';[20] Robinson's project as a science fiction writer seems to be a parallel move to seize hold of the *future* in a moment of danger and say, nonetheless, a better world still remains possible. And just as the protagonists of *New York 2140* take the tools available to them in their moment to transform their present, we are called on to change our own. After all, as Benjamin himself reminds us, 'every second of time' is one 'through which the Messiah might enter'.[21]

At one point in *New York 2140*, two of Robinson's characters imagine a utopian alternate history of the founding of America which was not predicated on the genocide of Native Americans:

"Why didn't anyone live there before?" Jeff asks from out of his sleep.

"Well, that's another story. Actually there were people there already, I have to say, but alas they didn't have immunity to the diseases that the new people brought with them, so most of them died. But the survivors joined this community and taught the newcomers how to take care of the land so that it would stay healthy forever. ... It took knowing every rock and plant and animal and fish and bird, that was the way they did it. You had to love the land the way you loved your mother, or in case you didn't love your mother, the way you loved your child, or yourself. Because it was you anyway. It took knowing all the other parts of your self so well that nothing was misunderstood or exploited, and everything was treated respectfully. Every single element of this land, right down to the bedrock, was a citizen of the community they all made together, and they all had legal standing, and they all made a good living, and they all had everything it took for total well-being for everyone. That's what it was like."[22]

Utopia is thus simultaneously a nowhere world – 'a kind of lullaby ... a tale for children' – *and* the world we might easily have built together, and the one we could still build, if we muster the collective will.[23] Utopia is a memory, a dream, and a plan, all at once. Every moment has within it the seeds of utopian possibility, as the arc of Robinson's *oeuvre* attests, as each novel locates the inflection point for the upswing of history at some different moment in the past or future but never finds it too late to try and make the world more liveable. Of course, Robinson does not promise it will be easy; 1990's ecotopian *Pacific Edge* defines utopia as 'struggle forever',[24] while 2312 reminds us 'There is still and always the risk of utter failure and mad gibbering extinction. There is no alternative to continuing to struggle'.[25] The deliberate lack of a period at the close of the sentence foregrounds the unfinishedness of utopia, while the words foreground its urgency, and the stakes of inaction. Robinson's most recent work at the time of this writing, *The Ministry for the Future* (2020), is in much the same mode. In much the same way that the 'Science in the Capital' trilogy before it pivoted from a far-future Mars to return to Earth, *Ministry* swings back from the distant future of 2140 to our own benighted moment. Organised around an NGO tasked by the signatories of the Paris Agreement 'to advocate for the world's future generations of citizens, whose rights ... are as valid as our own', and further charged with 'defending all living creatures present and future who cannot speak for themselves',[26] the book begins in the 2020s, and dares us to find hope, even here, even now.

Notes

1 D. A. Wollheim, *The Universe Makers: Science Fiction Today* (New York: Harper and Row, 1971).

2 The conflict between these two modes of galactic civilisation would later become the foundation stone for what is almost certainly the most influential science fiction narrative of all time, the *Star Wars* saga (1977–2019).

3 Wollheim, *Universe Makers*, 44.

4 *Star Trek: The Next Generation*, created by G. Roddenberry (Paramount and CBS, 1997–present); *Star Trek: Discovery*, created by B. Fuller and A. Kurtzman (CBS, 2017–present): *Star Trek: Picard*, created by A. Goldsman *et al.* (CBS, 2020–present).

5 K. S. Robinson, *Green Mars* (New York: Bantam Books, 1994), 555.

6 Robinson, *Green Mars*, 558.

7 F. Jameson, 'Future City', *New Left Review* 21 (2003), 76.

8 Robinson, *Green Mars*, 558.

9 The term 'divine violence' is adapted from Walter Benjamin; see his 'Critique of Violence' in *Reflections: Essays, Aphorisms, Autobiographical Writings*, trans. E. F. N. Jephcott (New York: Schocken, 1978), 277–300.

10 Left out of this reading is Robinson's transcendent alternate history novel, *The Years of Rice and Salt*, which posits a world in which the Black Plague nearly completely depopulates Europe in the fourteenth century. While this is a rare Robinson novel that does not mention the climate crisis, we do receive a hint in a section near the end of the novel titled 'What Remains to Be Explained', which asks, among other things, 'Will any mammals larger than a fox survive the next century?'; see *The Years of Rice and Salt* (New York: Random House, 2000), 742.

11 K. S. Robinson, *Sixty Days and Counting* (New York: Bantam, 2007), 516; original emphasis.

12 K. S. Robinson, *2312* (New York: Hachette, 2012), 303–34.

13 Robinson, *2312*, 90.

14 Robinson, *2312*, 124–5.

15 For more on the 'cowboy economy', the unbounded frontier, versus the 'space-man economy', maximum enclosure, see G. Canavan, 'Introduction: If This Goes On', in G. Canavan and K. S. Robinson (eds.), *Green Planets: Ecology and Science Fiction* (Middletown, CT: Wesleyan University Press, 2014), 6–8.

16 While somewhat outside the scope of this article, Robinson's career-long interest in ice-sheet collapse does see an interesting reversal in his prehistoric fantasy *Shaman* (2013), set 32,000 years ago during the last Ice Age.

17 K. S. Robinson, *New York 2140* (New York: Orbit Books, 2017), 33–4.

18 Robinson, *New York*, 144.

19 Robinson, *New York*, 144.

20 W. Benjamin, 'Theses on the Philosophy of History', in *Illuminations*, trans. H. Zohn (New York: Schocken Books, 1969), 255.

21 Benjamin, 'Theses on the Philosophy of History', 264.

22 Robinson, *New York*, 296–7.

23 Robinson, *New York*, 297.

24 K. S. Robinson, *Pacific Edge* (New York: Tom Doherty Associates, 2013), 95.

25 Robinson, *2312*, 553.

26 K. S. Robinson, *The Ministry for the Future* (New York: Orbit Books, 2020), 16.

12

GREGORY LYNALL

Solarpunk

... on May 14, 2061, what had been theory, became fact. The energy of the sun was stored, converted, and utilized directly on a planet-wide scale. All Earth turned off its burning coal, its fissioning uranium, and flipped the switch that connected all of it to a small station, one mile in diameter, circling the Earth at half the distance of the Moon. All Earth ran by invisible beams of sunpower.[1]

Isaac Asimov's short story, 'The Last Question' (1956), begins with a transformative moment in the Earth's history: when humanity becomes a fully democratic, planetary civilisation dependent entirely on space-based solar power for its energy needs. It imagines an instantaneous transition to this resource (of sunlight collected by photovoltaic panels above the atmosphere and then beamed to Earth as microwaves) which seems to involve no adaptation of existing energy infrastructure or consumption behaviours and, most of all, no acknowledgement that humanity's previous energy usage had transformed the climatic conditions of the planet.[2] It would be unfair, of course, to rebuke this 1950s story for failing to represent anthropogenic climate change, which, although considered in scientific papers of that decade, was not wide public knowledge until the 1980s.[3] My point, however, is to contrast 'The Last Question' (a story from one of the most famous science fiction authors) with more recent, similarly utopian-inflected science fiction (particularly 'solarpunk', the focus of this essay) which imagines both the technological and societal complexity of energy transition, and the conditions civilisations might face in adapting to living in damaged natural environments. Asimov's story appeared soon after Bell Laboratories announced its invention of silicon-based photovoltaic cells which, despite being only 4 percent efficient, pointed to a bright solar-energy future.[4] In more recent years, renewable energy technologies of various types have become credible alternatives to hydrocarbons or nuclear, and yet alongside them has developed an awareness that their adoption is dependent upon changes in policy and behaviour, which environmentally conscious authors are playing out in their works as kinds of thought experiment.

Science Fiction Climates and the Emergence of Solarpunk

Climate transformation has been a pervasive trope within science fiction (and speculative fiction more generally) almost from its inception.[5] Indeed, climate is bound up with the genre, since to imagine other worlds is to envision environments alien to Earth's upon those worlds. Moreover, those alien climates sometimes serve as projections of Earth's own future climate: one only has to think of H. G. Wells's *The War of the Worlds* (1897), in which the 'secular cooling' of the solar system affecting Mars prompts its inhabitants to invade and attempt to environmentally transform their nearest planetary neighbour.[6] Meanwhile, human alteration of climate has long been a common plot motif too, with early examples including Mark Twain's comic novel *The American Claimant* (1892).[7] In more recent science fiction, the soletta (space mirror) concept has been imagined as a way of terraforming a planet in order for it to sustain life.[8] Geoengineering projects are no longer merely the stuff of fiction, though, but technological possibilities. 'Solar Radiation Management', for instance, started as speculation in early pulp science fiction stories but is now considered seriously as a potential climate intervention, by scientists including Paul Crutzen, which in turn has given further impetus to more recent science fiction, notably the film *Snowpiercer* (2013).[9] Science fiction is, moreover, a genre of profound 'energy consciousness', pervaded by technologically sublime energy infrastructures, and with conflict over immense power sources a common plot in popular sf narratives.[10]

In the twenty-first century, science fiction occupies a significant cultural space, partly thanks to its success at the movie box office, but also because it is viewed by some as having a prognosticatory value in thinking through possible human and planetary futures. This transcends the genre itself, though, and can be observed as a mode within other kinds of work, particularly environmental non-fiction, which is increasingly adopting science fiction tropes to provoke audience action.[11] Jonathan Porritt's speculative non-fiction *The World We Made: Alex McKay's Story from 2050* (2013), for instance, simulates the voice of a fifty-year-old history teacher, giving snapshots of the social and technological changes between 2014 and 2050, with Porritt's intention being to 'connect that world in 2050 with what we can do today to help make it a reality'.[12] Meanwhile, Jeff Gibbs's controversial environmental documentary, *Planet of the Humans* (2020), frames itself as a science fiction dystopia via its title and opening credits, although it does little else with this premise for the rest of the film.[13] The connection between science fiction and climate change is therefore becoming almost ubiquitous in the popular imagination, although the value of this relationship is not without its critics.[14]

In some ways, at this time of climate crisis, it is our collective imagination which is the most important resource we should utilise to bring about sustainable futures via social transformation, by making us consider the consequences of our present lives and lifestyles. Yet, to date, it is difficult to find evidence of its effectiveness.[15] As Naomi Klein argues, the solution to global warming is to 'fix ourselves', yet the public dissemination of future climate projections has not resulted in the behavioural changes thought necessary to avoid environmental disaster.[16] Undeterred, authors of many different genres (but particularly cli-fi, science fiction, and environmental non-fiction) have sought to impart visions of the future, believing that they can enable readers to understand the full implications of present behaviours of consumption. However, there is much debate amongst climate psychologists as to whether radical change to the individual consciousness can be achieved via positive or negative images.[17] In particular, it is claimed that 'techno-optimism' (the belief that technological solutions to our problems will emerge) is as damaging in its ultimate effects as climate change denial. The Centre for Alternative Technology's manifesto for a 'zero carbon Britain', meanwhile, takes a nuanced approach, advising that 'action is better promoted by showing the positive benefits of mitigation'.[18] This all presupposes, of course, that individuals are in a position of agency anyway, which to some is unlikely, given the detrimental 'scale effects' of climate change.[19] Nevertheless, writers have deployed creative strategies explicitly in order to change the future of the planet, one mind at a time.

This aspiration to influence the individual consciousness is particularly apparent within the recently emerging counter-cultural movement of solarpunk, which imagines sustainable, post-oil futures, normally in terrestrial environments that have undergone significant climate change. Its ideas, narratives, and aesthetics are found across multiple platforms, disciplines, and art forms, especially architecture, art, and literature. Notable examples include the architectural designs of Vincent Callebaut, the concept art of Teikoku Shônen (known as Imperial Boy), and the anthologies *Solarpunk*, *Sunvault*, and *Glass and Gardens*.[20] In their modes of production and dissemination (such as the anthology, the blog post, the online discussion group), works of solarpunk often enact the community-driven, socially progressive, internationalist and inclusive ethos they depict within future societies and which they are intended to cultivate within the present day.[21] As solarpunk's own progenitors acknowledge, its tropes are still under negotiation, as one might expect from an artistic (and non-hierarchical) movement that has been in existence for only a short time (although renewable energy technologies themselves have a long cultural history, and works of what we might call 'proto-solarpunk' emerged alongside them).[22] Yet some common parameters of solarpunk can be identified. In particular, despite addressing the environmental costs of the Anthropocene, solarpunk narratives, scenes, and designs are frequently (but not always) optimistic in tone, and utopian in genre. Indeed, some of solarpunk's more prominent advocates claim that the 'solar' prefix refers to not only the genre's ecological aspect, but also its commitment to the 'idea of brightness and hope', making it distinct from its more dystopian 'cyberpunk' forebear.[23] Ultimately, solarpunk seeks to raise awareness of the possibilities for sustainable living and renewable energy infrastructures, and – as a 'speculative imaginary' – engages in thought experiments regarding the kinds of societies and behaviours they would support.[24] Solarpunk stories typically present liveable, not just survivable, futures of human societies existing (and even thriving) within their energy and material means.

Some long-form novels, such as Kim Stanley Robinson's *New York 2140* (2017), have been claimed as working within the genre, but solarpunk literature has been driven particularly by the anthology, and especially the short story. The anthology form reifies the sense of community intervention represented in many of the stories themselves, seeking to inculcate coordinated individual action within readers and, ultimately, society (and some of the anthologies have even sought financial subsidy via Kickstarter appeals). Moreover, the readers of solarpunk are encouraged to become its writers too, with every story itself seen as a valuable intervention that adds to the collective imagining of sustainable futures.[25] The communitarian ethos of solarpunk seems even more appropriate when we consider the emphasis upon the local within current energy transition strategies, which envision a move away from state- or corporate-run, grid-based energy supply, and towards microgeneration via individual-and/or community-owned systems.[26] The genre is itself styled similarly as 'decentralized' and 'localized',[27] placing creative power and social influence in the producer-consumer and the micro-fictions they generate.

Despite the expansiveness inherent in imagining new societies and environments, the short-story form grounds its narratives in individual lives, aiding the reader in projecting themselves vicariously into the future, but in order to consider simultaneously their own actions in the present. This is not to say, however, that solarpunk fictions always subordinate landscapes and weather patterns in favour of the individual experiences of the characters. For instance, in Antonio Luiz M. C. Costa's story 'Once upon a Time in a World' (2012), a trip across Brazil reveals: 'Where there was once the Caatinga, regular lines of wind generators and the rectangular and circular compositions of solar panels alternated regularly and geometrically with crops and pastures. There were reserves of fauna and flora of that and other biomes, but it was a world much altered by the human hand, mono-tonically symmetrical and tamed'.[28] The narrator's solastalgia reminds the reader that renewable energy technologies themselves come with an ecologi-cal cost, their aesthetic impact here serving as a synecdoche of their wider effect upon the ecosystem. Therefore, whilst not necessarily dystopian, some solarpunk stories offer a sobering sense that any future (other than a simple agrarian one) will not come with an environmental panacea.

Renewable Energies and Renewed Selves in Solarpunk

The above example also demonstrates that the renewable energy infrastruc-tures encountered in solarpunk fictions are often recognisable as such to the twenty-first-century reader. They do not push the envelope too far techno-logically, perhaps in order to maintain a closer sense of reader identification. Instead, solarpunk is often at its most inventive when embracing the biotech-nological possibilities of renewable energy, particularly solar power. Shel Graves's story 'Watch Out, Red Crusher!' (2018), for instance, is set in the community of Aberdonia, whose residents must agree to the 'Solar Pact', by which photovoltaic nanites are injected into the human body. By way of the nanites, each citizen not only 'help[s] power the community, providing electricity, running water, and warming the algae production ponds', but also ensures community safety and security, since the emotionally reactive nanites give a coloured glow according to a person's feelings. Whilst Aberdonia insists that the colour changes are just a 'side effect', they have nevertheless been harnessed by the governing 'elders', with all 'murderers and thieves' exiled to the 'uncivilized Freeway'.[29] Graves's story, therefore, uses photobiology as a conceit through which to explore the connections between technology and state surveillance and control.

The short story is currently the dominant literary genre of solarpunk, but poetry is increasing in prominence. Sara Norja's lyric poem in the *Sunvault* anthology (2017), 'Sunharvest Triptych', for instance, is a kind of georgic that ends with the speaker figuring herself as a solar panel, 'harvest[ing] the sun-light' within. The speaker presents her poetic labour as analogous to a form of photovoltaics that has been enabled by her ethical energy behaviours, the poem called a 'Triptych' because it has a tripartite stanza structure and has been generated out of (solar) panels. Meanwhile, Joel Nathanael's 'Light Sail Star Bound' (2017), from the same anthology, is an unabashed verse celebra-tion of the cosmic and poetic possibilities of 'photon propulsion', enabling journeys across other galaxies and with 'extradimensional / language'.[30] Both poems convey a belief that solar power benefits us not only ethically and economically, but also creatively. For both Norja and Nathanael, a new realisation of our dependence upon the sun renews our understanding of the natural world and of ourselves.

With this in mind, solarpunk simultaneously fetishises and obscures renewable technologies. The societies solarpunk depicts have had to adapt their energy and material production and consumption radically, and the human habitations and infrastructures are very different to those sustained by fossil fuels. Yet, part of solarpunk's ideological work is to normalise renewables as sources of energy within those societies. Some of the most successful stories in the genre, therefore, are set in worlds powered by renewables, but their narrative focus is not upon those renewables themselves.[31] Instead, they reduce renewable energy almost to the point of invisibility via their ubiquity. As part of this normalisation, solarpunk also considers renewable energy technologies at different kinds of scale. For example, in D. K. Mok's 'The Spider and the Stars' (2018) – a story principally concerned with biomimetics – the protagonist Del travels across what we might call stereotypical solarpunk vistas:

> there were towns, just like hers, speckled with solar arrays and water tanks. But there were also villages floating on inland seas, their bustling markets a crowd of floating tea houses and creaking junks with patchwork sails. There were forests of typhoon turbines ready to capture the rage of mighty storms, and enormous greenhouses in the desert, flanked by desalination plants powered by the sun.[32]

The landscapes Del encounters bear the scars of anthropogenic climate change, but also the marks of human adaptation and sustainability that can still support 'bustling' populations. Settlements and energy infrastructure are appropriate for the natural environments in which they sit, but are at the scale necessary to sustain human life. Their technological sublimity reflects the aesthetic and physical power of the natural resources they seek to capture, and in some cases they have also acquired a natural character themselves, with 'forests' of turbines sitting organically within the landscape. Later, though, at the 'Solaria Grande' world's fair, Del meets Xiaren, who is there to showcase a 'portable domestic biogas system', humorously christened 'Fromagerie 5000'.[33] What has inspired Xiaren to invent is her hometown's need for 'clean energy': 'And in my mind, gas is gas, whether it's happening inside a cow or a star. Or a round of cheese'.[34] Xiaren's method of renewable energy capture is unashamedly un-sublime, but no less valuable: indeed, the reader already knows at this point that Del's home laboratory is itself powered by cheese biogas.[35] Whilst during her journey Del has witnessed many large-scale energy interventions, there is still a place for the small and *ostensibly* ridiculous in the decentralised energy grid. It is not only grand schemes that have a place in the future.

But what of solarpunk's own future as a literary genre, particularly if it aims to necessitate social change? One possible model is offered by *The Weight of Light: A Collection of Solar Futures* (2018), the product of a 'narrative hackathon' between science fiction authors, visual artists, social scientists, and engineers, in which a science fiction short story is written and then made the subject of multidisciplinary analysis. This 'anticipatory design fiction work' potentially heralds a new phase of imagining sustainable futures: one that reifies disciplines working together, and places science fiction firmly in a central role.[36] As this collection recognises, the climate crisis is not only forcing different disciplines of knowledge to work collaboratively and across boundaries, but also transforming hierarchies and boundaries between kinds of writing.

In a short space of time, from the ground up, solarpunk has established itself as a recognisable aesthetic and movement with the potential to mobilise readers into climate action. Its tone is generally optimistic, but not without valuable nuance that subjects potential future scenarios to creative scrutiny. In whichever way solarpunk evolves, at its core is a hopeful global community spirit, yet one which recognises that the future cannot be changed at the flip of a switch.

Notes

1 I. Asimov, 'The Last Question' (1956), in B. Aldiss (ed.), *Space Opera: Science Fiction from the Golden Age* (London: Weidenfeld & Nicolson, 1974), 309. Asimov's fiction would later explore ecological catastrophe allegorically: see Asimov, *The Gods Themselves* (New York: Doubleday, 1972), 27, 56.

2 On the solar power space station concept, see chapter 5 of G. Lynall, *Imagining Solar Energy: The Power of the Sun in English Literature, Science and Culture* (London: Bloomsbury Academic, 2020), 144–56.

3 S. R. Weart, *The Discovery of Global Warming*, rev. ed. (Cambridge, MA: Harvard University Press, 2008), 23.

4 Lynall, *Imagining Solar Energy*, 171–2.

5 On the complicated distinction between 'science' and 'speculative' fiction, see S. Streeby, *Imagining the Future of Climate Change: World-Making through Science Fiction and Activism* (Berkeley: University of California Press, 2018), 19–20.

6 H. G. Wells, *The War of the Worlds*, eds. D. Y. Hughes and H. M. Geduld (Bloomington: Indiana University Press, 1993), 52.

7 M. Twain, *The American Claimant* (New York: Charles L. Webster, 1892), 272; see also J. R. Fleming, *Fixing the Sky: The Checkered History of Weather and Climate Control* (New York: Columbia University Press, 2010), 27–30.

8 See especially Kim Stanley Robinson's 'Mars' trilogy: *Red Mars* (New York: Bantam, 1993); *Green Mars* (New York: Bantam, 1994); *Blue Mars* (New York: Bantam, 1996); Lynall, *Imagining Solar Energy*, 151.

9 P. J. Crutzen, 'Albedo Enhancement by Stratospheric Sulfur Injections: A Contribution to Resolve a Policy Dilemma?', *Climate Change* 77 (2006), 211; *Snowpiercer*, dir. Bong Joon-ho (Weinstein Company, 2013); Streeby, *Imagining the Future*, 1–3.

10 G. Macdonald, 'Improbability Drives: The Energy of SF', *Paradoxa* 26 (2014), 111–44, reprinted in *Strange Horizons* (April 2016), http://strangehorizons.com/non-fiction/articles/improbability-drives-the-energy-of-sf/.

11 U. K. Heise, *Imagining Extinction: The Cultural Meanings of Endangered Species* (University of Chicago Press, 2016), 215.

12 J. Porritt, *The World We Made: Alex McKay's Story from 2050* (London: Phaidon Press, 2013), blurb.

13 *Planet of the Humans*, dir. J. Gibbs, prod. M. Moore (Rumble Media, 2019).

14 See especially A. Ghosh, *The Great Derangement: Climate Change and the Unthinkable* (University of Chicago Press, 2016), 72–3.

15 M. Schneider-Mayerson, 'The Influence of Climate Fiction: An Empirical Survey of Readers', *Environmental Humanities* 10.2 (2018), 473–500.

16 N. Klein, *This Changes Everything: Capitalism vs. the Climate* (London: Allen Lane, 2014), 279, and A. Davison, '"Not to Escape the World but to Join It": Responding to Climate Change with Imagination not Fantasy', *Philosophical Transactions of the Royal Society A*, 375.2095 (2017).

17 T. M. Marteau, 'Towards Environmentally Sustainable Human Behaviour: Targeting Non-conscious and Conscious Processes for Effective and Acceptable Policies', *Philosophical Transactions of the Royal Society A*, 375.2095 (2017).

18 Centre for Alternative Technology, *Zero Carbon Britain: Making It Happen* (Machynlleth, Powys: CAT Publications, 2017), 263.

19 T. Clark, 'Scale', in T. Cohen (ed.), *Telemorphosis: Theory in the Era of Climate Change*, vol. 1 (Ann Arbor: MI: Open Humanities Press, 2012), 148–66.

20 Vincent Callebaut Architectures, 'Bionic-Arch, A Sustainable Tower', *EVolo* 4 (Summer 2012); 'The Art of Imperial Boy', www.iamag.co/the-art-of-imperial-boy/; G. Lodi-Ribiero (ed.), *Solarpunk: Ecological and Fantastical Stories in a Sustainable World*, trans. F. Fernandes (2012; Albuquerque: World Weaver Press, 2018); P. Wagner and B. C. Wieland (eds.), *Sunvault: Stories of Solarpunk and Eco-Speculation* (Nashville, TN: Upper Rubber Boot, 2017); S. Ulibarri (ed.), *Glass and Gardens: Solarpunk Summers* (Albuquerque, NM: World Weaver Press, 2018).

21 A. Flynn, 'Solarpunk: Notes toward a Manifesto', *Hieroglyph* (4 September 2014). In D. K. Mok's 'The Spider and the Stars', an entire space station is crowd-funded; Mok, in *Glass and Gardens*, 29.

22 See Lynall, *Imagining Solar Energy*.

23 Ulibarri, 'Introduction', in *Glass and Gardens*, 1, and Ulibarri, 'Introduction', in *Solarpunk*, 2.

24 R. Williams, '"This Shining Confluence of Magic and Technology": Solarpunk, Energy Imaginaries, and the Infrastructures of Solarity', *Open Library of Humanities* 5(1).60 (2019), 3 n.3.

25 Ulibarri, 'Introduction', in *Glass and Gardens*, 2.

26 A. Hope *et al.*, 'Consumer Engagement in Low-Carbon Home Energy in the United Kingdom: Implications for Future Energy System Decentralization', *Energy Research and Social Science* 44 (2018), 362–70.

27 Ulibarri, 'Introduction', in *Glass and Gardens*, 1.

28 A. L. M. C. Costa, 'Once upon a Time in a World', in *Solarpunk*, 92.

29 S. Graves, 'Watch Out, Red Crusher!', in *Glass and Gardens*, 55, 53. See also C. Meyers, 'Solar Child', in *Sunvault*, 185–94.

30 S. Norja, 'Sunharvest Triptych', in *Sunvault*, 220, l. 71; J. Nathanael, 'Light Sail Star Bound', in *Sunvault*, 85, ll. 10, 14–15.

31 See, for instance, J. Goh, 'A Field of Sapphires and Sunshine', in *Glass and Gardens*, 107–18.

32 Mok, 'The Spider and the Stars', 19.

33 Mok, 'The Spider and the Stars', 20.

34 Mok, 'The Spider and the Stars', 21.

35 Mok, 'The Spider and the Stars', 13.

36 J. Eschrich and C. A. Miller (eds.), *The Weight of Light: A Collection of Solar Futures* (Tempe: Arizona State University, 2018), 11, 25.

Collective Climate Action

13

SHELLEY STREEBY

Indigenous and Black Feminist Knowledge-Production, Speculative Science Stories, and Climate Change Literature

Some of the most vital contributions to recent climate change literature come not in the form of cli-fi but in multi-form stories of speculative science written by Indigenous and Black women. These narratives defy boundaries among fiction, non-fiction, poetry, and theory as well as genre boundaries; they also trouble binaries of individual and collective action or individual authorship and collective voice by emphasising relations with activist communities and kinship with the more-than-human world. Making Indigenous knowledge foundational to literary experimentation, Robin Wall Kimmerer (Citizen Potawatomi Nation) builds on Indigenous sciences, place-based knowledge, Indigenous storytelling traditions, and futuristic internet forms, thereby connecting ecological and climate change literature to a spectrum of cultural practices inextricable from activism. Alexis Pauline Gumbs, on the other hand, centres Black and women of colour feminist knowledge-production in her contributions to transforming the literary, rethinking racial ecologies, and imagining different worlds in the face of colonialism, extractive racial capitalism, and climate change.

The ties between activism and writing that are explicit in Kimmerer's co-authored 'Letter from Indigenous Scientists in Support of the March for Science' (2017) also shape her classic *Braiding Sweetgrass: Indigenous Wisdom, Scientific Knowledge, and the Teachings of Plant*s (2013), her first book *Gathering Mosses: A Natural and Cultural History of Mosses* (2003), and her many essays, lectures, and public addresses. In 2017, Kimmerer joined Indigenous scientists and scholars Rosalyn LaPier (Blackfeet/Métis), Melissa Nelson ((Turtle Mountain Chippewa), and Kyle Whyte (Citizen Potawatomi Nation) in co-authoring the 'Letter from Indigenous Scientists', endorsed by more than 1,100 Native American and Indigenous scientists, scholars, and allies worldwide in the days leading up to the March for Science that took place on Earth Day that year. In a statement, Kimmerer declared that 'Indigenous science holds a wealth of knowledge' and is 'a powerful paradigm by which we understand our place in the living world', making it 'essential to the problems we face today', even though it has 'been historically marginalized by the scientific community'.[1] In the Letter, even as the co-authors 'endorse and support' the March, they insist 'that there are multiple ways of knowing that play an essential role in advancing knowledge for the health of all life'. The Letter, which circulated widely on social media, was a call to action for institutions of Western science to recognise the need for a productive symbiosis with Indigenous science in confronting climate change and ecological devastation. Early on, the Letter's writers invoke relations to the more-than-human world when they ask us to 'remember that long before Western science came to these shores, there were Indigenous scientists here', including 'Native astronomers, agronomists, geneticists, ecologists, engineers, botanists, zoologists, watershed hydrologists, pharmacologists, physicians and more – all engaged in the creation and application of knowledge which promoted the flourishing of both human societies and the beings with whom we share the planet'. They also insist on the need to heed Indigenous scientists' 'key insights and philosophical frameworks for problem solving that include human values, which are much needed as we face challenges such as climate change, sustainable resource management, health disparities and the need for healing the ecological damage we have done'.

Kimmerer's co-authored Indigenous ecological movement literature connects to both of her books, which I read as stories of speculative science. In her anthology *Walking the Clouds: An Anthology of Indigenous Fiction* (2012), Grace Dillon offers useful frameworks for thinking about how Indigenous writers engage 'Indigenous Scientific Literacies and Environmental Sustainability' in science fiction stories and novels, but also in other kinds of writing, experimental films, comics, and other cultural forms. Indigenous speculative science stories challenge conventional genre boundaries and connect to traditions of Indigenous storytelling that offer powerful alternatives to Western science.[2] As Dillon observes, many Indigenous cultures 'share the pattern of disseminating scientific knowledge in everyday teaching' since storytelling was 'the medium of choice' for transmitting and preserving 'botanical knowledge, knowledge of the land', as well as 'knowledge itself, teachings and ways of living'.[3] Kimmerer's speculative science stories build on Indigenous ways of knowing that depart from Western science's ways of knowing, especially in the emphasis on relations and responsibilities between the human and more-than-human world.

Kimmerer's interest in how different relations of looking and knowing shape Western and Indigenous science stories is evident in the Preface of *Gathering Moss*, as she recalls her first conscious memory of science in kindergarten, when her teacher handed her a magnifying glass to look at a snowflake. 'For the first time, but not the last', Kimmerer writes, 'I had the sense that there was more to the world than immediately met the eye'.[4] Reflecting on how she knew as an undergraduate she was 'committed' to studying mosses when she used part of her 'sparse college savings to send off for a professional grade Bausch and Lomb lens', she still insists that long before she went to the university, plants were her teachers. We 'learn each other's stories by looking', she suggests, and though Western science offers powerful ways to see and tell stories, it's 'not enough'.[5] Kimmerer's speculative science stories, on the other hand, are also about 'relationship' and 'coming to see the world through moss-colored glasses'.[6] Contrasting Indigenous with Western 'scientific ways of knowing', Kimmerer says the way she was taught plant science pushed her Potawatomi knowledge of plants to the margins. Thus, 'writing this book' was 'a process of reclaiming that understanding, of giving it its rightful place', in order to emphasise human relationships to the more-than-human world, which hold 'messages of consequence that need to be heard, the perspective of species other than our own'.[7] In addition to experimenting with literary strategies to centre more-than-human perspectives as a political and ethical necessity when confronting ecological disaster, Kimmerer also insists that recognising Indigenous science and knowledge-production is itself an important political act, one she has extended in impactful ways as founding Director of the Center for Native Peoples and the Environment at SUNY as well as in her activism, public talks, and her most famous second book.

Braiding Sweetgrass (2013) combines storytelling, speculative science, and pedagogical reflections while directly addressing human-caused climate change in relation to the more-than-human world. Each chapter emphasises Indigenous ways of seeing and knowing and takes speculative literary leaps to reorient the reader's understanding. In 'Maple Nation: A Citizenship Guide', Kimmerer suggests that a 'biologically inclusive census of the people' in her town would show that maples 'outnumber humans a hundred to one', for in 'our Anishinaabe way, we count trees as people, the "standing people"', she explains.[8] But 'maples of the United States face a grave enemy', since 'the most highly regarded models predict that the climate of New England will become hostile to sugar maples within fifty years'. As 'rising temperatures' reduce 'seedling success', maples will become 'climate refugees' who, in order to survive, 'must migrate northward to find homes at the boreal fringe'.[9] Recognising the personhood of the trees, Kimmerer blames their departure and exile on the demand for cheap gas no matter what the cost. Kimmerer unsettles capitalist common sense by pointing out that we 'do not pay at the pump for the cost of climate change, for the loss of ecosystems services provided by maples and others'. Calling for 'political action' and 'civic engagement' as 'powerful acts of reciprocity with the land', Kimmerer repeatedly connects literature to climate change activism and solidarity with the more-than-human world.[10]

In another chapter, 'The Sound of Silverbells', Kimmerer remembers taking students from an 'exclusive little college' located in coal country in the US South, known for its success in getting the sons and daughters of the 'bluegrass aristocracy' into 'medical school', into the field, 'through the sheared off mountain-tops of coal country, where the streams run red with acid'.[11] Though the students only seemed to be interested in 'a single species: themselves', Kimmerer hoped to give them a glimpse of 'the six million other species with whom we share the planet'.[12] So Kimmerer took them to the Great Smoky Mountains, where they studied an 'ecological map' of elevational zones as Kimmerer pushed them 'to see the world beyond the boundaries of their own skins'.[13] Once they arrived at the high mountaintops that reminded her of home, however, Kimmerer 'slipped the leash' of her 'lectures' to 'lay down on a carpet of moss and hold class from a spider's perspective'. This disorienting, speculative shift in point of view brings into relief the impact of 'global warming' on 'the world's last populations of the endangered spruce-fir moss spider', whose 'many lives', when 'this island of boreal forest' melts away, will also disappear, 'never to return'.[14]

Despite this epiphany, when reflecting on the unravelling of ecosystems and the dangers human-caused climate change poses to non-human species while heading home, Kimmerer worries she has failed to teach the 'kind of science' she 'had longed for' as a young woman.[15] But suddenly on the trail behind her, in a 'petal-strewn path in gauzy light', she becomes aware of the students singing 'Amazing Grace' in the 'same outpouring of love and gratitude for the creation that Skywoman first sang on the back of Turtle Island'. Humbled by how the 'land' was 'the real teacher', offering lessons that exceeded the knowledge of a teacher 'colonized by the arrogance of science', Kimmerer thereafter fundamentally changed her 'way of teaching' in recognition of how 'the mountains taught the students and the students taught the teacher'.[16] In these ways, she emphasises the power of the land and non-human species to cause us to reconsider the place of humans in the natural world.

Other non-human species threatened by climate change, including lichens, which are 'highly sensitive to air pollution', also hold important lessons for humans: they blur 'what it means to be an individual, as a lichen is not one being, but two: a fungus and an alga' that together become 'a wholly new organism'.[17] As lichens confound 'the distinction between individual and community', they 'remind us of the enduring power that arises from mutualism, from the sharing of the gifts carried by each species'. Humans, however, 'have not returned the favor' to lichens, instead creating 'a barrenness of our own making', in which 'whole species and entire ecosystems are vanishing before our eyes in the vanguard of accelerating climate chaos'. At the same time, lichens are 'also among the first to colonize post-glacial forelands today' as they emerge in formerly frozen lands in the wake of climate change, reminding Kimmerer of how 'our indigenous herbalists say to pay attention when plants come to you; they're bringing you something you need to learn'.[18] Throughout, Kimmerer situates Indigenous science as a source of knowledge that both contributes to and challenges Western science. Through speculative literary moves that centre Indigenous knowledge and ways of seeing, Kimmerer's stories of kinship to the more-than-human world and insistence on the personhood of other species provide a powerful alternative to the 'delusions of separateness' and myths of progress by destroying and transforming nature naturalised by intersecting, dominant stories of Western science, colonialism, imperialism, and extractive capitalism.[19]

In the chapter 'The Sacred and the Superfund', Kimmerer offers restoration of reciprocal relations with the more-than-human world as the antidote to environmental despair, which she predicts can create no vision other than 'woe and tears'.[20] Reflecting on the shared histories of 'wounded places' that an 'extractive economy' has extensively damaged, such as her home near Syracuse, New York, Kimmerer rejects 'shocking nightmare tableaux of environmental tragedies' that just provoke more 'dire predictions and powerless feelings'.[21] Instead, she insists on the 'participatory role of people in the well-being of the land'.[22] She calls restoration 'a powerful antidote to despair, which robs us of agency' and 'blinds us to our own power and the power of the earth'.[23] Humans must understand that they cannot find a quick fix to control the Earth, 'especially in an era of rapid climate change'. But though the climate and 'species composition' may change, 'relationship endures'.[24] Citing the activist Indigenous Environmental Network, Kimmerer suggests that Western science is a limited 'conceptual and methodological tool' that requires Indigenous knowledge to effect ecological restoration, 'care-giving', and 'world renewal'.[25] She also cites as exemplary the 'Onondaga Nation Vision for a Clean Onondaga Lake', which engages land as a 'community of respected non-human persons to whom we humans have a responsibility'.[26]

Kimmerer's speculations on the power of ways of knowing and seeing that centre human relations to the more-than-human world, and on the crafting of experimental cultural texts that connect to movements and problematise binaries between individual and collective voice in the face of climate change and struggles over sciences, ecologies, and environments, resonate with the work of many other Indigenous writers, thinkers, and activists, including many producers of Indigenous speculative fiction, futurisms, and science stories.[27] They also resonate with the work of Alexis Pauline Gumbs and other Black feminists who engage the speculative in recent art, literature, culture, and movement-building. Gumbs is part of a formation of Black feminist speculative thinkers and movement builders that includes adrienne maree brown, Walidah Imarisha, Dani McClain, and others involved in brown's and Imarisha's anthology *Octavia's Brood: Science Fiction Stories from Social Justice Movements* (2015). The 'visionary fiction' that the co-editors collect in this book often makes climate change and struggles over ecology, environment, and the more-than-human world central to speculative visions of the future, including brown's 'The River', which makes the Detroit River a more-than-human force that redresses inequalities and makes space for a different future, and McClain's 'Homing Instinct', which extrapolates from our present to imagine a world transformed by a US Executive Order that radically limits people's movements in response to climate change. Gumbs contributed to *Octavia's Brood* a short story called 'Evidence', structured as a series of time-travelling letters from the future to the present, which posits a future that is a radical break from capitalism and its 'scarcity-driven behavior'.[28] The *Octavia's Brood* project emerged from the activist work Gumbs, brown, Imarisha, McClain and many other Black speculative feminists and social movement organisers were doing, which partly comes together each year at the annual Allied Media Conference. Since its 2007 move to Detroit, the AMC is dedicated to the 'theory and practice of media-based organizing, or any collaborative process that uses media, art, or technology to address the roots of problems and advance holistic solutions towards a more just and creative world'. Many of the participants are involved in movements for which climate change is a central concern; there is a climate justice track that works on centring community-led solutions to climate change; and the AMC also sponsors environmental justice projects.[29]

Gumbs is a poet, theorist, and activist who has written a triptych of books in which she co-creates what she calls a speculative documentary form in dialogue with influential Black feminist writers Hortense Spillers, M. Jacqui Alexander, and Sylvia Wynter. Her first book, *Spill: Scenes of Black Feminist Fugitivity* (2016), signals its formal experimentation in the dedication to 'BLACK WOMEN who make and break narrative' and the acknowledgement that the text is written 'after and with' Spillers' *Black, White, and in Color, Essays on American Literature and Culture* (2003), which includes Spillers' seminal work on race, gender, sexuality, and psychoanalysis.[30] The second volume, *M Archive: After the End of the World* (2018), engages Alexander's *Pedagogies of Crossing: Meditations on Feminism, Sexual Politics, Memory, and the Sacred* (2005), crediting it with creating 'textual possibilities for inquiry beyond individual scholarly authority'.[31] In a note at the beginning, Gumbs names the form she imagines in *M Archive* 'speculative documentary', which is 'written in collaboration with the survivors, the far-into-the-future realities we are making possible or impossible with our present apocalypse', and which 'offers a possibility of being beyond the human'. Written 'from the perspective of a researcher, a post-scientist sorting artifacts after the end of the world', Gumbs imagines a world 'after and with the consequences of fracking past peak oil', as well as 'after and with clean water' and 'After the ways we have been knowing the world'.[32] Well aware of how exploiters and extractors have mobilised the speculative on behalf of capitalism (the 'erstwhile speculators' and 'speculative visionaries' who take over land and neighbourhoods), she nonetheless practises counter-speculation in conversation with Alexander and other 'Black speculative feminists', envisioning possibilities for Black life in the wake of climate and environmental devastation and future ongoing apocalypse.[33]

Climate change and racial ecologies are important in both *M Archive* and in *Dub: Finding Ceremony* (2020), which is written 'after and with published uncollected essays and one interview with Sylvia Wynter'. In the opening Note, Gumbs emphasises Wynter's experimentation with multiple literary forms, including 'theory, fiction, drama, and continual critical conversations that get at the underside of the stories so core to our existence that we don't even see them as stories'.[34] Wynter was also a 'participant in multiple social movements' who frequently wrote about 'the destruction of the physical environment' as she analysed the 'inhumane history of man' over time, in relation to colonialism, and imagined 'a different story'.[35] Although Wynter 'does not identify as a science fiction writer', Gumbs argues that her work illuminates how 'the history of the human has all been insidious science fiction, a fiction about what science is'.[36] Building on Wynter's analysis to ask, 'what if one group of people colonized the whole world with a story that survival meant destroying life on earth?', in *Dub* Gumbs attends to 'speakers who have never been considered human', expanding her understanding of 'family' and 'ancestors' to encompass 'relatives outside' the 'human species', who had some 'storytelling and untelling to do as well'.[37] Citing Wynter's classic 'No Humans Involved: An Open Letter to My Colleagues', Gumbs writes that 'the category of the never-considered-human' includes, among others, 'everyone subject to the police radio codes' about which Wynter writes, as well as 'whales, corals, barnacles, bacteria', and other 'kindred beyond taxonomy'.[38]

In 'No Humans Involved', written in 1994 in the wake of the acquittal of the police who beat Rodney King in Los Angeles, Wynter connects climate change and the destruction of the environment to anti-Black state violence and the inhumane history of Man told by colonial and imperial institutions of knowledge-production. The title, Wynter explains, came from a radio news report's account of how public officials of the LA judicial system used the acronym to 'refer to any case involving a breach of the rights of young Black males who belong to the jobless category of the inner-city ghettoes'.[39] Wynter's lead piece in the Stanford student organisation N.H.I. Institute's 1994 'Knowledge on Trial' issue takes the form of an 'open letter' to her colleagues in the university, asking them to consider that the officials who deployed this 'system of classification' were people 'whom we ourselves would have educated'.[40] Next, she emphasises how the present order of knowledge cannot even pose, let alone resolve, the plight of the 'poor and jobless' and the 'ongoing degradation of the planetary environment'.[41] Wynter repeatedly pairs the two problems, insisting that 'the hitherto discardable environment, its ongoing pollution, and ozone layer depletion' and the 'throwaway lives' at the 'global socio-human level' are 'hidden costs' that remain invisible to the 'inner eyes' of the mode of subjective understanding generated from the disciplines of her present and their representation 'of the human as if it were a natural organism'.[42] Wynter speculates that these costs are hidden 'within the terms of the hegemonic economic categories', which set the limits for 'our culture specific inner eyes' – the limits of 'how we can see, know, and behave upon our present global and national order'.[43] Thus the 'central issue' confronting us, Wynter wrote towards the end of the twentieth century, is 'whether we can move beyond the epistemic limits of our present "inner eye"' to address the plights of 'both the planetary as well as the global socio-human environment' in order to move towards a 'new, correlated human species, and eco-systemic ethic'.[44]

Gumbs writes in conversation with 'No Humans Involved' as well as other seminal pieces by Wynter that illuminate Wynter's significance as a major Black, feminist, climate-change intellectual speculating about racial and colonial ecologies and environments as early as the late twentieth century, including with 'Human Being as Noun?', an unpublished essay based on a talk Wynter gave in 2008 at Wesleyan University, just after the IPCC declared that humans had caused global warming. Wynter cites a 2007 *Time* article about the smoking gun report in an epigraph, criticising it for making *homo economicus* isomorphic with the human as such when making policy recommendations to address what she calls the already ongoing reality of global warming and climate change. Wynter's analysis clarifies the limits of this narrow understanding of the human and how it disappears underside costs of the Western capitalist growth model such as global warming and climate change. In Gumbs' documentary speculative science story-poems, she builds on Wynter's insights about the 'intra-Western' boundaries of this restrictive, colonising definition of the human to consider a planetarily extended vision of the intra-human beyond the idea of species, in relation to land and more-than-human kin.[45] Gumbs dedicates the book to '(all) my relations', thereby emphasising the expansive sense of kinship she explores throughout, and writes of how her sense of who her ancestors were changed through her practice of daily writing. These include her Caribbean ancestors, but also many others, including her 'coastal whale-listening Shinnecock ancestors' and 'untraceable Arawak ancestors' and 'finally the ocean itself'.[46] This process of exploration led her to seek 'to understand the species of whales, coral, barnacles, bacteria, and so forth, that were speaking from the bottom and the surface of the ocean' and to 'understand that the scientific taxonomy of what constituted a species' was 'as debatable and discursively unstable' as 'the narratives within my family of who was an inside or outside child, and who was related and why and how' and 'certainly as complex as what Wynter teaches us about: the discursive construction of man'.[47]

Gumbs also dialogues with Wynter's engagement with the sciences and the never-considered human as she considers Black people's relations to whales, in the middle passage, as commodities exploited and murdered by violent industry, as othered animals within inhumane histories of the human, as wondrous beings and more-than-human kin. In 'Instructions', she writes of African ancestors crossing the ocean and the 'whales who swam next to us, singing', who 'clicked sometimes louder than the chains'.[48] In a note, Gumbs references Wynter's thoughts on 'representation of origins' in 'Human Being as Noun?', where she discusses different origin stories that chart society's fictive modes and genres of being human; Gumbs imagines a more capacious origin story that doesn't sever Black people and the human from the more-than-human world even as she marks how both have been cast, in different ways, as sub-human.[49] In a section called 'Whale Chorus', Gumbs builds on this piece and 'Human Being as Noun?' as she speculates on the costs of the extractive economy undergirding this Western colonial conception of the human that turned Black people and whales into commodities, even as she raises questions about relations between and interconnected with material histories of Black people and whales. Thinking about the emergence of humanitarian concern for the whale, Gumbs writes, 'just because the singing of the whales had caused bumper stickers and rallies and international bans on their murder', did not mean 'it would work for us'. If 'singing could save, we'd be god', she suggests, insisting instead that 'it was the fact of other sources of oil to move onto, other deep black resources to extract' that made people want to 'save the whales once they knew they didn't need them'.[50] She also connects these speculations to Wynter's 'Ethnic or Socio Poetics', her contribution to a 1973 symposium on intersections between poetry and anthropology, in which she insists that the Old World's discovery of vast new lands was pivotal in the transition from feudalism to capitalism and fundamentally changed Europeans' 'relation to Nature' and to 'Other Men'.[51]

Gumbs' adaptation of Wynter's theories connects to Kimmerer's analysis of reciprocal relations and responsibilities among humans, the land, and the more-than-human world as she emphasises the relationships among what Wynter calls 'those defined and forced to accept their definition as sub-human'.[52] In their experimental, activist, speculative science stories, these writers refuse the amnesia about ongoing colonialism and white nationalism and the too-easy despair about the end of the world that dominates many contemporary US mainstream narratives of climate change. Instead, their climate change stories remember the knowledge of ancestors and the more-than-human world and imagine collective futures that swerve off the tracks of extractive capitalism's never-ending disaster story and facile hopes for a techno-fix.

Notes

1 R. W. Kimmerer *et al.*, 'Let Our Indigenous Voices Be Heard', www.esf.edu/indigenous-science-letter/Indigenous_Science_Declaration.pdf. All citations of this Letter that follow are from this source.
2 G. Dillon, 'Imagining Indigenous Futurisms', in Dillon (ed.), *Walking the Clouds: An Anthology of Indigenous Science Fiction* (Tucson: University of Arizona Press, 2012), 3.
3 Dillon, *Walking the Clouds*, 8.
4 R. W. Kimmerer, *Gathering Moss: A Natural and Cultural History of Mosses* (Corvallis: Oregon State University Press, 2003), vi.
5 Kimmerer, *Gathering Moss*, vii.
6 Kimmerer, *Gathering Moss*, vii.
7 Kimmerer, *Gathering Moss*, vii.
8 R. W. Kimmerer, *Braiding Sweetgrass: Indigenous Wisdom, Scientific Knowledge, and the Teachings of Plants* (Minneapolis: Milkweed, 2013), 168.
9 Kimmerer, *Braiding Sweetgrass*, 173.
10 Kimmerer, *Braiding Sweetgrass*, 174.
11 Kimmerer, *Braiding Sweetgrass*, 217.
12 Kimmerer, *Braiding Sweetgrass*, 218.
13 Kimmerer, *Braiding Sweetgrass*, 219.
14 Kimmerer, *Braiding Sweetgrass*, 220.
15 Kimmerer, *Braiding Sweetgrass*, 221.
16 Kimmerer, *Braiding Sweetgrass*, 221–2.

17 Kimmerer, *Braiding Sweetgrass*, 269.
18 Kimmerer, *Braiding Sweetgrass*, 275.
19 Kimmerer, *Braiding Sweetgrass*, 276.
20 Kimmerer, *Braiding Sweetgrass*, 327.
21 Kimmerer, *Braiding Sweetgrass*, 328, 327.
22 Kimmerer, *Braiding Sweetgrass*, 327.
23 Kimmerer, *Braiding Sweetgrass*, 328.
24 Kimmerer, *Braiding Sweetgrass*, 336.
25 Kimmerer, *Braiding Sweetgrass*, 336–7.
26 Kimmerer, *Braiding Sweetgrass*, 338.
27 I am thinking especially of the work of Leanne Betasamosake Simpson (Mississauga Nishnaabeg) and of the significance of climate change and the more-than-human world in many Indigenous futurist texts such as those collected by Dillon in *Walking the Clouds*.
28 A. P. Gumbs, 'Evidence', in W. Imarisha and A. M. Brown (eds.), *Octavia's Brood: Science Fiction Stories from Social Justice Movements* (Oakland, CA: AK Press, 2015), 40.
29 See 'About', *Allied Media Projects*, https://alliedmedia.org. On adrienne maree brown's leadership in the AMC, see S. Streeby, *Imagining the Future of Climate Change: Worldmaking through Science Fiction and Activism* (Berkeley: University of California Press, 2018), 103–5.
30 A. P. Gumbs, *Spill: Scenes of Black Feminist Fugitivity* (Durham, NC: Duke University Press, 2016), v.
31 A. P. Gumbs, *M Archive: After the End of the World* (Durham, NC: Duke University Press, 2018), ix.
32 Gumbs, *M Archive*, xi.
33 Gumbs, *M Archive*, 36, 171.
34 A. P. Gumbs, *Dub: Finding Ceremony* (Durham, NC: Duke University Press, 2020), ix.
35 Gumbs, *Dub*, x.
36 Gumbs, *Dub*, xi.
37 Gumbs, *Dub*, xi, xii, xiii.
38 Gumbs, *Dub*, xii.
39 S. Wynter, 'No Humans Involved: An Open Letter to My Colleagues', *Forum NHI: Knowledge for the 21st Century* 1.1 (Fall 1994), 43.
40 Wynter, 'No Humans Involved', 43.
41 Wynter, 'No Humans Involved', 59.
42 Wynter, 'No Humans Involved', 60.
43 Wynter, 'No Humans Involved', 61.
44 Wynter, 'No Humans Involved', 62, 69.
45 Gumbs, *Dub*, 262.
46 Gumbs, *Dub*, xiii.
47 Gumbs, *Dub*, xiii.
48 Gumbs, *Dub*, 6.
49 Gumbs, *Dub*, 261.
50 Gumbs, *Dub*, 18.
51 S. Wynter, 'Ethno or Socio-Poetics', *Alcheringa/Ethnopoetics* 2.2 (1976), 82.
52 Wynter, 'Ethno or Socio-Poetics', 88.

14

KELLY SULTZBACH

More-than-Human Collectives in Richard Powers' *The Overstory* and Vandana Singh's 'Entanglement'

Who Is the More-than-Human Collective?

Times of crisis seem to prompt a desire to extend beyond our species for more-than-human company and new insights. While on medical leave from fighting in the First World War, Wilfred Owen gave a talk for the Craiglockhart War Hospital Field Society titled 'Do Plants Think?', demonstrating how the vegetative will to survive is analogous to human behaviours, and that plants' 'astounding power' to transform soil into nutrients through photosynthesis 'was worth looking into "by us mere animals"'.[1] Such ideas have continued to take root not only in the imagination of science fiction authors such as Octavia Butler and Jeff VanderMeer, but also in new research on how trees communicate, from which Richard Powers' novel, *The Overstory* (2018), draws.[2] Of course, this recognition of the animacy and sentient value of non-human beings has long been a feature of Indigenous literature and culture, as Vandana Singh makes use of in her story 'Entanglement' (2014), drawing both from Baffin Island Inuit tradition and Hindu teachings.[3]

On the other side of the spectrum, but in a semantic parallel with Wilfred Owen, Alan Turing posed the question 'Can Machines Think?' in the years following the Second World War, when machinery's use in warfare and code-breaking augured the imitation-game test.[4] From the earlier stirrings of Karel Čapek's play *R.U.R.* (Rossum's Universal Robots) (1921), to Isaac Asimov's *The Robot* series (1940–86) and the *Bladerunner* films (1982, 2017), literature has also been considering how the more-than-human relationship with artificial intelligence (AI) – now used in algorithmic decision-making, chatbots, healthcare and cybersecurity – might expand. Powers' use of AI coding and Singh's use of biomimicry technology and AI watches place both of their stories within this lineage too.

The question of what constitutes a multispecies thinking community is becoming even more porous in the contemporary crisis of climate change.

Both Powers' *The Overstory* and Vandana Singh's 'Entanglement' depict a braided collective comprised of humans, intelligent botanical or zoological life, and AI. Further, both are overtly oriented to the problem of how to imagine collective action in the face of climate change – a pressing global conflict, if not an outright invitation to a third human world war. Moreover, they experiment with original narrative forms based on non-human models of dynamic systems: Powers models *The Overstory* on contemporary tree communication science, and Singh's 'Entanglement' uses her expertise in physics to construct a vision of collective action suggested by chaos theory and quantum entanglement. Using narrative forms that replicate non-human processes of large-scale synthesis, Powers and Singh grapple with how more-than-human collectives might work, both aesthetically and thematically. These non-human models also dictate the resolutions of their stories – eventualities of collectivity that may still be evolving, but gesture towards potential climate-changed futures.

Each story also integrates, albeit to differing degrees, inclusive approaches to races, ethnicities, and political groups dominated by conflict. Our destructive capacity toward each other is also embedded in the legacy of the Anthropocene, not only through wars, but even more pervasively through settler colonialism and genocide. Dipesh Chakrabarty warns: 'However much we speak of a human-induced climate change, humanity will remain a category of thought, even an ideal of political horizons, but perhaps never become a unified political agent acting in ways that are unjust to none.'[5] As a result, any widening of the collective of non-human organic or artificial agents in the world must be contextualised with the reality of white racism, promoted by nationalism and colonialism – treating some humans as less-thinking, or less-feeling, than other humans.

More-than-Human Collective Action as a Choice between Two 'Realities' in *The Overstory*

In *The Overstory*, trees suffuse the language of the text and at times even seem to direct the action of the plot, in a contemporary setting when the world is at the tipping point of climate destruction. What 'the world' truly is takes on a double meaning, revealing the simulacrum of the cultural 'world' humans think they inhabit versus the ecological one some have ruthlessly exploited. The overarching narrative is modelled on the arboreal structure of trees, from the underground symbiotic communications between a web of mycelium and roots, through rising capillary action, to the lofty tree crown habitats wafting pollen through the wind and dropping fruit to disperse new seeds of growth. This development is mirrored in the content titles: 'Roots' (where each of the nine human protagonists develops through generational backstories and has a pivotal epiphany about the significance of trees); 'Trunk' (where individual plots converge with a cluster of five characters becoming eco-activists together, while another character designs a world-making video game and another publishes a book on plant intelligence); 'Crown' (the denouement of the activists' failed attempts to change the world as they move from pacifists to eco-terrorists, resulting in the death of one character and incarceration of two others); and 'Seeds', the section this article will focus on.[6]

'Seeds' imagines the kind of action that might be produced by the more-than-human collective, after both pacifist and violent protests have failed. The novel as a whole suggests that if human minds were 'a slightly greener thing',[7] 'a slightly different creature',[8] then humans might become part of the ecological 'world' collective. The rich tenors of 'seed' involve all three main components of the 'collective': (1) the human characters that seemed to be lost (dead, imprisoned, or in a state of deep depression) whose fallen activist fruits still germinate cultural debate; (2) the actual seeds and floating spores of sentient trees, and (3) the 'living code'[9] of computer programming, initiated by virtual game-designer, Neelay Mehta. It is Powers' analogy between ecological pollen and genetic or computer coding that produces the most surprising and disturbing arc of action that might 'save' a world. But which world will be saved by Neelay's code? Will the AI program store an ecological seed-matrix that will one day grow a *real* flourishing plant and animal world after the human species, with its *false realities* of economy and consumerism, is extinct? Or will the game re-train the world of human culture through a simulacrum of green thinking, in which humanity persists in some improved ecocentric or even hybrid form?

Readers are first introduced to Neelay as 'The boy who'll help change humans into other creatures'.[10] In a fall from a tree that is described as both an attempt to injure himself a bit in order to get out of some trouble at home and a deliberate act of the tree itself, Neelay becomes paraplegic, encouraging his submersion into the digital mindscape. The revelation for the computer game he will create is inspired by a collection of colonised trees ringing an inner quad at Stanford University:

> He rolls from planter to planter, touching the beings, smelling them, listening to their rustles. ... He touches their bark and feels, just beneath their skins, the teeming assemblies of cells, like whole planetary civilizations, pulse and hum. ... The alien invaders insert a thought directly into his limbic system. There will be a game, a billion times richer than anything yet made, to be played by countless people around the world at the same time. And Neelay must bring

it into being ... in gradual, evolutionary stages, over the course of decades. The game will put its players smack in the middle of a living, breathing, seething, animist world filled with millions of different species, a world desperately in need of the players' help. And the goal of the game will be to figure out what the new and desperate world wants from you.[11]

This idea is a 'plan that now uses' Neelay, 'although he thinks it's his'. However, the references to 'alien invaders' and 'unearthly life' suggest not just arboreal dictates but pulsations of extraterrestrial origin or artificial intelligence – a double-helix of possibilities the novel doesn't fully unravel. Instead, the trees embody some larger cosmic system containing 'cells' and 'codes' that Neelay in his wheelchair literally seems to 'roll' or scroll through, touching and feeling real 'bark' or 'skin' as their messages pollinate his own cerebral limbic system of emotions and memory. The game itself, called Mastery, evolves from a botanical world-exploring platform to a game where players exploit natural resources, build civilisations, and even loot the lands of others, a re-enactment of Western patriarchy and colonial violence. Neelay eventually discards this conquest iteration of the game, even when revenues are at an all-time high, recognising 'Mastery has a Midas problem. Everything's dying a gold-plated death.'[12]

To convince his wealthy board and co-workers to embrace the game's next evolutionary stage, Neelay invites the now-famous ecologist and author Patricia Westerford to speak about the secret life of trees in an auditorium ironically 'lined with redwood questionably attained'.[13] Unbeknownst to her audience, she has brought along poisonous plant extracts, which she pours into her water while posing the question she was asked to address: 'What is the single best thing a person can do for tomorrow's world?'.[14] Neelay presumably expects her to talk about ideas that will justify changing the game into one that rewards conservation and ecological biodiversity. But Westerford's speech contains more than one message. At this point Powers splits time into two quantum realities: 'The speaker raises her glass, and the world splits. Down one branch, she lifts the glass to her lips, toasts the room – *To Tachigali versicolor* – and drinks. Down another branch, this one, she shouts, "Here's to unsuicide," and flings the cup of swirling green over the gasping audience'.[15] Thus, in one universe she ends her life as an embodied statement of the only solution to anthropogenic climate destruction – the self-abnegation of the human species. But in 'another branch, *this one*' (emphasis added) she throws the poisoned drink harmlessly over the heads of the audience, in an act of 'unsuicide', killing off the unreal version of the self, the one living only through constructed human culture, in order to realise a new, ecologically attuned form of human life, a becoming implied by the title of her next book,

The New Metamorphosis. If one reads 'unsuicide' as a symbolic gesture for Neelay's new computer programme too, one might interpret it as not merely about recording the natural world in anticipation of human annihilation, but rather an effort to change the way humans think about the 'real' world through the new game. But much depends on the interpretive hinge of '*this one*' in the description of Westerford's two branching realities; other readers I have spoken with finished the novel certain that Westerford kills herself, her second book *The New Metamorphosis* published post-mortem.

The code that Neelay uses to create his new programme is equally mired in multiple metaphors. The seeds of his programming codes are described as 'his children', 'his learners', though ones nurtured in a very corporate soil. They will 'see across the planet' as self-generating algorithms and accelerating returns that will 'eat every scrap of data', and yet they are also biologically inflected with 'the genes of their ancestors' in an effort to find out 'what life wants of people and how it might use them'.[16] Thus, towards the end of the novel when one of the activist characters, Mimi Ma, sees a vision of the future, what it portends is just as uncertain as Westerford's split reality:

> Messages hum from the bark she leans against. Chemical semaphores home in over the air. Currents rise from the soil-gripping roots, relayed over great distances through fungal synapses linked up in network the size of the planet. The signals say: *A good answer is worth reinventing from scratch, again and again* ... She sees and hears this by direct gathering, through her limbs. The fires will come, despite all efforts, the blight and windthrow and floods. Then the Earth will become another thing, and people will learn it all over again.

As the passage goes on, it adds that this new world, with 'seed banks ... thrown open', '[s]econd growth' returning, fresh '[w]ebs of forest ... with species ... dappled by new design', will begin only '[o]nce *the real world* ends'.[17]

There are, then, three possible interpretations of this passage. One invites a suggestion that, although there is no longer any action humans can collectively do to prevent the climate tragedy already unleashed by the demands of capitalist culture, the end of that solipsistic world which people only believe to be 'real' right now will be followed by another – whose seed banks will be 'thrown open', presumably by humans who have been able to collectively green their thinking in a mass 'unsuicide', radically transforming our very notion of what it means to be human. Neelay seems to intend this when he describes his design to dubious board members: 'A wrong choice in the game should lead to permadeath. ... Seven million users will need to discover the rules of a dangerous new place. To learn what the world will bear, how life really works, what it wants from a player in exchange for continuing to play'.[18] Alternatively, however, the passage doesn't specify that human hands will open that vault, allowing for a second interpretation: that regeneration will take place in a more literally posthuman future where the human species is both the cause and victim of the sixth extinction climate change poses. Further, opening a third interpretative possibility, a gaming lexicon tints this passage: 'testing all possibilities', 'new design', 'carpeted earth', 'surge', 'stacking themselves'. This vocabulary seems to come less from the terminology of ecology and more from the glossary of computer programming. Is the future only a simulation? In other words, an unreal 'natural' setting that exists only in the form of a game humans play in a post-apocalyptic world?

Although ambiguity is a powerful tool of the literary form, this expansively vague resolution courts evasion on multiple levels. Marco Caracciolo has dubbed it 'deus ex algorithmo', borrowing from 'the notorious narrative shortcut of Greek drama, wherein gods were lifted onto the stage by a crane (the 'machina') to solve a situation that would have been intractable in human terms'.[19] Although he acknowledges that this strategy 'has become mostly synonymous with a contrived, disappointing ending', he rescues Powers from this pitfall, in part because Caracciolo assumes that the coded learners represent 'the ethically significant caveat that it is the planet (not humanity) that will be saved', a conclusion that I propose is only one of three interpretive branches of possibility.[20] I am more persuaded by his defence that, 'when injected into narrative form, quantum uncertainty and self-organizing complexity turn a seemingly arbitrary "twist" (the traditional deus ex machina) into a far more compelling reconsideration of humanity's role in novelistic story and planetary history'.[21] Indeed, it is the very potential of AI to become a third actor in the collective – one which could employ anthropocentric, organic, or its own self-serving aims in the pursuit of finding out what life wants – which makes its use as a summation device into an important ethical question about AI. Yet the mechanisms of this overarching synthesising logos still present a troubling model that risks replicating capitalist and patriarchal structures.

A future of AI mastery with a human god at its germinating, code-twirling core is also envisioned by AI engineer and futurist Ray Kurzweil, for whom, 'by the end of this century', humanity's 'destiny' will be '[w]aking up the universe, and then intelligently deciding its fate by infusing it with our human intelligence in its nonbiological form'.[22] This language of god-like control, like Neelay's, lacks any discussion of to what use this technoscience will be put, who will influence its anomalies, who will create the algorithms that will organise data, or for what end such powers will be used. Donna Haraway states that 'The interface between specifically located people, other organisms, and machines turns out to be an excellent field for ethnographic inquiry into what counts as self-acting and as collective empowerment', but she also cautions against 'dogma where fundamental cultural and material values are both not shared and at stake. What must not be lost from sight in all of this complexity, however, is that power, profit, and bodily arrangements are at the heart of biotechnology as a global practice'.[23]

An attention to collective solutions emanating from a diverse constituency representing the risks to multiple ways of life is the most significant distinction between the collectives imagined by Powers and Singh. *The Overstory* includes humans from a variety of classes and immigrant backgrounds (with emphasis on the Norwegian, Chinese, and Asian-Indian characters' heritages). Yet, this gesture seems all the more problematic for leaving out African Americans – arguably the Americans with the most excruciating experience of how environmental conquest and the history of trees as places of lynching and slavery coincides with violence against human life. This is not to say that every writer is beholden to incorporate all social justice issues or create a token sense that every race and ethnicity is represented, but in a book entirely set in the United States, the complete absence of slavery and its coeval history with the felling of trees to build plantations seems odd. Additionally, the final scene, an encounter between the white American itinerant artist Nick and a few Indigenous Americans, teeters between two readings. One interpretation could suggest Indigenous Americans don't need the same ecological lessons of re-greening the mind: the Indigenous characters speak their own language without translating it for Nick, retort to Nick's statement that the trees talk with 'We've been trying to tell you that since 1492', and laugh when he seems not to recognise all that is edible around him.[24] Yet, another reading marginalises Indigenous peoples by representing them as nearly an afterthought at the novel's conclusion, mysteriously emanating from the Pacific Northwest old-growth forest, without specific tribal affiliation, or much need to talk, all in order to assist the white, male artist in his work.

That said, Powers' proliferating insistence on multiple branching buds of possible futures, in scenes that invite interpretations that both challenge and re-inscribe white patriarchal stereotypes, is a narrative strategy that underscores the novel's entire structure of roots and branches – growths that strive towards nutrients and light, but whose future is embedded in the decaying worlds (ecological and cultural) from which they spring. Therefore, the reader is called on to listen attentively, and forced to choose one destiny or the other.

More-than-Human Collective Action as Collaboration in 'Entanglement'

Singh's 'Entanglement' also considers what kind of collective action might synthesise physics, technology, and more cooperative world-building between species. Singh's prose does not have the poetic pull of Powers' lyricism, but its narrative design is satisfyingly clever. While her story is confined to an atom-charged fifty-odd-pages, it still manages to combine five separate ensembles of characters in five different regions of the globe, embracing the East Siberian Sea Arctic, Brazil, India, the United States, and an unspecified region of the Himalayas. The characters in each story are involved in combating the multi-farious forms of destruction which cause or result from climate change: in the first section of the narrative, characters work to restore Arctic ice, in the second to protect the Amazon from corporate deforestation, in the third to save a rural community from an unseasonal tornado, in the fourth to stop fracking, and in the fifth to develop a theory of empathy that might be embedded in a kind of orange smartwatch to help humans overcome the inertia of solas-talgia. All but one of the stories features non-human animals as well: a beluga whale saves the Arctic scientist, graffiti art animates jungle animals which then lure tourists to energy-saving garden rooftops, the life of a crow unites people from different social castes, and a mongoose's cry prevents a suicide.

Like *The Overstory*, Singh's narrative also has a unique structure, mod-elled on ideas from the intra-active dynamic systems of chaos theory and quantum entanglement.[25] Initially, the connection between each geographic section and set of new characters might seem random, creating a chaotic reading experience. Yet the titles and first sentences of each section hint at the story's preoccupation with linking larger movements of successful climate action to small moments of decision. Although all but one section title of 'Entanglement' are separated by ellipses on each side, when put together, these titles read: '... Flapping Its Wings ...' 'In the Amazon ...' '... Can Cause a Tornado ...' '... In Texas ...' 'The End' '... A Butterfly ...'. In a circular, end-defying sequence, they recall Edward Lorenz's statement about chaos theory: 'The flap of a butterfly's wings can be instrumental in generating a tornado, it can equally well be instrumental in preventing a - tornado'.[26] In the context of Singh's work, the different localised actions become a way for humans to generate system-wide solutions that mitigate climate change. However, not only does each section title link together on the large-scale Lorenz reference, but each can simultaneously be read as the beginning of the first discrete sentence of that section's narrative. For exam-ple, the first section '... Flapping Its Wings ...' starts '... and flying straight at her.'[27] As a result, the section titles enact a momentum of rhetorical engagement on both the small scale of each individual story and the com-bined work of the larger narrative.

Quantum entanglement is more subtly at play in how AI is used to connect human characters. In conventional physics, entanglement refers to the relationship between two partially known objects, where knowledge of the condition of one depends on knowing something about the condition of the other: they are entangled in some physical way. In quantum physics, however, quantum systems can be entangled even at great distance from each other: the state of one somehow complements the other and they are impossible to know independently. This notoriously tricky concept of quantum entanglement, what Albert Einstein called 'this spooky action at a distance', is key to Singh's story.[28] Discrete lines of dialogue, spoken by a character in a single episode, recur in another episode as something heard from an orange wristband. This wristband collects, collates, and reproduces seemingly disparate statements from physically distanced characters who are strangers to one another but who are prompted to respond to an image or recording of the other person. This often catalyses action the original, geographically remote, stranger could never have foreseen, providing the positive impetus to overcome loneliness or self-doubt, and leading to the successful completion of that other character's environmental activist task. In this way, the correlation between the two characters from separate places, working through distinct conflicts, and completely unknown to one another, roughly resembles quantumly entangled systems or particles. Via the wristband technology they are 'correlated' by their shared environmental concern, even if working on distant and distinct aspects of the climate problem. For example, in the first episode or story, Arctic marine researcher Irene has a kind of daydream of being in a storm and catapulted by something soft and feathery, so she shouts aloud a direction to run and seek out low ground, a dream that, in the context of her story, resonates with her concern that she may have 'run away' from her indigenous family connections.[29] In a later story, a small boy in India trying to save his village from a tornado, hears these words and acts on them, which saves his life, as well as the feathery bomb which ends up being a crow the boy then rescues.[30] Irene also becomes endangered during the course of her narrative by a small tear in her wetsuit that is certain to lead to hypothermia and death, but the wristwatch captures the voice of a character we encounter in a later story, an elderly woman who sees Irene's image and says 'Bless you and be careful up there; I'm praying for you.'[31] These words, which Irene hears as her own grandmother's, push her to move her arms towards the surface, which then registers her distress to a nearby beluga whale, who raises Irene to the surface, so that she survives to continue her work.[32] Thus, Singh envisions a consistent intertwining of actors in community, creating vital connections through an AI technology that seems to prompt, choose, and disperse bits of phrases of its own accord, in moments of need.

Readers eventually meet the young inventor of the wristbands, Yuan. Similar to Neelay, his vision for creating something that would dispel loneliness and create a network of empathy arises not just from his training but from a more mystic encounter. Yuan dreamed about a university, built from an old monastery, which he heard about in a lecture given by a Nigerian professor who 'changed everything I knew about the world': 'It was a place for those who sought to understand the world in a new way and to bring about its resurrection. I saw the humblest people come here to share what they knew, and the learned ones listened.'[33] When he arrives at the Himalayan monastery he saw in his dream, he finds it nearly destroyed by melting snowcaps and avalanche, but comes to realise that this scene of ending may in fact be the beginning of the school of his dreams. Yet he directly denies any god-like status when asked, 'Do you fancy yourself a Buddha, or a Jesus?', responding, 'I've no such fancies. I'm not even religious. I'm only trying to learn what my teacher called the true knowledge that teaches us how things are linked.'[34] When he needs affirmation, he hears through his own wristband the woman in the Amazon story saying, '... A Butterfly ...', both invoking the disruption of monarch butterfly migration and underscoring the systemic physics of the novel's prevailing motif.

Like Powers' novel, Singh's story relies on some form of AI within her representation of sentient collective action. Yet, unlike Neelay, Yuan is careful to situate the creation of the device within a series of events that emphasise collaboration. Debate and dissonance are refigured as a more genuine form of coherence when Yuan insists that 'true peace is dynamic and rests on a thousand quarrels'.[35] Whereas Neelay (though influenced by the dictates of trees, perhaps) becomes centred as forefather of the digitalised future re-greening, Yuan (albeit acting within socially entangled dynamics) is more modest about his invention, the product of chance occurrences and a more limited form of AI than Neelay's world-creating programme.

The orange wristband is not an all-powerful logos nor even the only species of AI technology in the story. The gigantic 'brollies' Irene and her research team create to record information about the ocean are able to know where they are needed without being summoned: 'Her original conception of linked artificial intelligences with information-feedback loops was based on biomimicry, inspired by natural systems like ecosystems and endocrine systems. She had a sudden vision of a multilevel, complexly interconnected grid, a sentience spanning continents and species, a kind of Gaiaweb come alive.'[36] Singh's AI presences don't recreate a new world as much as enable the sharing of knowledge among all thinking beings in the more-than-human collective. Additionally, the brollies' data, not just the purview of a corporation or scientists, is part of 'Million Eyes on the Arctic', 'the largest citizen science project in the world', sharing 'information about sea ice melt, methane leaks, marine animal sightings, and ocean hot spots'.[37]

Moreover, the technology is integrated with all the various actors in the collective. The transforming, saving powers of 'non-sentient' beings such as bacteria, are part of the rehabilitation effort of Irene, her team, and the intelligent brollies: 'Methanotrophs, like most living beings, didn't exist in isolation but in consortia. . . . With enough nutrients, they and their communities of cooperative organisms might take care of much of the methane'.[38] Other non-human animals become part of the 'million eyes' carbon-recapture project too as a 'mottled white crab' was 'sitting on top of one of the instrument panels, exploring the device with its claws'.[39] Here, Haraway's situated perspectives abound. All beings have specific bodies and lives at stake, for people and other animals both save and are saved: the whale saving Irene or the crow saved by the boy in India. Singh insists on an assemblage of plurality, forces arrayed against other complex systems of economics, profit, and nationalist power.

Thinking and Action

At the start of the Second World War, Virginia Woolf – who saw life as a suspended mist between the branches of trees and who composed her own experimental novel modelled on the light waves of physics[40] – wrote in her diary, 'Thinking is my fighting.'[41] Similarly, thinking and feeling is rendered active in these stories; inventive, supple forms of action are residual products of these initial reconceptualisations of the human self's relationship to an already ongoing, animate mesh of creative worlding. Powers and Singh prepare readers to imagine the interstices between biophilia and technophilia. Singh also spins spirituality, cultural respect, and international empathy into those currents of thought too, underscoring the fact that environmental change and social justice are inherently intertwined. Thus, the stories themselves become a form of fighting. As most ambiguous resolutions do, these stories require reflection and active reading choices. The reader is challenged to let themselves be changed. As Neelay says about gaming narratives, 'And what do all good stories do? . . . They kill you a little. They turn you into something you weren't.'[42] They are a call to action – for readers to enable their own greening of mind and choose futures, not through ecoterrorism or lone-hero activism, but rather through each reader influencing change within their own complex systems of workplace dynamics, investment in non-profit organisations, family influences, and community hope-building. It is a tremendous task – defying racism, hearing what the trees ask of us, trusting algorithms, rising up to become part of a rhizomatic, fractal, and evolving collective system. But how much time do we have? Can we change enough? Will we survive? Neither story provides assurances. But whether we are in an ending or a beginning, we can still work to become part of the larger living collective of beings that want to learn how life can use them.

Notes

1 W. Owen, 'Do Plants Think?', unpublished notes for lecture (1917), MS. 12282/ 5, Bodleian Library, Oxford.
2 R. Powers, *The Overstory* (New York: Norton, 2018).
3 V. Singh, 'Entanglement', in J. J. Adams (ed.), *Loosed upon the World: The Saga Anthology of Climate Fiction* (New York: Saga, 2015), 269–322.
4 A. M. Turing, 'I. Computing Machinery and Intelligence', *Mind* 59 (October 1950), 433–60.
5 D. Chakrabarty, *The Crises of Civilization: Exploring Global and Planetary Histories* (Oxford University Press, 2018), 212.
6 It has been noted that Powers' text draws heavily from Peter Wohlleben's *The Hidden Life of Trees: What They Feel, How They Communicate: Discoveries from a Secret World* (London: Harper Collins, 2016), and that the initials of the character Patricia Westerford echo that of its author, although the struggle to have her research recognised resembles the trajectory of Suzanne Simard; see N. Rich, 'The Novel That Asks: "What Went Wrong with Mankind?": Richard Powers's Climate-Themed Epic, *The Overstory*, Embraces a Dark Optimism about the Fate of Humanity', *The Atlantic* (June 2018).
7 Powers, *Overstory*, 4.
8 Powers, *Overstory*, 155.
9 Powers, *Overstory*, 493.
10 Powers, *Overstory*, 91.
11 Powers, *Overstory*, 110–11.
12 Powers, *Overstory*, 376–7.
13 Powers, *Overstory*, 450.
14 Powers, *Overstory*, 464.
15 Powers, *Overstory*, 466.
16 Powers, *Overstory*, 493–4.
17 Powers, *Overstory*, 499–500.
18 Powers, *Overstory*, 413.
19 M. Caracciolo, 'Deus Ex Algorithmo: Narrative Form, Computation, and the Fate of the World in David Mitchell's *Ghostwritten* and Richard Powers's *The Overstory*', *Contemporary Literature* 60.1 (2019), 48.
20 Caracciolo, 'Deus Ex Algorithmo', 50.
21 Caracciolo, 'Deus Ex Algorithmo', 53–4.
22 R. Kurzweil, *How to Create a Mind: The Secret of Human Thought Revealed* (London: Viking, 2012), 281–2.
23 D. J. Haraway, *Modest_Witness@Second_Millennium.FemaleMan©_Meets_Onco Mouse™: Feminism and Technoscience* (New York: Routledge, 1997), 52, 61.
24 Powers, *Overstory*, 493.
25 See M. Kurtz, '"Alternate Cuts": An Interview with Vandana Singh', *Science Fiction Studies* 43.3 (2016), 542–3.

26 E. Lorenz, 'Low Order Models Representing Realizations of Turbulence', *Journal of Fluid Mechanics* 55.3 (1972), 545–63.

27 Singh, 'Entanglement', 269.

28 F. Wilzcek, 'Entanglement Made Simple', *Quanta Magazine* (28 April 2016).

29 Singh, 'Entanglement', 269–81.

30 Singh, 'Entanglement', 291–302.

31 Singh, 'Entanglement', 275, 304.

32 Singh, 'Entanglement', 275–7.

33 Singh, 'Entanglement', 316, 313.

34 Singh, 'Entanglement', 318, 319.

35 Singh, 'Entanglement', 322.

36 Singh, 'Entanglement', 278.

37 Singh, 'Entanglement', 271.

38 Singh, 'Entanglement', 274.

39 Singh, 'Entanglement', 273.

40 See V. Woolf, *Mrs. Dalloway* (1925; New York: Harcourt, 2005), 9, and *The Waves* (1931), any edition.

41 Woolf, *The Diary of Virginia Woolf: Volume Five 1936–1941*, ed. A. O. Bell assisted by A. McNeillie (New York: Harcourt, 1984), 285.

42 Powers, *Overstory*, 412.

Love Letters to the Planet

15

THOMAS BRISTOW

Meteorology of Form

Preface (A Note on the Regionalism of an Island Continent)

This short study looks at fiction based in Australia, one of many places severely affected by anthropogenic global warming in the Global South. I elect not to refer to 'Western' cli-fi, or the 'Western' imaginary of anthropogenic climate change. I share a belief with other scholars in Australasia, Europe, and North America that it is time for a moratorium on the term 'the West'.[1]

Fictocritical Meteorology

Literature, like climate science, has 'worlds'.[2] Two such worlds within climate fiction are those determined by social collapse and loss of wilderness. The texts I have chosen for this chapter understand these aspects of global warming as 'simultaneously real, discursive, and social' as felt in Oceania.[3]

I turn to Australian literature to consider whether the arts and its analysis might yield models of socially symbolic acts that conceptualise life within a restricted field of immanence. Whether this helps to organise our responses to the ways materiality exhibits affectivity is a political issue, I intuit, key to reorganising our thoughts around mobilising climate change emotions. Fictocriticism enables the integration of the component of animacy that seeks out affective intensities that pass through and between human and non-human bodies. I believe this genre permits me to foreground personal meditations on the ongoing experiencing of climate catastrophe, and it discloses a space for dialogue between scholarly abstractions and personal ones. The unfolding cultural story that comes from these impulses is one of witness and embodiment that portends representations of climate as an intra-active being.

Literature is not tasked with identifying survival mechanisms; writers, however, are vastly more skilled at communicating anxiety, grief, and loss with human feeling than scientists who articulate our precarious state with empirical data. Both groups appear to orbit a representational polis governing commitments that range from privatised environmental literacy to the revolution of world spirit. The humanities refract this challenge as the difficulty of situating our self-reflective practices as generative of other practices, not merely descriptions of our state. The examples that follow are grouped by headings that by design homogenise various affective temporalities and emotional practices (including grief work).

*

A fan is spinning in an empty motel room. It commingles with the faint sound of traffic rolling past a cathedral in the near distance. I sit outside on the bare balcony hanging over the back of a gasoline station on Smith Street in Darwin's magnificent December sun.

Things move fast. I haven't had time to fully reflect on a recent trip to Sydney when the bushfire season started. I was at an Environmental Humanities workshop in the State Library of New South Wales. An hour before our session began, the buildings on Macquarie Street were surrounded by climate change protesters. Days later as I flew over the fires and the desert, burning ancient phytoplankton for research purposes, cricket matches in Canberra were cancelled owing to huge clouds of smoke arriving from Sydney.

Figure 1 Darwin motel

Figure 2 Sydney protest footprint

Inside Darwin T4 *is running* The Day the Earth Caught Fire *(dir. Val Guest, 1961). The lightning storm comes in and I adjust my chair to face it then reach for the novel on the concrete floor that scorches my bare feet.*

> The pioneers had difficulty in establishing permanent settlements, having several times to abandon ground they had won with slaughter and go on slaughtering again to secure more. This abandoning of ground was due not to the hostility of the natives, hostile enough though they were, but to the violence of the climate.[4]

As a paradigm for climate change novels, the ironic glee of the syntactically unkempt narrative is paradoxically infuriated by injustice; such textual configuration modulates social practices of grieving and shaming. I feel compelled to write myself into the atmosphere moving between texts and worlds.

*

Affects of Air

Gabrielle Lord's novel *Salt* (1990) opens mid-air, with the frustration of a helicopter pilot seeking out the crash scene of his colleague while undertaking routine, life-risking investigations of the environmental destruction and lawlessness of the capital of New South Wales. The opening page prepares us for an anxious journey towards an even darker state than the already present noir: 'He swung the craft due south so that the mass of mountains seemed to move to be suddenly beside them. Then he dipped and angled and billions of salt crystals glittered on the desert floor as the rising sun struck their microscopic facets'.[5] It's 2047 and Australia is in the grip of devastating saline levels that are on the rise. 'Swung', 'seemed', 'dipped', 'angled', and 'glittered' betray the immanent force of the sun's 'rising' energy 'suddenly' seen to animate all things: 'sickly billabongs, pools of acid-coloured scum flashed the brilliance of oil'.[6] How might we read climate as an agent with will?

In the novel, human occupation is commonly tested by the blazing westerly buffeting buildings. Physically tangible currents of air are figured mightily as unstoppable tormenting beats: '[the] blazing westerly that blew almost constantly now from the red-hot heart of Australia', reducing visibility and intensifying: 'it would swing to the north-west in the late afternoon, bringing a dust storm with it and an increase in temperature'; it can be felt through feet ('like the coming of a train') and it brings severe turbulence knotted in wind and mist.[7] An agent of destruction, it is literally and metaphorically coupled to water: known for how it 'chopped the littered surface of the water into waves', 'from its lair in the sunset' the westerly would charge up rushing thermals making the pilots' job difficult in 'an airy surf'.[8] The narrator refers to rising saline levels and progress of 'de-sal plants' at a distance (they comprise radio news reports) while running with the fusing power of metaphor to marry meteorological events to geophysical change:

> Wind and water erosion, irrigation and dryland salinity poisoned the once fertile soils of the nation. The millions of tonnes of superphosphate locked into the soil increased the killing acidity. Huge gullies split the structure and fabric of the earth once the trees and grasses were gone so that the poor land gaped under the sun's attack by day and the frost's by night.[9]

'Locked', 'split', 'gaped': ever-increasing degrees of participles remarking on things falling apart. The geophysical world is represented through scientific narrative pinned down by the following facts: humans are dependent upon narcotics to function at $57°C$; animals and birds exhibit unique survival instincts (feral pigs attack and eat humans); sun exposure kills in hours. The novel exhibits vulnerability owing to its own materiality; as a porous and open process of storytelling it is permeated by climate as demonstrated by contagion from continual exposure to a narrative of wind.

One-third of the way through the novel, we find our female protagonist, Hedda, standing alone, searching her feelings after discovering her (long-desired) pregnancy. We're told, 'she didn't know what she was feeling', and then:

> It was a gale of emotion, blowing her about in her deepest soul. Joy, that she was to be a mother; sorrow that the man who was the father could never make a husband; sorrow that the end of her own girlhood and daughterhood had finally been marked with this surprising event. Sorrow that the person she was, the world she lived in and the very life she lived every day were all finished now. A sort of grieving was in order, she felt sure, even though her previous life had been so riskless, so banal.[10]

The main thrust here is to expose us to complicated emotions articulated with climate literacy that gives rise to anterior conjoined affects: joy, burdened with its antonym, 'sorrow'. The word is drawn to our attention three times here. Regret and distress are but two aspects to this complicated emotion that is part of the intra-action (separate and knowable) of climate grief.[11] Our affective openness to apocalyptic messages might result in broken confidence from political manipulation and thus lead to a sense of powerlessness (see *Heat and Light*, below); conversely, raw feelings given narrative scaffolding – such as that provided by climate literacy – might generate new practices from the 'event of abysmal sorrow' (climate change). This is worth further examination as loss paradoxically reveals 'a connection between human dominion and total powerlessness that had not been so visible before anthropogenic global warming accelerated'.[12]

Anthropocene Anxiety

Ellen Van Neerven's *Heat and Light* (2014) situates the first-person narrator as an unassuming science research assistant thrown into the biopolitics and state control of an island. Set in the 2020s on Russell Island, Queensland, the 'plant-people', half-human half-plant, encounter scientists working under the guise of *Australia 2*, which is a fake attempt at providing land and rights to Aboriginal Australians. Thus, the emotion 'loss' is complexified by colonial history. The story opens with a lost ferry ticket, taken by the wind and water. This event instils a sense of 'misplaced grief' in the narrator, who pursues appropriate grieving for loss driven by a connection to water understood as 'an old anxiety, not forgotten'.[13]

The dormant affect is triggered into a psychologised emotion later in the novel when one Aboriginal Uncle tells us that the *sandplants* 'are "old people" that rose with the sea when it was raised up'.[14] The narrative binds personal feelings (of loss) with radical human–non-human interdependency; moreover, latent emotions previously understated in themes of anger and a desire for justice begin to open up in *Heat and Light* as climate literacy increases.

Our narrator's thoughts on climate change bring to mind her father's house and the very place from which she is speaking, further back in time when the old people walked barefoot. On one hand, the tension we witness between the cultural practices of colonial modernity and the near past of Indigenous stewardship of the island is tangible to such a degree that our political literacy enables us to critique ongoing colonial power and to sympathise with non-human communities. On the other hand, there is an intangible tension that reads like worry and conflict fused together, seeking out ways that the reader might invest their idiosyncratic climate emotions into the contract with our author. The narrator helps mediate this relationship by modifying her bodily comportment; her feelings find a voice as flesh touches soil from taking off her shoes: 'There is a groping sense of relief that I feel something: for this place, in this place. My country. My dad's country. But this relief quickly turns into a bitter sense of loss and regret, almost self-loathing in despair.'[15] Young adult fiction might not push much further than this in terms of complex psychological interiority; it often keeps with a millennial malaise condition.

*

I don't feel comfortable writing about latent emotions and complex interiority while bushfires are raging across the continent of Australia. I draw from fictocriticism's projection of a rival hermeneutic to those traditionally endorsed by literary studies, i.e., ideologies of the text (the inessential 'readerly', 'realistic', or 'referential' text; and the essential 'writerly' or 'open' text). I packed Fredric Jameson in my suitcase and discover over breakfast (with record-breaking humidity) that he has theorised the traditional double bind 'between antiquarianism and modernizing: relevance').[16] Fictocritical 'essays' might, like reflective journals, emphasise the process of discovery, stopping at what might ordinarily look like insignificant details rather than rush towards an argument. This form of slow writing becomes increasingly relevant when fictocriticism models a practice of empathy; for Heather Kerr, its tone and form 'belong to the larger category of "trauma studies"', including the feelings 'left out of historical narratives'.[17] One might add the feelings left out of traditional literary criticism.

*

Human anxiety for environmental catastrophe and its impact on individual lifeworlds, for Adeline Johns-Putra, achieves an apotheosis when felt as an existentialist threat.[18] Climate fiction and drama exhibit preoccupations

Figure 3 State of emergency

Figure 4 Violence of the climate

with parenthood: 'It is this emotional concern with the future and its increasing prevalence in climate change literature that deserves closer scrutiny in literary studies as it continues its engagement with the global crisis of climate change.'[19] Climate fiction takes parenthood to the question of a particularly acute affective state of the Anthropocene: anxiety. Parenthood as theme and catalyst for character and plot development helps illuminate a philosophical and existential problem, namely posterity.[20]

It is worth noting that these three Australian texts in this short study deal with offspring looking back in time at their parents. The inverse emotion of parenthood doubt and worry is at stake. In *Heat and Light*, the theme of *an inheritance of loss* runs throughout the trilogy, given adequate space in 'Light' to conflate sites of caring and concern, particularly in stories of multigenerational displacement and dreams of gardens and pregnancy.[21] These microworlds suggest control is out of reach in reality but imaginable in dream worlds and desires (potentially replicating the way parenthood concerns might veil the uncontrollable aspects of climate).[22] Children are few on the island; small beaches 'hold no people'; the lack of future for Aboriginal people here relates to failed cultural liaison that hasn't quite understood the extension of land loss – from displacement, that is, colonial violence, to mismanagement of mangroves and sea in reclaiming land – as 'loss of culture'.[23] Our narrator empathises with the plant-people, for her loss of culture (biological parents and cultural practices) seems to mirror theirs. Across the three stories of *Heat and Light* there are numerous failings of parents, lost parents, and troubled pregnancies.

'Water', for example, combines the narrator's desire to care with her dreams of gardening as she connects to her inner feelings about the loss of her father. This combination is backlit by the Australian sense of environment as vital physical reality, which I see as a critical counterpoint to the 'rhetorical overlay' of Northern Hemisphere texts that seek to veil the pain of climate injustice for an emphasis on resilience. As she sails on her own through the maze of sandbanks and islands in the former colony of Moreton Bay (where the plant-people live), a connection develops beyond that which might ordinarily be brokered solely by heightened phenomenological sensitivity:

> I make my way up a small hill and reach the treeline. It is a strange feeling. Other people may see the she-oaks and the sandy-coloured boulder with the skink on it. They might notice the air as quiet and crisp and the female magpie hopping on the grass, but I see something else, I feel something else.[24]

This feeling isn't named. Our narrator finds a vantage point from which she can better attune to it and share her feelings on the development of the sea into land:

> I can see most of the island and the sea stretched around it. I stay there as long as I can, but what can I do? It's a dying place, more or less. The beauty is dying – all around – the industry is strangling it. The wires they are putting under the sea and the water they will pump away will destroy all of this.[25]

To me, this appears a clear-cut case of 'the emotional impact of the extent of physical change to the environment' and humans pained by 'the lack of support and alienation caused by political powerlessness'; such affective emphasis is tonic to contemporary definitions of the genre resting on the loss of social institutions during intra-human conflict.[26]

Seasonal Destruction

Oblivia is the name of the protagonist; in the allusion to the stupor of climate denialism, she seeks the meaning of the swans' choice of a polluted swamp for a home 'where the summer sun was warming the dust spirit's mind'.[27] As with *Salt* and *Heat and Light*, Alexis Wright's *The Swan Book* (2013) is interested in interactions and exchanges.

The Swan Book is about a woman compiling a book of swan experiences across Australia. Such animal focalisation goes beyond inhabiting non-human minds and bodies; it speaks to and from the intensities that pass body to body, which can temporarily be 'seen' in isolation and felt.

To pass on stories is to pass on knowledge; in Aboriginal Australian stories the knowledge is wrapped up in tales of caring, that is, cultural memory is held within sustainable practices of human behaviour. Writing from within this tradition of cultural practice is important to us, for the goal is not only to formulate a workable epistemological stance that might encourage appropriate environmental behaviour; in Australia, it has the added responsibility to place country as consciousness.[28] For Deborah Bird Rose, country is 'a living entity with a yesterday, today and tomorrow, with a consciousness and will toward life'.[29] The secret to seeing this, as Raymond Evans has pointed out, lies in the Aboriginal sense of abidingness, a *cyclical* ontology. This ontology is registered in the Dreaming, 'existing independently of the linear time of every-day life and the temporal sequence of historical events',[30] its events 'created the hills and creeks, plants and animals, and imprinted their spirit on the place'.[31]

In its postmodern and posthuman contribution to the ongoing dream-time of the formation of living creatures, *The Swan Book* opens with the knowledge of a period 'when the world changed' by human hands.[32] This time is fused to the toxic swamp. Dreaming, then, is uniquely 'located' as a haunting drumbeat to the melody of anthropogenic global warming. Its signs and feelings are set in italicised speech, punctuating all chapters with a radical wisdom tying the environmental narrative of swan migrations to the loss of traditional land; thus, new nature writing landscape aesthetics do not figure in *The Swan Book*'s vitriolic critique of displacement by climate change.

Oblivia's people are given as much chance as anyone else, and any other species. Swamps are given and taken away by atmospheric storms; 'wild weather storms', 'droughts and high temperatures' play out while intolerable humidity wraps itself 'in a heavy haze' over the swamp and its dying trees.[33] Wright's spirited text (that might remind readers of magic realism) provides a space in which the haze and thermals can be figured as a 'black angel cloud playing harp music'.[34] And yet, the narrative often emphasises geophysical patterning in more accessible and exacting ways:

> A low-pressure weather system was unpredictable and nobody knew whether it would bring more dry storms or blue skies sulking through another year ... The ancestral sand spirits flew like a desert storm and backed themselves even further up against the mountain. ... This was the new story written in scrolls of intricate lacework formed by the salt crystals that the drought left behind.[35]

The environment is medium and message, sorcerer and scrivener of the sun's 'polluted glare ... broken into trails of rainbow made by the movement of swimming swans'.[36] The tropical canvas is the character that speaks for itself; it is a poetics of loss inflected by country that has a mind of its own (at one point a swan can be seen writing itself with a quill in its beak!). The country is locked 'in a tempestuous affair' born of the anarchic mix of tropical humidity (north country) and temperate climate (south country), confused by 'heavy cyclonic rain'.[37] As the novel progresses, the conditions for life become increasingly rarefied. Our narrator encapsulates masses of meteorological detail in roughly carved narrative blocks wherein an affective prose is discernible in three waves of weather fronts.

First, the environment envelops life to the point of entrapment: 'the valley became a box when clouds settled on this hills'.[38] Second, deranged species accumulate and increase in the post-apocalyptic cities with winds whistling through the turbulent skies.[39] Third, environment and animals bring ghosts into view, expanding the population further into 'bedlam' with 'erratic, unexplainable weather'.[40] These escalations occupy foreground, middle ground, and background to plot development hijacked by the assemblage of people united in grief at a lost leader, Warren Finch (mistakenly thought of as a saviour of the environment and Aboriginal society). This fourth and final element is magnificently coloured by emotions as practices: 'paranoia', 'anguish', and 'embracing grief escalate into a stranglehold of destruction'. As we have seen with other texts above, grief 'finds its own language' – here, in looting and protest in sight of the State funeral and the city's sprawling suburbs.[41]

Feelings lead to actions, yet Wright casts a cold eye on causality. A lasting contrast of grief and hope are set within a circular story of faith in what is, and what is to be as bequeathed by the imagination. Circularity offers nuances that the reader must feel as counterpoints to the pursuits of Oblivia's adversary (whose inquisitive despair we share as he attempts to locate self in the landscape in a linear, spatialised movement). Less determined by vanishing points, the migratory paths of a depleting population of swans (subject to the fluctuating seasons themselves reconfigured by climate change) are rehearsed for the last time in the terrible beauty of the cyclical aesthetic of the closing pages that map distinct climate seasons:

> Bushfires came in walls across their paths. Each kilometre was achieved by wing flapping and slow glide through floating ashes that flickered with fire and dazzle-danced the sky in the full-throated blizzard of heat … The swans, their strength crippled, breathed hot smoke-filled air, and the smell of their own singed feathers crawled into their lungs. Wrapped in fear, they whistle up the dead to see how they are going, before surrendering to the air, plummeting thousands of metres into the fire.
>
> …
>
> Then the winds grow warmer and disappear in the atmosphere laden with dust. Without a breeze, the land becomes so still and lonely in the silence, you know that the spirits have left the skies. It does not rain any more. The land dries. Every living thing leaves in the seemingly never-ending journeys that migrating creatures take.[42]
>
> The drought searches out the swans, blowing smoke across the land on fast currents. Some swans survive and multiply. One of these swans is left in the care of Oblivia. Its life incubates a desire that is curious in the cli-fi context: desire not to care for offspring, but desire for ancestors to relieve Oblivia of her responsibility for the swan's life.

All these temporalities figure in the same continent story, told again and again, forming character as it is with the first pinch of anxiety: 'This might be the same story about some important person carrying a swan centuries ago', we are told; 'it might be the same story in centuries to come when someone will carry a swan back to this ground where its story once lived'.[43] All we know is that things merely are, that they return, and they signify difference.

New-World Formations

These Australian texts present event-driven negative scenarios in which climate change is depicted as both a psychological problem and a physical reality *in the present* that has a force of its own. For Johns-Putra, futuristic dystopian and post-apocalyptic climate novels do not fail to deal with psychological and political ramifications of anthropogenic warming, yet research has found a tendency to 'emphasize its physical dramas over its emotional or mental ones'.[44] This might portend a defining issue for our analysis of first-wave climate fiction. In the contemporary Australian context, however, in the first analysis it appears less true. The emotions found in this study are considered for the multiple and contradictory ways in which they register in public and private spaces as delineated by warming and cooling, weather fronts, and immanent meteorological phenomena; in one text, the emphasis extends out to the praxis of writing about climate change itself. Furthermore, narrative impulses that gain momentum recursively mirror cyclical climate events to threaten the privatised, modern, and secular imagination with models of explanation and storytelling attuned with eco-cultural practices of collective memory and public practice. In the Australian novel, an emphasis on offspring trumps that of parenthood. This socially symbolic tilt, if you will, takes the novel into a domain much like that in which the contemporary museum space affords dialogic interactivity: a complex emotional terrain of conflict and confluence reconciling the sensorial and the pedagogical but remaining open to possibility and doubt. Much like our weather forecasts.

*

Figure 5 Chinooks leave North Queensland for bushfires in Victoria

The rain was coming in, finally and forcibly as the lightning storm last night foreshadowed. Moments pass. I'm preparing to return to Townsville. I pick up the 22nd Australian printing of Herbert's Capricornia, *which was gifted to me on the banks of the Macquarie River in Bathurst. I do not foretell what is to follow. It passed hands during Easter festivities. As it did, I looked over the gathered crowd in the country's first European inland settlement to see a cluster of stones neatly defining a space where Governor Macquarie camped to view the site for Australian pastoral extension westwards from Sydney (a ghostly heritage spot that might now symbolically mark out communal graves for the devastation wrought by the climate to farms of New South Wales).*

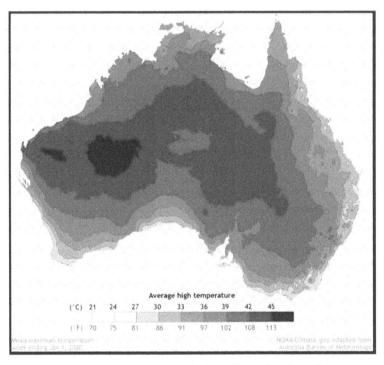

Figure 6 Average maximum temperature in Australia, week ending 1 January 2020. Reproduced with permission of the Bureau of Meteorology.

I decide to flick through the text to see if anything jumps out. The binding is falling apart and a fan of pages drops to the floor. My gaze catches the words 'abashed', 'guilty', 'weakness', and 'shame'.[45] *I'm feeling clammy. It's humid again. I grab my hat, air ticket, and hire-car keys. Imagine the view of Carpentaria from the aeroplane, before the white matter of clouds, on the way to sleep. The semi-arid plain; the irregular flow of inland rivers lost in the Simpson Desert.*

Notes

1 Gregers Andersen refers to the 'broader cultural analytical mapping of the most persistent worlds and modes of existence' that the Anthropocene brings to light; G. Andersen, *Climate Fiction and Cultural Analysis: A New Perspective on Life in the Anthropocene* (Abingdon: Routledge, 2020), 10.
2 Andersen, *Climate Fiction*, 19.
3 B. Latour, *We Have Never Been Modern*, trans. C. Porter (Cambridge, MA: Harvard University Press, 1993), 64.
4 X. Herbert, *Capricornia* (Sydney: Angus & Robertson, 1939), 1.
5 G. Lord, *Salt* (Sydney: McPhee Gribble, 1990), 1.
6 Lord, *Salt*, 2–3.
7 Lord, *Salt*, 4, 41; see also 4, 6, 50, 32.
8 Lord, *Salt*, 32, 26, 6.
9 Lord, *Salt*, 5, 120, 30.
10 Lord, *Salt*, 101.
11 See K. Barad, *Meeting the Universe Halfway: Quantum Physics and the Entanglement of Matter and Meaning* (Durham, NC: Duke University Press, 2007).
12 Andersen, *Climate Fiction*, 135.
13 E. Van Neerven, *Heat and Light* (Sydney: Read How You Want, 2014), 69, 38.
14 Van Neerven, *Heat and Light*, 113.
15 Van Neerven, *Heat and Light*, 107.
16 F. Jameson, *The Political Unconscious: Narrative as a Symbolic Act* (Ithaca, NY: Cornell University Press, 1981), 18.
17 H. Kerr, 'Fictocritical Empathy and the Work of Mourning', *Cultural Studies Review* 9.1 (2003), 194.
18 A. Johns-Putra, *Climate Change and the Contemporary Novel* (Cambridge University Press, 2019), 203–5.
19 Johns-Putra, 'Climate Change in Literature and Literary Studies: From Cli-fi, Climate Change Theater and Ecopoetry to Ecocriticism and Climate Change Criticism', *WIREs Climate Change* 7 (2016), 277.
20 See also the figure of the female scientist who 'breeds a new kind of human through manipulation of women's bodies and surrogate motherhood'; D. Jordan, *Climate Change Narratives in Australian Fiction* (Saarbrucken: Lambert, 2014), 19.
21 Van Neerven, *Heat and Light*, 208–9, 218.
22 Van Neerven, *Heat and Light*, 225.
23 Van Neerven, *Heat and Light*, 85, 74.
24 Van Neerven, *Heat and Light*, 106.
25 Van Neerven, *Heat and Light*, 107.
26 G. Albrecht, 'Solastalgia: The Distress Caused by Environmental Change', *Philosophy Activism Nature* 3 (2005), 41–55.
27 A. Wright, *The Swan Book* (New York: Washington Square Press, 2018), 14.

28 N. Easterlin, *A Biocultural Approach to Literary Theory and Interpretation* (Baltimore, MD: Johns Hopkins University Press, 2012), 93.

29 D. B. Rose, *Nourishing Terrains: Australian Aboriginal Views of Landscape and Wilderness* (Australian Heritage Commission, 1996), 7.

30 R. Evans, *A History of Queensland* (Melbourne: Cambridge University Press, 2007), 8.

31 S. Macintyre, *A Concise History of Australia*, 4th ed. (Cambridge University Press, 2018), 10.

32 Wright, *Swan Book*, 6.

33 Wright, *Swan Book*, 25.

34 Wright, *Swan Book*, 111.

35 Wright, *Swan Book*, 53.

36 Wright, *Swan Book*, 58.

37 Wright, *Swan Book*, 18.

38 Wright, *Swan Book*, 198, 214.

39 Wright, *Swan Book*, 264.

40 Wright, *Swan Book*, 272.

41 Wright, *Swan Book*, 285–92.

42 Wright, *Swan Book*, 323, 327.

43 Wright, *Swan Book*, 333.

44 Johns-Putra, 'Climate Change in Literature and Literary Studies', 269.

45 Herbert, *Capricornia*, 32, 35, 36, 41.

16

ISABEL GALLEYMORE

Perspective-Taking, Empathy, and Virtuality in Jorie Graham's *Fast*

In 2013, psychologists initiated a study in which participants watched a slideshow portraying a woman in the year 2105 adversely affected by environmental change.[1] Participants were also asked to listen to her narrative. Although the study never made it explicit, much of the future scenario suggested a climate-changed environment. In the narrative, the woman describes going outside with no protective measures and, as a result, burning her skin. This was accompanied by an image of a blistered hand. The participants were organised into three groups. While watching and listening to the narrative, one group was asked to take the perspective of the woman. The second group was to remain objective. Acting as a control group, the third was not exposed to the slideshow or narrative. A behaviour-intentions scale was used to record all participants' responses to statements such as 'I will take care to take short showers only in order to save energy and water', from 1 (extremely unlikely) to 7 (extremely likely).[2] After completing the process, participants were told that the study was finished, when the opposite was true. As participants were thanked for taking part, they were also invited to take brochures on sustainability. If participants began to look at, or take, these brochures, this was surreptitiously recorded by the experimenter.

The hypothesis of the study is that a participant who takes the woman's perspective is prompted into feelings of empathy. The results support the premise: enhanced pro-environmental intentions and behaviour (picking up said brochure) were recorded in the perspective-taking condition. The study is one of many undertaken in the field of social psychology. Taking the perspective of an otter in an oil spill increases biospheric concerns;[3] imagining oneself to be a dead bird or cut-down tree results in more willingness to fund community campaigns relating to environmental protection;[4] conservationist intentions appear stronger after perspective-taking of a local park.[5] While much connects these studies, Sabine Pahl and Judith Bauer, citing the work of Nira Liberman and Yaacov Trope, believe that their focus on a future scenario affected by climate change sets it apart because it evokes 'four dimensions of psychological distance – temporal (later rather than now), spatial (elsewhere rather than here), hypothetical (possible rather than certain), and social (others rather than me/my family)'.[6] The idea that perspective-taking can, as the title of their study suggests, 'overcome the distance' recurs in literary approaches to climate change, influenced by long-standing arguments on fiction's capacity to improve 'theory of mind'. '[Climate change] fiction can serve as a way for readers and viewers to empathize with people across time, and thus with future generations, as well as with people in different social, economic, and ethnic contexts', writes Antonia Mehnert.[7] Indeed, Adeline Johns-Putra develops a model of reading cli-fi novels that emphasises readers' identification with fictional characters.[8] With an emphasis on cognitive science, Alexa Weik von Mossner explores the relationship between narrative and empathy, attending to 'embodied simulation'.[9]

It is difficult to ignore that the vocabulary involved in these literary discussions – involving, for example, 'simulation' and 'immersion' – is fundamental to those concerning virtual reality (VR). VR has prompted academic debate with its own set of positive findings on the benefits of perspective-taking, while also popularising the argument in contemporary culture. Owing to VR's ability to allow a user to (virtually) experience any situation from any point of view, journalists, filmmakers, and advocacy groups have claimed that VR is the ultimate 'empathy machine' with regard to racism, the refugee crisis and climate change. Examples abound, perhaps most pertinently in *This Is Climate Change*: a VR docu-series that promises to plunge participants into Greenland's melting landscapes and drought-induced famine in Somalia.[10] The aim is to provide a 'compassionate, immersive, and motivating view of climate change', explains director Eric Strauss.[11] Like the processes of perspective-taking summarised above, VR is also thought to deliver a 'green nudge': 'hopefully this series causes you to think a little harder about what we can control – personal choices, and to some extent, our local governments'.[12] But such claims have not gone without controversy. As the pervasive (and physically oriented) clichés of 'walking in someone else's shoes' or 'seeing through another's eyes' have been adopted by VR, many have proposed renaming VR as an 'appropriation machine', commodifying the experience of others and producing a new (simulated) form of disaster tourism.

As the latter criticism begins to illuminate, the medium through which perspective-taking occurs is important. This essay explores the prospects and problems of perspective-taking, paying close attention to the ways in which technology and print may work against the very connections they seek to enable. Jorie Graham is an American poet whose work has, over numerous collections, increasingly reflected on ecological crisis. In her 2017 collection, *Fast*, which I take as the literary subject of my study here, she explores the possibility of connecting with the perspectives of others – human, non-human, and virtual.[13] Weik von Mossner's focus on novels and films explores how readers' bodies interact with ecological narratives to produce emotional engagements. As such, empirical research in cognitive science (including discussion on mirror neurons) is paramount to her study. A more traditional literary approach is taken in Johns-Putra's work, which applies a 'eudaemonistic' framework to understand how novels allow readers to empathise with characters that present (in some cases challenging) views on posterity.[14] While my intention is to join such discussion on empathy, or 'feeling-with' as I go on to explain with regard to Graham, my approach differs slightly in its focus. In the first instance, this study looks at perspective-taking as an empathic act enacted through, and affected by, different types of virtuality. Moreover, throughout this discussion, and as Graham strikingly articulates in her poems, I explore the complications involved in empathic connection and what this can tell us about the difficulty of 'overcoming the distance'. After all, a tendency exists (as is evident in some of the summary above) for perspective-taking to be understood as an easily accessible state. Perhaps, in the light of VR, it can even be 'switched on'. In the first half of this essay, I investigate how a deliberately unstable process of addressing an otherwise absent 'you' in Graham's *Fast* expresses the difficulty of connection with another person. After suggesting how apostrophe relates to perspective-taking in terms of interaction between self and other, this essay's second half engages with debates concerning analogue and digital technology to propose that Graham's perspective-taking is distinguished by self-reflexivity: a valuable trait in the context of climate change.

Apostrophe and Virtuality

Ecocritics have studied Graham's desire for connection in the context of climate change that permeates her 2008 collection *Sea Change*.[15] Here, Sam Solnick tends to 'global connectivity' enacted through water, as well as via Graham's manipulations of the poetic line.[16] Connection between the present and the future is explored by Matthew Griffiths, who considers the poet's representation of 'phenomena ... beyond the purview of immediate sensation'.[17] This question influences Garth Greenwell, who highlights Graham's address to future readers and her own imagined inhabitation of a time centuries from now.[18] Indeed, my own work on Graham has pursued this time-travelling technique within her poems as empathic engagement with future humans as a pedagogic opportunity.[19] While *Fast* can be understood as continuing this desire for connection, the collection's sensitivity to the digital age and the idea that we are better connected because of it, also sets it apart and necessitates attention.

'The just-dug pit / fills up like a comment box', she writes in 'From Inside the MRI'.[20] In an interview with Graham, Sarah Howe pursues the disturbing simile between mass graves and online discussion in the context of online trolls – an interpretation Graham elaborates upon by explaining that, for trolls like these, the 'supreme vice is taking anything too seriously ... emotions are a severe liability ... empathy being just the most inconvenient'.[21] As is clear from the interview, and from the poems I go on to study, she positions empathy in opposition to technological advancements that are supposedly intended to increase communal feeling. Empathy is, for Graham, an 'ancient and bodily state ... it needs to take place at the level of instinct': social media 'likes', on the other hand, represent 'a substitute emotion, a mock emotion'.[22] The emphasis put on 'bodily' empathy is contextualised by her belief that 'the ethical impulse requires the pressures of physical accountability': technology is the enemy, or at least it is in the United States, she argues, because it entails a 'removal from the experience of materiality, of three-dimensionality'.[23] Graham is not alone in her critique. In his work on 'psychoterratic' feelings, ecocritic Glenn Albrecht suggests that 'technological isolation from raw nature in the digital age' can lead to 'emotional death' in which humans no longer have any reaction to the loss of nature.[24] Speaking to nature's three-dimensionality, the prominent environmental educator David Sobel also argues that, 'if our fingers continually just float above the keyboard, our minds will similarly just drift across the surface, never settling down, never developing a sense of place'.[25]

Some care needs to be taken so as not to dismiss digitality altogether, which of course includes the insightful creative practice of electronic ecopoetry led by such figures as Stephanie Strickland and J. R. Carpenter.[26] Using hypertext and online platforms, this work invites readerly collaboration, often interrogating the wired world as it does so. As my specific focus here is on considering the relationship between empathy and virtuality in Graham's writing, I have chosen to engage with Robert Hassan's argument for 'analogue' over 'digital' paths to empathy as a nuanced text that complements my topic, while continuing aspects of the critique of digitality above.[27] The value Graham sees in 'physical accountability' is akin to the value Hassan posits in 'the link between action and effect' that is visible in analogue technologies such as the wheel, but not in those which are digital.[28] This point is representative of a larger argument Hassan makes on the importance of interactivity as a 'zone of porosity, where "I and thou" commingle'.[29] Although VR may include interactive elements, it is deficient: 'The virtual world responds to the user's actions ... but the virtual world cannot'.[30] Drawing on Hassan, as well as Graham's interview responses, the reading I propose of Graham's *Fast* focuses on interactivity (or lack thereof) in relation to the media that is intended to enable empathic perspective-taking.

'I do not want the 3D glasses, friend, it's all already 3D', begins 'from The Enmeshments'.[31] Although the glasses may recall those worn for a 3D film, a more serious situation is at hand: 'Look up look out. *Out* – what is that. Will you come out? Can you? Why don't you try'.[32] The real world and the simulated world appear enmeshed for the 'you' addressed by Graham, as well as for us as the poem continues. 'Those are people', we read, before recognising that they are 'people made a from a file. Someone printed them'.[33] An uncanny landscape of 3D printing and social media profiles prevails. When the command to 'look up look out' comes again, it is followed by the advice that 'you *can* make you *you*'.[34] The repetition of 'you' elevates the disorientation: is this advice that suggests one can find one's physical self by leaving the virtual world one inhabits, or, conversely, is this advice issuing from the world of social media itself, in which the act of profile-building is integral? This virtuality encompasses the landscape: 'oh look the / damselfly → can it land (no) on each of these wafer-thin strata'.[35] Although 'strata' might be associated with geological formation, such is quickly subsumed within the context of digital layers manipulated to provide the illusion of a solid environment. Yet, the speaker turns this latter description on its head too: 'such as / the world. Or time. Sintering, fusing. Such that the thing before you appears whole'.[36] Inherently subjective, is our perception of the world no less constructed than a simulated 3D world?

At the end of 'from The Enmeshments', Graham returns to the 'you' (who is, presumably, still unable to come out of the virtual world she inhabits) and states, 'I extend my arm and you, you ... // I will say "you"'.[37] Like the repetition of 'you' earlier in the poem, the scare quotes prompt uncertainty as to the realness of the other person. Intimacy and distance are set side by side: the ability to reach out to another person compromised. This apostrophic tension recurs in 'Reading to My Father', a poem that, while not addressing climate change directly, addresses non-human and planetary deaths that may well result from the climate emergency. Here, the speaker sits with her father in the moments following his death and continues what she had been reading to him when he was alive – a news article on extinction:

> how lonely are we aiming for – are we there
> yet – the orange-bellied and golden-shouldered parrots –
> I read them out into our room ...
> most of the ecosystem's services, it says,

will easily become replaced – the soil, the roots, the webs – the organizations
of – the 3D grasses, minnows, mudflats – the virtual carapace – the simulated
    action of
forest, wetland, of all the living noise that keeps us
company. Company. I look at you.[38]

What kind of company does the father offer in death? The juxtapositions within the poem suggest that this elegy for the deceased father is also an elegy for ecological loss. The father's body is now akin to the simulated noise of the natural world in the sense that it, too, only *represents* life, rather than being alive itself.

Virtuality is evoked by the prospect of simulated environments replacing those which are real, but virtuality is present in a more sustained, not to mention self-reflexive, manner in 'Reading to My Father'. The phrasing above that finds the speaker 'reads them [endangered and extinct species] out into the room' may reinstate the fact that the speaker no longer reads them out to a living person. There is, however, an interesting physicality to this act of reading 'out' and 'into'. It is as though the parrots (and other species listed) enter the room as the speaker names them. Could it be that the text itself functions as a kind of virtual reality? Earlier in the poem, we overhear the speaker reading out '*grove, forest, jungle*' to her deceased father, only to find similar landscapes replaced by simulation in the quotation above: 'forest, wetland'.[39] Increasingly, the poem flickers before us as another 'virtual carapace'. The poem's conclusion brings this tension to the fore. The speaker, addressing her father for the last time, says, 'and I caress you now with the same touch / as I caress these keys'.[40] Perhaps the caress is similar because the father is now no more animate than the computer keyboard to which the speaker turns. Yet, more might be said about the way these lines effect a strange simultaneity. Although the father is being caressed 'now', it would seem that this action is undertaken via the touching of 'these keys': a process that generates the poem itself. Like the 'you' framed in scare quotes in 'from The Enmeshments', the 'you' of the father is at once intimately accessible and distant; reachable, but only via the simulated world of the text.

Jonathan Culler argues that apostrophe is a strategy that can be used to overcome the distance in lyric poetry: address sets forth 'a play of presence and absence governed not by time but by poetic power'.[41] The '*now*' of apostrophe 'is not a moment in a temporal sequence', Culler continues, but 'a *now* of discourse, of writing'.[42] Graham exposes this effect by drawing attention to the act of writing (via 'these keys'). Consequently, the poem's artifice is foregrounded: the final caress that might be understood to embody empathic feeling is unsettled. Earlier in the poem comes the question, 'how lonely are we aiming for – are we there / yet', which may well be answered in the affirmative as simulation appears the only way forward. And yet, in 'Deep Water Trawling', we are given a different outlook: we find a poem populated with many voices, not all of them human. Set in the overfished, polluted, and warming seas, the poem speaks to environments damaged by climate change. As I quote later, whether it be the burning of fossil fuels, deforestation, or pesticide use, all can be understood as symptomatic of what Graham calls 'human supremacy'. As the last section of this essay will explore, the 'I' and 'you' in the poem are both unstable and lead to perspective-taking of both ecological victim and aggressor, enabling and disabling the empathic impulse in thought-provoking manner.

Self-Reflexive Perspective-Taking

The first-person speaker in the poems studied so far has been reliable, even if the circumstances described have not. This changes in 'Deep Water Trawling': 'Am I human we don't / know that – just because I have this way of transmitting – call it voice'.[43] Who asks this question? Who answers it? Is it even a question? The destruction central to the poem's subject is caused by trawling nets, but another net features: a 'net of your listening and my speaking we can no longer tell them / apart'.[44] The relatively unpunctuated syntax dissolves the boundaries between addresser and addressee. 'I' shapeshifts into 'you', 'we' into 'they'. The lines, 'They don't want to know you they want to / own you', identify the 'you' as the marine species, but, contrastingly, a few lines later the 'you' becomes representative of the consumer: 'There is nothing in / particular you want – you just want ... not / regulated are you?'.[45] Perhaps the most startling shift comes when Graham blurs human and non-human voices in the first-person:

> Did you ever kill a fish. I was once but now I am
> human. I have imagination. I want to love. I have self-interest. Things
> are not me. Do you have another question. I am haunted but by what?
> Human supremacy? The work of humiliation. The pungency of the pesticide.[46]

For a poem that explores oceanic depths, the issue of whether imagination and self-interest are possessed by the marine species or the human is suitably murky.

Describing the writing process, Graham explains that she did not give a voice to the non-human, but found a voice – or several. 'Fleeing the first person is not the same as letting the *other* flow into it ... When the seabed in "Deep Water Trawling" first "spoke" I almost dropped my pen ... so I kind of *listened*, maybe one could say I *channelled*'.[47] Using this vocabulary,

Graham suggests that instead of *taking* a perspective, she *received* it. On the idea that we can inhabit other viewpoints, she explains:

> Before writing this book I would have said (and have) 'of course it is an illusion, but it is an operative illusion'. Now I am wondering whether the imagination might not have the capacity for such seepage – its technae perhaps not entirely tapped-out by us yet … And maybe, even more than language or imagination itself – the amazing instruments of form and syntax. They tap into non-human unknowns beyond.[48]

The illusion presented in 'from The Enmeshments' is of a 3D world that is so convincing it seems one becomes lost within it ('Will you come out? Can you?'). But illusion is not present in 'Deep Water Trawling'. Despite immersion seeming apt for a poem about the sea's depths, the process of hearing other perspectives is described as 'seepage'. This tentative approach is, of course, appropriate, given Graham's uncertainty as to whether we can really access non-human worlds, but, as I conclude with further reference to Hassan's arguments on VR, this self-reflexive quality proves interesting with regard to overcoming the distance associated with climate change.

As outlined earlier, Hassan argues that we are 'analogue agents from an analogue world', and that digital technologies are ineffective in reproducing reality to prompt empathy because they provide experiences that are disembodied and ultimately withdrawn from the real world.[49] He uses an appealing comparison between VR and music as illustration. The introduction of MIDI, the Musical Instrument Digital Interface technology, in 1983 removes the 'noise and mistakes, the emotional and visceral, and anything unexpected in-between … the sound becomes "clean" and the music, if one accepts the opinion of many audiophiles, becomes "sterile" and "cold" if compared to the analogue recording'.[50] We might compare this account of listening to the listening that Graham undertakes in 'Deep Water Trawling'. In her poem we are refused a straightforward experience of overhearing other perspectives. We are confused; we strain at knowing who is speaking when. The shifting between voices yields wonder and some degree of connection, but, far from simulated smoothness, we are given texture. Voices appear and disappear, or interrupt one another, usually mid-sentence, resulting in a glitch-like quality. This glitching has significance with regard to the transatlantic communications cable laid under the ocean floor, which Graham explicitly alludes to in the poem's conclusion: 'Hold on→just a minute please→hold on→there is a call for you'.[51] An analogy between the poetic line and the telephone line becomes apparent, especially if we recall the poet's choice of words earlier, in which the poem is a tool to 'tap into non-human unknowns' that conjures the tapping of phone calls.

By choosing what Hassan would call an analogue technology as a metaphor for the act of listening to non-human perspectives, Graham subtly reiterates that 'the ethical impulse requires the pressures of physical accountability'. And yet, as noted, the voices glitch. The physicality of the telephone line is unreliable; the line may be bad, the voice indistinct, or the call dropped altogether. This is crucial. After all, committing to perspective-taking as an empathetic act is challenging. In Graham's words, 'empathy is not easy to "do" as a sensation – which is where it needs to start. And it is even harder to "do" as an emotion ... It's not easy and it's not fast'.[52] In his study on Graham, Griffiths, quoting from *Sea Change*, draws attention to the poem as an inadequate response to ecological collapse:

> am suddenly
>
>> aware
>> of having written my poems, I feel it in
>> my useless
>
> hands.[53]

Although Graham is not suggesting that empathy is an inadequate response, the self-reflexivity Griffiths points to is pursued in Graham's understanding that connection is fallible. The belief that VR can generate instant empathy, according to Hassan, 'valorises the spectacle-generating power of the digital and therefore subordinates the human scale, the proportional context, the analogue subjective experience, and the liminal zone that constitutes the "extension" of the individual into her environment'.[54] What Graham's poem emphasises is this very liminality – a voice heard and then not, a perspective inhabited, but only momentarily. 'I am not you. You are not me', she explains, and, as she provides us with an unstable process of perspective-taking, we become more aware of 'that gap [and of] crossing that gap'.[55] In turn, the poem serves as a reminder that connection is a relative state: if we are to strive for 'feeling-with', attention must also be paid to 'feeling-without'.

Hassan comes to the conclusion that VR is not an 'empathy machine', but a 'spectacle' with 'a capacity to stupefy through an immersive representation'.[56] As I have suggested, Graham occupies a series of positions on the nature of reality, simulated and otherwise. In 'from The Enmeshments', the speaker addresses a 'you' who is perhaps more paralysed than stupefied by the simulated world she inhabits. Connection appears impossible as the speaker's commands to 'look up look out' have no effect. Digital technologies cross space and time with ease, but it is the contingency of analogue connection that is vital for Graham. Indeed, in 'Deep Water Trawling', the telephone cable reflects the provisional quality of the connection we hold with other perspectives and thus may be read as a self-reflexive commentary on the difficulty of listening to, and empathising with, others. This essay opened with a study that focused on perspective-taking as a strategy for 'overcoming the distance' applicable to climate change. Although there are moments of connection with others in Graham's work, she also lays bare our struggle to overcome the distance in a manner that reflects our flaws. By doing so, the poems are not solely committed to exploring the interaction between self and other, but also committed to how we interact with our own failure. Instead of suggesting an answer to overcoming the spatial or temporal distance that serves to estrange us from rising temperatures and tides among much else, the poems function as a reminder that the quest for connection continues. Inverting the affirmative arguments on perspective-taking, Graham provokes the thought articulated as a question in 'Reading to My Father', but presented without a question mark: 'how lonely are we aiming for'.

Notes

1 S. Pahl and J. Bauer, 'Overcoming the Distance: Perspective Taking with Future Humans Improves Environmental Engagement', *Environment and Behaviour* 45 (2013), 155–69.

2 Pahl and Bauer, 'Overcoming the Distance', 161.

3 P. W. Schultz, 'Empathizing with Nature: The Effects of Perspective Taking on Concern for Environmental Issues', *Journal of Social Issues* 56 (2000), 391–406.

4 J. Berenguer, 'The Effect of Empathy in Pro-environmental Attitudes and Behaviours', *Environment and Behaviour* 39 (2007), 269–83.

5 G. J. Walker and R. Chapman, 'Thinking Like a Park: The Effects of Sense of Place, Perspective-taking, and Empathy on Pro-environmental Intentions', *The Journal of Park and Recreation Administration* 21 (2003), 71–86.

6 Pahl and Bauer, 'Overcoming the Distance', 156; N. Liberman and Y. Trope, 'The Psychology of Transcending the Here and Now', *Science* 322 (2008), 1201–5.

7 A. Mehnert, *Climate Change Fictions: Representations of Global Warming in American Literature* (London: Palgrave Macmillan, 2016), 188.

8 A. Johns-Putra, *Climate Change and the Contemporary Novel* (Cambridge University Press, 2019).

9 A. Weik von Mossner, *Affective Ecologies: Empathy, Emotion, and Environmental Narrative* (Ohio State University Press, 2017).

10 *This Is Climate Change*, dir. D. Danfung and E. Strauss (Condition One, 2018).

11 K. O'Reilly, 'Is Virtual Reality the Secret Sauce for Climate Action? Inside the "This Is Climate Change" Experience', *Sierra* (29 July 2018). www.sierraclub.org /sierra/virtual-reality-secret-sauce-for-climate-action.

12 Strauss, qtd. in O'Reilly.

13 J. Graham, *Fast* (Manchester: Carcanet, 2017).

14 Johns-Putra, *Climate Change*, 45.

15 J. Graham, *Sea Change* (Manchester: Carcanet, 2008).

16 S. Solnick, *Poetry and the Anthropocene.* (London: Routledge, 2017), 206.

17 M. Griffiths, *The New Poetics of Climate Change* (London: Bloomsbury Academic, 2017), 164.

18 G. Greenwell, 'Beauty's Canker: On Jorie Graham', *West Branch* 63 (2008), 115–34.

19 I. Galleymore, *Teaching Environmental Writing* (London: Bloomsbury Academic, 2020), 80–9.

20 Galleymore, *Teaching Environmental Writing*, 67–8.

21 S. Howe, 'Interview with Jorie Graham', *Prac Crit* (January 2017), www .praccrit.com/poems/cryo/.

22 Graham, qtd. in Howe.

23 Graham, qtd. in Howe.

24 G. Albrecht, *Earth Emotions* (New York: Cornell University Press, 2019), 67.

25 D. Sobel, *Childhood and Nature* (Portland, ME: Stenhouse, 2008), 114.

26 S. Strickland, *Zone: Zero* (Boise, ID: Ahsahta Press, 2008); J. R. Carpenter, *The Gathering Cloud* (Axminster: Uniform Books, 2017).

27 R. Hassan, 'Digitality, Virtual Reality and the "Empathy Machine"', *Digital Journalism* 6 (2019), 1–18.

28 Hassan, 'Digitality', 6.

29 Hassan, 'Digitality', 13.

30 Hassan, 'Digitality', 13.

31 Graham, *Fast*, 1.

32 Graham, *Fast*, 2.

33 Graham, *Fast*, 4.

34 Graham, *Fast*, 10.

35 Graham, *Fast*, 13–14.

36 Graham, *Fast*, 18–19.

37 Graham, *Fast*, 45–6.

38 Graham, *Fast*, 65–7, 69–73.

39 Graham, *Fast*, 33.

40 Graham, *Fast*, 92–3.

41 J. Culler, *The Pursuit of Signs* (New York: Cornell University Press, 1981), 150.

42 Culler, *Pursuit of Signs*, 152.

43 Graham, *Fast*, 3–4.

44 Graham, *Fast*, 14–15.

45 Graham, *Fast*, 2–3; 10–11; 16–17.

46 Graham, *Fast*, 33–6.

47 Graham, qtd. in Howe, 'Interview with Jorie Graham'.

48 Graham, qtd. in Howe.

49 Hassan, 'Digitality', 1.

50 Hassan, 'Digitality', 9.

51 Graham, *Fast*, 54.

52 Graham, qtd. in Howe.

53 Griffiths, *New Poetics*, 170.

54 Hassan, 'Digitality', 11.

55 Graham, qtd. in Howe.

56 Hassan, 'Digitality', 15.

Diverse Indigenous Voices on Climate

17

HSINYA HUANG

Climate Change and Indigenous Sovereignty in Pacific Islanders' Writing

In October 2018, I presided over a press conference with a number of chief scientists from Taiwan and Germany for the grand opening of a bilateral collaboration for the German research vessel *Die Sonne* to drill in the Formosan ridge, southwest offshore to the main island of Taiwan, for gas hydrate as an alternative source of energy. I was amazed by the cutting-edge science and technology and instrumentation involving the collective effort of the scientists across international borders to reduce global carbonate emission. In response to a journalist's enquiry as to how much time we needed for the skills to mature and the new energy to be in use, the scientists paused and responded with a degree of uncertainty – one to two decades, perhaps. This is the point at which disciplines in the humanities can intervene. As the only humanist in the group, I felt privileged to pull the threads that the scientists left off and to articulate the co-values of treasuring our planet as an interconnected web. There is no ultimate solution to the environmental enigma unless we empower people and communities with trust, ethics, stories, experiences, and action of survival and resilience. This study draws on my own work, which includes more than five years of research and field investigations, as well as over a decade of collaboration between academics, scientists, and Taiwanese Indigenous artists and writers that has contributed to the development of a school of cultural study linking Taiwanese Indigenous studies to other Pacific Islanders' and Native North American frameworks of Native and Aboriginal cultures and environmental humanities. It highlights the results of scholarly collaboration and dialogues with researchers, artists, and activists from the humanities for the environment network across the globe.[1]

This chapter examines the relationship between climate stress and Indigenous sustainability and sovereignty in the trans-Pacific context. Using the work of Keri Hulme (Māori), Craig Santos Perez (Chamorro Guam), Kathy Jetñil-Kijiner (Marshall Islands), Nequo Soqluman (Bunun Taiwan), and Rimuy Aki (Atayal Taiwan) as counter-narratives, I challenge readers to reconsider the centrality of the Indigenous subject by retrieving trans-Pacific Indigenous experiences, responses, and cultural practices, which have so far been over-looked in both the scholarship and the conceptual frameworks of the Anthropocene. These Indigenous communities share the same ocean and its resources. Instead of 'islands in the far sea', as Epili Hau'ofa puts it, the Pacific/Oceania should be re-visioned as 'a sea of islands', which has given rise to traditional Indigenous ways of life that are unique to the region and expressed through outstanding cultural landscapes and seascapes and in the intangible heritage of traditions, knowledge, and stories.[2] The Pacific is a pathway rather than a separation. The Pacific Islanders are united in their experiences of how they address the shared concern of rising ocean levels, the connection between militarisation and colonialisation of the seas and the ecological impacts of climate change on the ocean. I argue that narratives and poetry from the Pacific Indigenous communities forge a constellation of resistant practices in the era of global climate crisis. The reciprocal insights from the Indigenous texts in the trans-Pacific context propel us to reconsider the human transformation of the planetary networks in which Indigenous agency plays an important role. They help formulate environmental problems in the Anthropocene and recon-ceptualise the connectivity between humans and other species, lands, and waters, as possible solutions.

In addressing the impact of climate change on the Pacific Islanders or small islands, some focus on the vulnerability of these island commu-nities, even as others investigate the policies, costs, sources, and loca-tions of climate change migration.[3] Still others put forth discourses of apocalypse and the Anthropocene, envisioning the submersion of small islands and gesturing towards the present and future of these islands as a bleak apocalyptic revelation of humankind in the face of environmental degradation of our planet.[4] All these, however, fail to recognise the significance of Indigenous/native/local stories in combating the global challenges evoked by climate change. Indigenous stories focused on the values and experiences of the islanders during extreme weathers embody the islanders' (ancestral) wisdom in righting/writing the impact of cli-mate change. They provide (alter)native models of resilience in the face of climate change, rendering sea-level rise as everyday life experience. The examples abound.

Climate Change: (Mis)representation and Native Voice

Mainstream culture has appropriated climate issues/crisis according to its thought-world: its logic, ontology, epistemology, value, etc., representing climate change as extreme events and projections of catastrophe, creating 'a language of imminent terror' as well as visions of a world facing apocalypse.[5] This (mis)representation downplays and bypasses the impact of global warming on the local, territorial, and Indigenous communities, and their social, economic, and cultural practices. Climate change is in effect the everyday lived experiences of the Pacific Islanders communities as they witness the levels of the ocean rise.

Māori writer Keri Hulme, for instance, provides an alternative to the apocalyptic vision of climate change and island world in her volume *Stonefish* (2004), rendering cycles of mutation and transformation of the island. In the initial short story 'Floating Words', she retrieves the islanders' daily realities to question media representations and logics of climate change:

> Once upon a time, we were a community *here*, ten households of people pottering through our days. We grumbled at taxes and sometimes complained about the weather. ... We sometimes sang when we were sad. We knew – the television told us, the radio mentioned it often – that the oceans would rise, the green house effect would change the weather, and there could be rumblings and distortions along the crustal plates as Gaia adjusted to a different pressure of water. And we understood it to be one more ordinary change in the everlasting cycle of life.[6]

The word '*here*' orients us towards continuous cultural connections to an original source and community, calling for Indigenous resistance to Western media representation. This resistance takes the form of reclaiming a geography which has been lost elsewhere in space and time, but which is powerful as a political formation of *here* and *now*. Climate change is not what is represented on the television or on the radio, but rather what happens as daily realities and experiences for the islanders. This resistance also indicates an alternative mode of thinking on a planetary scale – by evoking 'Gaia' as a complex entity involving the planet's biosphere, atmosphere, oceans, and soil, Hulme refers to the powers which emanate from the planetary body. She inserts disasters and catastrophes as everyday life experiences, not as apocalyptic images or representations on the television or radio. Just as there would be sea-level rise, there would be 'rumblings and distortions along the crustal plates as Gaia adjusted to a different pressure of water'. She notes an Indigenous/island tradition of nature's law, which resists submersion into (mis)representation and ideology. Her vision of climate change as 'ordinary change in the everlasting cycle of life' remains consistent with the Pacific ethics and tradition of genealogical connection among living beings, positing no divide between animal and human, between nature and culture.[7]

In a similar vein, Craig Santos Perez pushes readers to reconsider Western stereotyping of Indigenous peoples as powerless victims of climate change, and he notes:

> In the climate movement, Indigenous peoples are the new polar bears.
> We sport a vulnerable-yet-charismatic-species-vibe, an endangered-yet-resilient-chic, a survive-and-thrive-swagger.
> Plus, we cry 'native tears,' which are the saddest kind of tears.[8]

The contradictory images of the islanders as both 'vulnerable' and 'yet-resilient' bypasses native agency in a changing climate. Framing Indigenous peoples as victims in visual representations or political movements does not provoke action to safeguard the vulnerable. In the mainstream movement, Indigenous people are hailed as icons of urgency like polar bears in the faraway Arctic as vanishing species in the face of climate change. The poet not only challenges the Western modernist logics in the climate movement and other (mis)representations in films, documentaries, and narratives, but also calls for the creation of space for Indigenous voice, forging the Indigenous subject as currency in the debates of contemporary environmental issues. Featuring climate catastrophe in a deteriorating environment, Perez's 'Rings of Fire, 2016' shows the excessive heat of the planet cumulating in the bodily fever of a young daughter, conflating the Earth with the human body:

> after years of drought, fueling catastrophe.
> When my daughter's body first hosted fever,
>
> the doctor said, 'It's a sign she's fighting
> infection.' Volcanoes erupt along fault lines
>
> and disrupt flight patterns; massive flames
> force thousands to evacuate tar sands
>
> oil country . . .[9]

The fever of the body echoes the poignant drought of the lands. The poet evokes disastrous outcomes of global climate crisis in both human and Earth bodies. Fever or heat can yet be a mechanism to fight harmful pathogens in the infected body. The alliance between the body and the island, between fever and drought, between the infected body and altered planet, furthermore suggests the totality of Indigenous resistant practices, which essentially constitute a way out of the foreclosure of Western empire and disease. As Perez puts it brilliantly in one of his 'Love Poems in the Time of Climate Change':

> I love you as one loves most vulnerable things,
> urgently, between the habitat and its loss.

. . .
I love you like this because we won't survive any other way,
except in this form in which humans and nature are kin
so close that your emissions of carbon are mine,
so close that your sea rises with my heat.[10]

For Perez, climate change is inextricable from other global and environmental injustices: a changing climate leads to the loss of species and habitats of 'vulnerable things', both human and non-human, hence the suppression and disenfranchisement of Indigenous peoples as 'othered' sentient beings. Whereas mainstream representations ironically re-patch the severed ties between Indigenous peoples and polar bears as climate victims, the poet re-visions the planet as an interconnected web in which the impact of carbon emission, global warming, and sea-level rise is expansive.

Climate Change and Indigenous Poetics

Whereas Perez emphasises the ugly reality of US militarism on his home island of Guam and the Pacific at large, Kathy Jetñil-Kijiner of the Marshall Islands concentrates on Indigenous poetics and aesthetics as a form of activism. For her, after each passage through a loop of poetry and images, we become more sensitive and more reactive to the fragile planet that we inhabit. It is through such a poetics in combination with aesthetics that the poet builds a capacity to become sensitive and concerned, to perceive and understand the environmental degradation in the ocean world and face and solve the crises.

In this way, Jetñil-Kijiner represents another powerful voice from the Pacific to articulate trans-Pacific Indigenous resistance against environmental infliction in the island nations. Like Perez, she fights climate change with poems inspired by the real experiences of real people in the planetary context. She, however, is more dedicated to images and poetics, through which to forge alliance across islands. She empowers the Indigenous communities across the oceans by disseminating knowledge and awareness through poetics and aesthetics as the foundation for her activism. In reading and performing a collaborative poem with Inuk poet Aka Niviâna, 'Rise: From One Island to Another', Jetñil-Kijiner demonstrates that climate change as a poignant environmental crisis is not to be limited to one region but entails a trans-border scale. The story of sea-level rise faced by Pacific Islanders correlates with that of a melting Arctic, both regions being the frontlines of climate change. In places geographically remote from one another, colonisation, militarisation, and capitalism have been equally pervasive; these poets from the Marshall Islands and the circumpolar jointly testify as they:

come ... in grief
mourning landscapes
that are always forced to change

first through wars inflicted on us
then through nuclear waste
dumped
in our waters
on our ice[11]

The poets demand that 'the world see' that 'our lives matter more than their power'.[12] The drastic land-, ice-, and seascapes present climate change as such that the Indigenous peoples across land and water are implicated in each other's trauma:

Do we deserve the melting ice?
the hungry polar bears coming to our islands
or the colossal icebergs hitting these waters with rage
Do we deserve
their mother,
coming for our homes
for our lives?
...

Let me show you
airports underwater
bulldozed reefs, blasted sands
and plans to build new atolls
forcing land
from an ancient, rising sea,
forcing us to imagine
turning ourselves to stone.[13]

Both regions are vulnerable to climate change. As temperatures in the Arctic are high, resulting in massive glacier melt, such drastic changes cause sea levels to rise in the Pacific, putting homes and livelihoods in both regions at risk. Indigenous peoples become immediate victims of an interconnected circle of hazards. Jetñil-Kijiner of the Marshall Islands in Micronesia and Aka Niviâna of Greenland recite their poem on top of a melting glacier. With appallingly vivid visual narrative, dramatic orchestration, and mournful cries sounding in the background, the poets tell of their respective lands, of submerging islands, sunken volcanoes, and hidden icebergs. The marine species upon which both Indigenous groups rely for subsistence harvests and traditional knowledge transfers are affected, too, making climate change not only an environmental crisis but also a cultural and spiritual threat.

Climate Change and Indigenous Agency

Their islands contained in a cycle of disasters and traumas and addressing each other as 'sister of ocean and sand' and 'sister of ice and snow', Jetñil-Kijiner and Niviâna ceremoniously exchange gifts of shells and stones from their ancestral lands as tokens of sisterhood and connectivity. This connectivity provides spiritual and cultural affirmation, and Indigenous agency remains a key to passing values, knowledge, practices, and messages of action across national and international borders.

Taiwan Aboriginal writer Nequo Soqluman of the Bunun, one of the sixteen recognised tribes in Taiwan (from the European imaginary of Taiwan as *Ilha Formosa*, the beautiful island), focuses on Indigenous agency as he narrates stories about the resilience of ecosystems. He tells of islanders' everyday practices to cope with environmental catastrophes in the island geography by retrieving Bunun traditional knowledge of the land embedded in the name of *Tongku Saveq*.[14] *Tongku Saveq* is the Bunun sacred mountain and their traditional territory, the highest mountain in Taiwan and the main peak of Jade Mountain. In the context of Bunun flood myth, *saveq* means shelter or escape; therefore, *Tongku Saveq* denotes a place of shelter during the floods. As islanders, the Bunun's ancestors always had a sacred place where they sheltered the community, both human and non-human, to prolong the line of Indigenous linkage in the time of flooding. Bunun legend has it that a giant snake (or eel) blocked the flow of rivers and caused unprecedented flood. People then fled from one mountain to another while the water flooded everywhere they went, and finally, the whole world was submerged under water. The only exception was the highest peak in the world – *Tongku Saveq* – which stood above the water's surface, where escaping humans and animals fortunately survived. Later on, brave toads and black bulbuls found tinder for humans and a gigantic crab dived underwater and cut the snake in half to release the flood. This Bunun mythological version of the flooding denotes the intrinsic value of a natural being, as though there could be a law defending existence per se. It refers to a cycle of life which is everlasting – forms of life that have managed to survive in their respective environments over time, over history, that is, in geological time beyond the human span.

Soqluman sustains the ancient tale by retelling it and stresses the significance of interspecies relationship in sustaining human survival. It is a gigantic crab that dived underwater, cut the snake in half to release the flood and save the Bunun, who then took refuge in *Tongku saveq*. The mountain becomes the sacred 'storied place'. The poet demonstrates the oceanic planet as the contested site of ecological crisis and opportunities. Whereas, in the modern world, this piece of traditional knowledge has been largely suppressed, as with other Indigenous writers of the Pacific, Soqluman's method is through storytelling and narratives of their 'storied residence' in the oceanic planet. These transformative stories from the Indigenous Pacific are living materials that delineate climate change not only as everyday experiences and 'ordinary futures' but as a pivotal event when contemporary writers come together and tell their respective '(is)landed' stories to inspire ambition and action.[15] Through their powerful agency, as Jetñil-Kijiner has brilliantly put it in her poem, 'Dear Matafele Peinam', with which she ended her 2014 United Nations Climate Summit Address, the Indigenous writers of the Pacific show the world how they 'deserve more than just to survive, they deserve to thrive'.[16]

Rimuy Aki's novella, *The Homeland of Mountain Sakura* (2010), maps the route of Indigenous survival, resilience, and thriving in fighting climate crisis.[17] While growing climate change results in numerous deaths and environmental refugees from Indigenous communities, a rapid disappearance of Indigenous rituals, beliefs, values, and spirituality alerts the writer to a crisis of another kind. Aki translates this devastating reality into fiction: 'Surprisingly, the torrential rain at night transformed the tiny creek into a rolling river flooded with mud and stones, which scoured a passage into the mountains and cut it into two halves. What's worse, there was no hope for them to get away by wading across the muddy river, which flooded over the banks.'[18] Aki depicts how an Atayal family faces violent storms with despair. While fierce weather has been a common experience for mountain people in Taiwan, the mudslides and flooding in the novella represent the disastrous outcome of Typhoon Morakat in 2009, the year before the novel was published. In her novella, however, there are numerous references to tribal foodways, names of traditional herbs, ceremonies and rituals, and insights and stories about the sky, environment, and land while tribal people face climate change and natural disaster. The novella presents a search for the 'recovery' of Atayal values and beliefs in the midst of fierce weather extremes, which she describes in the preface. She recalls the grief she experiences when she hears news about the people who gave her the Atayal stories featured in her novella: 'Namasia, where I did my fieldwork in February 2009, was hit badly by Typhoon Morakot. Mountains, rivers, and the Indigenous homelands were destroyed and can hardly be recovered at present.'[19] All this, as

Aki's novella demonstrates, results from colonisation and capitalistic development impacted on the Indigenous home-place.

Aki's frame story is organised according to the time of 'linear history' (that is, history imposed by Han Chinese colonists), and yet she implicates tribal continuance and survival in ceremonial history and time. Multiple modalities of time permeate Aki's narrative. Ceremonial time retains a sense of 'cycles, gestations, the eternal recurrence of a biological rhythm which conforms to that of nature', to borrow Julia Kristeva's words.[20] Its regularity corresponds to what is experienced by tribal people as cosmic time and vertiginous visions, which cut across the linear time frame. Aki inserts Atayal vocabulary within her modern text of Han Chinese writing and this vocabulary disrupts the flow of the dominant Chinese language. In so doing, she retains not just her tribal language but the foodways embedded in that language, which, in times of crisis, hold together the Indigenous community as a whole. Atayal women gather *qarauw* (bamboo pieces) and *ziluk* (wild cherries) to prepare dishes; *maqaw* (mountain peppers) chicken soup and *cimmya* (salted bacon), which illustrate different means of production and consumption of meat, rich with cultural meanings; and *tgwil tayal* (mountain cucumber), which is especially appealing for migrant aboriginals as it is 'big, juicy and handy'.[21] Aki depicts a modest life of subsistence practised by women who take care of both the family and the social (cultural) body in the face of crisis and danger as 'state-owned forestry encroached on [their] ancestral *gyunam* (hunting ground)' and '*gaga* was broken and scattered'.[22] While the bonds that tie all living things, human and non-human, into an interconnected web were once widely understood, these beliefs and practices have now nearly been lost. Atayal women's gatherings and cooking in contemporary times provides a material basis for return to *gaga*, the traditional concept of the 'natural order of things in the universe', which represents ancient teachings the Atayal people pass down from generation to generation. Aki prizes ecologically sustainable management of Indigenous foods and resources in accordance with *gaga* and is urging readers to practise self-sufficiency as the community faces drastic changes. By taking back control over the food system, she illustrates how the Atayal are resisting oppression and structural inequality and forging new routes to Indigenous 'roots'.

Coda

'The Anchorage Declaration', drawn up at the Indigenous Peoples' Global Summit on Climate Change in April 2009, illustrates how Indigenous peoples formulate their solidarity, as they are deeply alarmed by the accelerating climate devastation and experience 'disproportionate adverse impacts on their cultures, human and environmental health, human rights, well-being, traditional livelihoods, food systems and food sovereignty, local infrastructure, economic viability, and [their] very survival as Indigenous Peoples'.[23] Not only must the rights of Indigenous peoples 'be fully respected in all decision-making processes and activities related to climate change', but the predominant quality that defines humanity is our obligation and responsibility towards the other, an other that Gayatri Spivak defines in planetary terms.[24] She writes, 'to be human is to be intended toward the other'.[25] In defining what she means by 'planetary', Spivak speaks of an 'other' that involves millions of people who experience and see the Earth as a family as well as communities consisting of beings and humans of all colours, beliefs, and classes, transcending physical, cultural, and national boundaries. In her view, therefore, the planet is viewed as a commons instead of private property. Given that nature is a complex web of interconnected systems, climate change is not just a change of weather patterns over a certain period of time or a change in the distribution of weather events with respect to an average temperature. Climate systems involve a complex web of interconnected events. It is this fact of interconnectedness that can make the challenge of climate change so overwhelming and disorienting.

The Indigenous stories from the Pacific embody a unique worldview. They disclose a Native voice and science, an alternative knowledge system, which can be more attuned to complex interdependencies between human and environment. This knowledge exists and is inherited by way of storytelling and transformed into daily practices in the face of environmental challenges. Their narratives and poetics help translate ambiguous and abstract theoretical or scientific knowledge systems and bring them into the mediated presence of their 'storied residence'. The complex terrain of the imagination remains a way of understanding and exploring the manifestations of anthropogenic climate change in Indigenous culture and community. It is a way of seeing, sensing, thinking, and interpreting that creates the conditions for human interventions in ecology. It is an expression of human sensibilities to their home-places in connection with other species, landscapes, and seascapes. It plays a critical role in thinking through our representations of environmental change and offers insights to envision the future of the islands' world. Ultimately in the climate futures, there are visions, adaptive/transformative strategies, and daily practices from the cumulated frames of Indigenous cultures and everyday practices of the Pacific Islanders. In response to climate change and the erosion of their island landscape, the Pacific Islanders offer their points of view that dismiss apocalypse and inspire us to imagine resilience and adaptive/transformative strategies as our common ecological opportunities.

Notes

1 For detail, see HfE Asia-Pacific Observatory, *Between Land and Sea: Toward the Blue Humanities*, http://hfe-asiapacific-observatory.nsysu.edu.tw/.

2 E. Hau'ofa, 'Our Sea of Islands', *The Contemporary Pacific* 6.1 (1994), 152.

3 See W. Kempf, 'A Sea of Environmental Refugees? Oceania in an Age of Climate Change', in E. Hermann *et al.* (eds.), *Form, Macht, Differenz: Motive und Felder ethnologischen Forschens* (Universitätsverlag Göttingen, 2009), 191–205.

4 See L. Buell, *The Environmental Imagination: Thoreau, Nature Writing, and the Formation of American Culture* (Cambridge, MA: Belknap, 1995) and *The Future of Environmental Criticism: Environmental Crisis and Literary Imagination* (Malden, MA: Blackwell, 2005); and B. McKibben, *Eaarth: Making a Life on a Tough New Planet* (New York: Times Books, 2010).

5 M. Hulme, *Why We Disagree about Climate Change* (Cambridge University Press, 2009), 432.

6 K. Hulme, *Stonefish* (Wellington: Huia, 2004), 18.

7 For more on Keri Hulme, see E. DeLoughrey, 'Ordinary Futures: Interspecies Worldings in the Anthropocene', in DeLoughrey *et al.* (eds.), *Global Ecologies and the Environmental Humanities: Postcolonial Approaches* (London: Routledge, 2015), 352–72. This reading of *Stonefish* first appeared in H. Huang, 'When the Sea-Level Rises : (W)ri(gh)ting Climate Change in Pacific Islanders' Literature', in S. LeMenager *et al.* (eds.), *Teaching Climate Change in Literary and Cultural Studies* (London: Routledge, 2017), 258–64.

8 C. S. Perez, '"This Changes Everything" (Earth Day Poem)', *Craig Santos Perez* (22 April 2018), https://craigsantosperez.wordpress.com/2018/04/22/this-changes-everything-earth-day-poem/.

9 Perez, 'Rings of Fire, 2016', *Poets.org* (2017), https://poets.org/poem/rings-fire-2016.

10 Perez, 'Sonnet XVII', 'Love Poems in the Time of Climate Change', *The New Republic* (4 March 2017), https://newrepublic.com/article/140282/love-poems-time-climate-change.

11 K. Jetñil-Kijiner and A. Niviâna, 'Rise: From One Island to Another', *350.org* (2018), https://350.org/rise-from-one-island-to-another/.

12 Jetñil-Kijiner and Niviâna, 'Rise'.

13 Jetñil-Kijiner and Niviâna, 'Rise'.

14 See Huang, 'When the Sea-Level Rises' and Nequo Soqluman, *Tongku Saveq* (Taipei: INK, 2007).

15 DeLoughrey, 'Ordinary Futures'.

16 Jetñil-Kijiner, 'Dear Matafele Peinam' (United Nations Climate Summit Opening Ceremony – A Poem to My Daughter', *Kathy Jetñil-Kijiner* (24 September 2014), https://www.kathyjetnilkijiner.com/united-nations-climate-summit-opening-ceremony-my-poem-to-my-daughter/.

17 See Huang, 'Climate Justice and Trans-Pacific Indigenous Feminisms', in J. Adamson and K. N. Ruffin (eds.), *American Studies, Ecocriticism and Citizenship: Thinking and Acting in the Local and Global Commons* (London: Routledge, 2013), 158–72.

18 R. Aki, *Saninghua de guixiang (The Homeland of Mountain Sakura)* (Taipei: Rye Field, 2010), 176.

19 Aki, *Saninghua de guixiang*, 7.
20 J. Kristeva, 'Women's Time', trans. A. Jardine and H. Blake, *Signs* 7.1 (1981), 16.
21 Aki, *Saninghua de guixiang*, 68.
22 Aki, *Saninghua de guixiang*, 82–3.
23 'The Anchorage Declaration', *Indigenous Peoples' Global Summit on Climate Change* (24 April 2009), http://unfccc.int/resource/docs/2009/smsn/ngo/168.pdf.
24 'The Anchorage Declaration'.
25 G. C. Spivak, *Imperatives to Re-Imagine the Planet* (Vienna: Passagen, 1999), 73.

18

JENNY KERBER AND
CHERYL LOUSLEY

Literary Responses to Indigenous Climate Justice and the Canadian Settler-State

Indigenous peoples often exist on the front lines of climate change, finding their lives and livelihoods threatened by the effects of rising temperatures even as they have been excluded from many of the benefits afforded by carbon-intensive economies. Within a context of cultural- and land-based Indigenous resurgence, contemporary Indigenous writers, artists, theorists, and activists have made the settler-state and extraction economy of Canada a flashpoint of the global climate emergency. This chapter examines how Indigenous writers place climate change within a long, ongoing history of colonial resource appropriations, ecological loss, and violent suppression of Indigenous bodies and cultures in Canada. The chapter also addresses the diverse ways they respond to its challenges, including: crafting texts and practices of political dissent, solidarity-building, and land reoccupation; grounding present experiences in enduring stories of Indigenous response to environmental and political change; and refashioning genres such as science fiction, horror, or post-apocalyptic imaginaries to explore Indigenous futurisms in a climate-altered world. Above all, though, Indigenous writers make clear that climate change cannot be extricated from decolonisation and matters of sovereignty. The restoration of Indigenous lands and land-based ways of knowing is the starting point for the pursuit of climate justice.

Respectful Reading, Reciprocal Responsibilities, and Indigenous Climate Justice

Indigenous texts are important to read for many reasons, including their wit and humour, narrative and poetic craft, imaginative brilliance, distinct perspectives, historical significance, and cultural influence. However, the long, conjoined history of misrepresentations of Indigeneity and enforced suppression of Indigenous voices means that critics should discuss Indigenous texts respectfully and responsibly. The most common ways in which Indigenous peoples and cultures appear in climate discourse are, first, as quintessential victims of a changing climate, where sea-ice loss, sea-level rise, or increased drought and bushfires undermine traditional livelihoods; second, as land defenders, which can mean being either idealised as heroic resisters to global climate change or derided as antimodern barriers to progress; and, third, as sources of traditional ecological knowledge that can offer guidance for living well on the Earth. When disconnected from dialogue with Indigenous communities and lived Indigenous experiences, these representations can become simplistic, 'static portrayals' that position Indigenous people as symbols within other people's narratives and as tools for other people's empowerment.[1]

Indigenous literatures are not a subset of climate literature. Rather, they emerge from and are most subtly understood through the interpretive lenses of distinct Indigenous intellectual communities and practices.[2] These include long-enduring and adaptive land-based experience, storytelling, political activism, visual and language arts, scientific knowledge, international diplomacy and migration, and political, social, ethical, and philosophical thought.[3] Literary works can be accessible to non-experts but it is important that non-experts be attentive to their own social positioning, practising what self-labelled Canadian 'settler' scholar Sam McKegney describes as 'reciprocal responsibility', an ethico-epistemological approach he has learned from Indigenous writers and thinkers.[4] A story, a poem, a novel, a film, a critical analysis, a song, a dance – these are gifts.[5] How will our readings receive, honour, and reciprocate the gift? Reciprocal responsibility involves: recognising the limits of one's knowledge and being willing to learn from Indigenous people, including the theoretical and literary scholarship published by Indigenous people about Indigenous texts; entering into responsive and trustworthy relationships with Indigenous people; and learning the most appropriate contexts through which to study Indigenous texts. The co-writers of this chapter are non-Indigenous scholars, and we aim to share with other scholars working on climate change and literature what we are learning by listening to Indigenous colleagues, theorists, activists, and storytellers, as well as from our readings of Indigenous texts, analysis, and theory.

Canada, like the United States, New Zealand, Australia, and South Africa, is a settler-colonial state. Settler colonialism, as Potawatomi environmental theorist Kyle Whyte describes, is a system of governance and associated social practices 'in which at least one society seeks to move permanently onto the terrestrial, aquatic, and aerial places lived in by one or more other societies who already derive economic vitality, cultural flourishing, and political self-determination from the relationships they have established with the plants, animals, physical entities, and ecosystems of those places'.[6]

Land and related ecological appropriations are foundational to settler colonialism in its ongoing history of disrupting Indigenous lifeworlds, families, knowledge systems, languages, social resilience, and kinship responsibilities. Colonialism was not a single event, nor is it restricted to the past; it is a persistent form of injustice that systemically undermines and disrupts 'collective continuance' of particular Indigenous peoples.[7] Yet colonisation's brutality tends to be obscured by myths of settler legitimacy and belonging, ranging from heroic, *terra nullius* 'discovery' narratives, to tales of Indigenous savagery or laziness, to the tragic figure of the 'vanishing Indian', to idealisations of wilderness as uninhabited space. Most of these myths erase Indigenous presence and deny its legitimacy in the present. In the land now claimed as Canada, nation-to-nation treaties were negotiated between Indigenous peoples and, over time, with the French and British Crowns and the Canadian nation-state across much of the southern and eastern territories. As legal cases at the Supreme Court continue to affirm, these treaties emphasise reciprocal responsibilities among the parties and recognise the existing lands and societies of Indigenous peoples, including the right to harvest food.[8] These treaties and the rights of Indigenous people in Canada were not honoured for much of the twentieth century – and remain contested today.

Climate change is a further, compounding, form of colonial dispossession and violence, part of what Whyte terms the 'insidious loops' whereby historic patterns of settler dispossession and ecological disruption are implicated in further environmental injustices.[9] With global heating, all of those implicated in the rise of greenhouse gas emissions are party to the ongoing imposition of settler ecologies in Indigenous lands. In Inuit diplomat Sheila Watt-Cloutier's memoir *The Right to Be Cold* (2016), she describes how climate change presents many challenges for Inuit in the Arctic, where temperatures have increased at twice the global average: the ice has diminished and weather has become less predictable, thereby weakening access to nourishing food, changing the rivers, affecting the health and migration of the land and sea mammals, undermining infrastructure, and making it harder to pass on knowledge and survival skills. 'To Arctic Indigenous peoples, therefore', she asserts, 'climate change is emphatically a cultural issue'.[10] She also proclaims it a violation of internationally recognised human rights, for 'without a stable, safe climate, people cannot exercise their economic, social, or cultural rights'.[11] The memoir recounts her loss of language and connection to country, food, family, and culture by being sent south for schooling; it details the devastating effects of the Canadian government's sled dog slaughter in the 1950s and 1960s; and it recounts the years of negotiations to reach an international agreement to restrict persistent organic pollutants (POPs) from southern regions that bioaccumulate in Inuit food sources.

Climate injustice is thus situated within a cumulative degradation of Inuit ecologies and relationships.

Decolonisation, Resurgence, and Land Pedagogy

As the severity of the climate crisis escalates and the Canadian nation-state shows itself committed to expanding fossil-fuel extraction and pipeline and tanker transport from and across Indigenous lands, Indigenous activism has grown stronger, with new energies in the wake of the Idle No More grass-roots movement.[12] The assertion of Indigenous territorial use is often one of the few things left standing in the path of climate-warming resource extraction and other destructive settler land-use patterns, evident in strategic Indigenous actions like the anti-pipeline Unist'ot'en and Wet'suwet'en camps in northern British Columbia, the Tiny House Warrior encampments in Secwepemc territory in southern British Columbia, resistance to the cross-border Dakota Access Pipeline, or the Mi'kmaq road blockades against fracking developments in Elsipogtog, New Brunswick. Indigenous peoples currently find themselves at the forefront of climate protest, though, for many, it is as part of a broader movement for decolonisation. Political theorist Glen Coulthard (Yellowknives Dene) notes that protests and block-ades tend to be understood as acts of refusal and resistance: disrupting the resource economy and saying 'no' to the appropriation and exploitation of Indigenous land.[13] Less appreciated, Coulthard argues, is how they are also a 'resounding "yes"' to revitalising Indigenous ways of being on their lands – what theorists and activists like Coulthard, Leanne Simpson (Nishnaabeg), Jeff Corntassel (Cherokee), and Audra Simpson (Kanien'kehá:ka) are calling 'resurgence'.[14]

These thinkers argue that Indigenous peoples ought to turn away from narratives that orient their primary relationships towards the state as seekers of rights, recognition, and reconciliation – known as the 'politics of recognition' – and, instead, turn towards narratives and actions that prioritise the resurgence of their own nationhoods in matters of govern-ance, language, education, and land-based practices.[15] They insist that the continuance of Indigenous nations depends on it. Coulthard explains that the anti-colonial Indigenous struggle over land is 'not only for land in the material sense'. It is also about 'what the land as *system of reciprocal relations and obligations* can teach us about living our lives in relation to one another and the natural world'.[16] For Corntassel, the answer to whether future generations will recognise him as Indigenous hinges on how he enacts long-standing responsibilities to kin and creation. Such responsibilities can be carried out through small, everyday gestures of renewal, such as gathering medicinal plants, ensuring the health of a native habitat by removing invasive species, or telling a story that invites others to learn from the actions of animal kin.[17] In each case, more resilient, life-enhancing forms of attachment are developed by enacting the lessons of stories that reinforce reciprocity between people and land.[18]

Simpson names this principle 'land as pedagogy' and explains it through stories in which 'the land, Aki, is both context and process'.[19] The stories teach and require land-based experience, which is threatened by colonial practices that prevent Indigenous people from living on and harvesting from the land *and* by colonial practices that destroy the land. Referring to the main character of one story, she asks, 'What if Binoojiinh had no access to the sugar bush because of land dispossession, environmental contamination, or global climate change?'[20] Collective continuance, Simpson insists, requires flourishing lands and waters. The project of Indigenous resurgence must therefore 'take on global capitalism and its link to global warming, which is a direct threat to Indigenous presence and our visions for the future'.[21] The urgency of the climate situation prompts Anishinaabe-Nehiyaw curator Lindsay Nixon to similarly observe, 'we cannot wait for some faraway time when the land has been returned to heal the embodied effects of colonialism that are literally killing us every day. We must liberate both land and life by actively honouring our responsibilities to kinship in this moment'.[22]

The role of hunting and harvesting in these forms of ethical praxis can conflict with Western approaches to animal rights and environmental protection that individualise and de-contextualise species and landscapes in order to save them from change. What is missing in such approaches is a broader perspective on how global climate change, large-scale resource extraction projects, agribusiness, and urbanisation are dramatically transforming animal and plant habitats. In contrast, relational approaches to land and animal kin are key to two Inuit films, Alethea Arnaquq-Baril's *Angry Inuk* (2016) and *Tungijuk* (2009), produced by celebrated director Zacharias Kunuk and throat singer Tanya Tagaq.[23] Both defend the long-standing tradition of the Arctic seal hunt as a critical part of Inuit life. *Angry Inuk* shows how the hunt provides a way for Inuit to ground their relationships with particular coastal places via the enactment of knowledges and skills that are millennia old. The commercial hunt also provides them with material means of self-support, thereby reducing the pressure to turn to less sustainable resources, such as petroleum development on the Arctic seabed – a connection that international animal rights campaigners and policy-makers often fail to appreciate. The conduct of honourable harvests in lands and waters to which one has reciprocal obligations can have broad environmental benefits in a time of climate emergency, given that Indigenous lands contain many of Earth's largest repositories of biodiversity and stored carbon.[24]

While *Angry Inuk* is a documentary, the short film *Tungijuk* takes a figurative approach, depicting the seal and caribou hunts as ethical 'cycles of kinship and responsibility' by way of a bloody, shape-shifting female figure who is person and animal, hunter and hunted, dying and birthing.[25] These uncanny transmogrifications are depicted via an unstable viewer position that shifts down from the sky, across the land, and up from the ocean while repeatedly encountering the direct gaze of the hunter *as her prey*. It offers an estranging though also intimate perspective on the Arctic as an animate world of dynamic transformation to which climate change is increasingly contributing. More-than-human kinship in an Arctic homeland made precarious by climate change is also explored in Tagaq's genre-bending novel *Split Tooth* (2018). Like the film, the novel eschews conventional Western modes of seeing the Arctic through lenses of sublimity or naturalism, instead emphasising sensual bodily experiences through cycles of freeze and thaw, light and darkness, and good and evil. Coming of age amidst the climate crisis is both deeply personal and mythic in this story of erotic encounters, teenage malaise, and menacing powers: 'Global warming will release the deeper smells and coax stories out of the permafrost. Who knows what memories lie deep in the ice? Who knows what curses? Earth's whispers released back into the atmosphere can only wreak havoc'.[26] The Earth has always had its own stories to tell, the speaker suggests, but they may emerge in unsettling new forms as global temperatures increase.

Resurgence writers and theorists also emphasise how Indigenous land-based practices can cultivate the resilience needed to successfully negotiate present and future environmental stresses. Deborah and Hillary McGregor assert that Anishinaabe people have grappled with dramatic environmental and political changes in the past, and stories in the Oral Tradition provide ethical guidance on how to respond to challenges now. At a book launch for the climate change anthology *Rising Tides*, Hillary illustrated these ideas through the oral story of the Pipe and the Eagle, told first in Anishinaabemowin, then repeated in English translation. In a time when the people 'have become vain and unkind' and 'the teaching of peace, humility, and generosity are forgotten', it is Eagle who calls on the Creator to spare them and the Earth, promising to find one person each day 'who continues to live according to the principles of *mino-bimaadizawin* (living well with the earth – a good life)'.[27] This story, Deborah explained, shows how humility plays an important role within resurgence, recognising that humans alone cannot necessarily fix everything, and that we are also not the only climate change storytellers. Our other relations have the power of story too, if we are prepared to listen and attend. And yet, even as the value of relationship with creation endures, climate change also disrupts what might have been envisioned for the future. In some cases, new tools will have to be found and developed from the seeds of what has been re-gathered and carried forward.

Indigenous Futurisms

In his 2018 book *Why Indigenous Literatures Matter*, Cherokee scholar Daniel Heath Justice offers the term 'wonderwork' to encompass many of the literary strategies Indigenous writers are using – including speculative and science fiction, horror, and post-apocalyptic imaginaries – to depict climate-altered futures and Indigenous peoples' navigations through their acute and chronic challenges.[28] Indigenous imaginings of the future are also intimately connected to past and present. The imagery of apocalypse that is often applied to climate change, for instance, registers as eerily familiar to Indigenous peoples in the Americas given the mass disruptions they have already experienced at the hands of four hundred years of colonialism.[29] Colonisation's radical transformation of ecologies via the displacement of people, the introduction, diminishment and extinction of species, and practices of large-scale agriculture and extraction have altered climatic conditions in many places, and the effects of such changes continue to reverberate in Indigenous communities.

For many Indigenous peoples, then, dystopia is not located in the future; it was imposed on their past, it is ongoing, and, consequently, it requires urgent attention through grounded action and imaginative effort. Ecological disasters have already come, as several characters discuss in Anishinaabe writer Waubgeshig Rice's horror novel *Moon of the Crusted Snow*. Set in a boreal forest community where the electricity grid has collapsed, news and fuel supplies have dwindled, and deaths are multiplying, an Elder, Aileen, talks about the idea of apocalypse that fascinates young people. 'The world isn't ending', she explains, '[it] already ended . . .. When the Zhaagnaash cut down all the trees and fished all the fish and forced us out of there, that's when our world ended'.[30] Aileen tells of a history punctuated by repeated violence, extraction, and endurance: 'then they followed us up here and started taking our children away from us! That's when our world ended again. And that wasn't the last time.'[31] Aileen's account is not the action-film version of apocalypse we are so familiar with, which offers instant disaster and urban rubble rather than ongoing removals and loss. Imagining apocalypse can sometimes give an audience the fantasy of a clean slate, where a small band of good people can start afresh rather than dealing with the messy complexities of our accumulated colonial history – a history of building new worlds by maximising what we can take from nature and less powerful people with the least capital expense.

An attention to kinship and the past proves to be a fundamental strategy of Indigenous survival and resistance in Métis writer Cherie Dimaline's much lauded young adult novel, *The Marrow Thieves*, which is set in the Georgian Bay region roughly seventy years in the future. Amidst climate change and other pollution that has poisoned the Great Lakes, a peculiar illness has afflicted white people, the loss of the ability to dream. Indigenous people still hold this power, supposedly in their bone marrow, and white people attempt to seize it for themselves: Indigenous dreams are 'harvested' on an industrial scale through a new variant on residential schooling that repeats the former system's structural violence. To cope with this situation, the Indigenous characters flee the cities and teach one another how to hunt and live on despite the poisoned waters and the loss of their families. They adopt a flexible idea of kinship, building cross-cultural solidarities among and beyond Indigenous peoples, and end up offering a picture of the future based on the recovery and reinvention of land-based traditions with the goal of becoming good ancestors for those who follow. Crucially, environmental deterioration does not inevitably lead to the theft and destruction of Indigenous dreams, children, and communities; rather, it is the unwillingness of the powers that be to change their way of doing things in the wake of clear evidence of environmental peril that generates the novel's central conflict. They fail to dream a different way of living into being when other choices are possible.

In Dene writer Richard Van Camp's stories 'Wheetago War I' and 'Wheetago War II', environmental impacts of extraction similarly bring about harrowing future conditions, as the expansion of the Alberta tar sands and warming global temperatures foster the return of the buried Wheetago and the expansion of their population and geographic range. In Van Camp's rendering, the mythic Wheetago serves as a foe of humanity, but also reflects the human capacity for greed that fuels indiscriminate extraction. Indeed, one of the most potent manifestations of the Wheetago's insatiable appetite is in the form of a Shovel Head, a narrative nod to the heavy equipment that strips off the surface of the land to get at petro-wealth beneath. Similarly, Métis writer Warren Cariou's 'An Athabasca Story' explores the Cree-Anishinaabe figure Elder Brother's susceptibility to greed when he visits northeastern Alberta. His appetite for the warmth petroleum generates leads him to try to seize all of the tar sands for himself 'until winter had been vanquished for good'.[32] Unfortunately, Elder Brother's short-sighted concern with his own comfort leads him to get stuck in the

Athabasca tar, and he winds up being mined and processed into fuel himself. The story's creative reworking of older stories thus serves as a cautionary tale for our own time, for while Elder Brother cannot die, humans and the rest of creation remain vulnerable to the perils of unrestrained appetite.

Anishinaabe filmmaker Lisa Jackson's virtual-reality experience *Biidaaban: First Light* (2018) is similarly set in a post-apocalyptic, climate-altered future, but it departs from the northern bush by portraying a large urban centre as a place of peaceful Indigenous dwelling and renewal.[33] The VR participant is encouraged to explore well-known downtown Toronto locales, witnessing how vegetation sprouts out of decaying skyscrapers and crumbling streets, and water fills abandoned subway tunnels to make pathways for canoes. Here, Wendat, Anishinaabe, and Mohawk languages are given predominance, and city plazas become airy places to dry fish and set up skin tents. The origins of such an altered future are not identified, but the soft sounds and morning light in the sacred time before sunrise suggests that this is a place of gradual resurgence rather than a site of deficiency. It requires everything necessary for the practice of a central concept in Anishinaabemowin, *biskaabiiyang*, which Grace Dillon explains is a process of 'returning to ourselves', a concept that is central to many forms of Indigenous futurism.[34]

The persistence of Indigenous life in these imagined futures does not suggest that nature is never a source of threat. Further, it does not posit Indigenous people as wholly immune to human impulses of greed or violence. However, it does challenge the death imaginary that is so often ascribed to Indigenous peoples in settler-colonial contexts. Indigenous characters, settings, and traditions continue to exist in climate-altered futures because of the care and forethought of generations that preceded them. In turn, restoring kinship relations with human and non-human life is what might bring life back into renewed balance. Storytelling is key to this endeavour, for it continually reminds humans of their rights and responsibilities to their relations in the face of disruption, and helps to make the abstractions and unknowns of climate change more concrete and confrontable.

Notes

1 K. P. Whyte, 'Settler Colonialism, Ecology, and Environmental Injustice', *Environment and Society* 9.1 (2018), 125–44.
2 C. S. Womack, *Red on Red: Native American Literary Separatism* (Minneapolis: University of Minnesota Press, 1999); N. McLeod (ed.), *Indigenous Poetics in Canada* (Waterloo, ON: Wilfrid Laurier University Press, 2014); G. Younging, *Elements of Indigenous Style: A Guide for Writing by and about Indigenous Peoples* (Edmonton: Brush Education, 2018).

3 L. B. Simpson, *As We Have Always Done: Indigenous Freedom through Radical Resistance* (Minneapolis: University of Minnesota Press, 2017); Whyte, 'Settler Colonialism', 125–44.

4 S. McKegney, 'Writer–Reader Reciprocity and the Pursuit of Alliance through Indigenous Poetry' in N. McLeod (ed.), *Indigenous Poetics in Canada* (Waterloo, ON: Wilfrid Laurier University Press, 2014), 43–60.

5 K. Martin, 'The Hunting and Harvesting of Inuit Literature', in D. Reder and L. Morra (eds.), *Learn, Teach, Challenge: Approaching Indigenous Literature* (Waterloo, ON: Wilfrid Laurier University Press, 2016), 445–65; L. B. Simpson, *As We Have Always Done*, 6.

6 Whyte, 'Settler Colonialism', 134–5.

7 Whyte, 'Setter Colonialism', 131–6.

8 A. Manuel and R. M. Derrickson, 'The End of Colonialism', *Journal of Canadian Studies* 51.1 (2017), 244–7.

9 Whyte, 'Settler Colonialism', 138.

10 S. Watt-Cloutier, *The Right to Be Cold: One Woman's Story of Protecting Her Culture, the Arctic and the Whole Planet* (Toronto: Penguin Canada, 2016), 202.

11 Watt-Cloutier, *Right to Be Cold*, xii.

12 Kino-nda-niimi Collective, *The Winter We Danced: Voices from the Past, the Future, and the Idle No More Movement* (Winnipeg: ARP Books, 2014).

13 G. Coulthard, *Red Skin, White Masks: Rejecting the Colonial Politics of Recognition* (Minneapolis: University of Minnesota Press, 2014), 169–70.

14 Coulthard, *Red Skin, White Masks*, 169

15 Coulthard, *Red Skin, White Masks*; L. B. Simpson, *As We Have Always Done*; J. Corntassel, 'Re-envisioning Resurgence: Indigenous Pathways to Decolonization and Sustainable Self-Determination', *Decolonization: Indigeneity, Education and Society* 1.1 (2012), 86–101; A. Simpson, *Mohawk Interruptus: Political Life across the Borders of Settler States* (Durham, NC: Duke University Press, 2014).

16 Coulthard, *Red Skin, White Masks*, 13.

17 Corntassel, 90–1, 93–4, 96, 98; L. B. Simpson, *Dancing on Our Turtle's Back: Stories of Nishnaabeg Re-creation, Resurgence and a New Emergence* (Winnipeg: ARP Books, 2011), 68–81.

18 L. B. Simpson, *As We Have Always Done*, 43–4, 180–5.

19 L. B. Simpson, *As We Have Always Done*, 151.

20 L. B. Simpson, *As We Have Always Done*, 153.

21 L. B. Simpson, *As We Have Always Done*, 70.

22 L. Nixon, 'Visual Cultures of Indigenous Futurisms', *GUTS Magazine* 6 (2016).

23 *Angry Inuk*, dir. A. Arnaquq-Baril (National Film Board of Canada, 2016).

24 R. W. Kimmerer, *Braiding Sweetgrass: Indigenous Wisdom, Scientific Knowledge, and the Teachings of Plants* (Minneapolis: Milkweed Editions, 2013), 28, 328; N. Klein, *This Changes Everything: Capitalism vs. the Climate* (Toronto: Vintage Canada, 2015), 264, 271.

25 *Tungijuq*, dir. F. Lajeunesse and P. Raphaël, prod. T. Tagaq and Z. Kunuk (Isuma Productions, 2009).

26 T. Tagaq, *Split Tooth* (Toronto: Viking Canada, 2018), 6.

27 D. and H. McGregor, 'All Our Relations: Climate Change Storytellers', in C. Sandilands (ed.), *Rising Tides: Reflections for Climate Changing Times* (Halfmoon Bay, BC: Caitlin Press, 2019), 125–9.

28 D. H. Justice, *Why Indigenous Literatures Matter* (Waterloo, ON: Wilfrid Laurier University Press, 2018), 142–3.

29 K. P. Whyte, 'Is It Colonial Déja Vu? Indigenous Peoples and Climate Injustice', in J. Adamson *et al.* (eds.), *Humanities for the Environment: Integrating Knowledges, Forging New Constellations of Practice* (New York: Routledge, 2016), 88–104; H. Davis and Z. Todd, 'On the Importance of a Date, or Decolonizing the Anthropocene', *ACME* 16.4 (2017), 771.

30 W. Rice, *Moon of the Crusted Snow* (Toronto: ECW Press, 2018), 149.

31 Rice, *Moon of the Crusted Snow*, 149.

32 W. Cariou, 'An Athabasca Story', *Lake: Journal of Arts and Environment* 7 (2012), 74.

33 *Biidaaban: First Light*, dir. L. Jackson with M. Borret and Jam3 (National Film Board of Canada, 2018).

34 G. Dillon, 'Imagining Indigenous Futurisms' in Dillon (ed.), *Walking the Clouds: An Anthology of Indigenous Science Fiction* (Tucson: University of Arizona Press, 2012), 10.

Redefining 'the Real'

19

ADELINE JOHNS-PUTRA

Transtextual Realism for the Climatological Collective

Literary realism entails the imaginative and imaginary recreation of see-mingly actual events, experienced, effected, and sometimes narrated by individuals. At stake in the Anthropocene, in contrast, is the truly networked nature of our existences, an awareness of how human and non-human agencies are linked, nested, meshed with each other, a connectedness further complicated by the starkly and unjustly different levels of responsibility and agency that mark human activity. The kind of collective thinking this demands occurs at the scales of what one may call climatological time (that is, geological time expressed in long-term climatic trends, such as glaciation, which has led in part to the identification of geological epochs such as the Anthropocene) and climatological space (that is, the web of meteorological, ecological, and geographical complexity within which individual humans live). How can, how might, the realist representations of literature do justice to humans' experience within climatological collectives?

This chapter speculates on the possibility of a strain of realism that not only allows its readerships to participate and intervene in the disclosure of climate catastrophe but also evokes a global and transhistorical intercon-nectedness by invigorating readers with both ecological and evolutionary awareness. That is, I argue for the continuing relevance of realism's evoca-tion of readerly immersion while, at the same time, I seek to revise realism's situatedness in place, time, and individualistic (that is, anthropocentric) perspective. I do this by focusing on realist fiction's usually disregarded para-literary dimensions – the paraphernalia of publication and reception. Deploying Gerard Genette's structuralist theories of transtextuality, I argue for a recognition of the increasing relevance of these ostensibly external, but deeply integrated, aspects of narrative in engendering readerly sympathy on the one hand and building a sense of trans-temporal, trans-spatial collectivity on the other. Using this as a framework, I then discuss two authors whose work, textually and transtextually speaking, responds to the Anthropocene, if not climate crisis specifically: Kim Stanley Robinson and Liu Cixin. At the heart of my analysis is an interest in the scales of realist narrative – its relationships with time, space, and species – and the implications of these for readerly engagement.

Realism, in Brief

First, however, the fraught term 'realism' demands definition. I draw on Fredric Jameson's analysis, which traces the realist effect to a dialectic between two impulses that he labels récit and *roman*.[1] The first names the realist storyteller's imperative to convey a tale of individual destiny that gives the reader the satisfaction of a story told 'as it happened' or 'as it was meant to be'. The second refers to the affective appeal of the scenes of realism that work to draw the reader into its storyworld – a world that, as Erin James has astutely shown, is built through a range of narrative techniques, and that, as Alexa Weik von Mossner suggests, is key to engendering affective response.[2] Realism depends on the interplay between these two effects: it has an imaginative appeal that also possesses moral traction, built through readerly engagement with actions and consequences and through empathy with these, and thus with questions (not necessarily resolved, of course) of desert, fairness, and justice. It possesses, in other words, ethical potential in a time when human damage to climatic and other physical forces seems reversible or redressable only by human intervention.

Even while the dialectic interplay of récit and *roman* holds this promise for addressing climate crisis, it might equally be construed as being responsible for it. Timothy Clark suggests that the conventional novel's focus on the personal or national bespeaks an anthropocentrism that only embeds anthropogenic damage deeper, while Amitav Ghosh laments the capacity for 'serious fiction' (referring – it would seem – to realist novels) to grapple with climate change.[3] In asking 'Where are the novels of the Anthropocene?', Kate Marshall flags up the need for a 'speculative realism', which would engage with not just individual and national spaces but the durations in which the damage of the Anthropocene is measured.[4] The context of these critiques is Clark's influential work on scalar derangement and Dipesh Chakrabarty's call for a new historiography that he calls 'species history'.[5] Their aim is squarely at the narrowness of the realist novel, specifically, that emphasis on the here and now at the heart of the realist effect described by Jameson.

It would seem that, broadly speaking, suggestions for a realism fit for the Anthropocene have tended either to adopt or to reject the antinomic realist effect. Jameson implicitly suggests that realism's antinomies should continue to pertain in some form when he points out that they have re-emerged in science fiction. He views science fiction as the rightful inheritor of realism (which he traces back to the nineteenth-century historical novel) in our Anthropocenic times, for 'historicity today ... demands a temporal span far exceeding the biological limits of the individual human organism: so that the life of a single character – world-biological or not – can scarcely accommodate it; nor even the meager variety of our own chronological experiences of a limited national time and place'.[6] In Jameson's terms, science fiction is utterly realist, presumably because the science fiction novum (the internally coherent and consistent rationale for a futuristic and/or planetary otherworld) arises directly from the antinomy between récit and *roman.*

In contrast, explicit calls for alternative or new Anthropocene realisms have celebrated narrative features that reject récit, *roman*, or their combined effect, for example, open-endedness (which gives up on récit and plumps for *roman*), fabular plots (whose appeal depends much on récit), or metafiction (which consciously and sometimes suspiciously critiques the realist dialectic). The kind of speculative realism Marshall recommends and the critical-empathetic framework, interruptive realism, or revitalised magical realism I have proposed elsewhere have all relied on interference in realism's power on the reader, stalling its manipulation of the affective, identificatory pull on the one hand (the empathetic appeal of récit) and the understanding of the significance of causes and effects between actors within a self-contained story on the other (the moral weight of actions carried by *roman*).[7] All these Anthropocene realisms (including those that I have put forward) have advocated rupturing the text to allow for a critical reflection.

But what if such disruptions to the careful choreography of realism's antinomy actually risk instilling in the reader a cynical detachment from moral considerations? Might there be ways to harness, rather than disrupt, realism's ethical power, while yet avoiding anthropocentrism? How might this power be conveyed to the reader in terms not of the individual but of the collective, namely, the climatological collective? The answers I venture here take account of the potential for transtexts to instigate readerly empathy and moral concern.

Transtextuality in the Anthropocene

Transtextuality deals with all the textual information that surrounds a given text. Genette defines 'transtextuality' (termed 'paratextuality' in his early writing) as 'all that sets the text in relationship, whether obvious or concealed, with other texts'.[8] He identifies five types of transtextuality. The first, *intertextuality*, borrowed from Julia Kristeva's conceptualisation of the many and sometimes indiscernible layers of textual influence, is narrowed by Genette to refer to the 'relationship of copresence between two texts or among several texts ... eidetically or typically as the actual presence of one text within another'.[9] The second, the category of the *paratext* proper, refers to texts that accompany the core text's presentation as a literary work: 'a title, a subtitle, intertitles; prefaces, postfaces, notices, forewords, etc.; marginal, infrapaginal, terminal notes; epigraphs; illustrations; blurbs, book covers, dust jackets, and many other kinds of secondary signals, whether allographic or autographic'.[10] Next, *metatextuality* encompasses secondary, often critical, texts that provide commentary on the text.[11] Meanwhile, *hypertextuality* describes more ostensibly creative texts that aim to continue the core text (which, in this case, is the 'hypotext'), for example: sequels, either official or unofficial (and by either the original or new authors), imitations, parodies, and pastiches.[12] Finally, *architextuality* names the generic conventions and codes within which a text announces itself and is read.[13]

Transtexts, emanating from the 'institutional conditions of literature and its reception', might seem external to narrative elements of point of view, style, plot, characterisation, and so on – and thus might appear to detract from textual meaning.[14] Yet, because transtexts are an essential part of any textual interpretation, they actually remind us that meaning does not lie solely with the text or author. Florian Sedlmeier argues that some transtexts become 'an integral part of the repertoire of narrative techniques', producing 'collisions' with the text.[15] I would contend that, indeed, *all* transtexts end up colliding or cohering with the narratological elements of the core text. Transtexts inevitably participate in the readerly process, and, as reader-response theory reminds us, 'the reader is a producer of meaning; what one reads out of a text is always a function of the prior experiences; ideological commitments; interpretive strategies; and cognitive, moral, psychological and political interests that one brings to the reading'.[16] And this also means (although Genette, as an arch-structuralist, disregards historicist considerations) that a text's transtextuality changes over time. As Hans Robert Jauss writes of the text's 'horizon of expectations', 'a literary work is not an object which stands by itself and which offers the same face to each reader in each period'.[17]

To acknowledge the transtextuality of fiction written in today's climate crisis is to place that fiction within a wider discursive – and morally inflected – reality, in which readers live with questions of responsibility and agency for a biospherical catastrophe. This requires also that we revisit the vexed question of didacticism in literature, particularly, the tendency to separate 'pure' art from jeremiad or even propaganda. But, as Mark Van Doren long ago recognised, there is only a thin line between literature and propaganda, for persuasion and rhetoric are among their techniques in common.[18] Michaela Bronstein has more recently asked why it is that to 'see the novel as offering a meaning seems an embarrassment to its literary achievement', specifically identifying how, 'finally, the real problem of singling out a work as "climate fiction"' is that 'the idea seems awkwardly message-oriented'.[19] However, she argues, 'we may need to get over our fear of literature as public-service announcement'.[20] After all (and thinking again of Van Doren), climate fiction may be positioned within a long line of protest literature, while climate criticism extends and, crucially, develops a tradition of social criticism that includes feminist and postcolonial criticism.[21]

At the same time, an interest in political intent should not be misconstrued as a blinkered concern with authorial intent. The premise of transtextuality is that, within the ambit of the original text, all its transtexts are worthy of study, including those not produced or even sanctioned by the original author. To take account of the moral and political implications of climate fiction is to trace the text–author–reader interactions in and amongst those transtexts.

Questions of political intent and effect have further corollaries. As I have already suggested, the study of the transtexts of today's climate fiction must keep in focus the timeframes around these core texts, their transtexts, and wider concerns around climate crisis. Thus, texts and their transtexts can work to place readers more firmly within a climatological collective comprising the present human generations of the Anthropocene, even while they invite that collective to respond to a greater collective across species borders and temporal bounds. That is, the first-order collective is formed by climate texts and transtexts and positioned to interact with second- and third-order (and, perhaps, infinite orders) of collectivity. The climate crisis forces cross-temporal thinking. Climate change, suggests Srinivas Aravamudan, is a 'catachronism', because its most profound effects, while they are anticipated in the present, can only be understood 'from some future standpoint that could very well be a vantage point beyond human existence'.[22] Climate fiction is a 'model of literature written under the pressure of futurity', in Bronstein's words, while Stef Craps calls this pressure 'anticipatory memory'.[23]

Moreover, even as transtexts might play a role in clarifying and amplifying the text's socio-political or ethical power through their commentaries, responses, and elaborations (author-sanctioned or not), they can do this while allowing the text itself to maintain the illusion of impartiality, that tricky balance between what Bronstein calls 'representation and exhortation'.[24] In realist fiction, this means that the antinomic legerdemain of narrative immersion and suspension of disbelief described by Jameson remains, while the connections between the 'real' and the realist worlds are emphasised through transtexts. And transtexts achieve this without the kind of readerly cynicism and detachment demanded by critiques of realism that take place within the text, such as those performed by metafiction.

A final point to bear in mind is that the Anthropocene coincides with the onset of the digital age, with its new – and still poorly understood – formations of discourse, power, and publics. Yet, as Bradley Reina points out, the 'novel has remained a mostly textual form' in the age of digital publishing; fictional texts are composed and typeset with a pre-digital format in mind, and are not even necessarily read digitally (e-readers excepted).[25] Climate fiction publishing occurs mostly within these pre-digital parameters. That said, however, transtexts such as metatexts and hypertexts are increasingly discovered or accessed virtually, as is the infrastructure of architextuality, as genres and conventions are comprehended by readers not simply through traditional forms of education, browsing, and purchasing, but through online shopping and reviewing experiences. Most compellingly of all, that brand of sequel known as fan fiction has found a new life thanks to the Internet.[26] In the 'blogosphere' or 'blogsphere' (the online realm of serial, user-generated discourse in the form of blogs and microblogs), fan fiction is readily composable at a computer keyboard, within reach of other hypertexts, metatexts, and architexts.[27] This creates what Courtney Hopf, drawing on the work of Edward Soja, identifies as a crucial 'thirdspace' between the 'real' and realist worlds of the reader and text, respectively.[28] One could say that this space not only melts the boundaries between text and transtext but dissolves the line between solitary fandom and interactive fan community (while further transforming this into an author community). Though climate fan fiction has not yet proliferated, the popularity of fan fiction in science fiction – itself characterised and shaped to a large extent by fandom – suggests the potential for fan-authored, virtual transtexts (hypertexts) to expand the novums of science fiction texts (hypotexts), which in turn raises the possibility that this could occur in climate fiction too, especially in climate fiction that relies on science-fiction-style novums.[29]

Two Studies in Climate Fiction Transtextuality

Kim Stanley Robinson has enjoyed a long career as an author of science fiction and, more recently, climate fiction. His novels, even when not explicitly climate-themed, are concerned with how economic and political decisions interact with ecological phenomena and how societies might evolve to take seriously their responsibilities of environmental stewardship. Robinson made his name with the award-winning Mars trilogy (1993, 1994, 1996), in which the Red Planet is transformed into an ecologically and economically sustainable home by humans fleeing the collapse of their biosphere.[30] From here, his interest in the 'terraforming' of planetary atmospheres pivoted towards a concern with what such practices could achieve on Earth, in the 'Science and the Capital' trilogy (2004, 2005, 2007), subsequently abridged and published as the single novel, *Green Earth* (2016).[31] Since this trilogy, Robinson has released other novels that address climate crisis: implicitly, as the reason for humans' interplanetary and even intergalactic travel, in *2312* (2012) and *Aurora* (2015); tangentially, as an analogue of extreme climatic environments both historic and futuristic, for example, in *Shaman* (2013); and explicitly, as the condition of a future Earth, in *New York 2140* (2017) and *The Ministry for the Future* (2020).[32]

While Robinson's narratives about space exploration and planetary settlement depict a climate-ravaged Earth, his terrestrial climate novels are firmly optimistic about humans' capacity to redress climate crisis. Indeed, Robinson has been clear, at least since 'Science in the Capital', that his work is utopian, which he defines as expressing a hopeful and dynamic outlook rather than static perfection.[33] Moreover, Robinson's climate fiction implies that such an effort would be holistic, involving an overhaul of existing politico-economic systems, underpinned by data-driven analysis. In the trilogy, for example, American scientists, politicians, and policy-makers unite in order to reimagine the praxis of scientific research and therefore to enable bold geoengineering projects. Meanwhile, in *New York 2140*, the residents of a half-drowned apartment block in Manhattan function within a cooperative economic system that resists a property development takeover and challenges the market forces that have led to sea-level rise in the first place. In short, Robinson's novels envision a wholesale transformation of human activity: community-spirited, evidence-based, and socially and environmentally just and progressive.

Together, these novels might be read as intertexts, in addition to the hypertexts that form the sequels in the trilogy. Moreover, the first appearance of Robinson's climate fiction coincides with the emergence of a key external component in its architextuality, that is, the rise of the idea of climate fiction as a literary category in the first decade of the twenty-first century.[34] What is most notable, however, is that Robinson actively produces, singly and collaboratively, metatexts and architexts that provide direct critique of his creative works, flesh out the ideas within them, and help to construct conceptual frameworks in which to read them. These range from his contributions at academic conferences to a co-edited volume of scholarly essays on environmental issues in science fiction.[35] They also encompass interviews, media commentaries, and public talks, which explicate the intellectual underpinnings of Robinson's work, from an optimistic view of humans' sociobiological evolution into a cooperative species, to a post-capitalist, socialist-democratic political economy of, among other things, carbon taxation, a 'Green New Deal', universal basic income, and progressive taxation.[36]

Significantly, this set of transtexts occurs across different media and audiences, reaching beyond Robinson's initial readership within science fiction and his newer fans of climate fiction to the general consumer of news media, and inviting interaction with audiences in open forums. While some of these non-fictional communications provide publicity for the novels, they are not strictly promotional pieces or events, for they are also instalments in an extended Robinsonian philosophy. All Robinson's work in the twenty-first century, when taken as a transtextual whole, resembles a coherent ideological infrastructure. Moreover, readers are incorporated into this structure, to form part of the collective, utopian enterprise that Robinson depicts in his fiction and elaborates on in his media and public appearances.

Thus, Robinson's novels, as examples of what Jameson calls the 'Science-Fictional' phase of the historical novel, make their political and ethical points through the interplay between récit and *roman*: the morally worthwhile, vividly described actions of empathetic and believable actors are shown to achieve morally desirable and politically effective consequences.[37] At the same time, in engaging with Robinson's oeuvre of texts and transtexts, readers have recourse to a veritable user-instruction manual for turning this realist antinomy into a thought (and feeling) experiment for a time of climate crisis, experiencing the richness of its récits in our daily lives and re-enacting its *romans* as we do so.

The work of Liu Cixin, when considered alongside the many transtexts (specifically, hypertexts) it has generated, is a more explicit example of mass participation between author and readers. Liu is often regarded as China's most successful science fiction author, having won the country's Galaxy Award for science fiction nine times, as well as the Hugo Award. His best-known novel, *The Three-Body Problem* (2014), first published in Chinese as *Sān Tǐ* (2008), is part of the 'Remembrance of Earth's Past' (*Dìqiú Wǎngshì*, or 'Earth's Past') trilogy.[38] This trilogy of text and hypertexts has, further, motivated a rich internet discussion in China, with fans analysing and fantasising about the trilogy's storyworld. Strikingly, this discussion has generated not just metatexts but hypertexts, creating a large body of fan fiction and music. This includes a sequel, *Three-Body X: Aeon of Contemplation* (*Sān Tǐ X: Guān Xiǎng Zhī Zhòu*), by a fan identifying pseudonymously as Baoshu, eventually published in 2011 with Liu's blessing and rendered into English as *The Redemption of Time* (2019) by Liu's translator; it includes, too, unofficial soundtracks to the narrative, now available in albums.[39] Of course, the English version of the trilogy, along with Liu's postscript to *The Three-Body Problem* for American readers, also count among the hypertextual paraphernalia.[40] Meanwhile, a prominent architext is Barack Obama's praise for *The Three-Body Problem* in an interview with *New York Times* chief book critic Michiko Kakutani, an endorsement that led to a similarly high-profile meeting between Obama and Liu in China later that year.[41]

Unlike Robinson's transtexts, the body of work surrounding Liu's fiction tends to be – to invoke Genette's distinction – allographic rather than autographic. Moreover, the virtual nature of this authorial collective allows for an immediacy of interaction and intimacy of community, as what Hopf calls the 'thirdspace' of keyboard authorship seamlessly connects realist and 'real' worlds. Increasingly, too, Chinese cyberfiction is enhancing its reach and respectability; Jie Lu notes that it 'is now a large industry; literary websites have millions of registered users, offer hundreds of thousands of works, and collaborate with print publishers, the awards systems, training workshops, the film industry, and mass media, including TV drama'.[42] In the words of cyber-author Dong Mingxia, 'Internet literature is a new folk literature and a broad mass cultural movement' in China.[43] In the case of Liu's transtexts, this facilitates a seemingly endless expansion of the original trilogy's novum, as it crosses from hypotext to virtual hypertext, which in turn becomes more hypotext – virtually and in print, and variously recognised and accoladed within a burgeoning industry – that enables further hypertexts. As the storyworld proliferates, it activates imaginations to an unprecedented extent, as readerly identification and authorial creativity reciprocally regenerate each other. One could describe this ongoing process as organic.

The trilogy's transtextual collective echoes the idea of collectivity inherent in its storyworld – specifically, the presence of collectives on a climatological scale. The internecine plotting of the original hypotext – the trilogy – defies easy synopsis, but it deals primarily with an intergalactic battle between Earth and a distant planet referred to as Trisolaris because it has three suns. This creates the 'three-body problem' of the first novel's title, a well-known scientific conundrum that refers to the gravitational unpredictability exerted by three massive bodies on each other. In the narrative, it creates climatic havoc for the Trisolarians, prompting them to try to colonise Earth. As this journey takes seven hundred Earth years to complete, Trisolarians first send a sortie, using lightspeed nanotechnology that disrupts Earth's physical properties, throwing science into disarray and even prompting scientist suicides. The preparation of Earth's defences and ensuing battles then span thousands of years, and much of the trilogy. However, the Trisolarian invasion actually comes at the invitation of Ye Wenjie, a Chinese scientist so traumatised by the Cultural Revolution and inspired by the polemic of Rachel Carson's *Silent Spring* that she is intent on destroying the human species and ridding the Earth of its genocidal, ecocidal behaviours. Thus, the imaginative leaps and identificatory jumps enabled by the trilogy take place on a planetary scale, in terms not just of time and space, but of species, as they are concerned with the moral agency and destiny of the human species in relation to others, whether terrestrial or extraterrestrial, and to entire biospheres.

To this, the narrative adds another journey – into cyberspace – for the first novel also depicts a virtual reality. In so doing, it re-enacts its own enactment of other worlds. Another scientist, Wang Miao, part of an intergovernmental effort to uncover the reasons behind the scientific disruptions and deaths, discovers – and becomes expert in – a bizarre virtual-reality game that faithfully simulates Trisolaris. Indeed, much of the first novel focuses on Wang's experiences in the 'Three Body' game and, through this, his discovery that the three-body problem is the reason for the Trisolarian climate crisis. For readers, Wang's affective and intellectual encounters within the game replay their engagement with the narrative's *roman* and récit; moreover, for readers-turned-fan-authors, these encounters anticipate their creation of new twists and turns in and through these imaginative worlds.

Liu's work may not be strictly regarded as climate fiction, for its treatment of Trisolarian climatic disorder is tangential to its plot. Yet, it generates a concern not just with ecocide but with scaled-up, climatological thinking. In his postscript, Liu writes of his distinctive, scale-defying imaginative capacity: 'I realized I had a special talent: Scales and existences that far exceeded the bounds of human sensory perception – both macro and micro – and that seemed to be only abstract numbers to others, could take on concrete forms in my mind. I could touch them and feel them, much like others could touch and feel trees and rocks'.[44] His fans' cyber-collective response to such scalar criss-crossing within the realist novum of the Trisolarian saga is, therefore, a communal exercise not just in reading, writing, and imagining these seemingly impossible scales but in dealing with humanity's place within them.

*

Realist fiction's anthropocentrism – its emphasis on human-sized problems, priorities, fears, and dreams – has prompted a critical search, rightly so, for fictional approaches that would encourage readers in an ecocentric, Anthropocenic awareness through the scales of space and time and across species boundaries, that would position them within the evolutionary and ecological collective that I have here labelled climatological. But the climate fiction being written in the Anthropocene has activated another collective, one that has always co-existed with literature, and no less so when it comes to realist fiction. This discursive collective is the transtextual infrastructure around a given text, comprising that text's many textual companions and embodied in author–text–reader relationships. Increasingly, the texts of climate fiction are surrounded by contemporary transtexts that mirror, support, and enact the collectivity narrated within that fiction. Perhaps it is time climate change criticism paid heed to the extent to which politically and ethically motivated authors and readers are reaching across the line between real world and realist storyworld, and understanding their place at the intersection of the discursive, material, and moral universes of the Anthropocene.

Notes

1 F. Jameson, *The Antinomies of Realism* (London: Verso, 2015), 16.
2 E. James, *The Storyworld Accord: Econarratology and Postcolonial Narrative* (Lincoln: University of Nebraska Press, 2015); A. Weik von Mossner, *Affective Ecologies: Empathy, Emotion, and Environmental Narrative* (Columbus: Ohio State University Press, 2017), 1–13.
3 T. Clark, *Ecocriticism on the Edge: The Anthropocene as a Threshold Concept* (London: Bloomsbury Academic, 2015), 164–5; A. Ghosh, *The Great Derangement: Climate Change and the Unthinkable* (University of Chicago Press, 2016), 9.
4 K. Marshall, 'What Are the Novels of the Anthropocene? American Fiction in Geological Time', *American Literary History* 27.3 (2015), 530–1.
5 T. Clark, 'Derangements of Scale', in T. Cohen (ed.), *Telemorphosis: Essays in Critical Climate Change*, vol. 1 (Ann Arbor, MI: Open Humanities Press, 2012), 148–66; D. Chakrabarty, 'The Climate of History: Four Theses', *Critical Inquiry* 35.2 (2009), 212.
6 Jameson, *Antinomies of Realism*, 298, 301–2.
7 Marshall, 'What Are the Novels?', 523–38; A. Johns-Putra, *Climate Change and the Contemporary Novel* (Cambridge University Press, 2019), 45–51; 'Climate and History in the Anthropocene: Realist Narrative and the Framing of Time', in Johns-Putra (ed.), *Climate and Literature* (Cambridge University Press, 2019), 246–66; 'The Rest Is Silence: Postmodern and Postcolonial Possibilities in Climate Change Fiction', *Studies in the Novel* 50.1 (2018), 26–42.
8 G. Genette, *Palimpsests: Literature in the Second Degree*, trans. C. Newman and C. Doubinsky (Lincoln: University of Nebraska Press, 1997), 1, original emphasis; Genette, *The Architext: An Introduction*, trans. J. E. Lewin (Berkeley: University of California Press, 1992), 83–4.
9 Genette, *Palimpsests*, 1–2, original emphasis.
10 Genette, *Palimpsests*, 3, original emphasis.

11 Genette, *Palimpsests*, 4, original emphasis.

12 Genette, *Palimpsests*, 9, original emphasis.

13 Genette, *Palimpsests*, 8, original emphasis.

14 F. Sedlmeier, 'The Paratext and Literary Narration: Authorship, Institutions, Historiographies', *Narrative* 26.1 (2018), 64.

15 Sedlmeier, 'Paratext and Literary Narration', 70.

16 P. P. Schweickart and E. A. Flynn, Introduction, in Schweickart and Flynn (eds.), *Reading Sites: Social Difference and Reader Response* (New York: Modern Language Association, 2004), 1–2.

17 H. R. Jauss, *Toward an Aesthetic of Reception*, trans. T. Bahti (Minneapolis: University of Minneapolis Press, 1982), 21–2.

18 M. Van Doren, 'Literature and Propaganda', *Virginia Quarterly Review* 14.2 (1938), 203–8.

19 M. Bronstein, 'Taking the Future into Account: Today's Novels for Tomorrow's Readers', *PMLA* 134.1 (2019), 126.

20 Bronstein, 'Taking the Future', 127.

21 M. E. Rollé, 'Climate Fiction as Protest: Predicting, Portraying, and Confronting the Trauma of Climate Change', in 'Solastalgia', PhD dissertation, University of Surrey, 2021; G. Garrard, *Ecocriticism*, 2nd ed. (London: Routledge, 2012), 3–4.

22 S. Aravamudan, 'The Catachronism of Climate Change', *Diacritics* 41.3 (2013), 8.

23 Bronstein, 'Taking the Future', 127; S. Craps, 'Climate Change and the Art of Anticipatory Memory', *Parallax* 23.4 (2017), 479–92.

24 Bronstein, 'Taking the Future', 127.

25 B. Reina, 'Digital Print in the Material World: Paratext in Service of Narrative', *Word and Image* 35.1 (2019), 86.

26 K. Busse and K. Hellekson, 'Introduction: Work in Progress', in Busse and Hellekson (eds.), *Fan Fiction and Fan Communities in the Age of the Internet: New Essays* (Jefferson, NC: McFarland, 2006) 13.

27 Busse and Hellekson, 'Introduction', 14. Genette's term 'hypertext' in this context should not be confused with its more common meaning of website text that includes hyperlinks to other websites.

28 C. Hopf, 'Story Networks: A Theory of Narrative and Mass Collaboration', *Rhizomes* 21 (2010); E. W. Soja, *Thirdspace: Journeys to Los Angeles and Other Real-and-Imagined Places* (Cambridge, MA: Blackwell, 1996).

29 For fan fiction genres and hierarchies, see K. Busse, *Framing Fan Fiction: Literary and Social Practices in Fan Fiction Communities* (Iowa City: University of Iowa Press, 2017), 196. For more on climate fan fiction, see John Parham's chapter in this volume.

30 K. S. Robinson, *Red Mars* (New York: Bantam, 1993); *Green Mars* (New York: Bantam, 1994); *Blue Mars* (New York: Bantam, 1996).

31 Robinson, *Forty Signs of Rain* (New York: Bantam, 2004); *Fifty Degrees Below* (New York: Bantam, 2005); *Sixty Days and Counting* (New York: Bantam, 2007); *Green Earth* (New York: Del Rey, 2015).

32 Robinson, *2312* (New York: Orbit, 2012); *Aurora* (New York: Orbit, 2015); *Shaman* (New York: Orbit, 2013); *New York 2140* (New York: Orbit, 2017); *The Ministry for the Future* (New York: Orbit, 2020).

33 Robinson, *Imagining Abrupt Climate Change: Terraforming Earth* (Seattle: Amazon Shorts, 2005).

34 A. Goodbody and A. Johns-Putra, 'The Rise of the Climate Change Novel', in Johns-Putra (ed.), *Climate and Literature* (Cambridge University Press, 2019), 229–45.

35 G. Canavan and K. S. Robinson (eds.), *Green Planets: Ecology and Science Fiction* (Middletown, CT: Wesleyan University Press, 2014).

36 A full list of interviews, conference appearances, and non-fiction writings is available at 'List of Interviews', *KimStanleyRobinson.info*, www.kimstanleyro binson.info/content/list-interviews. For his political economics, see, for example, Robinson, 'To Slow Down Climate Change, We Need to Take on Capitalism', *BuzzFeed* (16 November 2018).

37 Jameson, *Antinomies of Realism*, 298.

38 C. Liu, *The Three-Body Problem*, trans. K. Liu (New York: Tor, 2014); *Dark Forest*, trans. J. Martinsen (New York: Tor, 2015); *Death's End*, trans. K. Liu (New York: Tor, 2016).

39 Baoshu, *The Redemption of Time*, trans. K. Liu (New York: Tor, 2019). For a list of the trilogy's literary and musical hypertexts, see S. Hu, 'Derivative Works of Liu Cixin's *The Three -Body Problem*', *Amazing Stories* (28 July 2015).

40 C. Liu, 'Author's Postscript for the American Edition', *The Three-Body Problem*, 391–6.

41 M. Kakutani, 'President Obama on What Books Mean to Him', *New York Times* (16 January 2017).

42 J. Lu, 'Chinese Historical Fan Fiction: Internet Writers and Internet Literature', *Pacific Coast Philology* 51.2 (2016), 160.

43 Lu, 'Chinese Historical Fan Fiction', 174.

44 C. Liu, 'Author's Postscript', 393.

20

SAM SOLNICK

Critical Climate Irrealism

In a striking moment within one of the sections of Arundhati Roy's novel *The Ministry of Utmost Happiness* (2017), which explores the horrors of the Kashmir conflict, the narrative turns away from a broadly realist account of disappearances and torture to a description of the floods that inundated Kashmir's regional capital Srinagar in 2014. The floods leave not just a 'drowned city' but a 'drowned civil war'. Roy's descriptions of the media spectacle of massive floods, and the very muddy aftermath, are punctuated by the recurring daydream of one of the main characters: fish turn into machine guns, militants and soldiers do battle underwater, interrogation transcripts turn into paper boats, and politicians prance around in sequined bathing suits.[1] This moment in the novel marks an eruption of a climate-change-related environmental crisis during a geopolitical conflict, but also an eruption of what Michael Löwy calls the 'irreal' – as in the fantastic, oneiric, or surrealistic – within a predominantly realist text. For Löwy, the 'term "critical irrealism" can be applied to oeuvres that do not follow [realism's] rules governing "accurate representations of life as it really is" but that are nevertheless critical of social reality. The critical viewpoint of these works of art is often related to the dream of another, imaginary world, either idealised or terrifying.'[2] This chapter argues that irrealism is one of the most significant emerging features in fiction focusing on climate change, enabling authors to capture the complexity and radical upheavals of environmental change in a manner that realism's tendency towards recognisable individual experience cannot.

Critical irrealism has increasingly been seen as a notable feature of fiction from what World Literary Studies calls the 'periphery'. In this context, 'periphery' denotes a structural (as opposed to cultural hierarchy) relation to the 'cores' of the capitalist world system.[3] These cores, typified by the 'violent imposition of capitalist modes and structures as a result of colonization and/or imperialism', extract both labour and resources from the periphery.[4] As the Warwick Research Collective (WReC) explain, this core/

periphery structure has had an impact on literary form: 'something of an elective affinity exists between the general situation(s) of peripherality and irrealist aesthetics'.[5] In other words, critical irrealism is a notable feature of peripheral literatures that attempt to render the processes of capitalism and globalisation. This is particularly true of those fictions addressing the drastic upheavals felt by territories that undergo environmental change related to the radical upheavals of the Anthropocene such as pollution or intense resource extraction. This chapter identifies an emergent strand of such fictions that employ what I call 'critical climate irrealism', a term that adapts Löwy's notion of critical irrealism by combining it with a sense of 'climate crisis'.

Locating Critical (Climate) Irrealism

The concept of critical irrealism has been used to describe quite varied strategies within fiction. At one end of the scale is a sense of irrealism that does not impact on the plot but might, say, be experienced by characters to mark the way technological modernity ruptures a pre-existing feeling of a stable socio-ecological lifeworld: Michael Niblett identifies one such moment in Chinua Achebe's *Arrow of God* (1964) where the priest's nightmare serves as an embodiment of the novel's concern with the disruption of the agricultural cycle by imperial incursion into Nigeria.[6] At the other end of the spectrum are full-blown fantastic elements central to plot and action, such as the zombies in certain Caribbean texts that Kerstin Oloff sees as an instance of critical irrealism because 'the employment of the zombie cannot be read as the eruption of a socio-ecological unconscious, but rather works as a critique of the material and ideological legacy of capitalist colonialism'.[7]

Oloff's distinction here is an important reminder that critical irrealism cannot be used as a catch-all term for any texts that defy realism. Critical irrealism describes fiction that contains critique of society's material conditions as well as deploying irrealism as an aesthetic response to those conditions. Not just any instance of fantasy, dream, or Gothic horror does this, but any of those modes could be used as part of a text's critical irrealism. As Sourit Bhattacharya puts it, instances of critical irrealism 'question, critique, protest against the hegemonic forms of reality, seek alternatives and find ways to liberate the characters from the oppressive social contingencies'.[8] Moreover, critical irrealism should not (generally) be applied to science fiction because, even though science fiction might engage in comparable modes of critique via non-realist modes, it operates by a different set of logics, founded on the scientific and the technological rather than the oneiric or surreal. This is not to say that a text could not contain both critical irrealist and science-fictional elements. Indeed, one text that does just that is David Mitchell's genre-spanning 2014 novel *The Bone Clocks*, which brings together a narrative about oil scarcity that runs from the 1980s to a climate-collapse future, that sometimes intersects with another thematically related plotline about warring factions of immortal beings.[9]

It is important to note that peripheralisation does not simply fall across national lines. As WReC explain, the processes of 'peripheralisation are multi-scale – neighbourhood, city, nation, region, macro-region – in addition to that of the world-system itself'.[10] So, the core/periphery model might describe the relationship between Nigeria and the countries to which it exports its oil – a relationship that has given rise to one of the most-discussed forms of critical irrealism, 'petro-magical-realism'.[11] But the core/periphery structure can also work within a country, or on even smaller levels. Take Max Porter's *Lanny* (2019), a novel about a UK village in the London commuter belt, with its central character of 'Dead Papa Toothwart', a kind of centuries-old spirit-of-place-cum-Green-Man who can move across different species and materials. Toothwart is used as a device to render intermingling social, political, and ecological processes across time, fore-grounding the village's deteriorating relationship with nature – with its fields poisoned by chemicals and its wildlife diminishing.[12] The novel is an instance of a mode of irrealism that Robert Macfarlane calls the 'English eerie', where 'suppressed forces pulse and flicker beneath the ground and within the air (capital, oil, energy, violence, state power, surveillance), waiting to erupt or to condense'.[13]

Lanny is an interesting case for thinking core/periphery.[14] The village and its environs are a peripheral territory to the city, marked and marred by the pesticides and foot-and-mouth culls of agribusiness. But, with its home-counties, financial-worker inhabitants, the village is also very much part of the core of the capitalist world system. The village itself is not easily dividable into a core/periphery structure: government housing and rich commuters' cottages sit amongst each other. The sense that the village is both victim of and complicit in the depredations of globalisation, is borne out in the sections of the novel where the prose shifts to a modernist intermingling of different voices, with the typography swirling on the page in snippets of unidentified villagers' interior monologues. These sections display a toxic brew of homo-phobia, misogyny, and racism (including prejudice against Caribbean, travel-ler, and European Union communities) alongside concerns about diminishing wildlife and a sense of loss over changes in the landscape. This stigmatisation and exclusion of certain groups itself reflects a familiar kind of populist back-lash, where the economic concerns of rural peripheries are co-opted by far-right political parties such as the UK Independence Party (UKIP) or *Rassemblement*

National, and local anxiety over conservation can mutate into socially regressive conservatism. Neither easily core nor periphery then, but displaying features of both, *Lanny*'s village fits with the more nebulous term 'semi-periphery', described by WReC as a site 'in which "local" and "global" forces come together in conflictual and unsteady flux'.[15] These spaces of the 'semi-periphery' become increasingly important when critical irrealism intersects with climate change.

Climate change complicates World Literature's model of the core's ecological and environmental exploitation of the (semi-)periphery. One reason for this involves questions of causality and vulnerability, where the impacts of climate change emissions are unevenly distributed both geographically and temporally. Unlike the impact of a toxic spill or land seizure for monoculture cultivation, it is sometimes hard to directly attribute, say, a particular extreme weather event to climate change. Yet the frequency and severity of floods and hurricanes is increasing. Climate change impacts are driven by collective global carbon emissions, but their occurrence does not easily map onto regional or national activity. Rather, the impacts of climate change are bound up with meteorological, geographical, anthropogenic, and other factors across multiple scales. Some societies least responsible for per-capita climate emissions will face severe challenges, Pacific islands lying barely above sea-level being one of the most extreme and pressing examples. On the other hand, there are cities such as Perth in Australia that face global-heating-induced water crises. And yet, despite the risks to its population centres from climate change, Australia itself continues to have the highest per-capita carbon emissions in the Anglosphere.[16] This speaks to the second issue, that of temporality. There is an increasing incidence of events potentially attributable to, or exacerbated by, climate change (not least the Australian bushfires burning at the time of writing). But the most extreme events of the climate change imaginary, those that shatter our conception of the planet's relatively stable ecologies, are still mostly located in a possible (and sometimes probable) future – a future that might well contain the sorts of sea-level or temperature rises that would render swathes of the Earth uninhabitable, but that currently exists primarily in scientific predictions, fictional prognostications, and societal forebodings.

Niblett explains that 'irrealism comes to the fore' when ecological revolutions 'dissolve pre-existing ecological regimes' and that therefore irrealism might wane as an aesthetic strategy in peripheral regions where 'emergent conditions have been stabilised and new socio-ecological unities created'.[17] Conversely then, if climate change has disrupted socio-ecological unities on a global scale (albeit with local manifestations), then it should be no surprise that we have seen the emergence of irrealism in climate-oriented literature, including from territories normally considered very much part of the core and not (yet) suffering from extreme climate change effects, though very much conscious of local and global threats. These include, but are not limited to, core territories that might become (semi-)peripheral due to climate change. Indeed, some such territories might have already been condemned to the radical environmental upheavals normally associated with the periphery, due to the world economy's carbon emissions, the effects of which have yet to fully manifest (though are beginning to be felt as well as feared). I suggest that these literatures constitute the emergence of a 'critical climate irrealism' that shares many of the features of a peripheral irrealism but is not always bound by the same logics of core/periphery. In what follows, I offer two contemporary short stories as test cases of 'critical climate irrealism' at either end of the spectrum of irrealism.

Feeling Irreal in *Florida*

'Flower Hunters' appears in Lauren Groff's 2018 short-story collection *Florida*. This story is narrated from the perspective of an unnamed woman in central Florida on Halloween. She waits at home while her husband and children trick or treat, she herself having been distracted by reading about the eighteenth-century travels of the naturalist William Bartram. Readers are led to believe that this woman has fallen out with her best friend – Meg, the director of a local abortion clinic – because Meg needs 'a break' from the woman's worries about climate change and associated environmental concerns, including marine-ecosystem collapse. As the woman sits inside, talking to her dog, the rain intensifies outside and she increasingly dwells on a small sinkhole that has opened near her house and which she fears may augur a much larger one. The story closes with her using the sinkhole as an excuse to summon back her family who are sheltering from the rain at a nearby Halloween party.

The irrealism is subtle but persistent, continually linked to consciousness of the material conditions present in relation to a climate-changed future and colonial history. The Halloween setting engenders a Faulkner-esque persistence of a traumatic past in the present, especially the moment when the woman dresses her son as an 'old-style ghost' and realises that this 'white boy in a white sheet' rankles, given the connotations of the Ku Klux Klan in a state which is 'still the Deep South'.[18] However, as the story proceeds, the motifs of haunting exceed the historical violence associated with the Southern Gothic to encompass the weather and climate: the 'brilliant orange' of the sky is paralleled with a jack-o'-lantern and the woman 'is inside the pumpkin'; there is a 'change in the air', with 'a lot of wind now, sense of something lurking. The spirits of the dead, she'd think, if she were super-stitious'. What is lurking *is* environmental crisis: 'she is frightened of climate change', which destabilises not only her sense of planetary ecosystems, but also the very solidity of her own suburban existence ('she is frightened of the small sinkhole') and of her own children's future ('she is frightened of her children, because now that they've arrived in the world she has to stay here for as long as she can').[19]

It is not the spirits of the dead rising this Halloween that lurk in the weather, but the overconsumption and gluttony associated with the holiday and indeed with the suburbs themselves. (As Andrew Pendakis puts it, by 'bunkering the family, expanding the scope and desirousness of our priva-cies, and fire-walling any real sense of social limit or obligation the suburban has abetted a colossal wastage of finite planetary treasure'; the suburb and not the skyscraper is the true architecture of the Anthropocene.[20]) Towards the end of the story, the woman's husband texts her to say that he and the children are at a party in a nearby house 'with tons of food' but she does not go because 'this would be the third circle of hell for her'.[21] In Dante's *Inferno* the third circle is the hell of gluttons where those who have consumed too much are beset by endless rain, wallowing on putrid ground.[22]

The allusion reinforces the links between the sense of haunting, the eerie stormy weather, the sinkhole(s), and environmental change driven by human activity. On the one hand, the sinkhole can be read as a realist(ic) climate change threat: if climate change triggered a rise in groundwater levels, it would exacerbate Florida's sinkhole problem.[23] But the larger sinkhole that the woman imagines becomes an irrealist encapsulation both of climate change and the mother's fears about it – destabilising not just her property but the socio-ecological foundations of her suburban life. As the mother prods the sinkhole with her mind, worrying at it 'like a hole in the mouth where a tooth used to be', she succumbs to a vision where she and her house tip into an imagined sinkhole 'so far down that nobody could get her out, they could only visit' and she must stay there with 'her family's heads peering once in a while over the lip'.[24] This vision becomes emble-matic of the way her climate anxiety separates the woman from her family and community, not least Meg, who, the story implies, is too caught up in dealing with anti-abortion activists to attend to issues that seem less immediate and real.

There is also a strain of irrealism in the way in which the woman is haunted by visions of Bartram and the eighteenth-century landscapes he would have encountered: 'A damp, dense tangle' an 'Eden of dangerous things' that existed 'before the planned communities, before the swarms of Mouseketeers'.[25] This is another haunting of the present by the past, and one typical of irrealism's attempts to render and critique the material conditions of the present:

> Insofar as the mode of representation is (ir)realist, the writing will take the present social order as its object. But the epistemology of irrealist representation is quite often historicist: the attempt will be made to peer back into the past, by way of recovering both the specific history of the present and the alternative histories that might have been but were not, yet that (paradoxically) still might be.[26]

The 'New World' that precedes and subtends the suburbs and Disneyland is not romanticised – Groff reminds us that both the naturalist Bartram and the Seminole chief he encounters are slave owners. What the sections on colonial-era America offer, as well as a reminder of the history of new frontiers being opened up for the exploitation of people and resources, is a sense of impermanence emphasised by quotations from Bartram's own writing. Under every step he discovers 'remains and traces of ancient habitations'.[27] This idea of one civilisation being built on top of another adds further poignancy to the woman's vision of her and her house disappearing into the sinkhole forged by the rain of gluttony. The implication is that perhaps the Florida suburbs too will be discovered by members of a future civilisation marvelling at the ruin of this one. Such a sense of our present as the ruins of the future is itself a common trope within fiction about the Anthropocene.[28]

Petrospectral Presence in East Anglia

China Miéville's 'Covehithe', with its fantastic animation of energy extraction, stands at the other end of the spectrum from Groff's depiction of a feeling of irrealism in bourgeois, suburban existence. In this short story, first published in *The Guardian* in 2011, an ex-military operative named Dughan and his daughter visit Covehithe in Suffolk. In this alternative present, sunken oil rigs have come back to life. These metal and concrete behemoths occasionally stride ashore and wreak havoc, zoomorphic icons of energy infrastructure that not only move like animals (or monsters) but, it transpires, also lay eggs that spawn baby rigs. (It is not clear whether the rigs also fornicate, though Dughan does dwell on the thought of this 'inhuman pornography ... where one rig mounted another' in front of 'horrified whales'.[29]) The rigs do not necessarily emerge near where they have sunk: at Covehithe, Dughan and his daughter encounter a Petrobras rig that sank in the Roncador field off Brazil in 2001.

The zoomorphic re-animations of hydrocarbon infrastructure are an example of the way that the spectre of petroleum haunts late-capitalist aesthetics. From films such as George Romero's *Night of the Living Dead*

(1968) to the uncanny Niger Delta landscapes of Helon Habila's *Oil on Water* (2010), depictions of oil have made use of an aesthetics of the monstrous or spectral to capture both the spectacular and insidious effects of hydrocarbon extraction.[30] In the words of Oloff, 'Oil-as-relation, oil-as-system, is difficult to either imagine or cognitively map. It therefore resurfaces in the symbolic economy of the monstrous that threatens to bring life as we know it to a halt. The unpaid debts – of cheap oil, water exhaustion, soil erosion and increasing social inequality – always return'.[31] The 'petrospectral presences' of 'Covehithe' remind readers that, while they may remain unconscious of hydrocarbons' materialities below the waves (whether as spills, decommissioned platforms, or carbon emissions locked in marine ecosystems), there is always a return of the repressed.[32]

The story acknowledges the world economy's creation of destructive petroleum frontiers such as the Niger Delta. The history of exploitative (neo)colonialism is also brought out by Miéville's self-conscious echoing of H. G. Wells's *War of the Worlds* (1898) in the description of the rig staggering 'like a crippled Martian out of the water'. As Andrew Hageman explains:

> Just as Wells's speculative fiction was an inverted colonization narrative that brought to light England's extractivism of land, resources, and aboriginal labor in Tasmania, so 'Covehithe' presents an inverted invasion that places a contemporary human extractivist relationship with petroleum in a disturbing allegorical light. In this reading, the rigs embody the history of petroleum cultures and markets, as their jerky movements and struggles to avoid collapse come to reflect the long history of economic and ecological booms and busts that have been integral to a world built on fossil fuels.[33]

The rigs are overdetermined. Focusing directly on climate change rather than the (admittedly inextricably linked) petroleum industry shifts the nature of the irrealist allegory, particularly if we think about the specificities of the Suffolk setting that Miéville details, right down to the actual names of roads and churches. The coast of East Anglia around Covehithe is not marked by petroleum infrastructure in the manner of the Niger Delta or even Merseyside or Aberdeen. Southwold and Walberswick, the two inhabitancies namechecked in the story, are monied seaside communities full of second homes and middle-class London retirees. The main energy infrastructure visible from the cliffs at Covehithe are wind turbines far offshore, and the dome of Sizewell B nuclear power station (itself on an attractive beach) that glints to the south. Coastal Suffolk is not part of a petro-exploited periphery. But it is one of the areas of the United Kingdom most vulnerable to sea-level rise; indeed, Dunwich, the hamlet where Dughan and his daughter stay, was once a thriving port that mostly disappeared into the sea in the thirteenth century. (This process of coastal erosion continues; while I was writing this chapter a house a kilometre from Covehithe was condemned to the encroaching sea.[34]) In contemporary novels and plays such as James Bradley's *Clade* (2017) or Steve Waters's *The Contingency Plan* (2009), East Anglia frequently features as an embodiment of the United Kingdom's shoreline vulnerabilities.

What the Suffolk setting does, then, is to move the story from a tale of irrealist oil encounter into one that turns Covehithe into a synecdoche for all communities at risk from climate change (including those very much considered 'core', such as coastal Canada, mentioned elsewhere in the tale). The petrospectrality that is made tangible by the monstrous rigs is not just the extractive infrastructure and economy, but future sea-level rises that we are haunted by, driven by emissions already in the atmosphere. This reading is supported by Miéville's terming the rigs a 'hydrocarbon Ragnarök'.[35] As Hageman reminds us, Ragnarök would see the submerging of the world in flood: death by water, not by fire. The attack on the coast by the zoomorphic rigs points towards a future inundation due to rising sea levels globally, hitting core and (semi-)periphery alike. As such, the story expands from a (semi-)peripheral critical irrealism to a more general critical climate irrealism that addresses global as well as local vulnerabilities and uncertainties.

Conclusion: Notes towards a Supreme Climate Fiction

Turning back to Roy's flooded civil war. The irrealist daydream captures both a response to the 2014 floods – where climate change was one of several possible drivers – and also a nightmare of floods and civil wars that have yet to emerge.[36] Climate change acts as a threat multiplier. Kashmir (and other territories possibly affected by the melting glaciers of the Himalayas) does not yet know what sorts of emergent socio-ecological transformations might exacerbate existing geopolitical tensions. But the same is true all over. No territory can fully predict the emergent factors of climate change. Not just extreme weather events but related resource conflicts or mass migrations might affect any country or city, even those less likely to bear the brunt of floods or hurricanes. If critical irrealism is the aesthetic response to the dissolution of socio-ecological unities, then it should be no surprise to see critical climate irrealism emerge at both cores and (semi-)peripheries as an aesthetic strategy to render and interrogate the possible climate-changed futures to come.

Notes

1 A. Roy, *The Ministry of Utmost Happiness* (London: Hamish Hamilton, 2017), 264–5.

2 M. Löwy, 'The Current of Critical Irrealism: "A Moonlit Enchanted Night"', in M. Beaumont (ed.), *Adventures in Realism* (Oxford: John Wiley & Sons, 2008), 196.

3 S. Deckard, 'Editorial', *Green Letters* 16.1 (2012), 8.

4 M. Niblett, 'World-Economy, World-Ecology, World Literature', *Green Letters* 16.1 (2012), 16.

5 Warwick Research Collective, *Combined and Uneven Development: Towards a New Theory of World-Literature* (Liverpool University Press, 2015), 68.

6 Niblett, 'World-Economy', 26.

7 K. Oloff, '"Greening" The Zombie: Caribbean Gothic, World-Ecology, and Socio-Ecological Degradation', *Green Letters* 16.1 (2012), 33.

8 S. Bhattacharya, 'The Margins of Postcolonial Urbanity: Reading Critical Irrealism in Nabarun Bhattacharya's Fiction', in M. Chakraborty and U. Al-wazedi (eds.), *Postcolonial Urban Outcasts: City Margins in South Asian Literature* (New York: Routledge, 2016), 40.

9 For a summary of the novel's combination of the fantastic and dystopian science fiction, see B. Smith, 'David Mitchell's *The Bone Clocks*', in A. Goodbody and A. Johns-Putra (eds.), *Cli-Fi: A Companion* (Oxford: Peter Lang, 2018), 203–10.

10 Warwick Research Collective, *Combined and Uneven Development*, 55.

11 J. Wenzel, 'Petro-Magic-Realism: Toward a Political Ecology of Nigerian Literature', *Postcolonial Studies* 9.4 (2006), 449–64. Wenzel's petro-magical-realism is a version of 'critical irrealism' avant-la-lettre, as Wenzel herself acknowledges in an interview with Lucy Potter, 'Postcolonial Resources, Pedagogical Resistance: An Energy-Driven Interview with Professor Jennifer Wenzel', *Journal of Postcolonial Writing* 53.3 (2017), 380–92.

12 M. Porter, *Lanny* (London: Faber, 2019), 64–6.

13 R. Macfarlane, 'The Eeriness of the English Countryside', *The Guardian* (10 April 2015).

14 Macfarlane, 'Eeriness of the English Countryside'.

15 Warwick Research Collective, *Combined and Uneven Development*, 67.

16 Global Carbon Project: www.globalcarbonproject.org/ using their tool, the Global Carbon Atlas: www.globalcarbonatlas.org/en/content/welcome-carbon-atlas.

17 Niblett, 'World-Economy', 23.

18 L. Groff, 'Flower Hunters', in *Florida* (London: Penguin Random House, 2018), 157.

19 Groff, 'Flower Hunters', 161–3.

20 A. Pendakis, 'Suburbs', in C. Howe and A. Pandian (eds.), *Anthropocene Unseen: A Lexicon* (Earth, Milky Way: Punctum Books, 2020), 449. Note that Howe and Pandian have explicitly listed this as their place of publication on their copyright page.

21 Groff, 'Flower Hunters', 157–65.

22 Dante Alighieri, *Inferno*, trans. G. Carlyle (London: George Bell & Sons, 1869), canto VI, lines 7–12.

23 C. Bodenner, 'The Science behind Florida's Sinkhole Epidemic', *Smithsonian Magazine* (24 May 2018).

24 Groff, 'Flower Hunters', 168.

25 Groff, 'Flower Hunters', 160.

26 Warwick Research Collective, *Combined and Uneven Development*, 72.

27 Groff, 'Flower Hunters', 168.

28 See S. Solnick, 'Anthropocene', in D. O'Gorman and R. Eaglestone (eds.), *The Routledge Companion to Twenty-First Century Literary Fiction* (Abingdon: Routledge, 2018), 225–38.

29 C. Miéville, 'Covehithe', *The Guardian* (22 April 2011).

30 For a discussion of Habila in this context, see B. Caminero-Santangel, 'Witnessing the Nature of Violence: Resource Extraction and Political Ecologies in the Contemporary African Novel', in E. DeLoughrey *et al.* (eds.), *Global Ecologies and the Environmental Humanities: Postcolonial Approaches* (New York: Routledge, 2015), 226–41; for Romero, see K. Oloff, 'From Sugar to Oil: The Ecology of George A. Romero's *Night of the Living Dead*', *Journal of Postcolonial Writing* 53. 3 (2017), 316–28.

31 Oloff, 'From Sugar to Oil', 320.

32 Miéville, 'Covehithe'.

33 A. Hageman, 'Bringing Infrastructural Criticism to Speculative Fiction: China Miéville's "Covehithe"', *C21 Literature: Journal of 21st-Century Writings* 7.1 (2019), 6.

34 J. Adams, 'Couple Must Leave Their Home of 12 Years before It Falls into the Sea', *The Daily Mail* (12 December 2019).

35 Miéville, 'Covehithe'.

36 S. A. Romshoo *et al.*, 'Climatic, Geomorphic and Anthropogenic Drivers of the 2014 Extreme Flooding in the Jhelum Basin of Kashmir, India', *Geomatics, Natural Hazards and Risk* 9.1 (2018), 224–48.

SELECTED BIBLIOGRAPHY

2040. Dir. D. Gameau. Madman Entertainment, 2019.

Abbasi, D. R. *Americans and Climate Change: Closing the Gap between Science and Action*. New Haven, CT: Yale School of Forestry and Environmental Studies, 2006.

Abdullah, S. *Rani in Search of a Rainbow*. Ann Arbor, MI: Living Healing Press, 2014.

Abrams, M. H. 'The Correspondent Breeze'. *Kenyon Review* 19 (1957), 113–30.

Adorno, T. W. *Aesthetic Theory*. Minneapolis: University of Minnesota Press, 1998.

The Age of Stupid. Dir. Franny Armstrong. Dogwoof Pictures, 2009.

Aki, R. *Saninghua de guxiang (The Homeland of Mountain Sakura)*. Taipei: Rye Field, 2010.

'The Anchorage Declaration'. *Indigenous Peoples' Global Summit on Climate Change*. 24 April 2009. http://unfccc.int/resource/docs/2009/smsn/ngo/168.pdf.

Anders, C. J. *All the Birds in the Sky*. London: Titan Books, 2016.

Andersen, G. *Climate Fiction and Cultural Analysis: A New Perspective on Life in the Anthropocene*. Abingdon: Routledge, 2020.

Anote's Ark. Dir. M. Rytz. Eyesteel Film, 2018.

Alaimo, S. *Bodily Natures: Science, Environment and the Material Self*. Bloomington: Indiana University Press, 2010.

    Exposed: Environmental Politics and Pleasures in Posthuman Times. Minneapolis: University of Minnesota Press, 2016.

    'States of Suspension: Trans-Corporeality at Sea'. *ISLE: Interdisciplinary Studies in Literature and Environment* 19.3 (2012), 476–93.

    'Thinking as the Stuff of the World'. *O-Zone: A Journal of Object-Oriented Studies* 1 (2014), 13–21.

    'Trans-Corporeality'. In R. Braidotti and M. Hlavajova (eds.), *The Posthuman Glossary*. London: Bloomsbury Academic, 2018. 435–8.

Albrecht, G. *Earth Emotions: New Words for a New World*. Ithaca, NY: Cornell University Press, 2019.

    'Solastalgia: The Distress Caused by Environmental Change'. *Philosophy Activism Nature* 3 (2005), 41–55.

Alfar, D. F. *et al.*, eds. *Outpouring: Typhoon Yolanda Relief Anthology*. Manila: Kestrel DDM and Flipside Publishing, 2014.

Allen, P. G. 'The Ceremonial Motion of Indian Time: Long Ago, So Far'. In H. Geiogamah and J. T. Darby (eds.), *American Indian Theater in*

Performance: A Reader. Los Angeles: UCLA American Indian Studies Center, 2000. 69–75.

The Sacred Hoop: Recovering the Feminine in American Indian Traditions. Boston, MA: Beacon Press, 1992.

'The Almeria Statement on Desertification and Migration'. *Environmental Conservation* 21.2 (1994), 179–81.

Andersen, G. *Climate Fiction and Cultural Analysis: A New Perspective on Life in the Anthropocene*. London: Routledge, 2020.

Anderson, K. *Predicting the Weather: Victorians and the Science of Meteorology*. University of Chicago Press, 2005.

Ang, I. 'Television Fictions around the World: Melodrama and Irony in Global Perspective'. *Critical Studies in Television* 2.2 (2007), 18–30.

Watching Dallas: Soap Opera and the Melodramatic Imagination. New York: Routledge, 1985.

Angry Inuk. Dir. A. Arnaquq-Baril. National Film Board of Canada, 2016.

Appadurai, A. *Modernity at Large: Cultural Dimensions of Globalization*. Vol. 1. Minneapolis: University of Minnesota Press, 1996.

Après-Demain. Dir. C. Dion. Mars Films, 2018.

Arasanayagam, J. 'I Am an Innocent Man'. In Arasanayagam, *All Is Burning*. New Delhi: Penguin, 1995. 22–42.

Aravamudan, S. 'The Catachronism of Climate Change'. *Diacritics* 41.3 (2013), 6–30.

Arcari, P. *et al.* 'Where Species Don't Meet: Invisibilized Animals, Urban Nature and City Limits'. *Environment and Planning E* 3.3 (2020).

Aristotle. 'Critical Contexts: From *The Poetics*'. Trans. G. E. Else. In W. B. Worthen (ed.), *The Wadsworth Anthology of Drama*, 5th ed. Belmont, CA: Wadsworth, 2007. 123–4.

Armitage, K. C. *The Nature Study Movement: The Forgotten Popularizer of America's Conservation Ethic*. Lawrence: University of Kansas Press, 2009.

Armstrong, J. 'Land Speaking'. In S. Ortiz (ed.), *Speaking for the Generations*. Tucson: University of Arizona Press, 1998. 174–94.

Armstrong, P. *What Animals Mean in the Fiction of Modernity*. London: Routledge, 2008.

Arnoldi, J. *Risk: An Introduction*. Cambridge: Polity Press, 2009.

Arons, W. 'Queer Ecology/Contemporary Plays'. *Theatre Journal* 64.4 (2012), 565–82.

Arons, W. and T. May. 'Ecodramaturgy in/and Contemporary Women's Playwriting'. In L. Ferris and P. Farfan (eds.), *Contemporary Women Playwrights*. New York: Palgrave Macmillan, 2013. 181–96.

eds. *Readings in Performance and Ecology*. New York: Palgrave Macmillan, 2012.

Ashbery, J. *A Wave: Poems*. New York: Penguin, 1985.

Asimov, I. *The Gods Themselves*. New York: Doubleday, 1972.

'The Last Question'. In B. Aldiss (ed.), *Space Opera: Science Fiction from the Golden Age*. London: Weidenfeld & Nicolson, 1974. 309–22.

Bacigalupi, P. Foreword. In J. J. Adams (ed.), *Loosed upon the World: The Saga Anthology of Climate Fiction*. New York: Saga, 2015. xiii–xv.

'Bali Principles of Climate Justice'. 29 August 2002. EJnet.org.

Baoshu. *The Redemption of Time*. Trans. K. Liu. New York: Tor, 2019.

Barad, K. *Meeting the Universe Halfway: Quantum Physics and the Entanglement of Matter and Meaning*. Durham, NC: Duke University Press, 2007.

Barthes, R. *The Rustle of Language*. Trans. R. Howard. Berkeley: University of California Press, 1986.

'Where to Begin?' *New Critical Essays*. Trans. R. Howard. Los Angeles: University of California Press, 1990. 79–89.

Bastasa, R. 'The Typhoon Last Night'. *Poem Hunter*. 17 April 2009.

Baudelaire, C. *A Wave: Poems*. Trans. J. Ashbery. New York: Penguin, 1985.

Beasts of the Southern Wild. Dir. B. Zeitlin. Fox Searchlight, 2012.

Beck, U. *Risk Society: Towards a New Modernity*. Trans. M. Ritter. London: Sage, 1992.

Before the Flood. Dir. F. Stevens. National Geographic, 2016.

Benjamin, W. 'Convolute D: Boredom, Eternal Return'. In R. Tiedemann (ed.), *The Arcades Project*. Trans. H. Eiland and K. McLauhglin. Cambridge, MA: Belknap, 1999.

'Critique of Violence'. *Reflections: Essays, Aphorisms, Autobiographical Writings*. Trans. E. F. N. Jephcott. New York: Schocken, 1978. 277–300.

'The Work of Art in the Age of Mechanical Reproduction'. In H. Arendt (ed.), *Illuminations*. Trans. H. Zohn. New York: Schocken Books, 1969. 217–52.

'Theses on the Philosophy of History'. In H. Arendt (ed.), *Illuminations*. Trans. H. Zohn. New York: Schocken Books, 1969. 253–64.

Bennett, J. *Vibrant Matter: A Political Ecology of Things*. Durham, NC: Duke University Press, 2010.

Berenguer, J. 'The Effect of Empathy in Pro-environmental Attitudes and Behaviours'. *Environment and Behaviour* 39 (2007), 269–83.

Berger, P. L. and T. Luckmann. *The Social Construction of Reality: A Treatise in the Sociology of Knowledge*. New York: Anchor Books, 1990.

Bergthaller, H. *et al*. 'Mapping Common Ground: Ecocriticism, Environmental History, and the Environmental Humanities'. *Environmental Humanities* 5 (2014), 261–76.

Bernasconi, R. 'Who Invented the Concept of Race? Kant's Role in the Enlightenment Construction of Race'. In R. Bernasconi (ed.), *Race*. London: Blackwell, 2001. 11–37.

The Beverly Hillbillies. Created by P. Henning. CBS, 1962–71.

Bhattacharya, S. 'The Margins of Postcolonial Urbanity: Reading Critical Irrealism in Nabarun Bhattacharya's Fiction'. In M. Chakraborty and U. Al-wazedi (eds.), *Postcolonial Urban Outcasts: City Margins in South Asian Literature*. New York: Routledge, 2016. 39–55.

Biidaaban: First Light. Dir. L. Jackson, with M. Borret and Jam3. National Film Board of Canada, 2018.

Bilandzic, H. and F. Sukalla. 'The Role of Fictional Film Exposure and Narrative Engagement for Personal Norms, Guilt and Intentions to Protect the Climate'. *Environmental Communication* 13.8 (2019), 1069–86.

Bilodeau, C. *Sila: The Artic Cycle*. Vancouver: Talonbooks, 2015.

Birch, T. 'Friday Essay: Recovering a Narrative of Place-Stories in the Time of Climate Change'. *The Conversation*. 27 April 2018.

Bloch, E. *The Principle of Hope*. Trans. N. Plaice *et al*. Cambridge, MA: MIT Press, 1986.

Blum, H. '"Bitter with the Salt of Continents": Rachel Carson and Oceanic Returns'. *WSQ: Women's Studies Quarterly* 451–2 (2017), 287–91.

Bode, K. and P. L. Arthur. 'Collecting Ourselves'. In P. L. Arthur and K. Bode (eds.), *Advancing Digital Humanities: Research, Methods, Theories*. Basingstoke: Palgrave Macmillan, 2014. 1–13.

Böhme, G. *The Aesthetics of Atmospheres*. Abingdon: Routledge, 2016.

Bonneuil, C. and J. B. Fressoz. *The Shock of the Anthropocene*. London: Verso, 2017.

Bourdieu, P. 'The Aristocracy of Culture'. Trans. R. Nice. *Media, Culture and Society* 2 (1980), 225–54.

Boyde, M. 'Mining Animal Death for All It's Worth'. In J. Johnston and F. Probyn-Rapsey (eds.), *Animal Death*. Sydney University Press, 2013. 119–36.

'"Mrs Boss! We Gotta Get Those Fat Cheeky Bullocks into That Big Bloody Metal Ship!": Live Export as Romantic Backdrop in Baz Luhrmann's *Australia*'. In Boyde (ed.), *Captured: The Animal Within Culture* New York: Palgrave Macmillan, 2013. 60–74.

Bracke, A. *Climate Crisis and the Twenty-First-Century British Novel*. London: Bloomsbury Academic, 2016.

Breaking Bad. Created by V. Gilligan. AMC, 2008–13.

Brennan, T. *The Transmission of Affect*. Ithaca: Cornell University Press, 2004.

Bristow, T. and T. H. Ford. 'Climates of History, Cultures of Climate'. In Bristow and Ford (eds.), *A Cultural History of Climate Change*. Abingdon: Routledge, 2016. 1–14.

Broadway Green Alliance. www.broadwaygreen.com.

Bronstein, M. 'Taking the Future into Account: Today's Novels for Tomorrow's Readers'. *PMLA* 134.1 (2019), 121–36.

Brontë, E. *Wuthering Heights*. Oxford University Press, 2007.

Brown, L. 'Reading Race and Gender: Jonathan Swift'. *Eighteenth-Century Studies* 23.4 (1990), 425–43.

Buell, L. *The Environmental Imagination: Thoreau, Nature Writing, and the Formation of American Culture*. Cambridge, MA: Belknap, 1995.

The Future of Environmental Criticism: Environmental Crisis and Literary Imagination. Malden, MA: Blackwell, 2005.

'Toxic Discourse'. *Critical Inquiry* 24.3 (1998), 639–65.

Burnett, L. 'Firing the Climate Canon: A Literary Critique of the Genre of Climate Change'. *Green Letters* 22.2 (2018), 161–80.

Büscher, B. and V. Davidov. 'Environmentally Induced Displacements in the Ecotourism–Extraction Nexus'. *Area* 48.2 (2016), 161–7.

Busse, K. *Framing Fan Fiction: Literary and Social Practices in Fan Fiction Communities*. Iowa City: University of Iowa Press, 2017.

Busse, K. and K. Hellekson. 'Introduction: Work in Progress'. In K. Busse and K. Hellekson (eds.), *Fan Fiction and Fan Communities in the Age of the Internet: New Essays*. Jefferson, NC: McFarland, 2006. 5–32.

Butler, O. *Dawn*. New York: Grand Central, 1987.

Calarco, M. *Zoographies: The Question of the Animal*. New York: Columbia University Press, 2008.

Caminero-Santangel, B. 'Witnessing the Nature of Violence: Resource Extraction and Political Ecologies in the Contemporary African Novel'. In DeLoughrey *et al.* (eds.), *Global Ecologies and the Environmental Humanities: Postcolonial Approaches*. 226–41.

Camuffo, D. 'History of the Long Series of Daily Air Temperature in Padova, 1725–1998'. *Climatic Change* 53 (2002), 7–75.

Canavan, G. 'Introduction: If This Goes On'. In Canavan and Robinson (eds.), *Green Planets*. 1–21.

Canavan, G. and K. S. Robinson (eds.). *Green Planets: Ecology and Science Fiction*. Middletown, CT: Wesleyan University Press, 2014.

Caracciolo, M. 'Deus Ex Algorithmo: Narrative Form, Computation, and the Fate of the World in David Mitchell's *Ghostwritten* and Richard Powers's *The Overstory*'. *Contemporary Literature* 60.1 (2019), 47–71.

Cariou, W. 'An Athabasca Story'. *Lake: Journal of Arts and Environment* 7 (2012), 71–5.

Carpenter, J. R. *The Gathering Cloud*. Axminster: Uniform Books, 2017.

Carson, R. 'Chincoteague: A National Wildlife Refuge'. *Conservation in Action*. Washington, DC: Fish and Wildlife Service, Department of the Interior, 1947.

The Edge of the Sea. Boston, MA: Houghton Mifflin, 1956.

'Help Your Child to Wonder'. *Woman's Home Companion*. July 1956.

The Sea Around Us. New York: Oxford University Press, 1951.

Silent Spring. Boston, MA: Houghton Mifflin, 1962.

Under the Sea-Wind. New York: Oxford University Press, 1941.

Caterpillars Count! https://caterpillarscount.unc.edu.

Cates, D. F. 'Hope, Hatred, and the Ambiguities of Utopic Longing'. In D. Boscaljon (ed.), *Hope and the Longing for Utopia: Futures and Illusions in Theology and Narrative*. Cambridge: James Clarke, 2014. 23–40.

Celermajer, D. and A. Wallach. 'The Fate of the Illegible Animal: The Case of the Australian Wild Donkey'. *Animal Studies Journal* 8.2 (2019), 229–58.

Center for Sustainable Practice in the Arts (CSPA). https://sustainablepractice.org.

Centre for Alternative Technology. *Zero Carbon Britain: Making It Happen*. Machynlleth: CAT Publications, 2017.

Chakrabarty, D. 'The Climate of History: Four Theses'. *Critical Inquiry* 35.2 (2009), 197–222.

The Crises of Civilization: Exploring Global and Planetary Histories. Oxford University Press, 2018.

'Postcolonial Studies and the Challenge of Climate Change'. *New Literary History* 43.1 (2012), 1–18.

Chambers, R. *An Atmospherics of the City: Baudelaire and the Poetics of Noise*. New York: Fordham University Press, 2015.

'Nervalian Mist and Baudelairean Fog: An Essay in Textual Atmospherics'. In E. J. Mickel (ed.), *The Shaping of Text: Style, Imagery and Structure in French Literature*. Lewisburg, PA: Bucknell University Press, 1993. 88–104.

Chasing Ice. Dir. J. Orlowski. Submarine Deluxe, 2012.

Chaudhuri, U. Introduction. In U. Chaudhuri (ed.), *Rachel's Brain and Other Storms: The Performance Scripts of Rachel Rosenthal*. New York: Bloomsbury, 2001. 1–13.

'The Silence of the Polar Bears'. In W. Arons and T. May (eds.), *Readings in Performance and Ecology*. New York: Palgrave Macmillan, 2012. 45–58.

'"There Must Be a Lot of Fish in that Lake": Toward an Ecological Theater'. *Theater* 25.1 (1994), 23–31.

Chiari, S. *Shakespeare's Representation of Weather, Climate, and Environment: The Early Modern 'Fated Sky'*. Edinburgh University Press, 2019.

Christian Aid. 'Human Tide: The Real Migration Crisis'. May 2007. www
.christianaid.org.uk/sites/default/files/2017-08/human-tide-the-real-migration-crisis
-may-2007.pdf.

Chrulew, M. and R. De Vos. 'Extinction: Stories of Unravelling and Reworlding'.
Cultural Studies Review 25.1 (2019), 23–8.

Chun, W. H. K. 'On Patterns and Proxies, or the Perils of Reconstructing the
Unknown'. *e-flux architecture*. 25 September 2018.

Clark, T. *The Cambridge Introduction to Literature and the Environment.*
Cambridge University Press, 2011.

'Scale'. In Cohen (ed.), *Telemorphosis*. 148–66.

Ecocriticism on the Edge: The Anthropocene as a Threshold Concept. London:
Bloomsbury Academic, 2015.

'What on World Is the Earth? The Anthropocene and Fictions of the World'. *The
Oxford Literary Review* 35.1 (2013), 5–24.

Clarke, B. *Gaian Systems: Lynn Margulis, Neocybernetics, and the End of the
Anthropocene.* Minneapolis: University of Minnesota Press, 2020.

'The Planetary Imaginary: Gaian Ecologies from *Dune* to *Neuromancer*'. In T.
Clarke (ed.), *Earth, Life, and System: Evolution and Ecology on a Gaian Planet.*
New York: Fordham University Press, 2015. 151–74.

Clements, M. *Burning Vision.* Vancouver: Talonbooks, 2003.

Cless, D. 'Eco-Theatre, USA: The Grassroots Is Greener'. *TDR* 40.2 (1996), 79–102.

Climate Stories Project. www.climatestoriesproject.org.

Coen, D. R. *Climate in Motion: Science, Empire, and the Problem of Scale.* University
of Chicago Press, 2018.

Coetzee, J. M. *The Lives of Animals.* Princeton University Press, 1999.

Cohen, T., ed. *Telemorphosis: Essays in Critical Climate Change.* Vol. 1. Ann Arbor,
MI: Open Humanities Press, 2012.

Colebrook, C. *Death of the Posthuman: Essays on Extinction.* Ann Arbor, MI: Open
Humanities Press, 2014.

Corntassel, J. 'Re-envisioning Resurgence: Indigenous Pathways to Decolonization
and Sustainable Self-Determination'. *Decolonization: Indigeneity, Education
and Society* 1.1 (2012), 86–101.

Cory, A. L. '"Out of My Brother's Power": Gender, Class and Rebellion in
Wuthering Heights'. *Women's Studies* 34.1 (2004), 1–26.

Costa, A. L. M. C. 'Once upon a Time in a World'. In Lodi-Ribiero (ed.), *Solarpunk.*
83–115.

Coulthard, G. *Red Skin, White Masks: Rejecting the Colonial Politics of Recognition.*
Minneapolis: University of Minnesota Press, 2014.

Cowspiracy: The Sustainability Secret. Dir. K. Andersen and K. Kuhn. Appian Way
Productions, 2014.

Crane, K. 'Tracking the Tassie Tiger: Extinction and Ethics in Julia Leigh's *The
Hunter*'. In L. Volkmann *et al.* (eds.), *Local Natures, Global Responsibilities:
Ecocritical Perspectives on the New English Literatures.* Amsterdam: Rodopi,
2010. 105–19.

Craps, S. 'Climate Change and the Art of Anticipatory Memory'. *Parallax* 23.4
(2017), 479–92.

Craps, S. and R. Crownshaw. 'Introduction: The Rising Tide of Climate Fiction'.
Studies in the Novel 50.1 (2018), 1–8.

Crist, E. and H. Kopnina. 'Unsettling Anthropocentrism'. *Dialectical Anthropology* 38 (2014), 387–96.

Crutzen, P. J. 'Albedo Enhancement by Stratospheric Sulfur Injections: A Contribution to Resolve a Policy Dilemma?' *Climate Change* 77 (2006), 211.

Cubitt, S. *Finite Media: Environmental Implications of Digital Technologies.* Durham, NC: Duke University Press, 2016.

Culler, J. *The Pursuit of Signs.* Ithaca, NY: Cornell University Press, 1981.

Cummings, B. 'Literally Speaking, or, the Literal Sense from Augustine to Lacan'. *Paragraph* 21 (1998), 200–26.

Cunsolo Willox, A. 'Climate Change as the Work of Mourning'. *Ethics and the Environment* 17.2 (2012), 137–64.

Dallas. Created by D. Jacobs. CBS, 1978–91.

Davis, H. and Z. Todd. 'On the Importance of a Date, or Decolonizing the Anthropocene'. *ACME* 16.4 (2017), 761–80.

Davison, J. '"Not to Escape the World But to Join It": Responding to Climate Change with Imagination Not Fantasy'. *Philosophical Transactions of the Royal Society A* 375.2095 (2017).

The Day After Tomorrow. Dir. R. Emmerich. Twentieth-Century Fox, 2004.

Deadwood. Created by D. Milch. HBO. 2004–6.

Deckard, S. 'Editorial'. *Green Letters* 16.1 (2012), 5–14.

DeLoughrey, E. *Allegories of the Anthropocene.* Durham, NC: Duke University Press, 2019.

  'Ordinary Futures: Interspecies Worldings in the Anthropocene'. In DeLoughrey *et al.* (eds.), *Global Ecologies and the Environmental Humanities.* 352–72.

DeLoughrey, E. *et al.*, eds. *Global Ecologies and the Environmental Humanities: Postcolonial Approaches.* London: Routledge, 2015.

  'Introduction: A Postcolonial Environmental Humanities'. In DeLoughrey *et al.* (eds.), *Global Ecologies and the Environmental Humanities.* 1–32.

Demain (Tomorrow). Dir. C. Dion and M. Laurent. Mars Films, 2015.

Derrida, J. 'The Animal That Therefore I Am (More to Follow)'. *Critical Inquiry* 28.2 (2002), 369–418.

De Vos, R. 'Extinction Stories: Performing Absence(s)'. In L. Simmons and P. Armstrong (eds.), *Knowing Non-Human Animals.* Leiden: Brill, 2007. 183–95.

Dillon, G. 'Imagining Indigenous Futurisms'. In G. Dillon (ed.), *Walking the Clouds: An Anthology of Indigenous Science Fiction.* Tucson: University of Arizona Press, 2012. 1–12.

Dolan, J. 'Performance, Utopia, and the "Utopian Performative"'. *Theatre Journal* 53.3 (2001), 455–79.

Domínguez-Castro, F. *et al.* 'An Early Weather Diary from Iberia (Lisbon, 1631–1632)'. *Weather* 70.1 (2015), 20–4.

Downsizing. Dir. A. Payne. Paramount Pictures, 2017.

Easterlin, N. *A Biocultural Approach to Literary Theory and Interpretation.* Baltimore, MD: Johns Hopkins University Press, 2012.

Edwards, P. N. *A Vast Machine: Computer Models, Climate Data, and the Politics of Global Warming.* Cambridge, MA: MIT Press, 2010.

El Hinnawi, E. *Environmental Refugees.* Nairobi: United Nations Environment Programme, 1985.

Emmett, R. and T. Lekan, eds. 'Whose Anthropocene? Revisiting Dipesh Chakrabarty's "Four Theses"'. *RCC Perspectives: Transformations in Environment and Society* 2 (2016).

Enelow, S. *Carla and Lewis.* In U. Chaudhuri and S. Enelow, *Research Theatre, Climate Change, and the Ecocide Project: A Casebook.* New York: Palgrave Pivot, 2014. 87–116

Engels, F. 'Preface'. In K. Marx, *Capital.* Vol. 2. New York: International Publishers, 1972.

Eschrich, J. and C. A. Miller, eds. *The Weight of Light: A Collection of Solar Futures.* Tempe: Arizona State University, 2018.

Evans, Raymond. *A History of Queensland.* Melbourne: Cambridge University Press, 2007.

Evans, Rebecca. 'Fantastic Futures? Climate Fiction, Climate Justice, and Queer Futurity'. *Resilience* 4.2–3 (2017), 94–110.

Everything's Cool. Dir. J. Helfand and D. B. Gold. City Lights Pictures, 2007.

Fagan, B. M. *The Little Ice Age: How Climate Made History 1300–1850.* New York: Basic Books, 2002.

FanFiction. www.fanfiction.net.

Feldman, T. 'Late Enlightenment Meteorology'. In T. Frängsmyr *et al.* (eds.), *The Quantifying Spirit in the Eighteenth Century.* Berkeley: University of California Press, 1990. 143–79.

Ferguson, E. *Line 9 Communities.* https://line9communities.com.

Fine, G. A. *Authors of the Storm: Meteorologists and the Culture of Prediction.* University of Chicago Press, 2007.

Fleming, J. R. *Fixing the Sky: The Checkered History of Weather and Climate Control.* New York: Columbia University Press, 2010.

Fleming, J. R. and V. Jankovic. 'Revisiting *Klima*'. *Osiris* 26.1 (2011), 1–16.

Flynn, A. 'Solarpunk: Notes toward a Manifesto'. *Hieroglyph.* 4 September 2014.

Ford, T. H. 'Climate Change and Literary History'. In T. Bristow and T. H. Ford (eds.), *A Cultural History of Climate Change.* Abingdon: Routledge, 2016. 157–74.

Forest 404. Dir. B. Ripley. Written by T. X. Atack. BBC Radio 4, 2019.

Foster, J. B. *et al. The Ecological Rift: Capitalism's War on the Earth.* New York: Monthly Review, Press, 2010.

Franzosi, R. 'Narrative Analysis – Or Why (and How) Sociologists Should Be Interested in Narrative'. *Annual Review of Sociology* 24 (1998), 517–54.

Freeman, C. *Paper Tiger: How Pictures Shaped the Thylacine.* Hobart: Forty South Publishing, 2014.

Fried, L. K. and T. May. *Greening Up Our Houses: A Guide to a More Ecologically Sound Theatre.* New York: Drama Book, 1994.

Frow, J. 'Genre Worlds: The Discursive Shaping of Knowledge'. *Arena Journal* 23 (2005), 129–46.

On Interpretative Conflict. University of Chicago Press, 2019.

Fuller, R. B. *Operating Manual for Spaceship Earth.* New York: Simon & Schuster, 1969.

Gabrys, J. *Program Earth: Environmental Sensing Technology and the Making of a Computational Planet.* Minneapolis: University of Minnesota Press, 2016.

Gagliano, M. *et al.* *The Language of Plants: Science, Philosophy, Literature.* Minneapolis: University of Minnesota Press, 2017.

Galjour, A. *Alligator Tales.* 1997. Manuscript. Courtesy of Joyce Ketay Agency.

Galleymore, I. *Teaching Environmental Writing: Ecocritical Pedagogy and Poetics.* London: Bloomsbury Academic, 2020.

Gamper, M. 'Rätsel der Atmosphäre: Umrisse einer "literarischen Meteorologie"'. *Zeitschrift für Germanistik* 24 (2014), 229–43.

Garrard, G. *Ecocriticism.* 2nd ed. London: Routledge, 2012.

Garret, I. 'Theatrical Production's Carbon Footprint'. In W. Arons and T. May (eds.), *Readings in Performance and Ecology.* New York: Palgrave Macmillan, 2012. 201–10.

Gasland. Dir. J. Fox. HBO, 2010.

Ge, Q.-S. *et al.* 'Reconstruction of Historical Climate in China: High Resolution Precipitation Data in Qing Dynasty Archives'. *Bulletin of the American Meteorological Society* 86.5 (2005), 671–9.

Genette, G. *Palimpsests: Literature in the Second Degree.* Trans. C. Newman and C. Doubinsky. Lincoln: University of Nebraska Press, 1997.

The Architext: An Introduction. Trans. J. E. Lewin. Berkeley: University of California Press, 1992.

Ghosh, A. *The Great Derangement: Climate Change and the Unthinkable.* University of Chicago Press, 2017.

Gun Island. New York: Farrar, Strauss and Giroux, 2019.

The Hungry Tide. New York: Harper Collins, 2004.

Giddens, A. *Affluence, Poverty and the Idea of a Post-Scarcity Society.* Geneva: United Nations Research Institute for Social Development, 1995.

The Politics of Climate Change. Cambridge: Polity Press, 2009.

Gifford, T. 'Pastoral, Antipastoral and Postpastoral as Reading Strategies'. In S. Slovic (ed.), *Critical Insights: Nature and the Environment.* Armenia, NY: Salem Press, 2013. 42–61.

Glotfelty, C. 'Preface'. In G. Garrard (ed.), *The Oxford Handbook of Ecocriticism.* Oxford University Press, 2014.

Goffman, E. *Frame Analysis: An Essay on the Organization of Experience.* Boston, MA: Northeastern University Press, 2010.

Golinski, J. *British Weather and the Climate of Enlightenment.* University of Chicago Press, 2007.

'Robert Boyle: Scepticism and Authority in Seventeenth-Century Chemical Discourse'. In A. E. Benjamin *et al.* (eds.), *The Figural and the Literal: Problems of Language in the History of Science and Philosophy, 1630–1800.* Manchester University Press, 1987. 58–82.

Goodbody, A. and A. Johns-Putra. 'The Rise of the Climate Change Novel'. In Johns-Putra (ed.), *Climate and Literature.* 229–45.

Gore, A. *Earth in the Balance: Forging a New Common Purpose.* London: Earthscan, 1992.

Graham, J. *Fast.* Manchester: Carcanet, 2017.

Sea Change: Poems. Manchester: Carcanet, 2008.

Graves, S. 'Watch Out, Red Crusher!' In Ulibarri (ed.), *Glass and Gardens.* 53–68.

Gray, N. and S. Rabillard. 'Theatre in an Age of Ecocrisis'. *Canadian Theatre Review* 144 (2010), 3–4.

Green, M. C. and T. C. Brock. 'The Role of Transportation in the Persuasiveness of Public Narratives'. *Journal of Personality and Social Psychology* 79 (2000), 701–21.

Greenwell, G. 'Beauty's Canker: On Jorie Graham'. *West Branch* 63 (2008), 115–34.

Griffiths, M. *The New Poetics of Climate Change: Modernist Aesthetics for a Warming World*. London: Bloomsbury Academic, 2017.

Groff, L. 'Flower Hunters'. In *Florida*. London: Penguin Random House, 2018. 155–69.

Gruen, L. 'Empathy'. In Gruen (ed.), *Critical Terms for Animal Studies*. University of Chicago Press, 2018. 141–53.

Gruen, L. and F. Probyn-Rapsey, eds. *Animaladies: Gender, Species, Madness*. New York: Bloomsbury Academic, 2018.

Gumbs, A. P. *Dub: Finding Ceremony*. Durham, NC: Duke University Press, 2020.

'Evidence'. In W. Imarisha and A. M. Brown (eds.), *Octavia's Brood: Science Fiction Stories from Social Justice Movements*. Oakland, CA: AK Press, 2015. 33–42.

M Archive: After the End of the World. Durham, NC: Duke University Press, 2018.

Spill: Scenes of Black Feminist Fugitivity. Durham, NC: Duke University Press, 2016.

Hageman, A. 'Bringing Infrastructural Criticism to Speculative Fiction: China Miéville's "Covehithe"'. *C21 Literature: Journal of 21st-Century Writings* 7.1 (2019), 1–10.

Haider, J. 'The Shaping of Environmental Information in Social Media'. *Environmental Communication* 10.4 (2016), 473–91.

Hamblyn, R. 'The Whistleblower and the Canary: Rhetorical Construction of Climate Change'. *Journal of Historical Geography* 35 (2009), 223–36.

Hamilton, J. M. *This Contentious Storm: An Ecocritical and Performance History of King Lear*. London: Bloomsbury Academic, 2017.

Haraway, D. J. *The Companion Species Manifesto: Dogs, People, and Significant Otherness*. University of Chicago Press, 2003.

'A Cyborg Manifesto: Science, Technology, and Socialist-Feminism in the Late Twentieth Century'. In D. J. Haraway, *Simians, Cyborgs and Women: The Reinvention of Nature*. London: Free Association Books, 1991. 149–81.

Modest_Witness@Second_Millennium.FemaleMan©_Meets_OncoMouse™: Feminism and Technoscience. New York: Routledge, 1997.

Staying with the Trouble: Making Kin in the Chthulucene. Durham, NC: Duke University Press, 2016.

Harkins, A. 'The Hillbilly in the Living Room: Television Representations of Southern Mountaineers in Situation Comedies, 1952–1971'. *Appalachian Journal* 29.1/2 (2001–2), 98–126.

Hassan, R. 'Digitality, Virtual Reality and the "Empathy Machine"'. *Digital Journalism* 6 (2019), 1–18.

Hau'ofa, E. 'Our Sea of Islands'. *The Contemporary Pacific* 6.1 (1994), 148–61.

Heise, U. K. *Imagining Extinction: The Cultural Meanings of Endangered Species*. University of Chicago Press, 2016.

Sense of Place and Sense of Planet: The Environmental Imagination of the Global. New York: Oxford University Press, 2008.

Helgeson, J. *et al.* 'The Role of Knowledge, Learning and Mental Models in Public Perceptions of Climate-Change-Related Risks'. In A. Wals and P. B. Corcoran (eds.), *Learning for Sustainability in Times of Accelerating Change*. Wageningen: Wageningen Academic Publishers, 2012. 329–46.

Hell. Dir. T. Fehlbaum. Paramount Pictures, 2011.

Herbert, X. *Capricornia*. Sydney: Angus and Robertson, 1939.

Heringman, N. 'Deep Time at the Dawn of the Anthropocene'. *Representations* 129.1 (2015), 56–85.

Holding, S. 'What Is Cli-Fi? And Why I Write It'. *The Guardian*. 6 February 2015.

Hope, A. *et al*. 'Consumer Engagement in Low-Carbon Home Energy in the United Kingdom: Implications for Future Energy System Decentralization'. *Energy Research and Social Science* 44 (2018), 362–70.

Hopf, C. 'Story Networks: A Theory of Narrative and Mass Collaboration'. *Rhizomes* 21 (2010).

Houser, H. 'Climate Visualizations: Making Data Experiential'. In U. K. Heise *et al*. (eds.), *The Routledge Companion to the Environmental Humanities*. London: Routledge, 2016. 358–68.

  Infowhelm: Environmental Art and Literature in an Age of Data. New York: Columbia University Press, 2020.

How to Let Go of the World and Love the Things That Climate Can't Change. Dir. J. Fox. HBO, 2016.

Huang, H. 'Climate Justice and Trans-Pacific Indigenous Feminisms'. In J. Adamson and K. N. Ruffin (eds.), *American Studies, Ecocriticism and Citizenship: Thinking and Acting in the Local and Global Commons*. London: Routledge, 2013. 158–72.

  'When the Sea-Level Rises: (W)ri(gh)ting Climate Change in Pacific Islanders' Literature'. In S. LeMenager *et al*. (eds.), *Teaching Climate Change in Literary and Cultural Studies*. London: Routledge, 2017. 258–64.

Hudson, N. 'From "Nation" to "Race": The Origin of Racial Classification in Eighteenth-Century Thought'. *Eighteenth-Century Studies* 29.3 (1996), 247–64.

Huggan, G. and H. Tiffin. *Postcolonial Ecocriticism: Literature, Animals, Environment*. 2nd ed. London: Routledge, 2015.

Hulme, K. *Stonefish*. Wellington: Huia, 2004.

Hulme, M. 'How Climate Models Gain and Exercise Authority'. In K. Hastrup and M. Skrystrup (eds.), *The Social Life of Climate Change Models: Anticipating Nature*. New York: Routledge, 2013. 30–44.

Huxley, G. C. *A Human's Approach to Adaptation*. Wattpad. www.wattpad.com /112090524-a-human%27s-approach-to-adaptation.

Hyman, W. B. '"Deductions from Metaphors": Figurative Truth, Poetical Language, and Early Modern Science'. In H. Marchitello and E. Tribble (eds.), *The Palgrave Handbook of Early Modern Literature and Science*. London: Palgrave Macmillan, 2017. 27–48.

Ice on Fire. Dir. L. Conners. HBO, 2019.

An Inconvenient Sequel. Dir. B. Cohen and J. Shenk. Paramount, 2017.

An Inconvenient Truth. Dir. D. Guggenheim. Paramount, 2006.

Ingold, T. 'The Atmosphere'. *Chiasmi International* 14 (2012), 75–85.

Ingram, D. 'Hollywood Cinema and Climate Change: *The Day After Tomorrow*'. In M. Devine and C. Grewe-Volpp (eds.), *Words on Water: Literary and Cultural Representations*. Wissenschaftlicher Verlag Trier, 2005. 53–63.

Inuit Knowledge and Climate Change. Dir. Z. Kunuk and I. Mauro. Isuma, 2010.

Interstellar. Dir. C. Nolan. Paramount, 2014.

Irigaray, L. *The Forgetting of Air in Martin Heidegger*. London: Athlone Press, 1999.

The Island President. Dir. J. Shenk. Samuel Goldwyn Films, 2011.

Jackson, Z. I. *On Becoming Human*. New York University Press, 2020.

James, E. *The Storyworld Accord: Econarratology and Postcolonial Narratives.* Lincoln: University of Nebraska Press, 2015.

Jameson, F. *The Antinomies of Realism*. London: Verso, 2015.

'Future City'. *New Left Review* 21 (2003), 65–71.

The Political Unconscious: Narrative as a Socially Symbolic Act. Ithaca, NY: Cornell University Press, 1981.

Postmodernism, or, The Cultural Logic of Late Capitalism. Durham, NC: Duke University Press, 1991.

Jankovic, V. *Reading the Skies: A Cultural History of English Weather, 1650–1820.* University of Chicago Press, 2000.

Jauss, H. R. *Toward an Aesthetic of Reception*. Trans. T. Bahti. Minneapolis: University of Minnesota Press, 1982.

Jemisin, N. K. *The Fifth Season*. London: Orbit, 2015.

Jetñil-Kijiner, K. *Kathy Jetñil-Kijiner*. www.kathyjetnilkijiner.com

Jetñil-Kijiner, K. and A. Niviâna. 'Rise: From One Island to Another'. *350.org*. 2018. https://350.org/rise-from-one-island-to-another/?fbclid=IwAR2YSFAM5jRuw_cF1 VrREyK81vHX-9lJpYKHo32pDPbwazPOwOUlBYlS724.

Johns-Putra, A. *Climate Change and the Contemporary Novel*. Cambridge University Press, 2019.

'Climate Change in Literature and Literary Studies: From Cli-Fi, Climate Change Theater and Ecopoetry to Ecocriticism and Climate Change Criticism'. *WIREs Climate Change* 7 (2016), 266–82.

'Climate and History in the Anthropocene: Realist Narrative and the Framing of Time'. In Johns-Putra (ed.), *Climate and Literature*. 246–66.

ed. *Climate and Literature*. Cambridge University Press, 2019.

'Ecocriticism, Genre, and Climate Change: Reading the Utopian Vision of Kim Stanley Robinson's Science in the Capital Trilogy'. *English Studies* 91.7 (2010), 744–60.

'The Rest Is Silence: Postmodern and Postcolonial Possibilities in Climate Change Fiction'. *Studies in the Novel* 50.1 (2018), 26–42.

Johnson, B. 'Gender Theory and the Yale School' (1985). In P. Rice and P. Waugh (eds.), *Modern Literary Theory: A Reader*. London: St. Martin's Press, 1996.

Jones, G. *Shakespeare's Storms*. Manchester University Press, 2015.

Jordan, D. *Climate Change Narratives in Australian Fiction*. Saarbrucken: Lambert, 2014.

Julie's Bicycle. https://juliesbicycle.com.

Justice, D. H. *Why Indigenous Literatures Matter*. Waterloo, ON: Wilfrid Laurier University Press, 2018.

Kalaidjian, A. 'The Spectacular Anthropocene'. *Angelaki* 22.4 (2017), 19–34.

Kammen, M. *A Time to Every Purpose: The Four Seasons in American Culture.* Chapel Hill: University of North Carolina Press, 2004.

Kant, I. *Critique of Judgement*. Oxford University Press, 2007.

Karera, A. 'Blackness and the Pitfalls of Anthropocene Ethics'. *Critical Philosophy of Race* 7.1 (2019), 32–56.

Kate Has Things to Say. www.marvelclimate.blogspot.com.

Kaza, S. 'Rachel Carson's Sense of Time: Experiencing Maine'. *ISLE: Interdisciplinary Studies in Literature and the Environment* 17.2 (2010), 291–315.

Keen, S. *Empathy and the Novel.* Oxford University Press, 2007.

Keith, D. *A Case for Climate Engineering.* Cambridge, MA: MIT Press, 2013.

Keller, L. *Recomposing Ecopoetics: North American Poetry of the Self-Conscious Anthropocene.* Charlottesville: University of Virginia Press, 2017.

Kempf, W. 'A Sea of Environmental Refugees? Oceania in an Age of Climate Change'. In E. Hermann *et al.* (eds.), *Form, Macht, Differenz: Motive und Felder ethnologischen Forschens.* Universitätsverlag Göttingen, 2009. 191–205.

Kerr, H. 'Fictocritical Empathy and the Work of Mourning'. *Cultural Studies Review* 9.1 (2003), 180–200.

Kim, C. *Dangerous Crossings: Race, Species, and Nature in a Multicultural Age.* Cambridge University Press, 2015.

Kimmerer, R. W. *Braiding Sweetgrass: Indigenous Wisdom, Scientific Knowledge, and the Teachings of Plants.* Minneapolis: Milkweed, 2013.

  Gathering Moss: A Natural and Cultural History of Mosses. Corvallis: Oregon State University Press, 2003.

Kimmerer, R. W. *et al.* 'Let Our Indigenous Voices Be Heard'. www.esf.edu/indigenous-science-letter/Indigenous_Science_Declaration.pdf.

Kingsland, S. *The Evolution of American Ecology, 1890–2000.* Baltimore, MD: Johns Hopkins University Press, 2005.

Kino-nda-niimi Collective. *The Winter We Danced: Voices from the Past, the Future, and the Idle No More Movement.* Winnipeg: ARP Books, 2014.

Kittay, E. F. 'Woman as Metaphor'. *Hypatia* 3.2 (1988), 63–86.

Kiwifruitini. *They Watched. Wattpad.* www.wattpad.com/630764661-they-watched.

Klein, N. 'Dancing the World into Being: A Conversation with Idle No More's Leanne Simpson'. *Yes! Magazine.* 5 March 2013.

  This Changes Everything: Capitalism vs. the Climate. Toronto: Vintage Canada, 2015.

Kristeva, J. 'Women's Time'. Trans. A. Jardine and H. Blake. *Signs* 7.1 (1981), 13–35.

Kuhn, T. *The Structure of Scientific Revolutions.* University of Chicago Press, 2012.

Kurtz, M. '"Alternate Cuts": An Interview with Vandana Singh'. *Science Fiction Studies* 43.3 (2016), 534–45.

Kurzweil, R. *How to Create a Mind: The Secret of Human Thought Revealed.* London: Viking, 2012.

Langeslag, P. S. 'Weathering the Storm: Adverse Climates in Medieval Literature'. In Johns-Putra (ed.), *Climate and Literature.* 76–91.

Langseth, T. 'Liquid Ice Surfers: The Construction of Surfer Identities in Norway'. *Journal of Adventure Education and Outdoor Learning Ontologies* 12.1 (2012), 3–23.

Latour, B. *We Have Never Been Modern.* Trans. C. Porter. Cambridge, MA: Harvard University Press, 1993.

Lavery, C. *Performance and Ecology: What Can Theatre Do?* Abingdon: Routledge, 2018.

Lawson, R. 'When Will Hollywood Actually Tackle Climate Change?' *Vanity Fair.* 19 September 2019.

Lazarus, R. J. 'Super Wicked Problems and Climate Change: Restraining the Present to Liberate the Future'. *Cornell Law Review* 94 (2009), 1153–233.

Le Guin, U. K. *The Lathe of Heaven*. New York: Scribner, 2008.

'Vaster Than Empires and More Slow'. In R. Silverberg (ed.), *New Dimensions 1: Fourteen Original Science Fiction Stories*. New York: Doubleday, 1971. 99–133.

Lear, L. *The Lost Woods: The Discovered Writing of Rachel Carson*. Boston: Beacon Press, 1998.

Rachel Carson: Witness for Nature. New York: Henry Holt, 1997.

Lee-Wright, P. *The Documentary Handbook*. London: Routledge, 2010.

Lehoux, D. *Astronomy, Weather, and Calendars in the Ancient World: Parapegmata and Related Texts in Classical and Near Eastern Societies*. Cambridge University Press, 2007.

Leigh, J. *The Hunter*. London: Faber, 1999.

Leiserowitz, A. 'Before and After *The Day After Tomorrow*: A U.S. Study of Climate Risk Perception'. *Environment* 46.9 (2004), 23–37.

LeMenager, S. 'Climate Change and the Struggle for Genre'. In Menely and Taylor (eds.), *Anthropocene Reading*. 220–38.

'The Humanities after the Anthropocene'. In U. K. Heise *et al.* (eds.), *The Routledge Companion to the Environmental Humanities*. London: Routledge, 2016. 473–81.

Living Oil: Petroleum Culture in the American Century. Oxford University Press, 2014.

Lenton, T. *Earth System Science: A Very Short Introduction*. Oxford University Press, 2016.

Leopold, A. 'The Land Ethic'. In *Sand Country Almanac and Sketches Here and There*. Oxford University Press, 1949. 201–26.

Lévi-Strauss, C. *Totemism*. Trans. R. Needham. Boston, MA: Beacon Press, 1963.

Lewis, E. M. *Magellanica*. Portland, OH: Actors Repertory Theatre, 2017. Unpublished.

Liberman, N. and Y. Trope. 'The Psychology of Transcending the Here and Now'. *Science* 322 (2008), 1201–5.

Liu, C. *Dark Forest*. Trans. J. Martinsen. New York: Tor, 2015.

Death's End. Trans. K. Liu. New York: Tor, 2016.

The Three-Body Problem. Trans. K. Liu. New York: Tor, 2014.

Lockwood, A. 'H Is for Hypocrite: Reading "New Nature Writing" through the Lens of Vegan Theory'. In L. Wright (ed.), *Through a Vegan Studies Lens: Textual Ethics and Lived Activism*. Reno: University of Nevada Press, 2019. 205–22.

Lodi-Ribiero, G. ed. *Solarpunk: Ecological and Fantastical Stories in a Sustainable World*. Trans. F. Fernandes. 2012. Albuquerque, NM: World Weaver Press, 2018.

Lorcher, F. and J. B. Fressoz. 'Modernity's Frail Climate: A Climate History of Environmental Reflexivity'. *Critical Inquiry* 38.3 (2012), 579–98.

Lord, G. *Salt*. Sydney: McPhee Gribble, 1990.

Lorenz, E. N. 'Deterministic Nonperiodic Flow'. *Journal of the Atmospheric Sciences* 20 (1963), 130–41.

'Low Order Models Representing Realizations of Turbulence'. *Journal of Fluid Mechanics* 55.3 (1972), 545–63.

Lorenzoni, I. *et al.* 'Climate Change, Human Genetics, and Post-Normality in the UK'. *Futures* 39 (2007), 65–82.

Love, G. *Practical Ecocriticism*. Charlottesville: University of Virginia Press, 2003.

Löwy, M. 'The Current of Critical Irrealism: "A Moonlit Enchanted Night"'. In M. Beaumont (ed.), *Adventures in Realism*. Oxford: John Wiley and Sons, 2008. 193–206.

Lu, J. 'Chinese Historical Fan Fiction: Internet Writers and Internet Literature'. *Pacific Coast Philology* 51.2 (2016), 159–76.

Lynall, G. *Imagining Solar Energy: The Power of the Sun in English Literature, Science and Culture*. London: Bloomsbury Academic, 2020.

Macdonald, G. 'Improbability Drives: The Energy of SF'. *Paradoxa* 26 (2014), 111–44.

Macfarlane, R. 'The Eeriness of the English Countryside'. *The Guardian*. 10 April 2015.

Macintyre, S. *A Concise History of Australia*. 4th ed. Cambridge University Press, 2018.

McGregor, D. and H. McGregor. 'All Our Relations: Climate Change Storytellers'. In C. Sandilands (ed.), *Rising Tides: Reflections for Climate Changing Times*. Halfmoon Bay, BC: Caitlin Press, 2019. 125–9.

McGurl, M. 'Gigantic Realism: The Rise of the Novel and the Comedy of Scale'. *Critical Inquiry* 43 (2017), 403–30.

McHugh, S. *Love in a Time of Slaughters: Human Animal Stories Against Genocide and Extinction*. University Park: Pennsylvania State University Press, 2019.

McKay, L. J. *The Animals in That Country*. Brunswick, Vic.: Scribe Publications, 2020.

McKegney, S. 'Writer-Reader Reciprocity and the Pursuit of Alliance through Indigenous Poetry'. In McLeod (ed.), *Indigenous Poetics in Canada*. 43–60.

McKibben, B. *Eaarth: Making a Life on a Tough New Planet*. New York: Times Books, 2010.

The End of Nature. New York: Random House, 1989.

ed. *I'm With the Bears: Short Stories from a Damaged Planet*. London: Verso, 2011.

'What the Warming World Needs Now Is Art, Sweet Art'. *Grist*. 22 April 2005.

McLeod, N., ed. *Indigenous Poetics in Canada*. Waterloo, ON: Wilfrid Laurier University Press, 2014.

McPhee, D. *Environmental History and Ecology of Moreton Bay*. Clayton, Vic.: CSIRO, 2017.

Mad Max: Fury Road. Dir. G. Miller. Roadshow Films, 2015

Marder, M. *Plant Thinking: A Philosophy of Vegetal Life*. New York: Columbia University Press, 2013.

Markley, R. '"Casualties and Disasters": Defoe and the Interpretation of Climatic Instability'. *Journal of Early Modern Cultural Studies* 8 (2008), 102–24.

'Climate Science'. In B. Clarke and M. Rossini (eds.), *The Routledge Companion to Literature and Science*. New York: Routledge, 2010. 63–76.

Marshall, K. 'What Are the Novels of the Anthropocene? American Fiction in Geological Time'. *American Literary History* 27.3 (2015), 523–38.

Marteau, T. M. 'Towards Environmentally Sustainable Human Behaviour: Targeting Non-Conscious and Conscious Processes for Effective and Acceptable Policies'. *Philosophical Transactions of the Royal Society A* 375.2095 (2017).

Martin, C. 'The Invention of Atmosphere'. *Studies in History and Philosophy of Science Part A* 52 (2015), 44–54.

Manuel, A. and R. M. Derrickson. 'The End of Colonialism'. *Journal of Canadian Studies* 51.1 (2017), 244–7.

Martin, K. 'The Hunting and Harvesting of Inuit Literature'. In D. Reder and L. Morra (eds.), *Learn, Teach, Challenge: Approaching Indigenous Literature*. Waterloo, ON: Wilfrid Laurier University Press, 2016. 445–65.

May, T. 'Beyond Bambi: Toward a Dangerous Ecocriticism in Theatre Studies'. *Theatre Topics* 17.2 (2007), 95–110.

Earth Matters on Stage: Ecology, Environment and American Theater. London: Routledge, 2020.

Mayer, S. 'Explorations of the Controversially Real: Risk, the Climate Change Novel, and the Narrative of Anticipation'. In S. Mayer and A. Weik von Mossner (eds.), *The Anticipation of Catastrophe: Environmental Risk in North American Literature and Culture*. Heidelberg: Universitätsverlag Winter, 2014. 21–37.

Mazzocco, P. J., M. C. Green, J. A. Sasota, and N. W. Jones. 'This Story Is Not for Everyone: Transportability and Narrative Persuasion'. *Social Psychology and Personality Science* 1.4 (2010), 361–8.

Mazzolini, E. 'Materialism's Affective Appeal'. *The Goose* 17.1 (2018).

Meeker, N. and A. Szabari. *Radical Botany: Plants and Speculative Fiction*. New York: Fordham University Press, 2020.

Mehnert, A. *Climate Change Fictions: Representations of Global Warming in American Literature*. London: Palgrave Macmillan, 2016.

Mellencamp, P. 'Prologue'. In Mellencamp (ed.), *Logics of Television: Essays in Cultural Criticism*. Bloomington: Indiana University Press, 1990. 1–13.

Melson, G. *Why the Wild Things Are: Animals in the Lives of Children*. Cambridge, MA: Harvard University Press, 2001.

Menely, T. '"The Present Obfuscation": Cowper's *Task* and the Time of Climate Change'. *PMLA* 127 (2012), 477–92.

Menely, T. and J. O. Taylor, eds. *Anthropocene Reading: Literary History in Geologic Times*. University Park: Pennsylvania State University Press, 2017.

'Introduction'. In Menely and Taylor (eds.), *Anthropocene Reading*. 1–24.

Mentz, S. 'Hurricanes, Tempests, and the Meteorological Globe'. In H. Marchitello and E. Tribble (eds.), *The Palgrave Handbook of Early Modern Literature and Science*. London: Palgrave Macmillan, 2017. 257–76.

'Strange Weather in *King Lear*'. *Shakespeare* 6.2 (2010), 139–52.

Meyers, C. 'Solar Child'. In Wagner and Wieland (eds.), *Sunvault*. 185–94.

Miéville, C. 'Covehithe'. *The Guardian*. 22 April 2011.

Mills, J. *Dyschronia*. Sydney: Pan Macmillan, 2018.

Milner, A. and J. R. Burgman. *Science Fiction and Climate Change: A Sociological Approach*. Liverpool University Press, 2020.

Mitman, G. *Reel Nature: America's Romance with Wildlife on Film*. Seattle: Washington University Press, 1999.

Mok, D. K. 'The Spider and the Stars'. In Ulibarri (ed.), *Glass and Gardens*. 10–30.

Moraga, C. 'Heroes and Saints'. In *Heroes and Saints and Other Plays*. Albuquerque, NM: West End Press, 1994. 85–149.

Mortenson, P. 'Reading Material'. *Written Communication* 18.4 (2001), 395–439.

Morton, T. *The Ecological Thought*. Cambridge, MA: Harvard University Press, 2010.

'Guest Column: Queer Ecology'. *PMLA* 125.2 (2010), 273–82.

Hyperobjects: Philosophy and Ecology after the End of the World. Minneapolis: University of Minnesota Press, 2013.

Mukherjee, U. P. *Postcolonial Environments: Nature, Culture and the Contemporary Indian Novel in English*. Basingstoke: Palgrave Macmillan, 2010.

Murphy, C. *The Breathing Hole*. Toronto: Playwrights Canada Press, 2020.

Murray, R. L. and J. K. Heumann. *Ecology and Popular Film: Cinema on the Edge*. Albany: State University of New York Press, 2009.

Musil, R. *The Man without Qualities I*. New York: Vintage, 1996.

Murthy, D. 'The Ontology of Tweets: Mixed-Method Approaches to the Study of Twitter'. In L. Sloan and A. Quan-Haase (eds.), *The SAGE Handbook of Social Media Research Methods*. Los Angeles: Sage, 2016. 559–73.

Myers, N. 'Environmental Refugees: An Emergent Security Issue'. 13th Meeting of the OSCE Economic Forum. Prague. 22 May 2005.

'Environmental Refugees in a Globally Warmed World'. *Bioscience* 43.11 (1993), 752–61.

Nagle, M. K. *Fairly Traceable*. Los Angeles: Native Voices at the Autry, 2014. Unpublished.

Nathanael, J. 'Light Sail Star Bound'. In Wagner and Wieland (eds.), *Sunvault*. 85.

Naughten, K. *ClimateSight: Climate Science from the Inside*. https://climatesight.org.

Nealon, J. T. *Plant Theory: Biopower and Vegetal Life*. Stanford University Press, 2015.

Post-Postmodernism, or, The Cultural Logic of Just-in-Time Capitalism. Stanford University Press, 2012.

Neimanis, A. and J. M. Hamilton. 'Weathering'. *Feminist Review* 118.1 (2018), 80–4.

Neimanis, A. and R. Loewen Walker. 'Weathering: Climate Change and the "Thick Time" of Transcorporeality'. *Hypatia* 29.3 (2014), 558–75.

Nelson, M. K. 'Indigenous Science and Traditional Ecological Knowledge: Persistence in Place'. In R. Warrior (ed.), *The World of Indigenous North America*. New York: Routledge, 2015. 188–214.

Neyrat, F. 'Elements for an Ecology of Separation: Beyond Ecological Constructivism'. In E. Hörl and J. Burton (eds.), *General Ecology: The New Ecological Paradigm*. London: Bloomsbury Academic, 2017. 101–28.

Niblett, M. 'World-Economy, World-Ecology, World Literature'. *Green Letters* 16.1 (2012): 15–30.

Nixon, L. 'Visual Cultures of Indigenous Futurisms'. *GUTS Magazine* 6 (20 May 2016).

Nixon, R. 'Rachel Carson's Prescience'. *Chronicle of Higher Education*. 3 September 2012.

Slow Violence and the Environmentalism of the Poor. Cambridge, MA: Harvard University Press, 2011.

No Impact Man. Dir. L. Gabbert and J. Schein. Eden Wurmfeld Films, 2009.

Norgaard, K. M. 'Climate Change Is a Social Issue'. *The Chronicle of Higher Education*. 17 January 2016.

Living in Denial: Climate Change, Emotions, and Everyday Life. Cambridge, MA: MIT Press, 2011.

Norja, S. 'Sunharvest Triptych'. In Wagner and Wieland (eds.), *Sunvault*. 218–20.

Noske, B. *Beyond Boundaries: Humans and Animals*. Montreal: Black Rose Books, 1997.

Nottage, L. *Ruined*. New York: Theatre Communications Group, 2009.

Nowra, L. *Into That Forest*. Sydney: Allen & Unwin, 2012.

Oleson, E. P. 'After the Super Typhoon'. *Poem Hunter*. 11 November 2013.

'Typhoon, Typhoon, an Appeal'. *Poem Hunter*. 21 October 2015.

Oloff, K. 'From Sugar to Oil: The Ecology of George A. Romero's Night of the Living Dead'. *Journal of Postcolonial Writing* 53.3 (2017), 316–28.

'"Greening" the Zombie: Caribbean Gothic, World-Ecology, and Socio-Ecological Degradation'. *Green Letters* 16. 1 (2012), 31–45.

The Overnighters. Dir. J. Moss. Mile End Films, 2014.

Owen, J. *The Boy Who Fell from the Sky*. *Wattpad*. www.wattpad.com/story/46949633-the-boy-who-fell-from-the-sky.

Owen, W. 'Do Plants Think?'. Unpublished notes for lecture. 1917. MS. 12282/5, Bodleian Library, Oxford.

Pachirat, T. *Every Twelve Seconds*. New Haven, CT: Yale University Press, 2011.

Pahl, S and J. Bauer. 'Overcoming the Distance: Perspective Taking with Future Humans Improves Environmental Engagement'. *Environment and Behaviour* 45 (2013), 155–69.

Parham, J. *Green Media and Popular Culture: An Introduction*. London: Palgrave Macmillan, 2015.

Pascoe, B. *Dark Emu, Black Seeds: Agriculture or Accident*. Perth: Magabala Books, 2014.

Paull, L. *The Bees*. London: Fourth Estate, 2014.

Pearson, K. A. *Germinal Life: The Difference and Repetition of Deleuze*. Abingdon: Routledge, 1999.

Pendakis, A. 'Suburbs'. In C. Howe and A. Pandian (eds.), *Anthropocene Unseen: A Lexicon*. Earth, Milky Way: Punctum Books, 2020. 447–50.

Perez, C. S. '"This Changes Everything" (Earth Day Poem)'. *Craig Santos Perez*. 22 April 2018. https://craigsantosperez.wordpress.com/2018/04/22/this-changes-everything-earth-day-poem/.

'Love Poems in the Time of Climate Change'. *The New Republic*. 4 March 2017. https://newrepublic.com/article/140282/love-poems-time-climate-change.

'Rings of Fire, 2016'. *Poets.org*. 2017. https://poets.org/poem/rings-fire-2016.

Pezzulo, P. *Toxic Tourism: Rhetorics of Pollution, Travel and Environmental Justice*. Tuscaloosa: University of Alabama Press, 2007.

Pfister, C. *et al.* 'Daily Weather Observations in Sixteenth-Century Europe'. *Climatic Change* 43 (1999), 111–50.

Planet of the Humans. Dir. J. Gibbs, prod. M. Moore. Rumble Media, 2019.

Plantinga, C. 'Trauma, Pleasure, and Emotion in the Viewing of *Titanic*: A Cognitive Approach'. In W. Buckland (ed.), *Film Theory and Contemporary Hollywood Movies*. London: Routledge, 2009. 237–56.

Porrit. J. *The World We Made: Alex McKay's Story from 2050*. London: Phaidon Press, 2013.

Porter, M. *Lanny*. London: Faber, 2019.

Potter, L. 'Postcolonial Resources, Pedagogical Resistance: An Energy-Driven Interview with Professor Jennifer Wenzel'. *Journal of Postcolonial Writing* 53.3 (2017), 380–92.

Powers, R. *The Overstory*. New York: Norton, 2018.

Price, J. 'Stop Saving the Planet! – and Other Tips via Rachel Carson for Twenty-First -Century Environmentalists'. In L. Culver *et al.* (eds.), *Rachel Carson's* Silent Spring: *Encounters and Legacies*. Special issue of *RCC Perspectives*, 7 (2012), 11–30.

Pringle, T. P. 'The Climate Proxy: Digital Cultures of Global Warming'. PhD dissertation. Brown University. 2020.

'Principles of Climate Justice'. *Mary Robinson Foundation – Climate Justice*. 2011. www.mrfcj.org/wp-content/uploads/2015/09/Principles-of-Climate-Justice.pdf.

Probyn-Rapsey, F. 'Anthropocentrism'. In L. Gruen (ed.), *Critical Terms for Animal Studies*. University of Chicago Press, 2018. 47–63.

  'Dingoes and Dog Whistling: A Cultural Politics of Race and Species in Australia'. In K. Struthers-Montford and C. Taylor (eds.), *Colonialism and Non-Human Animality: Anti-Colonial Perspectives in Critical Non-human Animal Studies*. London: Routledge, 2020. 181–200.

Rahmstorf, S. *et al.* 'Exceptional Twentieth-Century Slowdown in Atlantic Ocean Overturning Circulation'. *Nature Climate Change* 5 (2015), 475–80.

Reina, B. 'Digital Print in the Material World: Paratext in Service of Narrative'. *Word and Image* 35.1 (2019), 76–88.

Reusswig, F. 'The International Impact of *The Day After Tomorrow*'. *Environment* 46.9 (2004), 41–3.

Rice, W. *Moon of the Crusted Snow*. Toronto: ECW Press, 2018.

Ricoeur, P. *The Rule of Metaphor: The Creation of Meaning in Language*. Trans. R. Czerny. 1977. London: Routledge, 2003.

RinkTalk. www.rinktalk.org.

RinkWatch. www.rinkwatch.org.

The Road. Dir. J. Hillcoat. Dimension Films, 2009.

Robertson, C. *et al.* 'Winters Too Warm to Skate? Citizen-Science Reported Variability in Availability of Outdoor Skating in Canada'. *Canadian Geographer/Le Géographe canadien* 59.4 (2015).

Robinson, K. S. *2312*. New York: Orbit, 2012.

  Aurora. New York: Orbit, 2015.

  Blue Mars. New York: Bantam, 1996.

  Fifty Degrees Below. New York: Bantam, 2005.

  Forty Signs of Rain. New York: Bantam, 2004.

  Green Earth. New York: Del Rey, 2015.

  Green Mars. New York: Bantam, 1994.

  Imagining Abrupt Climate Change: Terraforming Earth. Seattle: Amazon Shorts, 2005.

  The Ministry for the Future. New York: Orbit, 2020.

  New York 2140. New York: Orbit, 2017.

  Pacific Edge. New York: Tom Doherty Associates, 2013 (orig. 1990).

  Red Mars. New York: Bantam, 1993.

  'Science Fiction When the Future Is Now'. *Nature* 552 (2017), 329–33.

  Shaman. New York: Orbit, 2013.

Sixty Days and Counting. New York: Bantam, 2007.

The Years of Rice and Salt. New York: Random House, 2000.

Rochester, R. 'We're Alive: The Resurrection of the Audio Drama in the Anthropocene'. *Philological Quarterly* 93.3 (2014), 361–81.

Romshoo, S. A. *et al*. 'Climatic, Geomorphic and Anthropogenic Drivers of the 2014 Extreme Flooding in the Jhelum Basin of Kashmir, India'. *Geomatics, Natural Hazards and Risk* 9.1 (2018), 224–48.

Ronda, M. *Remainders: American Poetry at Nature's End*. Stanford University Press, 2018.

Rose, D. B. *Nourishing Terrains: Australian Aboriginal Views of Landscape and Wilderness*. Canberra: Australian Heritage Commission, 1996.

Wild Dog Dreaming: Love and Extinction. Charlottesville: University of Virginia Press, 2011.

Rosenthal, D. J. 'Climate-Change Fiction and Poverty Studies: Kingsolver's *Flight Behavior*, Diaz's "Monstro", and Bacigalupi's "The Tamarisk Hunter"'. *ISLE: Interdisciplinary Studies in Literature and Environment* 27.2 (2020), 268–86.

Rosenthal, R. 'Gaia, Mon Amor'. In U. Chaudhuri (ed.), *Rachel's Brain and Other Storms: The Performance Scripts of Rachel Rosenthal*. New York: Bloomsbury, 2001.

Roy, A. *The God of Small Things*. New York: Random House, 1997.

The Ministry of Utmost Happiness. London: Hamish Hamilton, 2017.

Ruskin, J. *Modern Painters*. Vol. 3. London: George Allen, 1904.

Sale, K. *Dwellers in the Land: The Bioregional Anthology of Northern California*. Philadelphia: New Vision, 1991.

Sankaran, C. 'Retrieving the Margins: Use of *Thinai* by Three Contemporary Tamil Women Writers'. *ISLE: Interdisciplinary Studies in Literature and Environment* 28.1 (2021).

Saussure, F. de. *Course in General Linguistics* (1916). In P. Rice and P. Waugh (eds.), *Modern Literary Theory: A Reader*. London: St. Martin's Press, 1996.

Schneider-Mayerson, M. 'Climate Change Fiction'. In R. Greenwald Smith (ed.), *American Literature in Transition: 2000–2010*. Cambridge University Press, 2017. 309–21.

'The Influence of Climate Fiction: An Empirical Survey of Readers'. *Environmental Humanities* 10.2 (2018), 473–500.

'"Just as in the Book"? The Influence of Literature on Readers' Awareness of Climate Justice and Perception of Climate Migrants'. *ISLE: Interdisciplinary Studies in Literature and Environment* 27.2 (2020), 327–64.

Schuller, K. *The Biopolitics of Feeling: Race, Sex, and Science in the Nineteenth Century*. Durham, NC: Duke University Press, 2018.

Schultz, P. W. 'Empathizing with Nature: The Effects of Perspective-Taking on Concern for Environmental Issues'. *Journal of Social Issues* 56 (2000), 391–406.

Schweickart, P. P. and E. A. Flynn. Introduction. In Schweickart and Flynn (eds.), *Reading Sites: Social Difference and Reader Response*. New York: Modern Language Association, 2004. 1–38.

Sedlmeier, F. 'The Paratext and Literary Narration: Authorship, Institutions, Historiographies'. *Narrative* 26.1 (2018), 63–80.

Seymour, N. *Bad Environmentalism: Irony and Irreverence in the Ecological Age*. Minneapolis: University of Minnesota Press, 2018.

'Irony and Contemporary Ecocinema: Theorizing a New Affective Paradigm'. In A. Weik von Mossner (ed.), *Moving Environments: Affect, Emotion, Ecology, and Film*. Waterloo, ON: Wilfrid Laurier University Press, 2014. 61–78.

Shannon, L. *The Accommodated Animal: Cosmopolity in Shakespearean Locales*. University of Chicago Press, 2013.

Shapin, S. and S. Schaffer. *Leviathan and the Air-Pump: Hobbes, Boyle, and the Experimental Life*. Princeton University Press, 1985.

Sharpe, C. *In the Wake: On Blackness and Being*. Durham, NC: Duke University Press, 2016.

Skinner, J. 'Editor's Statement'. *Ecopoetics* 1 (2001), 5–8.

Slovic, S. 'The Third Wave of Ecocriticism: North American Reflections of the Current State of the Discipline'. *Ecozon@* 1.1 (2010), 4–10.

Slovic, S. and P. Slovic. 'Introduction: The Psychophysics of Brightness and the Value of a Life'. In S. Slovic and P. Slovic (eds.), *Numbers and Nerves: Information, Emotion, and Meaning in a World of Data*. Corvallis: Oregon State University Press, 2015. 1–22.

Simpson, A. *Mohawk Interruptus: Political Life Across the Borders of Settler States*. Durham, NC: Duke University Press, 2014.

Simpson, L. B. *As We Have Always Done: Indigenous Freedom through Radical Resistance*. Minneapolis: University of Minnesota Press, 2017.

Dancing on Our Turtle's Back: Stories of Nishnaabeg Re-creation, Resurgence and a New Emergence. Winnipeg: ARP Books, 2011.

Singh, V. 'Entanglement'. In J. J. Adams (ed.), *Loosed upon the World: The Saga Anthology of Climate Fiction*. New York: Saga, 2015. 269–322.

Smartfin. https://.smartfin.org.

Smith, B. 'David Mitchell's *The Bone Clocks*'. In A. Goodbody and A. Johns-Putra (eds.), *Cli-Fi: A Companion*. Oxford: Peter Lang, 2018. 203–10.

Smith, L. T. *Decolonizing Methodologies: Research and Indigenous Peoples*. London: Zed Books, 1999.

Smith, N. 'The Return of the Living Dead: Unsettlement and the Tasmanian Tiger'. *Journal of Australian Studies* 36.3 (2012), 269–89.

Snowpiercer. Dir. Bong Joon-ho. Weinstein Company, 2013.

Sobel, D. *Childhood and Nature: Design Principles for Educators*. Portland, ME: Stenhouse, 2008.

Soja, E. W. *Thirdspace: Journeys to Los Angeles and Other Real-and-Imagined Places*. Cambridge, MA: Blackwell, 1996.

Solnick, S. 'Anthropocene'. In D. O'Gorman and R. Eaglestone (eds.), *The Routledge Companion to Twenty-First Century Literary Fiction*. Abingdon: Routledge, 2018. 225–38.

Poetry and the Anthropocene: Ecology, Biology and Technology in Contemporary British and Irish Poetry. London: Routledge, 2017.

Somaini, A. 'The Atmospheric Screen: Turner, Hazlitt, Ruskin'. In C. Buckley *et al.* (eds.), *Screen Genealogies: From Optical Device to Environmental Medium*. Amsterdam University Press, 2019. 159–85.

Sontag, S. *Illness as Metaphor*. New York: Farrar, Strauss & Giroux, 1978.

Soqluman, N. *Tongku Saveq*. Taipei: INK, 2007.

Souder, W. *On a Farther Shore: The Life and Legacy of Rachel Carson*. New York: Crown, 2012.

Spivak, G. C. *Imperatives to Re-imagine the Planet*. Vienna: Passagen, 1999.

Springwatch. BBC. 2005–19.

Stanlake, C. *Native American Drama: A Critical Perspective*. Cambridge University Press, 2009.

Stanner, W. E. H. 'The Boyer Lectures: After the Dreaming'. 1968. In *The Dreaming and Other Essays*. Melbourne: Black Inc Books, 2009.

Starbuck, S. T. *Trees, Fish, and Dreams Climateblog*. www.riverseek.blogspot.com.

Steffen, W. *et al. Cranking up the Intensity: Climate Change and Extreme Weather Events*. Canberra: Climate Council of Australia, 2017.

Steinfeld, H. *et al. Livestock's Long Shadow: Environmental Issues and Options*. Rome: Food and Agriculture Organization of the United Nations, 2006.

Streeby, S. *Imagining the Future of Climate Change: World-Making through Science Fiction and Activism*. Berkeley: University of California Press, 2018.

Strickland, S. *Zone: Zero*. Boise, ID: Ahsahta Press, 2008.

Sultzbach, K. 'How Can Scholarly Work Be Meaningful in an Era of Lost Causes?' *Green Letters* 23.1–2 (2019), 19–38.

Svoboda, M. 'Cli-Fi on the Screen(s): Patterns in the Representations of Climate Change in Fictional Films'. *WIREs Climate Change* 7.1 (2016): 43–64.

'The Long Melt: The Lingering Influence of *The Day After Tomorrow*'. *Yale Climate Connections*. 5 November 2014.

Swift, J. *Gulliver's Travels*. New York: Signet, 1960.

Szerszynski, B. 'Reading and Writing the Weather'. *Theory, Culture and Society* 27.2–3 (2010), 9–30.

Tabios, E. R, ed. *Verses Typhoon Yolanda: A Storm of Filipino Poets*. San Francisco, CA: Meritage Press, 2014.

Tagaq, T. *Split Tooth*. Toronto: Viking Canada, 2018.

Taste the Waste. Dir. V. Thurn. Schnittstelle/Thurn Film, 2011.

Taylor, J. O. 'Atmosphere as Setting, or, "Wuthering" the Anthropocene'. In Johns-Putra (ed.), *Climate and Literature*. 31–44.

The Sky of Our Manufacture: The London Fog in British Fiction from Dickens to Woolf Charlottesville: University of Virginia Press, 2016.

That Sugar Film. Dir. D. Gameau. Madman Entertainment, 2015.

There Once Was an Island. Dir. B. March. Roadshow, 2010.

Thin Ice. Dir. S. Lamb and D. Sington. Green Planet Films, 2013.

This Is Climate Change. Dir. D. Danfung and E. Strauss. Condition One, 2018.

Thompson, D. W. *On Growth and Form*. Cambridge University Press, 1992.

Tournier, M. *Gemini*. London: Collins, 1981.

Tuck, E. and K. W. Yang. 'Decolonization Is Not a Metaphor'. *Decolonization: Indigeneity, Education and Society* 1.1 (2012), 1–40.

Tungijuq. Dir. F. Lajeunesse and P. Raphaël. Prod. T. Tagaq and Z. Kunuk. Isuma Productions, 2009.

Trexler, A. *Anthropocene Fictions: The Novel in a Time of Climate Change*. Charlottesville: University of Virginia Press, 2015.

Trexler, A. and A. Johns-Putra. 'Climate Change in Literature and Literary Criticism'. *WIREs Climate Change* 2 (2011), 185–200.

Twine, R. 'Revealing the "Animal Industrial Complex": Concept and Method for Critical Animal Studies'. *Journal for Critical Animal Studies* 10.1 (2012), 12–39.

Turing, A. M. 'I. Computing Machinery and Intelligence'. *Mind* 59 (October 1950), 433–60.

Tyszczuk, R. and J. Smith. 'Culture and Climate Change Scenarios: The Role and Potential of the Arts and Humanities in Responding to the 1.5 Degrees Target'. *Current Opinion in Environmental Sustainability* 31 (2018), 56–64.

Uexküll, J. von. *Forays into the Worlds of Animals and Humans, with a Theory of Meaning*. Trans. J. D. O'Neill. Minneapolis: University of Minnesota Press, 2010.

Ulibarri, S, ed. *Glass and Gardens: Solarpunk Summers*. Albuquerque, NM: World Weaver Press, 2018.

'Introduction'. In Ulibarri (ed.), *Glass and Gardens*. 1–2.

'Introduction'. In Lodi-Ribiero (ed.), *Solarpunk*. 1–3.

Underworld, Inc. Prod. J. Hewes and C. Lent. Wall to Wall and National Geographic. 2015–16.

Van Doren, M. 'Literature and Propaganda'. *Virginia Quarterly Review* 14.2 (1938), 203–8.

Van Neerven, E. *Heat and Light*. Sydney: Read How You Want, 2014.

Varma, R. *Bhopal*. Toronto: Playwrights Canada Press, 2005.

Vialles, N. *Animal to Edible*. Trans J. A. Underwood. Cambridge University Press, 1994.

Wagner, P. and B. C. Wieland, eds. *Sunvault: Stories of Solarpunk and Eco-Speculation*. Nashville, TN: Upper Rubber Boot, 2017.

Wagner-Pacifici, R. *et al.* 'Ontologies, Methodologies, and New Uses of Big Data in the Social and Cultural Sciences'. *Big Data and Society* 2.2 (2015), 1–11.

Walker, G. J. and R. Chapman. 'Thinking Like a Park: The Effects of Sense of Place, Perspective-Taking, and Empathy on Pro-environmental Intentions'. *Journal of Park and Recreation Administration* 21 (2003), 71–86.

Wallace-Wells, D. 'The Uninhabitable Earth'. *New York Magazine*. 9 July 2017.

Walsham, A. *Providence in Early Modern England*. Oxford University Press, 1999.

Wang, P. K. and D. Zhang. 'An Introduction to Some Historical Governmental Weather Records of China'. *Bulletin of the American Meteorological Society* 69.7 (1988), 753–8.

Warwick Research Collective. *Combined and Uneven Development: Towards a New Theory of World-Literature*. Liverpool University Press, 2015.

Waters, S. *The Contingency Plan: On the Beach* and *Resilience*. London: Bush Theatre, 2009.

Watkins, E. *Everyday Exchanges: Marketwork and Capitalist Common Sense*. Stanford University Press, 1998.

Watson, I. 'Sovereign Spaces, Caring for Country, and the Homeless Position of Aboriginal Peoples'. *South Atlantic Quarterly* 108.1 (2009), 27–52.

Watt-Cloutier, S. *The Right to Be Cold: One Woman's Story of Protecting Her Culture, the Arctic and the Whole Planet*. Toronto: Penguin Canada, 2016.

Wattpad. www.wattpad.com.

Weart, S. R. *The Discovery of Global Warming*. Rev. ed. Cambridge, MA: Harvard University Press, 2008.

Weik von Mossner, A. *Affective Ecologies: Empathy, Emotion and Environmental Narrative*. Columbus: Ohio State University Press, 2017.

'Climate Change and the Dark Side of Translating Science into Popular Culture'. In F. Italiano (ed.), *The Dark Side of Translation*. London: Routledge, 2020. 111–25.

'Visceralizing Ecocide in Science Fiction Films: *The Road* and *Hell*'. *Ecozon@* 3.2 (2012), 42–56.

Wells, H. G. *The Time Machine*. Ed. J. Lawton. London: Everyman, 1995.

The War of the Worlds. Ed. D. Y. Hughes and H. M. Geduld. Bloomington: Indiana University Press, 1993.

Wenzel, J. 'Petro-Magic-Realism: Toward a Political Ecology of Nigerian Literature'. *Postcolonial Studies* 9.4 (2006), 449–64.

Westra, L. *Environmental Justice and the Rights of Ecological Refugees*. London: Earthscan, 2009.

Westworld. Created by L. Joy and L. Nolan. HBO. 2016.

Whatmore, S. *Hybrid Geographies: Natures, Cultures, Spaces*. London: Sage, 2002.

White, R. 'Are You an Environmentalist or Do You Work for a Living?' In W. Cronon (ed.), *Uncommon Ground: Rethinking the Human Place in Nature*. New York: W.W. Norton, 1996. 171–85.

Whyte, K. P. 'Is It Colonial Déja Vu? Indigenous Peoples and Climate Injustice'. In J. Adamson *et al.* (eds.), *Humanities for the Environment: Integrating Knowledges, Forging New Constellations of Practice*. New York: Routledge, 2016. 88–104.

'Let's Be Honest, White Allies'. *Yes* 85 (2018), 47–8.

'Settler Colonialism, Ecology, and Environmental Injustice'. *Environment and Society* 9.1 (2018). 125–44.

Wilkins, J. *The Discoverie of a World in the Moone*. London: Michael Sparl and Edward Forrest, 1638.

Williams, H. T. P. *et al.* 'Network Analysis Reveals Open Forums and Echo Chambers in Social Media Discussions of Climate Change'. *Global Environmental Change* 32 (2015), 126–38.

Williams, Raymond. *The Country and the City*. New York: Oxford University Press, 1973.

Williams, Rhys. '"This Shining Confluence of Magic and Technology": Solarpunk, Energy Imaginaries, and the Infrastructures of Solarity'. *Open Library of Humanities* 5(1).60 (2019), 1–35.

Willoquet-Maricondi, P. 'Shifting Paradigms: From Environmentalist Films to Ecocinema'. In Willoquet-Maricondi (ed.), *Framing the World: Explorations in Ecocriticism and Film*. Charlottesville: University of Virginia Press, 2010. 43–60.

Wohlleben, P. *The Hidden Life of Trees: What They Feel, How They Communicate: Discoveries from a Secret World*. London: Harper Collins, 2016.

Wolfe, C. *Animal Rites: American Culture, the Discourse of Species, and Posthumanist Theory*. University of Chicago Press, 2003.

Wolfe, P. 'Settler Colonialism and the Elimination of the Native'. *Journal of Genocide Research* 8.4 (2006), 387–409.

Wollheim, D. A. *The Universe Makers: Science Fiction Today*. New York: Harper & Row, 1971.

Womack, C. S. *Red on Red: Native American Literary Separatism*. Minneapolis: University of Minnesota Press, 1999.

Wood, G. D. Foreword. In A. Johns-Putra *et al.* (eds.), *Literature and Sustainability: Concept, Text and Culture*. Manchester University Press, 2017. xii–xv.

Tambora: The Eruption that Changed the World. Princeton University Press, 2015.

Woods, D. 'Accelerated Reading: Fossil Fuels, Infowhelm, and Archival Life'. In Menely and Taylor (eds.), *Anthropocene Reading*. 202–19.

'Genre at Earth Magnitude: A Theory of Climate Fiction'. Forthcoming.

Wright, A. *The Swan Book*. Sydney: Giramondo, 2013.

Wynter, S. 'Ethno or Socio Poetics'. *Alcheringa/Ethnopoetics* 2.2 (1976), 78–94.

'No Humans Involved: An Open Letter to My Colleagues'. *Forum NHI: Knowledge for the 21st Century* 1.1 (Fall 1994), 42–73.

Yeats, G. '"Dirty Air": *Little Dorrit*'s Atmosphere'. *Nineteenth-Century Literature* 66 (2011), 328–54.

Younging, G. *Elements of Indigenous Style: A Guide for Writing by and about Indigenous Peoples*. Edmonton: Brush Education, 2018.

Yunkaporta, T. *Sand Talk: How Indigenous Thinking Can Save the World*. Melbourne: Text Publishing, 2019.

Yusoff, K. *A Billion Black Anthropocenes or None*. Minneapolis: University of Minnesota Press, 2018.

Yusoff, K. and J. Gabrys. 'Climate Change and the Imagination'. *WIREs Climate Change* 2.4 (2011), 516–34.

Zhu, K. 'A Preliminary Study on the Climatic Fluctuations during the Last 5000 Years in China'. *Scientia Sinica* 2 (1973), 115–20.

INDEX

Cambridge Companions to ...

AUTHORS

For EU product safety concerns, contact us at Calle de José Abascal, 56–1°,
28003 Madrid, Spain or eugpsr@cambridge.org.

www.ingramcontent.com/pod-product-compliance
Ingram Content Group UK Ltd.
Pitfield, Milton Keynes, MK11 3LW, UK
UKHW042145130625

459647UK00011B/1187

* 9 7 8 1 0 0 9 0 6 0 8 1 3 *